ONE TRAIN LATER

ONE TRAIN LATER

A Memoir

ANDY SUMMERS

Thomas Dunne Books
St. Martin's Press ⚌ New York

Author's Note: This is a memoir, a recollection, a remembrance.
A few times and names of peripheral events and players from my youth have been changed.
The essence of the memoir and the direct quotes within are true to my memory.

THOMAS DUNNE BOOKS.
An imprint of St. Martin's Press.

www.thomasdunnebooks.com
www.stmartins.com

Photo on pg. 24 courtesy of Jean Summers; pgs. 43, 146, 242, 285, 287, 294, 315,
and 338, Andy Summers; pgs. 86, 92, 102, and 165, Andy Summers Collection;
pgs. 180 and 205, Lawrence Impey; pg. 197, Jill Furmanosky; pg. 246,
Watal Asanuma; pg. 268, Arturo Encinas.

ISBN-13: 978-0-312-35914-0
ISBN-10: 0-312-35914-4

First Edition: September 2006

10 9 8 7 6 5 4 3 2 1

For Richard

Acknowledgments

To Kate, my wife and partner, for her love, support, and unerring instinct for the truth. To our children, Layla, Mo, and Anton, who complete it all.

To my parents, Jean and Maurice, for being my parents and believing.

My brothers, Richard and Tony, and my sister, Monica, for the life shared.

To Sting and Stewart Copeland for the dream.

To Kim Turner, Miles Copeland, and Ian Copeland for being on the path with us.

To Zoot Money, with whom I began this adventure and who remains a touchstone.

To friend and poet Cathy Colman, who gave me invaluable editorial advice throughout the writing process.

To friend and writer Brian Cinadr, who read the manuscript more than once and reminded me of parts of my history that I had forgotten.

To my agent, Susan Schulman, for her counsel, wisdom, and staying power.

To John Parsley, my editor at Thomas Dunne Books, for nudging me down the path to resolution.

To Dennis Smith for making it all possible.

To all those along the way for support, friendship, and performing so well in the play: Ralph Gibson, Mary Jane Marcasiano, Jenny Fabian, Robert Wyatt, Kevin Coyne, Anthony and Martine Moore, Eric Burdon, Vic Garbarini, Morleigh Steinberg and The Edge, Stevo Glendenning, Christopher Burley, Bradley Bambarger, Robin Lane, Kit Lane, Norman Moore, Adrian and Lynn Boot, Chris Salewicz, Ben Verdery, The Shants, John Etheridge, Victor Biglione, Luiz Paulo Asuncio, Watal Asanuma, Coco Asanuma, Lenny Riggio, Louis Lepore, Robert Fripp, Jill Furmanosky, Lawrence Impey, Frane Lessac, Eberhard and Steffi Schoener, Karen Grey, Randall Kremer, Sonja Kristina, Jerome Lapperousaz, Nazir Jairazbhoy, Dittany Lang, Jodi Peckman, Jeff Seitz, Danny Quatrochi, Tam Fairgreaves, Cecila Miniucchi, Jeffrey Coulter, Gerry Casale, Phil Sutcliffe . . . sorry if I left anyone out . . .

Foreword

by The Edge

How to become a rock star? Plug in and wait for inspiration. That seems to have been the secret to Andy Summers's success in the music business, or so it would seem based on his autobiography.

In the age of "pop idol," when the order of the day is to commodify yourself to success, this book will hopefully be a welcome counterbalance. Full of anecdotes of near misses and false starts, the book's overarching theme is of a man blown by some supernatural wind along a road not of his choosing but of his calling: music, for better or worse, his mistress, his seducer, his lifeline.

And with every blind alley, every setback, there comes the increasing sense that the journey is the most important thing.

Starting, as his story does, with his first experiments with skiffle, taking us through his involvement in the U.K. blues explosion, and on into the high sixties of the Beatles and the Stones, no other apprenticeship could possibly have prepared Andy for the world-dominating success of the Police, just one of the bands that can claim him as a member, but the one that will surely be remembered by history.

It was during his time with the Police that I first met Andy. As a member of U2, then a junior band about to open for them at their 1982 Gateshead Stadium gig, I was somewhat intimidated by the sight of the three blond icons as they came bounding into the lobby of the hotel where we had all

gathered to await transport to the stadium. There was between Andy and his
bandmates, Sting and Stewart Copeland, this unmistakable sense of chemistry. They were not just a great band, they were a real band.

We had in fact opened for the Police once before—across the Irish Sea in
our homeland at the first ever outdoor concert at Slane Castle—but in 1981
such was the gulf between us that we never actually met.

Time passed, and in 1986 by some twist of fate U2 ended up playing at
an Amnesty International "Conspiracy of Hope" concert at New Jersey's Gi-
ants Stadium with the Police after they had decided to call it a day. It was a
major occasion for many different reasons. I certainly will never forget the
moment when Andy handed me his guitar in front of the 65,000 capacity
crowd at the end of the Police's final set, for U2 to play out the last song of
the event. There was more than a little symbolism in that handing over of
instruments.

That Andy absorbed the success of the Police, as he did all the other ups
and downs he experienced along the road, without losing a sense of himself,
his passion for, and his belief in the sacred and life-changing qualities of
music is a testimony to the purity of his motivation as a musician, songwriter, and artist. May we be lucky enough to see his like again.

BOOK ONE

BRIDGEHAMPTON, AUGUST 18, 1983

It's over.

I wake, my eyes fill with morning light. The band—it's over. Shea Stadium tonight; this is it. The soft dream voice confirms with a knife-edge what I already know.

Like a raft lashed together with anything at hand, we have managed to float this far without disintegrating. With strange chemistry and fragile nexus, we raised the flimsy sail of chance—and still we haven't sunk. But this—the concert tonight—is the signifier of a final destination, the abandoning of the craft. As the summer waves fall on the beach in the close distance and fans in Police shirts and scarves and badges and armfuls of vinyl records line up outside of Shea Stadium, I clasp my hands behind my head and stare at the stuccoed ceiling.

The facts: We have held the number one album spot on the *Billboard* charts for four months without a break. We have had the number one single in the United States for eight weeks. We are a phenomenon. We have countless number one records around the world. We are a multimillion-dollar industry. We are three. All this—and yet it seems like only a flickering five minutes ago that we were pushing a broken van back through the streets of London after a gig we played to no one. Tonight we play out the fantasy of millions.

This is the Cinderella moment; the hands are close to midnight, the spoked sun wheeling out of the sky.

I stare across the room into the mirror over the mantel, where the early light creates a soft chiaroscuro. Sting has been muttering about how this is the time to stop, to get off, to quit at the high point of the curve. He has repeated this as if it is a fait accompli, but instead of negating this idea or working out some slower form of dissolution or telling him to fuck off, I have murmured a sort of assent as if it's some kind of engaging concept, an interesting idea. But on the gut level it's devastating. I knew that this was inevitable, that it was always in the script; the question was when it would surface. Is it possible to walk away from this poppy, this opiated success, this deadly nightshade of stardom?

I arrive onstage almost as an afterthought—oh yeah, now play. We are in a state of siege, encircled twenty-four hours a day by lawyers, record companies, fans, and the yawning maw of the press. From this elevation, with its weird brew of light and claustrophobia, you see why the Beatles finally blew apart. We seem to be following the same route, with the saurian roar of the media filling our ears, drowning out our beautiful songs.

With my head full of this shadowed subtext and the sunlit wave we are surfing, I swing my legs out from under the sheets. My feet land on the floor to form a triangle with my torso.

In a few days my baby daughter, Layla, will arrive with her nanny to spend time with me, a joy and a sharp reminder of the pain that pricks beneath all the shiny rock and roll. My beautiful wife, my best friend, my inamorata—Kate—has gone. She divorced me two years ago, telling me to get on with it, she'd had enough. Now I am a father only once in a while, and it hurts. Yawning and stretching, I cross the room, lean on the mantelpiece, and look back at the rumpled bed. What a fucking cliché. I destroyed my marriage for this, and what is this anyway? A Faustian pact? A union shredding as the singer conjures a different future for himself.

But tonight Sting, Stewart, and I are on the other side. This is the apogee of our time together; with the words THE POLICE—SHEA

STADIUM on a little paper ticket, we are close to the stars, close to the golden sphere that casts a shadow.

I look up into the mirror and think, Get a grip, you wanker. . . . It's only fucking pop music. I have to wake up, take a shower, try to think about tonight.

After the shower I feel slightly more awake but with a craving for caffeine and the sense that I have lost something. The house is full of ghostly silence broken only by the waves in the distance beating gently on the sand. We have been camped out in this private mansion in the Hamptons for the past three weeks, using it as a base while we fly in a private plane each day to stadiums on the East Coast.

I go over to my black Samsonite, which lies on the floor by the window, and pull out a T-shirt. My Telecaster is lying in the corner, bathed in a patch of sunlight. The buttery rays strike the strings and from them streams an incandescent glow, a lutescent aura, a Buddha smile from what might truly be called my most loyal friend.

One

I am born at the edge of the River Wyre in Lancashire, where my dad is stationed with the RAF in the north of England. Housing is in short supply and he makes the purchase of a Gypsy caravan. It is a romantic move, but one of necessity. My mother is known as Red; she is pregnant, and works in a bomb factory alongside a gang of northern girls called the Fosgene Follies. One day, in her ninth month, she becomes intoxicated by the fumes leaking from a faulty bomb and, having contractions, is carried back to the field where she lives with my dad. I come into this world a few hours later, and the queen of the Romany vagrants in the next field pays a visit to my mother. She hands over a small piece of silver, six eggs, and a piece of white linen—all traditional gifts intended to bring a propitious future. Sitting on the floor with a pack of tarot cards and a meaningful look on her face, she looks up at the young flame-haired woman leaning back into the pillow with her baby and begins shuffling the cards. But Red, with her attraction to the occult still in place and me dangling from her nipple, struggles up and looks across expectantly.

Red gives up her job as a bomb packer, and as the war comes to an end my parents return to the south of England and the beaches of Bournemouth, with their huge rusting curlicues of barbed wire and lonely skeletal piers. I stand on the promenade, clutching my mother's hand as my dad explains to me through the biting wind that we have blown up the piers to prevent the Germans from getting onto our shore. My five-year-old brain is filled with hordes of helmeted men racing across the sand with thick stubby guns. Around the town are the ruins of several buildings, destroyed after the Luftwaffe dropped their remaining bombs before heading back over the Channel to Germany. *What if one lands on your head?* I wonder. *Would you blow up?*

Near our house on the outskirts of town is a large wooded area by the name of Haddon Hill. Filled with oak, pine, beech, chestnut, and birch that spread for miles, it becomes the arena of my childhood where other boys and I wrestle and fight in the dirt, throw stones at dogs, torture cats, start fires, steal birds' eggs, and piss on flowers. Sometimes we find old boxes of gas masks and other wartime paraphernalia that have been guiltily dumped among the trees. We instantly put these things on and race off into the elms and oaks, howling at the top of our lungs. At the end of an afternoon with hours of ambush, screaming, and cruelty under our belts, we return home. As the evening stars emerge and the lampposts in the street begin to create their yellowish flare, we trail into our mothers' kitchens looking like miniature versions of the home guard. With our gas mask tubes bouncing on our puny chests and sensible sweaters, we look upward to ask with a voice muffled by rubber tubing, "Can I have something to eat, Mum?"

The woods fill my imagination, because secretly I am a nature lover, something I don't betray to the other boys, and I become an expert on secret paths, trees with holes in them, owls' nests, places where you can find slow-worms and adders, the pale blue eggs of the chaffinch.

I scrawl weird signs in the dirt as if they contain hidden meaning, my keys to the whereabouts of a rookery or a dump of used wartime supplies. I spend every minute I can in this place until I feel as if I know every vein on every leaf, the knots in trees where rolling waves of beetles race from under rotting logs and where the venom-filled adders lie in wait. The thick smell of decomposition pervades my senses like a perfume, and under the low-piled clouds I kick my way through dense leaves, used condoms, tea-colored ferns, and tossed Black Cat cigarette packs, wearing a vivid blue cloak because I am Captain Marvel. I find a fragment of a letter in the ferns, but all I can make out in the rain-smeared writing are the words *Mike, it's been too long.* And I become obsessed with a man called Mike. Who is he? Who wrote this letter?

Where are they now? What happened? I stand at the local bus shelter with sheets of rain obscuring everything and stare at women in the queue, wondering if one of them is the one who wrote those words.

Between the ages of seven and twelve the overpowering sense of nature makes me feel drunk, and in a future filled with electricity, lights, and loud music, it will linger like a sanctifying echo, a chord I used to know. After my mother switches out the lights I sit in bed with the Dr. Doolittle books and read by holding back the curtain, which lets in the flickering light of the lamppost from the street below. Inspired by his adventures, I begin collecting birds' eggs, lizard skins, flowers, grasses, and weirdly shaped rocks. I make careful notes about these objects and look them up in my Observer's books. I fancy myself as Doolittle junior, a son of nature strolling through long grass with a pipe in my mouth. I pore over books about plants and animals and take to making long lists of names, which I give dimension by gluing lizard skin, bird feathers, and dead flowers onto pieces of cardboard until my bedroom becomes a personal museum and acquires a slightly strange smell.

As I pull myself closer and closer to these things both living and dead, the world—in my nascent imagination—becomes alive and vivid. Now, as if for the first time, I see it teeming with natural events, a connection between all things, a web, the underlying soul. *Animus mundi*.

A tragic moment occurs at the age of nine, when discarding Marvel's blue cape, I move into a Lash LaRue phase. Lash is a popular Western hero and features in a popular comic I read from cover to cover every week. In every story he escapes dire situations through his incredible ability with a bullwhip or his lash—hence the moniker. An inspiring figure, Lash dresses in black from head to toe, with a black eye mask and a broad stiff-rimmed black hat. With his whip and mask, he is the perfect embodiment of some kind of homoerotic fantasy that I am too young to comprehend.

Close to our house there is an apple orchard that contains a working beehive. Clothed in anything black I can find, and with my whip in hand, I decide one afternoon to see if I can emulate my hero by snaring the hive and pulling it to the ground. I creep through the long sun-dappled grass to spy on my target. Hiding behind a tree full of Granny Smiths, I calculate carefully. And then, raising the whip over my head like a king cobra, I strike and yell in triumph as the whip coils itself into a tight circle around the buzzing cone. I give it a strong tug and it crashes down, releasing about fifty million venomous and pissed-off bees that rise like a thick black cloud. I drop the whip and run like a man on fire, but they are faster and I am stung, pierced, and penetrated in every available piece of exposed flesh and through my lash outfit until I reach home, sobbing and panting with a face like a swollen river. "Mum!" I scream. "I've been stung! I've been stung!"

Stuck at home, the only diversions being reading or listening to the radio, I become a fan of a show that thrills me and many of my friends at school. It's called *Journey into Space* and has four protagonists: Jet, Lemmy, Mitch, and Doc. It's a serial that's on every Tuesday night at eight o'clock. Heralded by the dramatic fanfare of a rocket blasting into space, a masculine voice intones the program title and we pick up from where we left off last week. Usually the heroes are having a problem such as a control malfunction as they attempt to travel to the moon, and we crouch on the floor in front of the coal fire listening bug-eyed as our heroes grapple with martians, alien monsters, or a failed retro-rocket. As the show comes to an end my mum is standing there with a mug of Horlicks, telling me to get up the apples and pears. Stoned on the last half hour of space, stars, and planets, I stare at her in incomprehension. But I climb the stairs, calling out good night, and slide into bed to follow the adventures of Dan Dare and the Mekon in the *Eagle*, the yellowing flare of the streetlight through the crack in the curtains giving just enough light to ruin my eyes.

From time to time in the dream of life that spins from four to eleven years of age, there are points of gold—moments of completeness—the happiest of these times being when my parents take me to the cinema to see the latest film.

In the hours before the event—going to the pictures—there is always a sense of excitement in the house. My father disappears to fill the car with petrol while my mother rattles around in the kitchen to see that we have dinner before we leave. The phrase "What time does the big picture start?" becomes a mantra in our family. Finally we close the front door behind us. My mother squeezes into the car next to me, a cloud of perfume powder and makeup; my dad turns the ignition; and we lurch away from the wet curb toward the Moderne cinema. The tight confines of the car and the intoxicating haze of perfume combine with the leather seats and the smell of petrol to make the drive a voluptuous and sacred ritual.

Along with this heavenly bouquet comes my craving for chocolate. The dark brown stuff fills my head like a dark sea of unending pleasure, and as we pass through rain-filled streets with my dad cursing the faulty heater and wiping his hand across a befogged windscreen, I fantasize about it, dream of it, and plan to have so much of it one day that I will laugh out loud as I eat myself into a chocoholic coma.

But life for many young couples in postwar Britain is difficult and my parents have problems. "It's so hard to make ends meet," my mother will often say, as she washes another dish or darns another sock, and my dad never seems to be home because he is always working. A huge row between them one day ends in the kitchen with my mother sobbing and me on the floor with my arms around her legs, screaming, "Please don't cry, Mummy, please don't cry." The tension of trying to survive has an eroding effect on their marriage, and it breaks down. My younger brother and I are put into an orphanage for six months. We never see our mother, but Dad visits us on the weekends. We live with other kids in the top room of a farmhouse building, where we sleep in two-tier bunks and ridicule one another with cruel remarks. My bunk lies near a window and through it I can see across several fields to a river in the distance, and as the stars climb into the sky I fall asleep with these rivers and meadows in my mind like a map to a beautiful place and I wonder if my mum will be there. One day Dad comes to collect us, telling us that she is back from the hospital and that it is time to go home. My brother and I ask him about the hospital, but he is vague and just mutters something about an operation. An hour later we are back in our own house with our own mother, who weeps and hugs us, and then we get on with teatime as if nothing had happened.

Through the bright and shadowed years of childhood the pop songs of the time—"Twenty Tiny Fingers (Twenty Tiny Toes)," "You're a Pink Tooth Brush, I'm a Blue Tooth Brush," or "How Much Is That Doggie in the Window"—fill my head like a tinny pink-colored soundtrack: the optimism of a world now under the shadow of the bomb. As if in some premonitory act, I lie in bed giving imaginary solo concerts by making twanging guitar sounds with my mouth, although I have never seen a real guitar. Even-

tually my mother insists that I take piano lessons, and a small upright is purchased for the front room, where she sits at my side each night making sure
that I go through my scales and five-finger exercises.

Every Thursday evening around five I walk down the avenue to the house of
Mrs. Thorne, the local piano teacher, who is supposed to be good if a little
eccentric. "Practice, Andrew—practice," my mum says, and I drag myself to
the lesson, filled with a deep desire to take off into the woods at the end
of the street and chuck my spear at something. Mrs. Thorne—a throwback
to Victorian England—wears small wire-rimmed glasses and has her hair cut
like an English schoolgirl with a clip in it; and to round it off, she wears long
pink bloomers whose edges always poke out beneath the hemline of her
skirts. She has a permanent cold—or so it appears—because she is forever
sniffing and extracting a white hankie from her bloomers, blowing into it,
and then stuffing it back into place. This act always faintly disgusts me—
I imagine a line of transparent snot like a snail trail up her leg.

I play children's exercises and an odd assortment of simple pieces. The
highlight, and usually the grand finale of the lesson, comes when we play a
duet on the song "Wonderful Wonderful Copenhagen." I actually love this
tune and don't mind playing it with the old dear because I've seen the film,
which stars Danny Kaye, and adore it. So I go at it with considerable gusto
and not much finesse because it is on this one song that I feel I can actually
play the piano; knowing this, she always saves it for the end of the lesson so
that I can go home feeling less dour about the whole thing.

The room we play in reeks of mothballs and is filled with overstuffed
armchairs and pictures of dogs; on the piano is a framed color photo of the
queen. There is a rumor on the street that Mrs. Thorne has actually com-
posed music for the coronation. This is impressive, and we all vaguely wonder what she's doing in our part of the world, seeing as how she has written
music for royalty.

Mrs. Thorne's husband, who is a conductor for the Hants and Dorset bus
line, skulks about in the background. He is a short, stubby man with dark
greasy hair, a unibrow, and very thick glasses that look like the ends of a couple of beer bottles.

One lovely summer evening as I am shutting the front door after the lesson and about to walk home, Mr. Thorne appears on the path beside me. At first I think it is the garden gnome come to life but then realize it is the bus conductor. He smiles at me through stained English teeth and says, "Come with me, I want to show you something." Innocent as the first day of spring, I skip down the path behind him in the direction of the potting shed at the bottom of the garden.

The shed, with its pots, tools, bags of fertilizer, and smell of earth, is typical of the English garden. Dark and claustrophobic, it is the perfect spot for an Agatha Christie murder. *Maybe Mr. Thorne will show me some comics or a train set,* I think, but after a little preamble of showing me the serrated edge of a hacksaw, he produces a large leather belt and asks me to whip him. "Whip you?" I say, my cornflower eyes wide and innocent as Bambi's. "Why?" He stares at me through his beer-bottle lenses and grunts something about deserving it and come on, be a good boy. I notice that his face is flushed, I don't understand it, but I also can't see anything wrong with it if that's what he wants. Mr. Thorne bends over the bench and asks me again with a small sob in his voice to give it to him. So with a puzzled idea in my head and a momentary glimpse of Lash LaRue, I let him have it. He tells me to do it harder, so I oblige, giving him a good half a dozen strokes, feeling like Captain Bluebeard in the process. Then he thanks me and I trot off home, dragging my hand through the hedges at the side of the road and whistling the Danny Kaye song and looking forward to beans on toast. The event recedes like a summer tide; I don't say anything to my parents or consider that I might put a man away for life but continue happily on thumping away at "Wonderful Wonderful Copenhagen."

BRIDGEHAMPTON, AUGUST 18, 1983

I pull on a pair of shorts and head down to the kitchen. The house is still quiet; I realize that for some odd reason I am up before everyone else. The kitchen in the mansion is a vast, complicated affair with massive refrigerators and freezers unlike anything you would see in an English house, and I wonder if it is going to be possible to make coffee. But miraculously some gentle Maria has prepared the way and there in a gleaming new coffeepot is the lifesaving java, ready to kick-start the flesh robot.

I pour out a large mug and then search around for a spoon to stir the milk. Spoon—spoon, where are you hiding? I grunt and tug open a recalcitrant drawer to see if there is any sign of the implement in this labyrinth of kitchenware—surely it's somewhere. I see that beneath the gleaming silver cutlery the drawer is lined with a red-and-white-checked material, like my mum had, and I see a small boy walking into his mother's kitchen wearing a gas mask and asking for bread and butter and his mother with her copper hair in a bun wiping the suds from her arms. Ignoring the beastly visage and staring out the high window at the mass of clouds piling up over the green fields, she replies, "You know where it is, dear . . ."

I wake up from my reverie and take a large gulp of coffee. I'm hungry, but everything is behind cupboard doors and it's too early yet for the professional help. I cross the kitchen and start opening doors in the quest for food. Finding a large tin, I pull the lid off. It is packed with Danish pastries, all individually wrapped in plastic. Perfect. I fancy a sugar rush. I take one over to the table and begin taking off the plastic. There is a picture of the Little Mermaid on the front and an inscription that reads, "Anderson, the Best of Denmark," and as I bite into the soft dough a melody like a siren call floats into my brain: "Wonderful Wonderful Copenhagen."

Nursing my coffee and feeling like an extra from *The Night of the Living Dead,* I walk into the lounge. The owner keeps a small baby grand in this room, and we all plunk away on it at different times. I stick my coffee mug on a piece of sheet music on top of the piano and twiddle at a few high notes. I play fragments of "Take Five" by Dave Brubeck and then try to turn it into "Straight, No Chaser" by Monk and then into a series of descending thirteenth chords from Duke Ellington. Anytime I play this progression it takes me back to the dusty and noisy assembly hall at Summerbee, when I was eleven years old.

One day we are all gathered in the school hall for something or other and Mr. Furneaux, our music teacher, is idly playing a beautiful sequence of harmonies on the piano unlike anything I've ever heard him play before. It hits me right in the solar plexus and wakes me as if from a dream, and like a moth to the flame I go over to ask what it is that he is playing. "'Sophisticated Lady' by Duke Ellington," he answers without lifting his fingers from the keyboard. Neither name means much to me, but the chord progression creates a strange new excitement in my gut. I don't understand it—but whatever it is, I am hooked and want more.

Mr. Furneaux is a short, bald-headed man who wears tweed jackets and always has a pipe sticking up out of his breast pocket like a flag waving a truce at the oncoming horde. Classes with him are scenes of madness as he tries desperately to get us—a mob of rowdy little shits—to sing songs like "English Country Garden" or some other piece of Victoriana like "Nymphs and Shepherds," on which we are supposed to sing descant parts but which the whole class deliberately sings off-key so that it sounds like a roomful of rabid dogs. I actually feel some pain for Mr. Furneaux during this mayhem because somehow, in a way I can't articulate, I want to make music.

At age eleven I begin listening to the AFN radio station, which plays American jazz. One day Mr. Furneaux—who now regards me somewhat differently, maybe as an island in a sea of lunacy—asks me to stand up in class and talk about my interest in jazz as an example to the other miscreants (at least when it comes to music). I actually like this, and drop the names of Django Reinhardt, Radio Luxembourg, and Ellington with a bigheaded teacher's-pet smugness. After I sit down, Mr. Furneaux makes a couple of remarks to the class that maybe some of them could take a leaf from my book and take a genuine interest in music. I feel rather pleased with myself but also slightly apprehensive, knowing that I will probably get a kicking from the heavies after class. My best bet to avoid the pain is to be first out the door and piss off down the corridor before they get their hands on me, and surreptitiously I slide over a couple of desks.

Though the spiritual side of life slowly fills with music, the words of the Holy Bible fall on stony ground. Classes in religious instruction are anarchy beyond even the twisted behavior of the music class. Our teacher is Miss Jones, a minute Welsh lady with periwinkle blue eyes and hair tied up in a bun. Her entering the classroom is the signal for the ructions that start with a loud simulated fart, followed by a long period of people gasping for breath, choking, opening and shutting windows, lying on the floor and asking for first aid, etc. During this profane moment poor Miss Jones stands very still and fixes her eyes on some distant horizon as if seeing the fabled green hill itself; remarkably, after a while the very weirdness of her trancelike presence stills us. She then asks us in a very quiet voice to open our books to a Bible story, and once again the class erupts into hooligan antics and loud boos with off-color remarks about Jesus stabbing at the air. At this delinquent point Miss Jones goes down on her knees in the center of the classroom and begins to pray, but this doesn't help; in fact, if anything, it increases the violence in the classroom. The poor woman now rushes out of the room and to the headmaster's office and returns with him to a classroom that now is as quiet as a church, with the students' heads bent in diligent reverence over their books.

Once a year a physical fitness display is organized for the parents, to show the progenitors of the mob that when the fruit of their loins aren't actually in the bogs smoking or having a punch-up, they are being kept in good enough condition to go on to a life of meaningless labor in England's green and pleasant land. This display involves testicle-threatening handsprings over wooden horses and rapid climbing of ropes, which always causes an erection to rise cheerfully in one's skimpy shorts.

And then there are the dreaded boxing matches. Being an innate coward, I normally avoid anything to do with punching, but one year to my horror I am chosen to fight not one but two other kids, Smith and Evans. Smith is actually smaller and runtier than I am, so I breathe a sigh of relief when I hear his name; but Evans is a mean little Welsh boy who already has a reputation on the playground for a vicious fighting style, and at the thought of it I'm ready to crap in my pants.

On the night of the fight I go into the ring against Smith first, and it's like slapping a baby. I just slug the poor little sod senseless and then feel really terrible about it as he thanks me for the fight with his nose spurting blood and his eye closing up, and I mumble something about better luck next time. Evans is next, and now buoyed by the death blows I have just dealt, I feel confident that I can take the Welsh boy. Wrong—dead wrong.

Evans shoots out from his corner like a dog with its tail on fire and smacks me straight in the mouth. I reel back, my eyes filling with salt and my face stinging. I stagger after him as he nimbly bounces away, bobbing and weaving in front of me with a taunting look on his face. Bastard, I have to hit him; in fact, I want to kill him. But I can't get near him as he twirls past me like a marionette and slugs my right ear, which explodes like a meteor shower. My arms flail like a windmill in empty space, and I sob in frustration—he simply isn't there. Punches rain down on me like winter hail-stones, pain and humiliation flood my soul, jeering laughter fills my head. It's endless, and I have wild thoughts of the priesthood—anything, any-where, that is peaceful and away from this incessant hellish pounding.

A bell rings off in some distant place and I think it might be a nice old church bell or something, but it is the chime that signifies Evans's smirking and beastly triumph over me. I crawl from the ring like a whipped dog and a strong sense of the audience's schadenfreude. After the beating I limp home with some friends. Do I perceive hints of pity? Do I see faint smiles? We talk casually about giving Evans a collective bashing, but in the end we do nothing about it, probably because we think he could take the lot of us.

As members of the academic stream, we are privileged to receive a somewhat different style of teaching than the moron scum in the forms below us. En-glish literature, for example, in its relaxed and conversational style, is run like a club for insiders. Our teacher, Miss James—an oasis of sanity and reason in a school that seems to be filled with psychotic, deranged, and sexually per-verse teachers—is about seventy years old, dresses in tweed suits, covers her hair with a net, and speaks to us in the plummy tones of the aristocracy. I find her considerable enthusiasm for literature and the English language con-tagious, and whatever assignments she sets us are a pleasure rather than dull homework. A real teacher like Miss James is an accomplice as you discover parts of yourself at an early age, and although I am already a committed reader, this dear old lady stokes the fire.

We voyage through the plots of *Jude the Obscure, The Mayor of Caster-bridge, Far from the Madding Crowd,* and *Tess of the D'Urbervilles*, all of which have a resonance since they are written by Thomas Hardy, who might be termed a local. The pessimism of these books doesn't put me off. En-thralled by characters like Jude, Michael Henchard, and Sue Bridehead, and by the fragility of their relationships, I begin waking up to what appears to me a view of the world that is real. My mother also loves Hardy and has read all the novels, and suddenly we are able to talk about something that seems light-years from childhood. A few miles away the green hills of Dorset—the setting for Hardy's stories—take on a new significance. We study other literature with Miss James, but it is the tragedy of Jude, the travails of Michael Henchard, the adventures of Tess and Sergeant Troy that get me, come in like a dark knot and never leave.

To get to school, I have to trudge for two miles through a shady wood that seems to hold about two hundred homosexual men on a daily basis. In these benighted days in Britain the love that dare not speak its name is still deeply in the closet and regarded as a crime against nature. The term *gay* still means happy, carefree spirits and crinoline doilies à la Jane Austen, not yet the perfectly greased six-packs, San Francisco bathhouses, Zapata mustaches, and flashing muscle. If you are gay at this time, you are queer or ginger or nancy or a turd burglar, and you had better keep your identity hidden or risk not only being ostracized from "decent" society but also a prison term to boot, and many a day in yonder wood do I see a pink upraised willy twirling at me from behind a stout oak. They are usually pale middle-aged men who look lonely and no doubt will run like a frightened rabbit if challenged. Sometimes they trail behind us in the distance, dodging behind bushes and trying to work up the courage to unleash their spinnakers into the fresh spring air.

Each morning between eight-thirty and nine the entire school joins together in the assembly hall. We hear remarks about the supposed progress of the school, followed by a short Bible reading, and then we sing a couple of hymns before trudging off to our various classes. In the fifth form we stand in a shabby line at the back of the hall. We hate the hymn-singing part of assembly, and just as we did with Mr. Furneaux, deliberately sing as off-key as possible, pissing ourselves while doing so. It's a cacophonous racket and we do it as a matter of habit, thinking that no one can detect where it's coming from. One morning after the headmaster, a miserable old bastard named Mr. Legg, has advised us all to "hitch our wagon to a star," I for some reason get called up to the stage where I stand while the last hymn is sung. With the strains of "Jerusalem" echoing around the hall, I am filled with abject horror as I hear the caterwauling coming from the back row where I normally stand. It is loud, clear, awful, and desperately obvious who the culprits—my mates—are; I cringe and gain a new respect for the teachers who either have an excellent sense of humor or are tone-deaf.

A couple of months after my twelfth birthday, I am at the front of a line of kids waiting to go into class. Everyone is pushing and shoving and being stupid until suddenly the line surges and I get pushed through the door, which is made of glass. I push out my arms to save myself but go straight through the glass, shattering it in all directions. I hit the ground with blood pumping at warp speed from my right hand, all of its fingers now slashed open. I scream and scream, cry out for my mother, and eventually get raced off to the emergency ward, where everything is sewn back together and I live—but for the rest of my life with a right hand full of scarred fingers.

Somewhere in the middle of these chaotic days of inky pages and military-style school thrashings, I get the faint idea that I have a thing for music, an ear for it maybe, but no way in which to express it other than enthusiastic talk and humming the day's idiotic songs—the piano lessons now having faded because of my getting a pair of roller skates. But shortly after my thirteenth birthday things change when I am given a guitar by my uncle Jim.

Jim has recently returned to England after years of living in Africa. Because of his exploits he has a somewhat legendary status in our family, having lived with actual Africans, shot at lions, and been down the diamond mines. When I was six he sent me a present of a book called *The Man-Eaters of Tsavo,* a story of some wild lions that attack a camp in Kenya. Thrilled by the vision of flesh being ripped by wild cats, I love it and wonder if Uncle Jim has ever seen one, a lion.

One day he comes over and says, "Come 'ere a minute, I've got something for you." He stares down at me, his face brown and furrowed by years under the African sun, and from a battered case he pulls out an old and beaten Spanish guitar and says, "What do you think about this—I had it in Africa—would you like it?" My heart almost stops because to me it is complicated and exotic—a fabulous machine. He passes it to me and I feel a rush of blood as I whisper, "Thank you, Uncle," and carry it into my bedroom as if trying not to drop an egg. Scratched and dented with a string missing, it isn't much of an instrument, but I love it instantly and sit on the edge of the bed with it cradled in my arms, holding it in the position that I have seen used by guitarists on TV. I study it and gaze at its dents and scratches, its evidence of a long life, and wonder how many songs have been played on it, where it's been. It is an immediate bond, and possibly in that moment there is a shift in the universe because this is the moment, the point from which my life unfolds. I strike the remaining strings, which make a sound like slack elastic. It's horribly out of tune and I don't know even the simplest chord, but to me it is the sound of love.

It may be the sound of love, but with no idea of how to tune it and even less idea of how to play it, I don't know how to put one foot or finger in front of another. But Providence is at hand in the shape of a six-foot-seven ex-RAF serviceman by the name of David Ellis, a lodger my parents have recently taken into the house. We call him Cloudy because he literally towers over the rest of us, and we like to ask him how the weather is up there, but he's a genial personality and luckily for me a musician: a pianist. He immediately sees my plight and remedies the situation by returning one day with a new set of strings and a chord book with instructions on how to tune the guitar.

I watch, fascinated, as he wrestles the strings onto the guitar and proceeds to tune it to the family piano. He then hands me the guitar and asks me to try out a D7 chord as shown on page one of the book, a simple triangle shape. With the guitar now in tune, the chord comes out sounding like heaven and I laugh in amazement as if I have received a surprise kiss at a party. I try some of the other shapes, like E, A, and B7. At first it's slow and painful—this being the last moment in my life when my fingers will be without calluses—but I become obsessed and manfully struggle on into the night as the guitar gradually detunes itself and slides from the sound of an angel's harp to the moan of hell. Cloudy comes to the rescue and brings the strings up to pitch again. We go on like this for a couple of weeks until I slowly get my fingers around the open-position chords and learn to tune to the piano. I'm shaky and nervous but, taking a deep breath, decide to make an appearance at school with my guitar.

A few years earlier you would never have seen something as exotic as a guitar, but now it's beginning to establish its iconic presence as the trenchant symbol of youth. I notice a few other kids in the playground showing off to small groups during the morning or afternoon break and I start by joining these little throngs and looking over shoulders at the hands of the other boys as they form strange little triangles and parallelograms on the necks of their guitars. After school as I stumble home through the woods past the familiar trees, rotting logs, and spirals of pussy willow, I try to memorize these configurations, holding my left hand in the air, fingers clustered in three points against the dark wet greenness.

At first I am shy because I now have a new identity and have to grow into it like a new skin. I expect a certain amount of snideness from the playground yobs, but because I have given myself time to get at least the first few chords down, it goes smoothly, with a minimum of jeering, and I become one of the kids with a guitar. The instrument is a badge of power: it makes me different and also helps me overcome feelings of physical inadequacy that I have in comparison to some of the tall blond superathletes who seem to abound in my form. I pick up more chords from other kids who have been playing longer than me, for at this time there is no other way to learn—no videos, no DVDs, no CD-ROMs, few books. You get information—chord by chord—only if another kid takes pity on you, so I get it wherever I can and practice into the night.

I begin taking the guitar to school almost every day, slogging through the woods weighed down by the satchel on my back and the guitar in my hand. I am a fanatic now, and if I don't have it with me at school, I race home at night to get back on it. One of the first side effects I notice is that it attracts girls. The guitar, like the gun, sticks out from the body phallic and hard; even in the pubescent stage of consciousness, the boy with the guitar—unless he is impossibly ugly—becomes a more sexually desirable being, has the aura of a gunslinger.

Those of us who play the guitar in school tend to group together, and it's not long before we are strumming away in the front rooms of various mums' and dads' houses. Five of us decide to call ourselves the Midnighters, although none of us has ever been allowed to stay up past eleven. We fancy ourselves a skiffle group. Skiffle is a new movement and a new word that has recently entered the English vocabulary with the emergence of Lonnie Donegan, a former singer with the Chris Barber Jazz Band. Lonnie is very popular with his guitar and vocal style. He sings songs like "Rock Island Line" and "John Henry," and skiffle seems like a music that even we lowly schoolboys might achieve.

Mostly we just have guitars, but one day Graham White, our number three guitarist, brings along a tea chest bass. A primitive musical device made out of a box with a broom handle sticking out of it, a string is attached between the box and the handle so that when plucked, it gives a thudding atonal boom. Graham's homemade bass is bigger than he is, and after various sarcastic suggestions that maybe he should stand on it rather than play it, he gives up and uses it as a hutch for his pet rabbit, Sneaky. Another poor sod suggests that he play piano along with our strumming guitars, but that idea is greeted with hoots of derision: we are men with guitars, skifflers, and we stare with a steely-eyed gaze down railroad tracks that disappear into infinity.

Our repertoire is limited but we learn American folk songs like "Midnight Special," "John Henry," "Worried Man Blues," and "Tom Dooley," all of which we play with a grim enthusiasm as if battling our way out of hell. There is no concept of parts or dynamics other than just banging away like maniacs at E, A, and B7, and we probably resemble a bad Salvation Army band or an outtake of the Shaggs. The song lyrics are all about trains driving across the Deep South on errant time schedules and men who drive steel into the Missouri dirt or "wimin who dun me wrong," and the lace curtains and overstuffed couches of Graham White's mum are assaulted with the gutbucket feeling of black poverty squawked out by spotty-faced boys whose balls haven't dropped yet.

My guitarist profile takes a sharp turn upward when I not only get the leading role in the school Christmas play but then reappear afterward onstage to sing "Tom Dooley" and "Worried Man Blues" with our skiffle group. When I finish there's an audible gasp from the audience, but whether it's in disbelief at the gross ineptitude of the performance or the ghastly Americanized row that has sullied the assembly hall, one will never know. But the result is that my status at school goes up several notches, and from this moment on I often have a small group of girls trailing behind me through the woods as I walk home. This is followed in the evenings by anonymous giggling phone calls. My career as a rock star has begun.

My friends are now mostly other boys who have guitars, and I start to spend a lot of time with a kid named Eddie Evans because, older than I, he knows about players like Merle Travis, Chet Atkins, and Buddy Holly and he has records I have never seen or heard before. He plays me "Saturday Night Shuffle" by Merle Travis, and it knocks me to the floor. I have never heard playing like this before, with two parts going at once, and I am fascinated. Eddie has some EPs and we sit on the linoleum floor of his bedroom, leaning against his bed, guitars in position with a couple of Woodbines dangling from our lips, the windows open so his mum won't notice the smell. Eddie has a slight clue about how it's done, something about playing on the bass string at the same time as you play the melody on the treble strings. It's bloody difficult, and as we listen to the record above the din of the trolley buses that go droning by his mum's upstairs flat, Merle's fingerpicking pierces the blue smoke of our Woodies like a shamanistic spell.

"Peggy Sue" is a lot easier. I get it quickly and we strum through it a couple of hundred times with great enthusiasm until Eddie's mum starts banging on the wall with a broom and yells out that it's setting the parrot off and she can't hear the telly. Chastened, because we think we sound so great, we turn to another Buddy Holly item: the opening lick to "That'll Be the Day." A thing of beauty, this lick in the key of E major starts on an A on the third string, immediately slurs to a b flat note, which is then played as a triplet across the open B natural and E strings and then descends on down and into the open E major chord. This is pure rock-and-roll genius, a stunning piece of guitar devised by someone who is probably only seven or eight years older than we are.

To our thirteen-year-old minds almost everything about the guitar seems to come from or be over there, in America, at least everything we are interested in. All the best guitars are American, all the great players and the styles: rock and roll, jazz, and country music. We don't have a Buddy Holly, an Eddie Cochran, a Gene Vincent; we live in rural England, and the USA might as well be another planet, to go there would be like trying to book a flight to the moon.

The guitar and its players appear to us as if shrouded in a heavenly mist; we are utterly seduced by the glamour of the photographs on the sleeves of LPs that we stare at in the racks of the local record stores. The faces in these black-and-white photographs stare back at us from under greased and coiffed hair and turned-up collars as if to say, "Hey, baby, wanna little rock and roll?" We do, and it never occurs to us for an instant that they are human beings struggling with drugs, broken marriages, and lousy managers—for to us they are gods. We gaze at their glossy images, the glint in their eye as if they know something we don't, and hear them call with the scream of the blues, rock and roll, bent strings, and a yeah baby yeah that is about a million miles from a tea dance at the Bournemouth Pavilion.

As I get back on the twenty-nine bus to go home at the end of the afternoon, my head is swimming with guitar licks. I wanted to stay at Eddie's and play on through the night, but it's getting late; I have homework and my mum will be getting anxious. The conductor arrives at my seat and asks me where to. "Nashville," I reply dreamily, staring out the window into the rainy English night and the sputtering neon of Brown's fish-and-chip shop.

Sometimes I go over to Carl Hollings's house. Carl is an Elvis fan, and that is the only music he will play or listen to, anyone who doesn't like Presley getting a bloody nose for lack of respect. I prefer to stay on Carl's good side, and we sprawl on a fake fur rug in front of his mum's imitation coal fire—which features actual flickering flames—and croak along with the El, singing "Teddy Bear" or "Heartbreak Hotel." Other times, in a more pensive mood or depressed by homework, we get serious and play his EP *Peace in the Valley,* El's spiritual side coming through in the old-style hymns he sings with such sincerity. When we're not listening to the King, Carl and I sometimes go into the town center and try to nick sweets from Woolworth's while we hum along with Neil Sedaka in the background singing "Oh Carol."

There's a boy a year ahead of me named Peter Jones who some of the kids say is the best guitar player in school. He has this reputation because apparently he can play the intro to "Move It," which is a hit by Cliff Richard and the Shadows, but he won't show it to anybody, so I get friendly with him with the ulterior motive of capturing this lick. We get chummy and one afternoon after school he invites me to his house to have a session in his mum's front room. We play for half an hour, strumming along in unison on the simple chords that we know, and then I ask him if by any chance he knows the intro to "Move It." *Oh yeah,* comes the nonchalant and unsuspecting reply. He quickly rips it out, a very simple double stopping in fourths on the E and B strings ending on the E major chord. It's a knockout, this simple lick that seems to contain everything for which I lust: the blues, sex, glamour, electric guitar, and the far-off shores of America. But casually, as if I already vaguely know it, I say, "Oh, I get it, yeah—now I remember," for now that I have seen it, I possess it, and a new guitar door opens with the light of heaven pouring through.

With this lick under my fingers, it seems like a godlike coincidence when it's announced that they—Cliff Richard and the Shadows—are coming to town. All of us aspiring young guitarists go because Cliff and his group are about the nearest thing we have in England to Elvis or anything from the United States. They are on at the Winter Gardens, where previously I have been only on school outings to hear Sir Charles Groves conduct the Bournemouth Symphony Orchestra. The show, about an hour and a half in duration, is divided into two parts, with an intermission halfway through so that the proprietors can flog ice cream, chocolate, and orangeade. During the first half, naturally enough, the guitarist wannabes in the audience never take their eyes off of Hank Marvin with his red Stratocaster. Hank is already a guitar hero, although that phrase hasn't yet been coined. Black horn-rimmed glasses à la Buddy Holly make him cool, an interesting prototype nerd and the perfect nonthreatening foil to Cliff, who is a good-looking Elvis clone. We all think that Hank is a great guitarist, and to a man we all want to be him. But he's a long way in front of us, and the Shadows are already having hits on their own with instrumental pieces like "Apache." They play a pleasant English variant of surf music, pretty melodies played with a nice, clean twangy sound, like Dick Dale or the Ventures, but somehow lacking the grit of the original. Another thing about the Shadows that impresses us all is a little dance step they have worked out when backing Cliff. It's a neat backward two-step that makes a circle and can be repeated infinitely. Of course, we all ape it and try it when we practice; sometimes we even practice it with tennis rackets or a cricket bat, and it still looks cool.

During the intermission we pile out of the theater for a breather, and I separate myself from the mob for a moment to cogitate on what Hank is doing up there. I wander toward the back of the theater, and to my amazement standing there like Zeus is the man himself. "Hank, my G-G-God," I stutter, and I scream out, "H-a-a-a-a-n-k," and propel myself toward the skinny guitarist like an F-16. What Hank sees coming toward him is hard to be sure of, but while it is actually a slight fourteen-year-old with an ear-to-ear grin, I think for Hank the boy has morphed into a thousand-pound rhino or the Incredible Hulk because a look of cold white terror passes across the lead guitarist's face and he takes off like a reebok.

I zoom after him like a heat-seeking missile, the word *autograph* strobing across my brain like a red alert. Hank tears down into Bournemouth Square, shoots around it and back again toward the Winter Gardens. It's peculiar, to say the least, because it's only the two of us running, there are no other fans in sight, just the two of us, a bespectacled guitarist being pursued by a small boy at full tilt past bus stops, queues of bored-looking people, the upper pleasure gardens, and various assorted litter bins stuffed with ice-cream wrappers, old newspapers, cigarette stubs, and the shit of seagulls. Hank runs and I run. It becomes dreamlike, a film in slow motion—the world falls away, and I am pursuing not only Hank Marvin but the guitar itself, which seems far away and suspended in amber.

"Hank," I yell—my voice blending with the screech of the overhead gulls that wheel above us like rats with wings—"pleeeeeeeease." We shoot back toward the theater and my hero finally pulls over near a large rhododendron bush, panting like a racehorse at the end of eight furlongs. "Oh, alright," he gasps. I proffer my grubby little program, and Hank smiles in a dazed way and scribbles his name. I thank him, and he disappears back into the theater. Several years later when I sit down in a music shop in the West End with Hank one afternoon and exchange pleasantries, somehow I don't have the heart to mention our Keystone Kops chase a few years earlier, as it might have sullied the moment when I finally met one of my heroes on not quite, but almost, equal terms.

Two

I get up from the piano and stretch—what bloody time is it anyway? I remember that there is a clock in the hallway and I go to discover with a nasty jolt that it's barely nine A.M. This is horribly early; I don't have to be at the gig for fifteen hours, but it's only fucking Shea Stadium tonight (only the biggest gig) and I have to go back to bed. I climb back up the stairs and return to my room, pick up my guitar, and get into bed with it. The guitar lies next to me with its head on the pillow. I run a hand over its scarred surface, caressing the warm wood. *There's the metaphor,* I think dozily, *there's the marriage. It's to this, this bloody thing.* I lean back on the pillow with the guitar across my chest, and strum a few gentle chords that make me dreamy. Big one tonight—you'd better practice. . . . Lying back in the sheets, I run through some chord passages that are as familiar as old friends, always there when you want them.

Music and the suspension of time . . . I pick up a pen at the side of the bed and write down the phrase. *Time ceases to exist when you play—collapses. . . . You play in . . . real time. . . . Extemporization means to play outside of time . . . getting lost in the instrument, following your fingers, tracing a line of thought out onto the frets and strings, letting it become a maze through which you wander—learning to play means learning to forget yourself, to disappear into the thing you are doing. Like an act of meditation—the instrument is a sacred space you always return to. Just practicing is enough.* This has been my touchstone since the first obsessive years as a teenager, when I would sit in my bedroom at home and practice ten hours at a stretch, lost in the guitar.

In the first year or so I learn from other kids and the book my uncle gave me, but the great inspiration of the week is a radio program called *Guitar Club,* which is on at six-thirty every Saturday night. It's hosted with dry English humor by Ken Sykora and features the best British guitar talent—players such as Diz Dizley, Ike Isaacs, and Dave Goldberg. I never miss it. I listen intently and after a while I notice something that sounds like a crying or laughing sound in the middle of solo passages. I wonder what it is and how they do that. One day while practicing I accidentally push the B string over sideways and then release it to its correct position on the fret, and I hear the string make the crying sound I've heard on the radio and I almost fall on the floor. I have just played my first blues note! After that, I can't wipe the smirk from my face as I bend the strings when I am around other kids with guitars. Most of the guitarists on *Guitar Club* are jazz players whose playing—typical of the time—comes out of Charlie Christian and bebop, and I am knocked out by the effortless way they rip out solos. My fourteen-year-old response to this is from the gut; I have to get this stuff, no matter what it takes. This is the path to the stars. Most of my friends are content to get the hang of a few Shadows tunes, but I take the high road, sit on the edge of my bed, and struggle into the night.

On Sunday afternoon at two o'clock there's a TV show with vocalists, big-band numbers, and various soloists. One is the guitarist Dave Goldberg, and munching on a Birds Eye fish finger, I wait for his solo spot when I can watch his fingers dance across the pearloid double parallelograms of his Gibson ES 175. My mum usually stands there with a huge pile of ironing, murmuring little pieces of encouragement like "You'll be able to do that one day, love—just keep practicing," and then runs the iron down my cotton shirtsleeve as if heating it up for my future.

I spend hours in my bedroom hunched obsessively over my guitar, trying to sound like the records that I play over and over. Sometimes I think about girls and feel faint as I drown in a fantasy of women and music, and then I feel like a prisoner. I meet a kid named Mike, who plays guitar and also likes jazz. He invites me over to his house and we listen to his one Tal Farlow record together. He points out things to me about the guitarist's phrasing, and it thrills me to have found someone who is as excited as I am about this music. We turn up at each other's house with our guitars and practice together, swapping licks and trying to accompany each other on "Autumn Leaves" or "All the Things You Are," although we haven't really got the chords figured out. And we don't have the deep swing feel yet, so it doesn't sound like much. But we love it anyway and enjoy talking and studying the pictures on the back of our few records: cool Americans with great-looking guitars, dark suits, and button-down collars. We want to be like that, play like that, dress like that, and maybe this is the first inkling of what will later be called Mod.

Slowly I build my collection of LPs until I have a grand total of eight. They sit on the windowsill beneath damask curtains, and I stare at them and feel like a king. Holding my breath, I pull the precious fuliginous object from the sleeve, check it for imperfections, flick at it with my sleeve, and then lower it into place on the spindle that rises like a miniature cathedral from the center of the player. I set the volume and then gently lower the tone arm into place and nervously find the passage by dropping the stylus point into the black until I find it, carefully noting its distance from the perimeter of the disc so that I can find it again. I sit on the floor by the fireplace of my bedroom, playing them at 16 revs per minute instead of the prescribed 33⅓. Now I learn the solo by repeatedly dropping the needle into this spot, trying to match my notes to the player's. The disc spins like a black sun below me, and out comes the solo, a full octave below the speed at which it was recorded. Sometimes, if it is a slower passage, it sounds like a wolf howling into the night and I imagine the player drunk and staggering down a dark street.

This playing of LPs at half speed is a fairly common practice at the time, and if you want to learn the fancy stuff, this is how you do it. But I get better at it, become more adept at copying the phrasing and the flow of the musicians I am listening to. Sometimes it is beyond me, I can't always hear the intervals. I make mistakes, become frustrated but gradually get faster and begin to recognize patterns, grasp the vocabulary, and get the lick that always works over a minor seventh chord.

The neck of the guitar becomes a territory of chords, melodic lines, shapes, and colors, and the grid of strings and frets fills my head as if from a dream. I talk with others; we are all after the same thing: the flow, the cascade, the ripple and stream, the notes that rise like highlights over the burnt umber harmony below, the jazz improviser's swerving, reacting, parrying, and dancing lead. His ability—like an actor—to be sad, jubilant, poignant, and earthy. The Taoists described the act of meditation as facing an unsculpted block of time, and the musician as he extemporises creates a dream, a suspended state, a place that has slipped from the grasp of the ordinary; at the end of a good solo with the last phrase appearing as the final blossom of the first, the audience seems to wake as if from a trance.

The sessions with guitars and records become almost a sacred state, the dark whirling records like mandalas—the repeated solos, mantras running through my head like a distant train. I become reclusive and private about my practice session and add to the isolation by creating a barrier around my record player out of a couch, an armchair, and a reangling of my bed. My room looks strange, as if the furniture's been arranged by a madman, but I climb across my bed and down into my magic circle and sit for several hours with guitar and LPs, lost in surrender to this world.

Most of what I learn about jazz comes from my own rabid curiosity and whatever I can pick up by ear. But a friend tells me about a hard-to-find record shop in the center of town that sells American jazz imports, and I go looking for it that weekend. I find it buried at the end of an alley between Woolworth's back entrance and the British Home Stores. I stand outside and gaze at the window, which displays sleeves with pictures of men as they raise saxophones, hunch over a double bass, or lean back from a snare drum with whirling hands. This is real jazz. It seems beyond reach; what hope would I have of ever getting to understand this world? I don't recognize any of the names, and it hits me like a scary alien planet.

I take a deep breath and push open the door, which makes a loud chiming sound and blows my invisibility, making me even more nervous. Stepping down into the shop—which has the dank atmosphere of an old wine cellar—

I get a strange feeling in the pit of my stomach. This cave is filled from floor to ceiling with racks of American records: Blue Note, Riverside, Columbia, Contemporary Jazz Masters. There is no one in the shop except a small dark-haired man with olive skin who stands behind the counter, smoking a cigarette and exuding power. I look over at him and he appears enormous. He looks up, grunts, and then looks back down at an album he is holding.

This dingy hole is filled with everything I aspire to. Feeling like a thief, I start thumbing through the racks quietly, taking in the names, the faces, the song titles. Another man comes into the shop and goes over to the counter. I overhear their conversation as they smoke and talk with small world-weary laughs and references that I don't get. But I get the owner's name—Lenny—and begin returning to the shop every weekend. I don't have the money to buy anything, but I read the sleeves and try to take in the ambience. He sells only jazz albums, and it's as if he is giving up something from his personal collection when with an attitude of "are you worthy?" he lets someone walk out with an LP.

He seems remote, cynical, and I think he doesn't like me; I buy nothing and I know nothing. I feel anxious about Lenny, hoping that maybe he will become friendly, tell me something, share a joke with me. I finger my way through the racks of Cannonball Adderly, John Coltrane, and Miles Davis albums and furtively stare across the shop to where he stands like a priest at the altar, engaged in a sardonic conversation with one of his friends, who all seem to supplicate in front of him. As an expert on the subject of my desire, he wields an emotional power over me even though we have never exchanged a word. But one afternoon I approach the cash register and he leans across the counter, takes a long drag on his cigarette, blows a smoke ring toward the first rack, looks out through the window and says, "So, you like jazz."

I start talking with Lenny and nervously tell him what I know—not much—but that I really love it, and how can I learn? I explain that I am a guitarist, or would like to be one anyway. He nods and pulls a few records from the racks. Wes Montgomery, Jimmy Raney, Barney Kessel, Tal Farlow. Then he holds up a Blue Note LP and taps it, saying, "This one is great—just got it." It's Kenny Burrell's *On View at the Five Spot Cafe,* with Art Blakey on drums.

I leave that afternoon, my heart pounding with a strange mixture of relief and commitment, as if I've just been allowed into the priesthood. I can't wait to play the album, and when I get home and finally get it onto the turntable, it puts me in a trance and I play it over and over. I love Burrell's dark wine-stained sound and the atmosphere of this album, with its sound of low murmuring voices, clinking glasses, and laughter somehow conveying the impression of the jazz life, the living reality. I feel as if it is me right there on the stage, guitar in hand, moodily playing to the darkness of a small club in lower Manhattan. No doubt I romanticize it heavily, but the ambience of the club and the liquid voice of the guitar represent some kind of nirvana to me.

I decide to learn Kenny's solo on "Lover Man"—one of the best jazz guitar solos ever recorded—but he plays it in g minor, which takes me a while to understand. But eventually—as I work from a tattered piece of red-colored sheet music with a picture of Billie Holiday on the cover—I am able to transpose it from d minor and note by note learn to play it like a song on its own.

BRIDGEHAMPTON, AUGUST 18, 1983

I play a few more chords. My left hand drifts into a c# minor chord that I play with open E and B strings. I have been playing this configuration constantly over the past few weeks, making a new composition out of it as I hear a top line of a pretty descending chromatic melody. This c# minor area manages to sound both minor and major at the same time as it relates to E major and A major, both big guitar-friendly keys. I stop for a second and move to the fifth fret and the central position on the guitar neck. D minor and another set of feelings and constellations appear. This key is darker and brings to mind Django, the sound of a clarinet, rain forming deep puddles under my window, and my dad cursing as the roses get beaten into the dirt.

Lenny and I become more friendly and he begins to broaden my listening beyond the guitar. He gives me a heavily discounted price on albums, and after a while I have a collection of Monk, Coltrane, Miles, Sonny Rollins, and Ornette Coleman. I listen intently in an effort to have a view of jazz beyond the guitar. Lenny pushes my appreciation further when he gives me an album called *The Thelonius Monk Orchestra at the Town Hall*, a live recording of Thelonius Monk with a big band. As I listen to this LP, Monk's compositions and asymmetrical magic hit me like a revelation. I report back to Lenny, who is pleased that I "got" it and then tells me that Monk is coming to England in a few months.

Pop isn't rock yet, and like the nineteenth century turning into the twentieth, music hasn't reached the creative self-conscious stage where it will have edge, artiness, and expression with lyrics rooted in poetry and the hallucinatory ramblings of Bob Dylan. And as I struggle with the guitar in the first two or three years of playing, it is not pop that calls to me but the darker precipice of American music, with its blue underworld, edgy solos, loose drums, and dark-throated bass. I want to play the real outsider music—jazz. British pop and British culture at this stage are about as much fun as a Mcvities biscuit. We have Helen Shapiro, Alma Cogan, and the Beverley Sisters. They have Elvis, Little Richard, Chuck Berry, Link Wray, Lonnie Mack, Ray Charles, James Brown, Muddy Waters, Bo Diddley, Miles, Coltrane, and Monk. The words *rock* and *star* haven't cojoined yet, and you don't aspire to rock (because it doesn't exist), but you do effect a lip-curling insouciance, imagine blowing a smoke ring, calling girls "chicks," whistling a Miles solo. Rock music, guitars, and youth culure will eventually infiltrate everything, even the sacred ground of such luminaries as Miles Davis, and will shape the course that jazz takes in the late sixties and seventies.

Under Lenny's guidance, I continue to expand and add horn players and pianists to my listening: Bill Evans, Horace Silver, Clifford Brown, Hank Mobley. I begin reading *Really the Blues* by Mezz Mezzrow and Louis Armstrong's autobiography. I begin to feel more immersed in this jazz thing and I stare into my bedroom mirror, seeing the guy on the record sleeve, the cat in a dark suit, the man. Sometimes this vision fades and all I see is a boy with tousled hair, freckles, and a red-and-yellow school tie, and then I'm overcome with panic as my self-confidence hits the floor. But slowly my courage grows and I form opinions. Although I still like Cliff Richard and the Shadows, *Kind of Blue* and "Goodbye Pork Pie Hat" make "We're All Going on a Summer Holiday" seem like a piece of fluff.

Lying on a towel in the hot sand of Bournemouth Beach, with the high-summer mélange of ice cream, candy floss, sunburned skin, and the petroleum fumes of Nivea cream crowding in, I see another world, a place where things are broken, bittersweet—the lipstick smudge on the rim of the cup, the woman gone, a smoky blue drift in a cheap room, the croon of a tenor sax. I get up from the sand, vaguely thinking I want a Cornish mivvi, and begin picking my way through the thicket of red sunburned legs toward the water's edge. As I kick through the feeble waves that fall on the hot grit between my toes, my head is filled with the sad and beautiful vision of this other life: its drift from the brothels of New Orleans to the streets of New York, its high priests—Armstrong, Ellington, Parker, Miles, and Coltrane—the words I don't understand, *reefer, horse junk, ofay, Jim Crow, hoochie coochie.*

And then I notice a girl lying in the sand with two friends. Her name is Jenna; she goes to my school and she's in a tight blue bathing costume that's glistening and wet from a dip in the sea. I stare at her breasts swelling over the top of her costume. She looks like a woman, a flame bursts to life inside me, and my head feels hot. With my pulse thudding like an African drum, I go over to her. "Hi," I say. She turns away from her friends for a second and squints up at me. "Oh, hi," she says. I notice that there's a fly on her nose but that she doesn't flick it away. I wonder if the fly knows how lucky he is. I offer a small penguinlike wave and limp off.

"Moose the Mooche," "Sippin' at Bells," "Klact-Oveeseds-Tene," Jenna's breasts, mouths, legs, junkies, powder, horn solos, and zoot suits, Birdland, Manhattan, the stink of seaweed, the din of screaming gulls, and an aching lust pour into me like cider. I laugh like a parrot at the rusting girders of the pier as if sharing a joke with them and then, confused and sighing with desire for jazz and Jenna, I struggle past the Punch-and-Judy show, through the thicket of deck chairs, the screaming babies, and the snoring dads with handkerchiefs on their heads and buy a Lyons Maid choc ice and a can of Tango.

At home, after practicing, I lie on the eiderdown, my old Spanish guitar lying across my chest, and mentally project a movie onto the plastered ceiling. There it is—-flickering like a black-and-white Sennett film. A shadowy figure with the guitar that sings a phrase like the low moan of midnight and a thousand cigarettes out into the cinder blue ambience of the Five Spot. Jenna is sitting there, waiting, dressed in a sexy low-cut dress, her mouth like a scarlet flower—she exudes the scent of roses. After the second set I take her out. We go downtown to a little Italian restaurant—they know me here—we sit in the corner, drink red wine, touch under the table, the night ahead swollen with desire. . . .

I still have to do my homework but I pick up *Really the Blues* and my eyes flicker along the passage about Mezzrow's jail sentence and how he, a white Jew, passes himself off as black—the words are getting fuzzy . . . my eyes are ruined.

BRIDGEHAMPTON, AUGUST 18, 1983

Ten-thirty A.M. Finding it hard to sleep, I reach over the side of the bed into my travel bag for my cassette player and think, *Well, yeah, didn't work out quite like that, but still* . . . I am looking for a tape of the great Brazilian guitarist Luiz Bonfá, thinking that I'll relax and listen to some music. In the jumble of my traveling bag, with its tapes, headphones, cassette player, paperbacks, notebooks, and a half-chewed apple, I can't find it, so I lean back and, half asleep, play through a solo version of "Manhã de Carnaval," a song I first heard at sixteen in the underbelly of the Continental cinema.

The Continental is a place where, in an atmosphere reeking of stale cigarettes, ice cream, and sperm, you can vicariously experience the world out there. The specialty of this cinema is the double and triple Xers, films such as *And God Created Woman* with Brigitte Bardot, which would have us all sitting in the front row, gazing upward with lust at her tiny waist and swelling breasts as she writhes through yet another sultry melodrama. Or, as if correcting a moral imbalance, films about the perils of venereal disease or smoking marijuana, providing us with an educational double message. It's as if the programs at the Continental place a fabulous cake on the table with a small warning that it contains strychnine. But one film that transcends all this and knocks me for six is *Black Orpheus*.

Set in Rio de Janeiro, the film is a reworking of the Orpheus myth with an all-black cast and fantastic music by Luiz Bonfá. The haunting melody of "Manhã de Carnaval," the exotic sun-drenched vistas of Rio, and the sheer physicality of it all fill me with a wave of desire, a sun-, sex-, and music-filled world that comes at me like a Brazilian Shangri-la. Naturally, I miss the irony: the poor black folks from the *favelas* who are able to forget the grinding poverty and violence of their lives with a song. But in the dark of the Continental, with its Chinese lanterns and odor of seedy loneliness, I am transported. Bonfá's exquisite melodic line and harmonies cut like a knife through my teenage emotions and shower sunlight like a beam of truth across the rows of grubby seats. Years later I will manifest this dream by playing many concerts in Brazil and finally performing this song on the beach in Copacabana one night to a large crowd of swaying *brasileiros*.

Although I love them and they have the effect of reinforcing or shaping my idea of the world, films do not threaten my pact with the guitar. When my hands are on the strings and the flow begins to happen, all is well and I intuit that this is how I will make my way. I start sending away for guitar catalogs and breathlessly wait for their arrival, when I greedily rip open the envelopes and lie on my bed for hours, drooling over the black-and-white photographs of Hofner Senator, Committee, and President guitars. New terms enter my head: lustrous sunbrust finishes, resonating tailpieces, ivoroid tuners, spruce soundboards, and split backs. I lay in bed at night with visions of these desirable instruments drifting through my fevered imagination. The concept of a rock star isn't on the map yet. There is no rock scene, no MTV, no possibility of being able to retire world-famous at twenty-five or have your face on a T-shirt; the only thing you have is trying to get good on your guitar. That is the target. There are Cliff Richards and other hip-shaking rebels, but if you can learn to play, maybe you will get in the band at the local Locarno—and this lowly idea is enough to sustain the endless hours of practice.

My best friend around this time is another guitarist by the name of Dave Wilson, an intelligent dark-haired boy with looks that most women can't resist. Dave plays classical guitar and also knows some flamenco. In addition to incessantly swapping guitar licks, we read the same books in tandem, discuss them at length, and become an opinionated guitar/book club of two. After a while we develop our own view: generally a sneering attitude to anything that we consider a part of the straight world, mostly received from the nasty books we read together. We increase our knowledge of cutting-edge culture by going to see foreign films directed by Godard, Truffaut, and Antonioni. We go see *Last Year at Marienbad;* with its multiple editing, layering of time, flashback and flash-forward sequences, it is just confusing. But we walk out sagely nodding at each other as if in deep understanding, both afraid to admit that we don't have a clue as to what the hell it was all about. Pretending to a deep knowledge of sex and women, we speak in terms that would make Casanova pale, but the truth is that neither of us has probably got much beyond twanging a tight bra strap or an end-of-party knee trembler. Women are still a far-off mystery.

Sometimes we go to a Spanish wine bar. Although we are too young to get a drink, we can get an orangeade and listen to the resident flamenco guitarist. Eventually we work up the courage to speak to the guitarist (who is friendly), and he tells us a little bit about the compass of flamenco and the names of some of the rhythms: bulerías, seguiriyas, and soleares. It all sounds exotic and weird to me, but I make a mental note to revisit this kind of guitar playing in the future. He plays a couple of pieces by Villa-Lobos and tells us it's classical guitar from Brazil. The angularity of the lines and the exotic harmony excite me; it isn't jazz, but it gets to me and I tuck it away for future investigation.

One summer we hitchhike down the French coast and into San Sebastián, just across the Spanish border. We sleep in fields and then grab whatever lifts we can the next morning. One of the better rides we get is with a French priest who regales us the whole way with tales of how he became a priest to avoid going into the army. We arrive in San Sebastián at around ten at night with nowhere to stay, but luckily a local police officer takes pity on us and shows us to a small pension in the middle of town. The landlady, whom we only know as the señora, has one room available with two beds, so we grab it. It also turns out that she has two beautiful daughters, and we immediately began fantasizing about them, goading each other on to new erotic delusions.

We wander around San Sebastián for a few days and sit on the beach with our books by Kierkegaard and Camus while we fry in the Spanish sun and starve because we have close to no money; existential life is alright as long as you can eat. But the señora feels sorry for us and murmurs, "*Delgado, delgado,*" when she sees us in the house. Eventually we start to eat with the family, the señora realizing that probably the only way we are going to get food is if she invited us to sit down with them in the evening. Being Spain, dinner doesn't happen until about ten o'clock at night, by which time we are hallucinating with hunger. All Dave and I are eating at this point are oranges washed down with water.

We eat in the kitchen at a big table. The father sits at one end and apart from a *"buenas noches"* is silent. He works in the local fish market and has a scar over his right eyebrow and curiously red cheeks. We sit opposite Isabella and Graciella, the two daughters, which is unsettling: they are about sixteen and eighteen years of age, a couple of Spanish sex bombs. They say almost nothing because they are shy and don't speak English, but they smile a lot. Maybe it's just in my head, but there is a feeling in the sultry kitchen air of electric sexuality. The heat of the summer night seems to be in collusion with their bare brown arms and legs, their vermillion lips and pink flicking tongues, until it seems as if fire is emanating from their bodies, and this combines with the Rioja to produce a feeling of suffocation and clothes that feel too tight, and the hot little kitchen and checkered tablecloth spin before me.

At seventeen there is only one thing on our minds and it's there, inches away. I think the señora, who has a Mona Lisa smile wreathed across her craggy face, is enjoying this moment, feeding us with one hand and putting us through the most exquisite torture with the other, like a witch cooking two shrimps in her cauldron.

In the middle of the table sits a large bowl of pears, pomegranates, and grapes. Luscious and ripe, they seem to mock us with their echo of the young females. When Isabella, the younger sister, proffers the bowl and my hand touches hers, it feels as though an electric eel has just dived into my body.

The kitchen, with its strong, soulful aroma of garlic and olive oil, has the effect of igniting our salivary glands to the point of liquidity. And as the señora serves us a bowl of steaming meat and vegetables along with dark bread and Manchego cheese and olive oil, we eat like wolves. She leans over the table and pours two more glasses of Rioja and with a raised eyebrow murmurs, *"¿Vino?"* and although we aren't really used to it, we don't argue. Above the center of the table hangs a small lamp with a shade constructed out of an old mantilla shawl with pictures of flamenco dancers. It seems incongruous in the small, hot confines of the kitchen but gives a subdued ambient light, casting shadows on the wall that are reminiscent of a Goya. On the wall opposite, next to a small painting of the Virgin, is a San Sebastián bullfight poster from a few years earlier, and suspended from a nail next to it, an ancient-looking guitar with one string missing.

I think we both have the same thought of asking to take down the guitar to play it and impress the girls, but we are too busy stuffing our faces. At the end of dinner the señora smiles at us and says, *"¿Quieren helados?"* and we both grin back and say, *"Sì, gracias,"* then the four of us sit at the table and slurp our way through large dollops of vanilla. Seeing Isabella and Graciella with ice cream dribbling down their chins and their tongues licking away at the diminishing whiteness is like witnessing a Balthus painting in action. For a moment the four of us grin at one another and experience a kind of sensual unity. It isn't sex, but it's within licking distance. We can't touch them, to do so would be to risk a knife in the back or death by accidental drowning in San Sebastián Bay . . . but then again, maybe it would be worth it.

Replete with Spanish food to the point of pain, Dave and I limp off to our monk's cell and try to return to Jean-Paul Sartre and nothingness, with the faint hope that it will take our fevered minds off the vision of two hot, naked females next door tossing and turning in the sultry Spanish night. We have strong thoughts about staying in Spain and just being itinerant, but eventually we hit the road and hitch rides back across France. Starving and hallucinating about food the whole way, we sustain each other with dreams of the future, which for me has to contain the guitar. After two weeks, I'm really missing it.

The following summer we go to Paris.

This is a different deal because we are slightly older and have suits, which we think are what you need to wear in Paris. We arrive at Orly in a small commercial plane and make our way to the city. Again we have nowhere to stay but find our way to Pigalle and eventually a small boardinghouse with a landlady who is obviously the reincarnation of Madame Defarge. This time there are no daughters, but a rather cold atmosphere where our existence is barely acknowledged. So we amuse ourselves by wandering around Paris and visiting the sites and desperately hoping to be picked up by two sexy girls. No girls come our way, but we roam around Pigalle at night and watch the prostitutes at work, many of whom are stunningly beautiful. We dare each other to go off with one of them, but neither of us has the balls for it, so to speak, although we receive many lovely smiles from the Sisters of Mercy as we cruise the boulevard. We are young meat and probably a better bet than many of the old lags whom we laugh at as they form huge lines to go into one particularly popular brothel, Vive la France.

After a few days we move to the rue de la Huchette in St. Michell, where we get a room above a jazz club called La Chat Qui Pêche. As we take up residence upstairs above the jazz club, the cellar features the American jazz trumpet star Chet Baker. This is in a moment of Chet's decline; we go down to see him play, but he is playing with a French rhythm section who just clunk along behind him with no real feeling or connection. Although I can't yet articulate it, I feel something coming from Chet, who appears broken but is still playing with an undeniable and heartbreaking lyricism. He is suffering from bad drugs, bad health, and lousy accompaniment; I'm too green to comprehend the subtext, but I have an intuition that something is wrong.

Another night when left to my own devices while Dave is off with a skinny German girl by the name of Margueritte, I head across the river to the Right Bank and the Blue Note Club. I stand outside and study the poster of who is playing. It's a trio with Kenny Clarke on drums, Jimmy Gourley on guitar, and a French organist I don't know. I desperately want to go in but it's very expensive, so it's out of the question. "Are you going in?" they ask. "No," I say wistfully, "haven't got the money." "We'll take you," they say, and in we go.

Inside it's dark and sexy with a small bar at the side of the room and a postage-stamp-size stage; the musicians aren't on yet, so my new mentor Bill orders drinks. I ask for a beer because I think it sounds cool and grown-up, but I would rather have a Coke. The trio comes on with a sort of world-weary resignation and begins the set. I'm stunned, it all flows so beautifully: Jimmy Gourley seems to melt from one pattern to another, swimming with consummate ease in the flux and whirl of drumming and chord changes. I watch his fingers and try to fathom some kind of logic—how does he know how to do that? He has a way of roaming all over the guitar neck that I just don't have yet. Of course, I have been playing only a couple of years and haven't yet grasped that there is a system of clichés, patterns, and scales you can learn and study that take you through all kinds of harmonic structure. But I can taste it, feel it. It's like an ache inside; I have to be able to do that.

To improvise, to dance across the strings with eyes closed, lost in the river of time, to make music in the instant, to reflect like a mirror—this is the way to speak to the world, this is the spirit eternal. Seeing Jimmy Gourley at the Blue Note is my first exposure to a great jazz guitar improviser, and it cuts deep. After the show I wander out with my friends into the Paris night and thank them and then, scared and on fire, begin the long walk back to our room in the Latin Quarter.

On my own and with my head back over a guitar rather than homework, I begin to feel that if I am going to be a contender, I will have to get a better instrument—and that means money, and that means work, and that means a newspaper route. This tedious labor begins just as the moon fades from the icy black sky and before the rooster crows. Unfortunately, I am in the pernicious habit of crouching over my rhubarb and custard Dansette copping licks until the wee hours. This would be fine if I could sleep until three the following afternoon, but my mum now gets me up at six A.M. Like a freak of nature I crawl out of bed, put my feet on an icy patch of linoleum, and struggle into my clothes while trying to gulp down a cup of Ovaltine. At this point—being exhausted—it would be nice to get back into bed, but instead I stagger out the front door, with my mum calling out not to be late for school. I cycle through flooded streets, treacherous ice, vicious dogs, and gale-force wind. With my hands seared to the handlebars and the sleety rain howling through my woolly balaclava, the heat of the Ovaltine rapidly disappearing from my stomach, I try to think about the guitar but realize it's a waste of time because no doubt, my hands, thanks to the blackening frostbite that's now creeping over them, will have to be hacked off at the wrists. There is not one day in which the weather is not ripping me to shreds as if I were undergoing some preprogrammed extreme conditions test to ascertain whether or not I am worthy of the prize. In *Down Beat* magazine in America, they'd call this paying your dues.

Some mornings my mum remembers to give me "something to keep you going till breakfast," as she calls it, and on a good day will slip into my pocket a Mars bar or a Munchy Crunch Bolero. On a bad day it will be a Farley's Rusk or a few Peek Freans cheeselets, which I throw to the first Doberman that attacks. When I arrive home numb and shaking, she has breakfast ready: could be Scott's Oats porridge—always stored on the shelf next to the Omo—or Welgar shredded wheat with a slice of apple and just a hint of Windowlene. This handsome repast is usually washed down with lemon barley water, and then it's either back on the bike or the long trudge to school through the dark wood of waving willies. But the sum and reward of this mental and physical torture is the guitar that hangs like a bright flag in an impossible future.

Three

I look down at the guitar in my hands, this battered old Fender Telecaster with most of its paint scraped off and its hybrid character (due to a Gibson humbucker replacing the original Fender neck pickup). It is with this guitar, this mangled old thing I bought in 1972 off a kid in L.A. for two hundred dollars that I have made the journey. I idly wonder if he has noticed that his old guitar has become an icon. I offered it

back to him after making the purchase, saying, "Are you sure? There's something about this guitar," but he declined. I suppose I should have a nice shiny new guitar—I get offered one about every five minutes now—but I love it, this old relic: it has soul. Someone once said to me that like a woman, you get only one real guitar in your life. For me, it's this 1961 Tele.

By the approach of my sixteenth birthday, and after a couple of years of delivering newspapers, I have worked my way through a few guitars—a Voss, a Rogers, and a Hofner Senator—and a couple of amps: a Watkins Dominator and a Selmer True Voice (featuring the famous Selmer filtered sound). But finally after enduring the endless purgatory of newspaper rounds and other menial tasks—washing up, peeling potatoes in a hotel kitchen, dog walking, selling ice cream, working as a beachfront photographer—I have the money for a Gibson, the most iconic and desirable of all guitars. With a pocket full of pound notes and a head full of hope, I board the train to London.

Arriving at Waterloo, I am overwhelmed by the size of the station and the grey mass of city beyond and almost get back on the train to return to the west, but with a beating heart, I ask a black-capped porter the way to Charing Cross Road. He leans down and says, "Toob to Tottenham Court Road and jump aht there, aw right, Sunshine." I thank him and wander down the platform, having understood nothing. Eventually, and after asking many strangers, I grasp that the tube is a train, not a thing full of toothpaste, and it's down there—underground. And so by getting little niblets of information, I arrive on the right train and eventually (with several people now guiding me) manage to jump out at Tottenham Court Road and make my way south to Selmer's. The shop is large, impersonal, and intimidating, and I feel about as significant as a fly on the side of Westminster Abbey. The guitars, the bored-looking salesmen, the whole ambience, makes me as nervous as a rabbit, but hanging on the wall like an Aztec sun in all her sunburst glory is a Gibson, an ES 175. With a pulse pounding like an African drum, I croak, "Can I see that?" to the salesman who has diffidently asked me what I want. "You want to see 'that' guitar?" He looks at me incredulously, as if I have just asked for a date with Rita Hayworth. "Christ," he mutters to himself, but reaches up and unhooks it. I try a few chords—it's great, it's miraculous—and as I run my fingers over the neck it is as if angels whisper in my ear, *The future begins here.* I look up at the lapels of the blue suit. "I'll take it," I say with a grin.

On the train home I sit churning with excitement, gripping the handle of the case; there is no way I am putting this on an overhead rack or letting anyone get near it. Back in my bedroom I unveil my new bride in all her honeyed splendor. Lying there in the crushed pink velvet case, she's a perfect musical machine. I gently remove her from her bed and stroke a few chords, gm7,

C7♭9, FM7#11. The smell of new wood drifts into my senses like an ancient forest perfume, something takes wing, and I play the intro to "Move It."

Two weeks later, on a beautiful late October day, I arrange to meet a girl in the local park. Wanting to impress her, I decide to take the 175 along and show off with a few chords. We sit on the bench together like Romeo and Juliet. The wind is sending a cascade of red and brown leaves down from the trees across the grass and around the bench where we sit, me holding the guitar. The girl, Natasha, has long blond hair, a face with a hint of Russia, and the promise of a heartbreaking woman. She sits close to me and I feel her heat. I am desperate to kiss her and I try to play something for her on the 175 and am so overcome that I play badly, but she pulls a leaf from her hair and murmurs as if in assent. On an impulse I put my arm around her and pull her toward me with closed eyes. "No," she says, and lets out a loud laugh and takes off across the park. I put the guitar down and take off after her into the streets that lead to her house. She runs like a deer, and in the twilight I lose her. I run back to the park to get my guitar and go home. But when I reach the bench, there is nothing there except a few more leaves. She's gone. My ES 175—disappeared. In hallucination I run my hands over the wood of the bench. I feel sick, the guitar of my dreams lost forever. I walk home numb and shocked and go through a tearful and wrenching scene as I explain to my parents what happened. My dad immediately calls the local police station, and they agree to go out and look for it.

Days pass and nothing turns up. I become very quiet, stay in my room, and experience a black depression. I stare into space and strum listlessly on the Uncle Jim Spanish, but it brings me down even more. I lie on my bed and stare at the ceiling. Maybe it's a first lesson: a rite of passage, a convergence of guitars and desire—the fatal mix of frets and femme fatale—a marker of the future. Or maybe I should just pay more attention.

Meanwhile, the local constabulary—good lads—scour field and hedgerow for the stealer of my dreams and come up with nothing except a blank expression. But the universe turns and one day, as if a double six has fallen on the roulette wheel, I hear my dad in the hallway talking into the huge black rotary thing that he calls a telephone. "Yes, I see . . . oh, well, hmm . . . yes, of course, I'll tell him." It doesn't sound too good. There's a knock on my bedroom door as I morosely play. My dad frowns and does his best Captain

Bligh imitation, but he can't keep it up—he starts grinning and says, "The bastards are going to cough up." I let out a moan and roll off the bed in a mock epileptic fit. He smiles and quietly closes the door; whether it's relief or madness, I don't know, but I stand in front of my small pile of LPs, touch them, and then begin laughing as tears roll down my cheeks.

With the insurance company money safely deposited, I return to London and get my second Gibson. This time, now under the influence of ultrahip New York guitarist Grant Green, I buy an ES 335. The 335 is an innovative guitar that Gibson designed in 1958 and is slowly being accepted as a pretty cool instrument. They have come up with the concept of a semi-solid: a slimmed down version of an archtop jazz, maybe in answer to Fender's highly successful line of solid-body guitars. Not much more than two inches deep, it features a double cutaway that allows the player access to the highest frets and is a slick, fast guitar with two double humbuckers. In fact, the 335 turns out to be one of the best guitar designs ever, and from its humble beginnings in Michigan it begins its inexorable diaspora. How was I to know in this breathless moment as the first 335 passes into my hands that in the distant and magical future, Gibson will one day manufacture one of them as the Andy Summers Signature model? If the spirit had whispered into the sixteen-year-old's ear at that point, it would have been a cosmic joke.

Four

Right after I get my 335, Thelonius Monk arrives in England to play a concert at Fairfield Hall in Croydon, and I travel up to London by train to see him. After fifteen or sixteen hours of marvelous food and luxury travel with British Rail and several tricky station changes, I finally make it to the concert hall. On the bill are not only Monk but Dizzy Gillespie and Roy Eldridge. I am thrilled by all of it and love the jubilant sound of Dizzy and Roy playing "Groovin' High." But when Monk comes on and plays a solo rendition of "I'm Getting Sentimental Over You," it's as if the sun rises in my head. Monk plays from another place, pulling the order of notes and the sequence of chords from some private cookbook. With odd syncopation, minor seconds, and upside-downness, he creates a cracked perfection that hits me as the essence of jazz—the central message—and he does all this with big flat hands splayed out on the black and white keys to create a music that is beyond anything I have heard from a guitarist (or any other instrument, for that matter). Monk's playing cuts to the core experience of American life. After this I collect more Monk albums and become a lifelong fan, eventually recording my own album of Monk music, *Green Chimneys.*

Gradually my local reputation grows and I get invited to play at dances and private functions around town. For me, any chance to play is good enough, and I grab them like a man getting an extra slice of birthday cake. One night, driving back from a party I had played at in a village hall in the New Forest, Lenny (who has undertaken the task of driving me, my guitar, and amp out to the gig) turns to me in the front seat of his Morris Minor and says, "You know, if you keep practicing, you might just . . . ," and his words trail off, but I get it—this is benediction from on high. A small sob almost appears in my throat, and as we drive on through the night back to my parents' house, the stars above appear unusually bright and clear.

There are a number of young musicians in the town, and I try to form little groups with anyone who will play with me. My friend Nigel Streeter plays alto sax, and the two of us—both Sonny Rollins fans—spend hours listening to *The Bridge,* Sonny's latest recording. The word is that Sonny has spent two years away from the public, during which time he sat on New York's Williamsburg Bridge and practiced for hours every day, his horn sending myriad streams of notes out over the East River. He has been searching, trying to take the music to another place, trying to move beyond the conventions, and refusing to come back until he has something to say.

We are inspired by this idea: the search for truth through music, the quest for higher consciousness, the concept of transcendence. Although we are only half aware of them, these ideas are beginning to float in the air like pollen. Kerouac has written *On the Road* and *The Dharma Bums,* Esalen has been established, and Timothy Leary is being fired from Harvard for his experiments with LSD. There are murmurings in the pages of *Down Beat* of Asian spirituality and Eastern philosophies beginning to infiltrate the music scene, and suddenly it seems as if all the hippest cats are embracing Buddhism, Sufism, Islam, and yoga. It all sounds very exotic, and we ponder phrases like *avatars of the new consciousness* and wonder what that means. *Avatar?* It sounds like some kind of trombone.

The jazz community, with its long history of pot smoking and heroin, is a natural place for this to start. Altered states may arise from strict spiritual disciplines but are more likely with the imbibing of drugs, things with weird names like horse and tea. We sprawl on Nigel's mum's Axminster among endless cups of Darjeeling and Pontefract cakes and read articles in *Down Beat* about withdrawal, cold turkey, or monkeys on the back and musicians who have bad colds or are heaped to the gills. Rather than jazz, it sounds like the zoo or the butcher's shop or a visit to the doctor. But it is the quest, the search, that inspires us and we play the new Rollins LP over and over. We don't speak much with our parents about this world; it belongs to us, and our mums and dads, as they busily vacuum, dream about Sunbeam Talbots, and plan next summer at Butlins, are somewhere back in time—lost in a Pathé newsreel. We ignore the fact that they have survived the Second World War and may have spiritual reserves of their own, and in the arrogance of youth and the pebbledash frame of suburbia, we guard our secret code with grunts and snobbery.

Sixteen, and as my skin breaks out and I turn my collar up James Dean–style, my brain becomes a pastiche of bebop, Kerouac, *Down Beat* reviews, skyscrapers piercing the New York skyline, girls, women, dolls, chicks—the whole beat scene.

I get a job in the summer as a deck-chair-ticket collector on Bournemouth Beach and each afternoon wander through the crush of arms, legs, and perspiring foreheads to collect beachgoers' money, which goes to the Bournemouth Corporation. All day for seven pence. I realize that I have power over these poor begotten lumps trapped in striped canvas—I could turn in those who try to get away with not paying. But standing in the sand in a white corporation attendant coat and a heavy leather satchel around my neck, I punch tickets with a headful of riffing horn solos, foreign films, and the breasts of Brigitte Bardot. The red-faced mums with sticky little kids in the sand at their feet barely make it onto my radar.

"Hey, man, don't just stand there dreaming." A voice from behind penetrates my sun-bleached hallucination. It's Kit, another corporation employee but a guy who is different from the rest of us. He walks about in a cool, detached way, and it's rumored that he is a poet. He doesn't appear to have a home but carries all his worldly possessions in a small backpack. I work up the courage to talk to him one day and he gives me a small grim lecture about being beat, which he says is a state of mind and that to be cool, to be on the outside, is to be hip and the two things—hip and cool—combine to make you a hip outsider, who is cool, the very essence of beat, cool. The hip don't have regular jobs, don't get mortgages, don't buy bungalows, don't buy into this whole crock we call the straight world, man, they just keep moving.

A 250-pound woman heaves herself out of a deck chair with a struggle, and Kit swiftly slings it on top of the stack he is making. "Burroughs's *Naked Lunch*—read it," he says, spitting in the sand, stacking another deck chair. The sun sinks behind the pier in a swirl of circling seagulls and I feel a deep sense of insecurity, but I look at Kit and nod in an impassive but knowing way, in fraternity—yeah, brother. This deck-chair thing is just for kicks. But this thing that he's got in spades, I want it too; I desperately hope that playing jazz is cool—it must be, jazz musicians call each other "cats." I am very impressed—how could this guy know all of this? I decide to get a backpack.

I begin grunting in monosyllables, barely parting my lips to speak, and take to wearing sunglasses inside the house, even when sitting on the end of the bed practicing. "Are your eyes hurting again, dear?" my mum asks anxiously—or so I think, although she is probably smirking behind her hand. "Better pop down to the optician's with you, then." I merely grunt back in her general direction as I struggle with C7♭9. I read *On the Road* and *The Dharma Bums*. I don't really get them—it's another world—but I take in their aroma and realize that my fellow deck-chair stacker is the personification of Japhy Ryder, Kerouac's protagonist from *The Dharma Bums*.

Rebellion is still worth having a go at because it's not yet an over-the-counter item. In a few years the corporate world will suck up everything from the underground and brand it with a logo; coolness will be obtained by drinking sugary caffeinated confections, wearing prewashed jeans and sneakers made by people in the Third World. But on the beach as I hand five pennies' change back from an ice-cream-covered shilling, the underground is being raised into white consciousness by a few poets in the United States such as Kerouac and Ginsberg and Gary Snyder and William S. Burroughs, who take it from black culture, the jazz scene, and Buddhism. I make my way toward the pier, thinking about what I will practice tonight and that I must wear shades at all times from now on.

One night I go with Nigel to a club called with a disarming lack of originality the Blue Note. Every Friday night a quintet of ex–London jazz musicians set up and play in a local hotel, and when I hear the quintet roar through a repertoire of Cannonball Adderley, John Coltrane, the MJQ, Miles Davis, and Monk, my confusion about whether it is beat and hip to play music fly out the window. The music is so inventive and bursting with joy that it wipes out all concerns about being cool—this is what I want. This is it.

Although I am still in the early stages, I can improvise my way through standard chord changes, more by a visual interpretation than with full harmonic knowledge. I begin going to the club every weekend, and with pretty girls in the crowd and the surging solos, it becomes the high point of the week. I pluck up the courage one night to ask their sax player if I can sit in with them. Alan, the group leader, is pleasant but sarcastic and I think rather amazed that one so young could have the balls to propose such a thing. He kindly demurs but asks if I would like to play during their intermission.

I begin a long series of appearances in which I try out all number of trios, duos, and whatever I can cobble together for Friday night. All through the week I wait tremulously for the moment when I will get up and play during the break. This moment will be preceded throughout the evening by Alan Melly's mock solemn announcements that a living legend is to appear later in the evening, to be followed by a fan club meeting afterward in the telephone kiosk across the road. This is usually greeted by a fair amount of hilarity, but the result is that I become a pet feature of the club and taste very minor celebrity. Gradually, instead of heading straight to the bar, people begin stopping to see what I will do this week. As this goes on, Alan takes to including my name in the local ads for the club, and each week it is different: "Tonight Andy Summers plays West Coast blues" or "From New York City—the Andy Summers onetet" or, most winningly, "Andy Summers plays the Mao Tse-tung Songbook."

Every week I am forced to put together whatever musicians I can find to pull off this cliff-hanging twenty-five minutes, usually a trio of guitar, bass, and drums, but a couple of times it's just me and a trombonist, which puts an unintended avant-garde edge to the proceedings; I notice some people are on the floor splitting their sides with laughter. The highlight of all this comes one night when Alan suggests that I sit in with them for one song, and what would I like to play? I suggest an old standard called "Between the Devil and the Deep Blue Sea" and wait for the moment, trembling like Bambi in a forest glade.

A grandiloquent announcement is made and I get up onto the stage, plug in and look nervously over at Alan, who raises an eyebrow and, grinning, says, "Count us in, then." With a feeling on the inside of a stained-glass window shattering, I count the bastards in. I start playing and state the theme before I take off on a double-chorus solo that is about as good as I have ever played. I pass through it as if in a dream, locked into the notes, the frets, the strings, and no sense of anything other than the accompanying piano chords, the drums behind me, and maybe a far-off voice whispering as if through clouds, "This is what it is really like." I finish my solo and there is wild applause, which is probably the sound of an audience even more relieved than I am that I haven't blown it.

But I am sixteen years old; everyone here knows me, and it's possible that there's a lot of love in the room (even if laced with pity). The club swims in front of my eyes and I come very close to fainting but manage to stand there and keep a grip. I have just been chucked into the deep end. I don't sleep that night—or that week, for that matter—but just keep recycling the solo over and over again in my head. Somehow I have crossed a line, as if I have been shot full of junk.

I realize that my sense of self is in fact defined by the guitar, and that's that, which I suppose makes me a guitarist. I begin to feel worthy or unworthy according to the merit of the last solo I have played. If the last solo was shit, then so am I, but if I have pulled off a good one, then I feel like a king.

I become more confident with my Blue Note intermission sets and continue learning on the job, finally reaching a point where local musicians are actually importuning me to play. I affect a new confidence and swagger that is undermined only by the fact that my eyes are now so weak that I have to wear glasses, which make me look like a misplaced librarian. But without them I can barely see the frets on my guitar. I eventually cover this Achilles' heel by wearing a pair of clip-on sunglasses on top of them, much to the amusement of the quintet.

I survive by the largesse of my parents and whatever gigs I can find on the local scene, so it's a surprise and a relief when Don Hardyman, the brilliant pianist of the quintet, asks me if I would like to play in his other band, which holds a residency at a local hotel, the WhiteCliffs.

The bandleader, Cyril, is a mean old bastard from Yorkshire; he is supposed to be the bass player, but with a shit-eating grin on his face, he merely leans against it like a dog pissing against a tree. With scant musical ability, he is a networker on the Jewish hotel scene more than anything else, and he rules by fear. He's agreed to have a guitar in the band only because the teenagers at the hotel are asking for one. I don't like him but I have to keep in with him because he is paying me nine pounds a week, a royal sum at the time. He's always telling me to turn down the volume and not get so carried away in the solos. And so I plod on through the endless fox-trots and waltzes, trying to quench the fire within, but it's musical purgatory. The only thing that saves it is my relationship with Don Hardyman, who has taken to showing me hip changes and instructing me generally about jazz. We smile secretly at each other as Don slips a nifty little flat-five substitution into a standard that has been hacked to death while Cyril grins woodenly at the dance floor and thumps like a moron on his bull fiddle.

My electric guitar is an appeasement for the teenagers who stay at the hotel with their parents. So, to give the impression of a band that is fully contemporary, we play a small repertoire of pop songs during which I stand up and do a Hank Marvin or Duane Eddy imitation. This is well received by the cute girls who litter the dance floor. I have lustful thoughts in their direction, but Cyril sees it and warns me with a nasty glint in his eye not to go anywhere near them.

Dominating the proceedings most nights is the proprietor of the hotel, a matriarch of whalelike proportions named Mrs. Goldblatt (or Goldfart, as I call her under my breath). She watches over the dance floor with a laserlike scrutiny and rules with a fist of iron. All behavior has to be kosher, and teenagers are expected to conduct themselves like people in late middle age; snogging and jiving are banned.

So I sit behind my little bandstand and get through the night, sometimes so bored that I hardly know I'm there. And then I begin noticing an unusual phenomenon when on one or two occasions I suddenly wake up realizing that although I haven't technically been asleep, I've been in a dream state for the past twenty minutes and have actually been playing on autopilot without making any mistakes. I find this slightly disturbing and wonder if I should move on or start into a life of drug use, but somehow playing at the White-Cliffs with an arm full of heroin doesn't quite fit the bill, so I carry on risking the odd touch of teenage doziness.

Meanwhile, Cyril, who really wants to get the guitar out of the band, is looking for an excuse, and I provide him with one in the shape of a nubile girl by the name of Mona Silverman. We have been eyeing each other across the crowded room, and nature is working its chemistry. Mona glides by the bandstand in the arms of a Henry Kissinger look-alike and drops a small folded piece of paper onto the stage at my feet. I surreptitiously glance at it as Cyril announces the "Gay Gordons." It gets straight to the point: "Meet me at the cliffs . . . after the dance?" I start breathing faster and can't wait to get bloody "Hava Nagila" over with so I can get out of there and embrace this olive-skinned, almond-eyed girl. Sex is in the air, and all thoughts of Cyril's warnings and my future in the dance band business go out of my head as I pack up at warp speed, my brain now centered in the groin area.

I meet Mona on the cliffs at the designated spot, and we dive into one of the numerous shelters so kindly provided by the council elders for those who wish to have an illicit bunk-up in a public setting, or in full view of the English Channel. After a few pleasantries about pop music, Mona is primed to a point of about 75 percent. She is a fantastic kisser and we don't part lips for about forty-five minutes, by which time I have the most incredible case of blue balls known to man, and then she abruptly pulls away from me and says, "Got to go now—if my mum finds out, she'll kill me." Like a poisoned dart, the cold arrow of truth pierces my brain and I rapidly shrink back to reality. *Fuck*, I gulp to the now-empty wooden bench scarred with the names of lovers who actually had trysts here, who actually did it, *if Cyril hears about this, fuck*—with the black realization of an early death to my career, I imagine a samurai impaling himself on his own sword—*I'm done for*.

The next night as I am nervously packing up, Cyril comes over to me with the death ray in his eye and says, "I'd like a word with you, young man," and I feel icicles—or rather, stalactites—pierce my heart. He takes me into the kitchen and gives me a coruscating tongue-lashing that would break Attila the Hun. You would have thought I had just had it off with the Queen Mother, so dire, so evil, are my actions with a willing girl who in fact had importuned me. I try weakly to protest but can't get a word in edgewise. It turns out that Mona's little sister has told their mother that her sister was out on the cliffs snogging with one of the musicians in the band. The mother practically had a seizure, sent Mona back to London the next day, complained bitterly to Mrs. Goldblatt, and then shredded Cyril. Cyril was told to fire me—which, of course, is what he is doing, also knowing in his heart of hearts that anyone playing the guitar is probably of low character. He's right, but nevertheless he finds it necessary to strip me of any idea of manhood or hope of having a career.

At a young age these events assume a somewhat oversize legend in your life. I am terrified by this small, mean Yorkshire man who can't play his instrument and I slink home that night in a deep funk. About a week later I hear that I have been replaced by another local guitarist by the name of Robert Fripp.

But eventually it is the guitar itself that restores my spirit and sets me back on track, and as the great Saddhu Mahhamsarat Jinji Yoga said, "Music washes from the soul the dust of everyday life." I return to a life of subsistence, doing gigs when and wherever I can scrape them up, but about this time things change when I am introduced to a red-haired Italian rocker by the name of Zoot Money. Zoot sings and plays keyboards, and is already an accomplished performer. We start getting together and one afternoon we sit on the floor of his brother Bruno's bedroom and he plays me some records of Sonny Terry and Brownie McGhee and Ray Charles and sings along, demonstrating the deep blues feeling. Across the road on Horseshoe Common in the hazy summer heat, boys chase girls into the trees, hoping to cop a feel, get a kiss, make out. In the dark confines of the Victorian flat opposite, I am transfixed as I hear Ray Charles belting out, "See the girl with the red dress on . . ."

Gradually through the fixed point of the Blue Note, more like-minded young musicians around town get to know one another; before long there's a gang of us hanging around and playing together. On the weekends we crowd into the Downstairs Club, a dark, smoky cellar underneath a grubby Italian *ristorante* in the town center. On Fridays and Saturdays it's open all night, not closing until about six A.M., and in the claustrophobic darkness we attempt to outdo one another with our latest licks.

Frenetic and wired, we jam, joke, and jostle in the company of feverish young girls and play everything we can think of, from standards like "I Cover the Waterfront" to the rhythm and blues of "What'd I Say" and "Sack O' Woe" by Cannonball Adderley. We crowd on and off the stage, yap incessantly about music—everything from Miles to blues to Ringo's new bass drum patterns. In the hot little sweatbox the atmosphere is visceral and edgy. With heat and music pulsing through your veins, you come off stage and in a few minutes are pushing a girl against the back wall of the club in an impassioned embrace that will probably end in the backseat of a car or on the sand of Bournemouth Beach as the summer sun breaks in the eastern sky.

I feel euphoric all the time and live for the weekend, when we will pack into the dark again, when the future seems cloudless, a swelling balloon of endless possibility.

Unfortunately, this dirigible is not fueled by much other than hot air and a lust for music and girls, and to a man we are without a job. After the mind-numbing task of collecting our weekly dole packet of two pounds, we—a cluster of unemployed teen musicians—fill the blank days of the week by sitting upstairs in the El Cabala coffee bar with foamy cappuccinos and watching the girls walk by on the street below, talk about music, and listen to "Love Me Do" on the jukebox.

Typically after one of these grueling days and possibly after watching *Dixon of Dock Green* or *Opportunity Knocks,* we turn up at the Pinocchio Café, which stays open until four A.M. With its Formica tabletops and air of violence, it's a nasty little hole; but happy in one another's company, we sit around the tables, suck up more coffee, and eat pizzas until it's kick-out time. One night we are there as usual and bullshitting up a storm until someone foolishly tries to interject a note of culture by suggesting we all read a book called *Catcher in the Rye,* which is greeted with faint interest before we get back to the nasty sex talk.

Zoot and I play around in the local scene with a group that comes and goes depending on the gig, but after a while—and a round of church halls, women's institutes, and village community centers—it feels as though we need a bigger arena. We have to go to where the action is, and that means London. I try to talk the others into all of us going up to London together, but we don't have a consensus. Some think it too competitive, too risky; we wouldn't stand a chance. But for me the way is clear: we have to go or be doomed to the

Haggersley women's institute or the notice board outside of a church hall in Tolpuddle, with our names scrawled in biro on a small dog-eared piece of paper.

One night we are playing out at Ossemsley Manor in the New Forest, and my desire to move on presents itself in the shape of the manager of Alexis Korner's band. He emerges from the dark with a rattling glass of scotch in his hand and an invitation for Zoot to join the band in London— he's impressed with Zoot's singing. This is quite a coup; Alexis is on the BBC and already holds a legendary reputation on the English music scene as a bluesman. I feel threatened because Zoot and I were planning to go to London together to start our own band, so I attempt a bit of emotional blackmail by saying that if he's going up to London to be with Alexis, I'll go with him and wait until it's time to get started with our original plan.

Zoot doesn't seem to mind this idea, agreeing that it's important that he have his own outfit rather than just being someone else's singing turkey. I nod sagely and we make the decision to leave for the city. Somewhat nervously I have told my parents that I am going to live in London and be a musician. To my surprise and relief, I don't get a lot of argument; they see that I am determined on this course and don't try to stop me. I imagine their talking together in private: "Musn't stand in his way." "It's what he's always wanted." "He's a determined little bugger."

On the morning I leave, my mother stands on the pavement outside the house, her face a wrestling match between composure and anguish. Although I am light and casual about it, this is it: I am leaving home, never to return. She tells me to eat, be careful, and write as soon as I arrive. I give her one last hug and, with a ripping of the umbilical cord, sling my suitcase and guitar into the trunk. She bursts into tears and I pile into a secondhand Vauxhall Victor with Zoot and our friend Phil the hairdresser.

Five

We arrive at Alexis's house in Hampstead to hear how Zoot's illustrious future will go. It rather sounds like one gig as a tryout and there are no accommodations, but we are advised to try the Finchley Road area, somewhere south of where we are presently enjoying cups of tea in creamy Hampstead comfort. As we have just struggled in from the West Country with no clue about London, we find this prospect daunting. But we down the last half inch of tea from bone china, utter thank-yous, and project our fear and our bodies out into the strange and unfamiliar streets.

We trudge about, looking for somewhere to begin our life in London or even a friendly face that will take us in, but it seems hopeless. After knocking on endless doors and staring at hostile signs that say no vacancies, no blacks, no Indians, no dogs, no cats, we finally get a ray of mercy from Mrs. O'Donoghue, an Irish widow. It's a one-room flat on the second floor of her terrace house, the sole problem being that there is only one bed and three of us. Mrs. O'Donoghue mutters to herself that she shouldn't really, but we look so desperate, so cold, poor pets. Maybe she sees it as an act of charity, but she makes the sign of the cross and we enter the stygian gloom of her boardinghouse.

We can just make out that the walls are awash with religious icons of the Catholic variety, and it feels as if we have just volunteered for the priesthood rather than coming to London to be profligate musicians. There's nothing much we can do—it's this or a park bench, or return to Bournemouth with our tails between our legs—so we tiptoe into the small room, almost choking on the odor of mothballs. There is a large bed with a purple candlewick bedspread, and on the wall, buried in a sea of floral wallpaper, a sign about no smoking, drinking, spitting, or swearing.

After much short-straw-pulling about who doesn't get the dreaded middle spot, we retire for the night. Since the bed takes up all but a few inches of the room, there is no floor to sleep on. For about half an hour there is a great deal of loud fake snoring and trumpetlike fart sounds made from mouths on wrists as we desperately attempt to keep the humor high in case there's even the slightest hint of homosexuality. Above our heads—radiating the light of God—a plastic Virgin watches over us while we sleep frozen and corpselike, lest we touch another man's flesh.

Zoot performs two or three gigs with Alexis, one of which I witness, and then his gigs dribble to zero. One night we go to see Alexis in a trio setting that takes place on the Finchley Road in what might be called a tavern. A low dark room, it has a small stage at the far end with a few wooden tables covered in cardboard beer mats and large heavy ashtrays. The wall has an equestrian theme, with paintings à la George Stubbs of prizewinning horses that seem superior to the customers below. The band is Alexis on guitar and vocals, Jack Bruce on bass, and Ginger Baker on drums. Alexis sings Chicago and country blues and plays some bottleneck guitar. He is one of the first Englishmen to attempt authentic blues, and although he is not a natural singer, he puts it over with a certain amount of raw conviction. Something like "ooochy kooooochie maaaan—baaaack dooooor baaaby" surges forth from Alexis's throat with a guttural roar as he whips his bottleneck up and down the neck of his guitar with an intense alien chromaticism that covers every note and quarter tone in the book. At this early point in my musical life—despite my exposure to American folk music as a thirteen-year-old with the Midnighters—I am not yet steeped in the blues. This otherworldly racket confuses me and makes me nervous. On the Finchley Road among advertisements for Watneys brown ale and weary voices asking for a pint of bitter, it rings out like the voice of the devil—and I wonder if I have got it all wrong.

But leaning against the bar with half a pint of lager and lime and a packet

of crisps, I attempt a fake London sophistication, pretending to understand
and dig it—although I am much more comfortable with a jazzier version of
the blues and the virtuoso guitar playing of Wes Montgomery. Alexis comes
over to meet us and is an utterly charming man with a deep Oxbridge accent
who radiates only good vibes in our direction, and for a moment he lightens
the gloom. But despite Alexis's good cheer, we feel our enthusiasm flagging.
Compared to these weary beer-stained surroundings and the dismal weight
of the metropolis, Bournemouth seems like a simple sunny planet and it is
tempting to turn and flee. But we don't feel like running home just yet, although we are faced with the grim truth that we are without a gig, three men
to a bed, and close to penniless. We decide to stick it out and get our own
place; after that Herculean task is accomplished, we can try and restart the
band. Phil the hairdresser gives up and heads south. Zoot and I are now a
duo with no bass, no drums, no future. There is nothing but the locked
hearts and locked minds of the great sprawling mass that's called London.

We begin scouring the *Evening Standard* for a flat to rent, a hole in the wall,
or shelter. At the other end of London—in Ludgate, to be precise—are two
men whose dreams coincide nicely with our own. Mr. Smith and Mr.
Gardner-Brown, both pushing thirty-five, are two business partners who
seem to cradle a fantasy to become real estate barons, and they are starting
into this venture by advertising for tenants. We go to meet them one afternoon at the flat. The address, 11 Gunterstone Road, West Kensington W 14.

In the tea-stained penumbra that passes for light in London, we sit with
them in the front room of the basement. The afternoon is so leaden and
overcast that it is difficult to make them out and it's as if we are talking to
silhouettes. But through the gloom Gardner-Brown (in a dark blue pinstripe
and gripping a briefcase) and Smith (in a grey charcoal number with a crisp
white handkerchief poking from his breast pocket), speak in precise, clipped
voices redolent of topiary, manicured lawns, and freshly washed poodles.

We attempt to discuss terms—how to come up with the vast three
months' advance rent—but get the distinct feeling that we are not quite what
they are looking for. The difficulty is compounded by the fact that neither
Zoot nor I has a job or enough money to rent past the first week. We ask them
if we might get back to them tomorrow and in the evening put in a furtive

call to Colin Allen, our drummer from Bournemouth, who agrees to drive up to London, put his savings from De Havilland aircraft down as the deposit, and join the band. We return the next afternoon to try and take it one step further with Smith and Gardner-Brown, who don't appear to know quite what they are doing and seem slightly intimidated by scruffy musicians. But nevertheless, they seem eager to move along the road toward real estate riches and we at least are a start. We come to terms, they accept one month's rent rather than three, and like Alice down the rabbit hole, we're in.

We now have a home, and a drummer, but we still need a bass player. We ask around and are put in touch with Paul Williams, a singer who doesn't play an instrument but says that he will learn the bass if that's what we want. We do, and in a remarkably short time—being a natural musician—he is playing decently enough for it to work. We rehearse the songs we already know, the Ray Charles stuff and some other R&B hits, and through a friend of Paul's get an audition spot at one of the West End's premier clubs, the Flamingo, in Soho.

On a Sunday afternoon the crowd is sparse: a handful of American GIs, some Jamaicans, and a few assorted punters who look as if they haven't left from the night before. The room reeks of alcohol and cigarettes, and even the walls seem hungover. Yet we are full of adrenaline and play with all the fire and innocence that we have in these early days; as a result, we get a vociferous reception that makes us stare at one another in excitement.

The emcee for the afternoon show is Johnny Gunnell, who runs the club with his brother Rik. As we come off the stage into the dressing room at the side, which will become another home away from home, Johnny tells us—in a way we will come to recognize—that he sees a rosy future ahead for us: "You are the new house band." "You will replace Georgie Fame." "You start next weekend." We can hardly believe it. We have been in London for five minutes and have landed a plum gig in the West End; in fact, we have taken it right from under the noses of all the other London bands who want to play there.

The probable truth is that we have the sound and the music alright, but we are green and can be hired for next to nothing, which suits Johnny. One day he tells us that he's had the Stones on the stage and paid them four shillings and sixpence (about fifty cents by today's reckoning), but we don't care—we have a gig and we're here.

London, with its speed, noise, dirt, concrete, and multiracial society, is shocking. I wander around Soho through streets filled with prostitutes, betting shops, bars, private drinking clubs, and exotic food smells, trying to get used to the idea that this fast, cynical place is now my home. Security comes from being in the band, coming from the same town, and having moved here together. But gradually we settle into it and after a while I can't imagine being anywhere else.

As we gain popularity from our steady gig at the Flamingo we play six or seven nights a week and are able to add a couple of saxophones to the band. This regular work eventually provides enough money for Zoot to move upstairs to the ground-floor flat with his new girlfriend, Ronni, a tough and outspoken little Scot who acts as the voice of sanity, the shaper of events, and the mother hen in the madness of the next few years.

Our show, Zoot Money and the Big Roll Band, is a fast-paced rabble-rousing set of R&B featuring the songs of Ray Charles, the Isley Brothers, Rufus Thomas, and James Brown. Zoot is a great blues shouter/R&B singer with a natural flair for comedy and showmanship. From the stage he heckles the audience with insults and jibes about playing in the graveyard, etc., until he goads them into a full and heated response. At this point being in a band is about having a good time rather than being moody, artistic, and introspective. We are supposed to be entertainers, and the idea of calling ourselves artists is not on the dial yet. Artists are referred to as "arteeeests" with a French accent, and with a smirk you think of Mr. Teezy Weezy—hairdresser to the stars.

As our reputation grows we begin playing around the country and start an endless round of gigs that have us locked up in a Commer van, crisscrossing England on a daily basis. But we always return to the Flamingo and the sessions known as the all-nighters. These run from eleven P.M. till seven A.M. on the weekends and are almost Shakespearean in the way that tragedy and comedy play out in front of the stage and the dark recesses of the club. They become the fixed point, the true north of our universe.

The Flamingo on Wardour Street is directly opposite Garrard Street, a real Chinatown without the huge crowds of tourists (which belong to the future). It is seedy and run-down, and I enjoy walking through the alien smells, the odor of spice and rotting fish heads—the babble of language and sharp edge of threat. The Flamingo has a small door and two flights of dingy narrow stairs. It's an inky black pit with a small bar on one side, and the stage at the far end has a presence, as if music is being played even when musicians are absent. At each side of the stage there is a dank little hole laughingly called a dressing room, and the alternating bands get one each.

We always favor the one located at stage right, with its green paint, graffiti-covered walls, and broken overstuffed couch. It's a submarine space with nowhere to hang your clothes, be private, sit in meditation, study a racing form, scratch your ass, or stare at the wall, but this pit is where everyone wants to be. Here, out of sight, drugs are swallowed, sniffed, and snorted; booze downed; and the occasional fuck had. Johnny Gunnell reigns in this small kingdom, and these rooms signify the racetrack, the dogs, pubs, beer, hookers, pimps, violence, the East End, and people doing anything to stay alive. Maybe because of my own roots in the East End, I adjust without too much trouble, but unstated and lingering in the air is the unspoken word that "you are the band, and as long as you are the band, everything will be alright. You supply the sounds, Sunshine, but don't step out of line or I will do you a violence." The Gunnells preside like underworld princes and are reputed to have associations with the Kray twins, the notorious gangster brothers from the East End of London, and behind the Gunnells' sardonic repartee there is the perfume of extreme measures. Rik is the older brother and is the heavy. He likes to joke with us, but one night in the dressing room he picks me up in a bear hug and doesn't let me out for slightly too long while he whispers in my ear, "Wanna play with Uncle Rik, Sunshine?" and I feel that he might just break every bone in my body.

But from the stage you get a panoramic view, and as the fetid air of the club singes the hair in your nose, you feel that the decline of the West is progressing nicely—the Hieronymus Bosch scene of a Saturday night with beer, scotch, vodka, rum, Mandrax, purple hearts, whites, blues, purples, smack, charley, dilated pupils, seizures, and money for sex playing out in their own sweet rhythm. With saxophones and Hammond organ blaring at my back, I bend strings and shoot snake-tongue lines out into the dark, roiling swamp, where they flick through the Saturday-night inferno of grinding bodies, jabbering talk, and pill-driven excess.

In some ways doing the all-nighters is more like bearing witness or providing the swan song to the decadence of late-night London. Staring into the murky wound before me, I sometimes wonder—as the green hills of Dorset strobe across my memory—how the hell I came to be in this Dante's Inferno. But the moment passes and I continue to slur a seventh at some pilled-up young honey whirling within the mob.

Johnny, for his own amusement, is usually the emcee on Friday and Saturday nights. He sports a razor scar on his left cheek that runs from his mouth to his ear that seems emblematic of the Gunnells and their background. There is much whispered speculation about how he received it, but no one dares ask. He announces the bands as they arrive onstage to play their sets, and these intros are laced with deprecating acid humor that gets progressively worse as the night wears on and he becomes more and more inebriated. But Johnny is a true comedian, and his Cockney wit peppers the night with a spicy counterpoint to the enthusiastic efforts of the bands. Toward the end of the night, with red eyes, rolled shirtsleeves, and a sideways list, Johnny's intros become rambling and slurred. As he slouches over the microphone he picks on a girl in the audience and, instead of introducing the band, asks her with a soft, innocent look on his face if she is on the rag tonight or if she is getting any, and then staggers off the stage for another slug in the pit of the dressing room. But we always do good business for the Gunnells, and there is a thread of mutual affection between us. It's a family of sorts, and being associated with them brings a veil of protection—Rik and Johnny's boys.

Sometimes, to the audience's delight, a visiting celebrity gets onstage with us for a song or two. At different times we have various Tamla Motown stars: Ben E. King, John Lee Hooker, Sonny Boy Williamson, Eric Burdon, Long John Baldry, among others. The sit-ins with the band sessions, as they are known, have varying degrees of musical success. Ben E. King comes to sing "Stand by Me," and this is no problem because every musician knows this one and we pull off a decent backing job. But when

Solomon Burke arrives onstage to a version of "Maggie's Farm," it's a different story. For a start, he is a huge, heavy man with a fierce look on his face, and as we start into the song he turns and snarls at me, "Louder— louder." I turn and crank the Fender amp up a bit more; he turns again, this time with a foam-flecked mouth: "Louder—much louder." I start shaking and turn the fucking amplifier up to ten, now not caring if I drown him out. Eventually he departs the stage to vociferous applause and not even a glance back in our direction. I feel utterly wrecked and it takes a couple of lagers, several pats on the back, and words of consolation from the rest of the band before I recover. John Lee Hooker sits in with us and plays his blues all on one chord with a couple of five-four bars thrown in for good measure. This fucks us all up, and afterward we surmise that it wasn't that he didn't know what he was doing but that it was very, very African.

Long John Baldry is a gay six-foot-seven folk-blues singer from the Marquee scene and is popular in the West End. A talented singer and guitarist and the possessor of a dry urban wit, he is fun to be around. As everybody seems to hang out with just about everyone else on the scene onstage and off, it's not long before we are in Long John's semifurnished flat in Earls Court, drinking tea and smoking dope. He makes it clear during the evening that he wants me in the closest possible sense. Being straight hetero, I point out to him through a blue cloud of Tibetan temple ball that not before the Red Sea parts for a second time would such an event occur. But from that night on, whenever he is around us at the Flamingo, Long John never fails to point out that he is ready for love.

This culminates one night when, even more inebriated than usual, he picks me up bodily and shoves his way across the densely packed floor, up the stairs, and out into Wardour Street, where he hails a cab and throws me inside. I protest and struggle vigorously the whole way, but it's useless: my efforts to free myself from the clutches of this giant are like a worm struggling in the beak of a crow, and it's only when he has me in the confines of the taxi that he relents and lets me go. I croak out a good night and leap like a piece of live bait back down the stairs to the relative safety of the

Flamingo, happy that I am not going to be split in half in a seedy west London bedsit.

The womblike entrance of the Flamingo goes around a corner and down two flights of stairs, which like a spiral into Hades are a hazard to us, for somehow we always have to carry our Hammond organ down these stairs and across the crowded floor without dropping the lead coffin. The only way to do it is with a man at each corner, and there is a great deal of argument about who is on Hammond duty each night. It's amazing how musicians suddenly develop sprained wrists and bad backs when the time comes to lift a heavy weight. In these days the concept of help or roadies has not been thought of; we get a long way into our career before somebody has the bright idea of getting actual assistance, and it's a mighty big decision to actually pay out our hard-earned cash for such a service. But after a while we give in, mostly because of a brush with death on the point of a sharp blade.

One night we arrive as usual around eleven-thirty at the entrance to the club. Wardour Street is awash with a thick mob of pill-chewing mods, so dense in fact that getting from the back of the van and into the entrance of the Flamingo with drums, amps, and Hammond is a farce. The swirling sea of mods around us just doesn't seem to recognize that we are trying to cross six feet of pavement with a large heavy object that would crush a man like an egg if dropped, but as if by an act of God, one of the heavies from the club emerges and is threatening enough for the mass to part and let us through.

A reluctant pallbearer, I am on organ duty tonight and am hanging on like grim death to my corner, hoping the weight won't ruin the rest of my guitar-playing life or destroy my ability to father a child. We shuffle across the pavement and start making our way down the stairs with the Hammond, and halfway down we hear shouting and yelling from somewhere below, then two men come struggling around the corner, fighting their way up the stairs. We are on a steep angle, desperately hanging on to the Hammond with barely enough room to squeeze a mouse through as they reach us—two men intent on murdering each other. We press back against the wall like statues as they wrestle into our three feet of staircase, with one of them cursing in a thick Glaswegian accent, "You fickin' bastard," and then whipping out a knife and plunging it several times into the gut of the other man. *So,* I flash, *this is how it ends, halfway down the stairs of the Flamingo, stabbed and crushed beneath half a ton of Hammond organ.* Glasgow runs his dark whiskey-filled eyes over us; "Cunts," he spits, then takes off up the stairs while, groaning, the stabbed man slides down the stairs in the direction of the joyous dancing mob. The police arrive and we line up to give descriptions. Finally we are allowed to get on with the show, which we play with extra zest. By about 6:30 A.M. it's over and we wearily haul ourselves and our gear back out into the grey London light, our brains a strange turmoil of flashing blades and "Papa's Got a Brand New Bag."

Most of the bands playing around London eventually end up playing at the Flamingo also. Everyone likes to play in the clubs because it's such a vibrant scene and also smack in the middle of the West End. You can hang out with other bands, meet a willing girl, get stoned, and check out the action. The band you are in may fall apart, that's par for the course, and the club is where you can find out who is working and what's happening and get a sense of your own standing in the scene. We regularly share the stage with Chris Farlowe and the Thunderbirds, featuring the phenomenal Albert Lee; the Birds with Ronnie Wood; Georgie Fame and the Blue Flames; John Mayall and the Bluesbreakers, featuring at various times Peter Green, Eric Clapton, and Mick Taylor; the Action; Fleetwood Mac; and the Pink Fairies.

Among guitarists, there is circumspect but fierce eyeballing of one another's playing. The electric rock guitar is still in the childhood stage, and we all creep forward together, feeding off one another's playing and only discussing it tentatively, not wanting to give too much away.

During this period I am still more influenced by jazz than by pop music. I'm into Kenny Burrell, Grant Green, and Wes Montgomery, my taste being more for bluesy soulful jazz on the guitar rather than the more direct electric Chicago blues style. But everyone mixes it up, and jazz, R&B, and rock and roll are all hybrid styles anyway. I work on playing with chord changes, phrasing, and time within harmonic frameworks that are outside of the standard pop song. I can't always insert it into the Big Roll Band repertoire, but I can usually get a few off during a night.

When the blues boom hits London and everyone starts doing the Eric, I keep playing the way I hear it, ignoring the bovine mentality that's spreading like a flu epidemic through guitarists around London. As well as jazz, I'm pulled toward another sound that's more esoteric. Indian music, the oud playing of Hamza el Din, the East European flavor of the guitarist Gábor Szabó: these sounds catch my ear and I start to experiment with weird open voicings on the guitar that I cannot put a name to.

In a well-publicized moment Eric Clapton leaves the Yardbirds and joins John Mayall's Bluesbreakers. Mayall, like us, is a fixture at the Flamingo, and we often do all-nighters together. Being guitarists, Eric and I nod at each other, the way guitarists tend to, rather like medieval knights passing each other on horseback and acknowledging that the other fellow also has a weapon. Clapton gives off an air of intense seriousness that is really, really the blues as some of us refer to it, and it is an accepted fact that Eric has the blues deeper than anyone else. But his air of intensity and being lost in this music is seductive and is backed up by his great playing. Coupling intense volume and poetically bluesy phrasing, he creates an audience for himself alone. Undoubtedly he is the star of John Mayall's band. The songs are really just a framework for Eric to take off; and when he solos, the whole place moves. Graffiti with the words CLAPTON IS GOD start appearing on walls around London. Among white boys in London at least, he is the first to play this loud and distorted, to make the solos the high point of a set, and to create shock with the guitar.

About the time that we share a stage at the Flamingo, I acquire a new Gibson from a store on Charing Cross Road. When Eric sees me with it, a '59 Les Paul Sunburst, he asks where I bought it. I innocently tell him that they have another one on sale for eighty quid and he could go get it. At this time there is no market for these guitars, which in the future will go for $100,000, so it doesn't occur to me to whip back to the store and grab the other one. But Eric gets the other Les Paul and eventually changes the sound of rock guitar forever.

We become friends for a while and I drop over to his flat in Notting Hill; we go and get coffee and baklava nearby and talk about books, girls, and guitars. We trudge through the rainy streets of Marylebone, nudging each other at the achingly short miniskirts that pass by us, and then disappear into the fetid black of the cinema to watch Olivier act out the agonies of Richard III.

One night we meet after a gig in South London. There are a lot of fans hanging around, and within short order we pull two girls. We offer to drive them back to their flat, which is within striking distance. We arrive at their place and split off into two different rooms with the willing females and emerge about half an hour later, both from our respective corners, worthy of the title "lead guitarist." Driving back in my blue mini, Eric takes a long drag on his cigarette and remarks that we'll all be dead by the time we're thirty if we keep up this sort of behavior. I lean forward to turn up the pathetically underachieving heater and reply that I am already on an extended visa.

One morning in Notting Hill Eric puts on a record with some remarkable blues guitar. "Christ, that's great," I remark. "When dya do it?" "It's not me, it's Buddy Guy," he says. I sit down on the faded Turkish carpet and think, *So that's where it comes from*—the sound, the distortion, the vibrato. I am amazed; he's copied this sound and style perfectly and is now bringing it to a white English audience. It's not actually original unless it's the fact of being put through a white sensibility that makes it into something else, but it doesn't matter because Eric gets it across with conviction and intensity and in that sense he owns it. He often remarks during this time that he's not interested in pop music, that he is playing in a tradition, the blues. There is a kind of austerity to these remarks that seems to imply that everyone else is just skating around on the surface while he is in the gold mine.

Personally I admire Eric's philosophy and that he has tapped into a sort of guitar collective unconscious. But I have my own ideas and despite the new prevailing blues climate, like a fish swimming upstream, I stick to my own thoughts about music. I like harmonic change, weirder scales, asymmetry, and I still dig Monk. But Eric, with his simple but powerful style, has an enormous influence on guitarists in London and is emulated by eight out of ten players. Within a short time there are a great number of blues guitarists in London. Uniform in style and dress, they generally sport long hair, anoraks, and plimsolls. You imagine them in places like Hounslow and Ealing, cranking out a deep blues in their bedrooms while Mum downstairs tries to get the breakfast ready or Dad cuts himself shaving in the bathroom, distracted by the plangent whine of "Dust My Broom." The Les Paul becomes *the* guitar, and the London blues boom lifts off like a bent string at the fifteenth fret.

The most unlikely people now get and feel the music of the American South, young men who before might have had a nice office job or gone into undertaking become deeply committed blues players and are ready to sacrifice their lives on the altar of the Mississippi Delta. Clapton has had an effect: in retrospect, a rather great one because if this style is about anything at all, it's about playing with feeling; rather than being technically perfect or being a speed maniac, you are supposed to play with soul. Unfortunately, as time moves on, all these blues licks will become formulaic and dated—done to death—but probably no one will ever play them with Eric's power when he is ripping them out with the John Mayall Blues band.

In fact, the whole blues-boom thing is rather away from the style of pop music that has been dominant so far. What Eric is doing is something very different from the Beatles, who at this time rule the record charts, but this expansion and new expressive voice of the guitar keys in with the new face of pop music as it becomes more self-conscious, more searching, and calls itself art (and, as some critics like to point out, is the ruination of it).

But there's also a layer of snobbery that comes with the blues boom, just like New Orleans jazz versus Dixieland in the fifties. Some musicians—like the pigs in *Animal Farm*—are purer than others. Many a guitarist now adopts a pokerlike demeanor—born to play the blues—and drops a remark like "I don't play that kind of music, man" to us less-enlightened souls, the subtext being that if we are not playing the blues, we haven't yet seen the light and thus are inferior. *Fine,* we think, *except where would you be without Eric as your role model?* Somehow when you are white, English, and from somewhere thousands of miles east of the Mississippi, these kind of remarks seem puerile.

But Clapton becomes a star and leaves John Mayall to form Cream with Jack Bruce and Ginger Baker, and shortly thereafter his '59 Les Paul gets stolen. Knowing that I have the other one, Eric starts calling and asking me to sell it to him. By this time, in a telepathic flash on my own future, I have moved on to a Fender Telecaster, thinking it to be the hipper guitar. I also think that there's something wrong with my Les Paul, the back pickup doesn't work or something. We are still fairly naive about the technical aspects of guitars, and it probably just needs to be sprayed with switch cleaner. I decline because although it hasn't yet reached its future stratospheric price, the Les Paul is already becoming a sought-after guitar. But Eric persists and I weaken. He is offering me two hundred pounds, which is more than twice what I paid for it.

One night I drag it out from under the bed and open the case with its plush pink fur lining. I play it for a few minutes and stare at a poster of Ravi Shankar. I dunno: two hundred, back pickup doesn't work, it feels like the love affair with this one is over, I am not a Les Paul man. I reach for the phone. I tell him okay—I'll do it. He gets the Les Paul, I stay with the Telecaster, and both will be signifiers in our careers. We agree to meet tomorrow night at the Cromwellian, where Robert Stigwood, his hard-nosed manager, will give me the money. Twenty-four hours later, with the din of the Supremes singing "Baby Love" in the background, I lean across a table in a dark booth as Stigwood hands me a wad of notes, remarking that it's too much money for a bloody guitar.

The next day I drop off the Les Paul at Advision in the West End, where Eric's in the middle of recording with Jack and Ginger. Not wanting to hang around, I hand the guitar over to the kid at the front desk and tell him to give it to Clapton. I go into the toilet at the side of the reception area and when I come out I can hear Eric's voice over the PA system, which is inadvertently hooked into the foyer. He is remarking how great the guitar is, just like his old one. I feel a rush of seller's remorse and get the Green Line back to West Kensington with "I'm So Glad" rolling through my head.

Eric records *Fresh Cream* with my Les Paul, becomes a guitar hero, is identified with this guitar—the terms *Les Paul* and *Clapton* become synonymous—the star of the '59 Sunburst begins to ascend. Before Clapton it was regarded as a weird failure, but after *Fresh Cream* the little Gibson becomes the absolute guitar. What if I hadn't sold my guitar to Eric? Maybe it would all have turned out differently, and the Les Paul would have been merely another interesting historical clunker rather than a cultural icon. But possibly because of our little interchange, it becomes a Stradivarius of rock guitars.

The audience for the Big Roll Band continues to grow and we continue on in a life of nonstop gigging, sometimes managing up to thirteen shows a week. Most days I drag myself out of bed around noon and get picked up by the van at around three to head off for somewhere north of Hatfield. We play farther and farther away from London, from Swindon and Plymouth in the west, to the Twisted Wheel in Manchester, Durham University in the north, and the Cavern in Liverpool, which despite being just another dank basement, seems imbued with some sort of magic, as this was where John, Paul, George, and Ringo became the Beatles.

We get a gig in Newcastle at the Club A-Go-Go, which is run by Mike Jeffries, who later will manage Jimi Hendrix. Driving to Newcastle seems like an expedition of galactic proportions, and we decide to meet at five A.M. to start driving, guessing that it will take us the better part of a day to make the journey. At that ungodly hour we sleepily crowd into the front room of the basement flat and study the map on the floor, aiming flashlights at it as if planning a commando raid. I comment that it looks as if we have to travel a full three inches before we reached the frozen North. At any rate we set off with the length of England in front of us, but even with stopping for tea, etc., we arrive in Newcastle by about 10:30 A.M. This is not what we had planned, and all we can do is sit in the van until we play that night at eight. Outside in the black streets of Newcastle it's freezing and raining, and a few miles away a youth by the name of Gordon Sumner stares at a blackboard but thinks about music.

We become gigbots. Wake up, piss, get in van, drive to gig, do gig, piss, get back in van, drive home, piss, get back in bed, sleep. Get up—repeat previous day. At the beginning of each month we are handed a date sheet by our manager, Bob Hinds, a sharp young groover about our age who is from Hounslow but works in the Gunnell office and is working just about everything else. We play somewhere different every night of the week: Hull College of Art, Leeds College of Art, Huddersfield, Manchester, Liverpool, Bristol, Glasgow, Edinburgh, Sheffield. I dream of tarmac, road signs, cloud-torn skies, and seem to be moving even when lying in bed.

Through the rainy, befogged, mud-smeared windscreens, wiper motion, and endless blur of roads and motorway cafés, I numbly grasp that this is now my reality, this traveling zoo exhibit is where I live. We get to know all the best cafés and where to pull over for food stops, and can name the highways of England by heart. After a while we are occasionally greeted or rather grunted at by the staff who begin to recognize us. This is an assortment of paunchy middle-aged men with male pattern baldness accompanied by a variety of northern and midland "lasses" such as Sheila, Rita, Janet, and Sally, about whom various sordid remarks are made. We sit together at rickety Formica tables covered with white sugar granules, stray chips, and a light film of bacon fat. We eat with our hats, coats, and scarves on and see our breath in the air while staring at the walls decorated with black-and-white photos of rock groups posing with guitars and a grim determination to look heavy.

They always have names like the Raiders or the Rockets or Duane and the Tyros—it doesn't matter, they all seem interchangeable. Most of the pictures are autographed with flashy signatures indicating that not only are these stars resonant with glamour and at the top of the game but they also have the common touch and are happy to authenticate their dining experience with a glossy eight-by-ten. From the volubility of the messages, you imagine that they have just dined at the George V in Paris. There are long tributes to the high quality of the egg and chips at Bert's, and sometimes we wonder in the midst of our deprecating remarks and plates of grease if we are eating in the same place.

We have our own vocabulary for the various menu items. For instance, fried eggs are referred to as dead dog's eyes, beans on toast as a thousand on a raft, sausages are widows' memories, and chips are grease capsules. One can request a big five, which is basically all of the above, including bacon and tomatoes and half a pound of lard. Naturally, this style of cuisine results in the most evil sulfurous and stomach-wrenching kind of farting, and the next leg of the journey inside the van is a feat of grim endurance.

One night as we are on the way back into London, Zoot and Clive Burrows, our baritone sax players, are sitting in the front seat, and Zoot, who has been the happy recipient of a big five at the Blue Boar, imperceptibly raises a left buttock cheek, and seconds later the deadly fumes waft through the cabin like the last gasp of a dying star before it becomes a black hole. In the backseat we know that it's one of them, but while we moan about Auschwitz, heat death of the universe, and the Second Law of Thermodynamics, neither of them moves or says a word. The only giveaway is when Clive lights up a cigarette about five minutes later and starts humming a little ditty to himself as he stares out the window. It's a rather brilliant performance on his part, and one has to admire him for his incredible guts in withstanding Zoot's incredible guts. It's only when we arrive back at the flat in West Ken that he finally breaks down and admits that he wanted to scream and throw up and is now worried it might have given him an exotic disease.

We play in Frankfurt for three weeks at a famous club called Storyville. Every night it's crowded with not only young Germans but black American GIs who are rabid for American rhythm and blues. We play six sets a night, forty-five minutes on and fifteen minutes off, from eight o'clock to three o'clock in the morning. It's grueling, sweaty work and we play every single song we know or have ever heard of, and many that we don't know. The GIs love us and it's gratifying to think that we sound authentic to real Americans, because it's their music and we do a half-decent job with it. Storyville is a long, thin club with the dressing room at the far end of the room opposite the stage, and after every set we have to struggle back through the packed room all the way to our little sanctuary, nodding and smiling the whole way. The one advantage of this, despite the struggle, is that we get to meet a lot of the local girls who have turned up, pretty German girls. I meet one. Her name is Helga.

The band stays in a little *gästehaus* in a street behind the club, two to a room. The rooms are freezing and have only a tiny single-bar gas fire that barely dents the knife-edged cold. I curl up in my narrow cot with all of my clothes on top of the bed in an effort to keep from dying of hypothermia. Occasionally the bed is heated to a higher temperature by the presence of the lovely Helga, when she can get away from her parents. As we don't get back most nights until six or seven A.M., we sleep through the day until three or four in the afternoon, when we finally roll out of bed to start the late afternoon with a warming bratwurst and a cup of tea from the Weinerwold across the *strasse*.

After six exhausting sets we end the night in a dive called the Café Moderno. It's filled with workers, itinerant laborers, prostitutes, and Frankfurt's own variety of malcontent. We always sit together and keep our heads down; it's obvious enough that we aren't one of them. We also remind one another to shut the fuck up about the war and not to make loudmouthed jovial remarks about Hitler. English musicians in Germany have an innate ability to pop out an endless series of jokes about Germans and Hitler and usually at the worst possible time, such as when going through customs. I have seen whole bands goose-step onto a stage in Germany before fans who weren't even born during the time of the Führer. So we zip it and quietly eat our *spiegelei und strammer max.*

One night some nasty-looking brutes enter the café and we instinctively feel trouble. They have a couple of women with them who look like hookers and they sit down and start into the beer, stein after stein after stein. There's a palpable tension in the room, as if a fuse is burning slowly, and suddenly the place explodes into an imitation of Custer's Last Stand as a murderous fight erupts. The whole café becomes an inferno of flying tables, broken glass, crunching fists, and tearing flesh involving every man in the joint except us little English boys. The violence is extreme and filled with screaming and bloodcurdling moans as knives and broken bottles rip into flesh. Most of us run out into the street and disappear into the dark, but for some reason, I see a small piano in the upstairs section and leap up the stairs like a frightened rabbit to hide behind it while the carnage rages below. Bottles and table legs hurtle across the room and bounce off the piano keys, making some rather beautiful Scriabin-like chords, which I think the perfect accompaniment to the mayhem as my heart attempts cardiac arrest.

And then as suddenly as the fight started, it goes completely quiet, the silence broken only by the sound of a body moaning softly to itself in the corner. I poke one eye around the edge of the piano. The café is destroyed, there is blood everywhere, the band has gone. As the scream of a police car siren fills the night, I leap down the stairs and run like a dog with its tail on fire.

BRIDGEHAMPTON, AUGUST 18, 1983

I stretch and yawn and throw the counterpane off the bed. It's getting hot in here and I still want to sleep. I reach over for the Tele and pick it up again. I begin strumming a simple rhythm pattern. One of the first and most important things I learned was to play tight metronomic rhythm. One of the defining things of a great musician, to me, is great and natural timekeeping ability. It seems that if you have that, you can go anywhere. If you don't have it, music will always be hard. I am not sure if it can be taught, because it seems to be in the realm of a natural gift, like a singing voice. Having played with many other guitarists, I have found it a rarer attribute than might be thought. Many players can learn dazzling licks, but only one in five can turn it into a developed solo with interesting time. The ability to play with time—to play inside and outside of it—is what you hear when you listen to the really great players. In the Big Roll Band we listened over and over to James Brown, and I took in as many of the rhythm guitar patterns as I could. I cradle the Tele and amuse myself by playing the E9 chord rhythm lick of "Papa's Got a Brand New Bag" and recall how that line about James Brown— "the hardest working man in showbiz"—became like a mantra for the Big Roll Band as we started up another endless stretch of motorway.

Although it's a daunting prospect, we are thrilled when we are invited to Paris to play on a rhythm-and-blues extravaganza as support for our hero James Brown. Not only do we get to share the stage, but we are also actually going to see him perform—fantastic. We're on just before the great man and don't expect much other than to do our usual show and clear off before the real thing happens, but as things turn out, we just about upstage him.

As we play and try to get the Parisians to move their chic little derrieres, there is noise and heckling from the audience. We stare in the direction of the hecklers, who turn out to be Eric Burdon and drummer Barry Jenkins from the Animals. As we're raving away on the last number of our set, they leap up onto the stage. This gets a big cheer from the audience that swells in volume and they proceed to debag Zoot—in other words, pull his trousers off until he is left with only his underpants on, still singing and hammering away at the organ the entire time. Of course, this is hugely entertaining for the crowd and is greeted by a wild reaction, which James Brown—the Godfather of Soul—will now have to top. Later while drinking with the perpetrators and calling them bastards, etc., it's all deemed very amusing. In fact, it is a turning point in the fortunes of the Big Roll Band, and in a way the beginning of the end.

The next issue of *Melody Maker* has a full page devoted to our little lark in Paris, with a strip of photographs running along the top of the page replete with sardonic captions, and is in effect a great piece of publicity. A day after the paper hits the streets, we have a gig at the Manor House. We drive across London as usual through traffic and bitter rain, chortling away about this unexpected piece of publicity. When we pull up outside of the Manor House, there's a line around the block and we wonder if we have gotten confused with someone else's gig. But it turns out that the line is for us. The *Melody Maker* article has made a serious impact and from nowhere people turn out in droves.

As a result of this publicity our fee and our percentage go up, but also at the end of the show (which we almost always end with the song "Barefootin'") it becomes almost mandatory for Zoot to end the show by prancing about on the top of his Hammond, singing and slowly stripping down to his Y fronts, which is greeted with roars of delight from the audience. This act develops as we go on, with Zoot eventually having on not one pair of underpants but two and at the climax daringly removing the outer pair to find yet another pair underneath. At first these garments are of the common garden Marks & Sparks variety but later evolve into brilliantly colored pantaloons with large polka dot patterns of which there are several pairs. Zoot gets up to about seven pair in the end, with fans tossing special designs with little messages sewn on inside.

It's great fun for a while and we are sure to sell out everywhere we play, but it's beginning to feel like a circus. Something else is happening with music, the Big Roll Band is more like a novelty act than a serious band, and it suddenly feels like we are getting left behind.

Six

I roll over in bed and stare at the clock. Am I mad, or are the hands actually going backward? Maybe my mind is unraveling.

I stare at the wall, unable to sleep: "Madman Running Through the Fields," the one song of our next band that is still regarded as a classic of the era. With Dantalian's Chariot, I felt freer and planted the seeds of many of the guitar parts I play in the Police. Decades seem to blend seamlessly from one to another and then assume their own true identity. How different the sixties are from the eighties, although in a way I have always thought of the Police as the last great sixties band. In Dantalian's Chariot we tried to swallow the zeitgeist whole, even if it came in a small white capsule.

'Sixty-six and the rainbow flag of freedom rolls out, flaps in the breeze, and climbs the pole to herald the news.

It's happening. The revolution rolls out from West Ken tube station, lays a fiver in the betting shop, gets a curry at the New Delhi, drops off a couple of shirts at the dry cleaner's, and flops onto the coconut mat by the front door. The Beatles spearhead the charge and set the style as they write their own songs, grow long hair, and swallow acid. Suddenly everything seems possible, and we all want to be the Fab Four. The bomb-shadowed fifties and the Cold War seem to melt away like spring snow, and what has just been an intimation now leaps into the outer world with bright clothes, hair like Jesus, and a roaring guitar.

In the Big Roll Band we continue on with a strong following around England, but I begin to feel as though we are rapidly becoming an anachronism. The new thing is here and we aren't part of it. I begin to feel uncomfortable with the music we're playing, the nightly funny entertainment we are putting on, playing other people's songs. Our show suddenly feels too jolly—too showbiz. In the new mode you write your own songs, crank the amp, and dress in the coat of many colors. A great cultural shift is taking place; I want to be a part of it and express this desire to the band, hoping we'll all feel the same way and freak out together. It falls on deaf ears, but with all the changes that are happening around us in London, a double rainbow is beginning to arc through my skull—and this needs a different kind of musical expression.

We have been friends for a while with the Animals, who are a hit group, almost at the level of the Stones or the Beatles. Constantly touring in the United States, they sit at the edge of the new scene and frequently mention something called acid. They chuckle to themselves about Owsley, sunshine, and windowpane and we don't really know what they are talking about but are intrigued. I sit in a doctor's office in Earls Court one afternoon and read about the dangerous new drug that is now epidemic in the United States, how it's ruining the minds and lives of young people. I can't wait to try it.

Inevitably, via the Animals, it will come our way—and the redbrick greyness of West Kensington, with its moldering architecture, Carlsberg signs, sublets, and language schools, will be the initiation scene of the orgasmic, kaleidoscopic mindfuck known as acid.

Almost every night when we return to London after a gig there will be a rave or a get-together in Zoot's flat. The word spreads and it reaches the point where most of showbiz London seems to pass through or pass out. By eleven-thirty or midnight there will be a motley group of the famous, the semifamous, and their suppliers, all in an elevated state and having a jolly good time. These include musicians, entertainers, girls, hangers-on, and drug pushers, all of whom lie around in the flat and usually partake of illegal substances accompanied by large amounts of alcohol. The Animals are regular visitors and, already pioneers of the new consciousness, seem to be in an advanced state of chemical usage.

Their talk is full of California, San Francisco, the Fillmore, Jim Morrison, L.A., and Owsley. Hilton Valentine in particular appears to be the leading head, and it is he who tells me with enthusiasm about acid and its effects. I am nervous but willing to try it—my head is already full of tripped-out psycho material, the books of Thomas de Quincey, Aleister Crowley, Jean Cocteau, William Burroughs, Coleridge, and Blake—I tell myself this is just another step in that direction.

Eventually the night arrives when we are to try acid for the first time, but for me it is preceded by a complicated little event on the mundane plane. Naturally, it involves a woman, a girl I have been living with, a very pretty Anglo Indian girl from Chingford in Essex named Angela.

Angie had been the girlfriend of Chas Chandler, the bass player for the Animals, for a while, but has moved in with me. I am hung up on her in a way that isn't healthy because we are patently unsuited for each other and, apart from the sex, there is no way I can relate to her—a full-tilt hedonist with no visible boundaries. Most nights I arrive home around one or two A.M. to an empty flat and then twitch in an empty bed until about five A.M., when she will stagger in, reeking of alcohol and cigarettes. I can't handle her, I'm suspicious that she's having sex all over the place, and I simply don't have the experience yet to deal with someone like this. I should kick her out and move on, but instead, I moon about in a feeble way.

I read books about Zen and Scriabin's experiments with synesthesia; she swallows another vodka martini and fucks the next drummer. Later I recognize that it was nothing more than an early rite of passage and give a hollow laugh about it. We break up for a while but I get sick. Every time I try to eat I vomit, as if I have some form of bulimia. I grow thin and weak to the point where people start to notice and make comments. This goes on for a couple of months. I lose weight and become listless. But finally, as if the hex has finally worn off, I wake up one morning with the smell of food in my head and rush to the nearest Chinese restaurant to wolf down a plate of noodles. It's over. I remember where I was before and gradually start to recover. It's as if I have been under some sort of shamanic curse. I have had dozens of girlfriends in London but for some reason with Angie I have lost all sense of myself.

So tonight Zoot and I are going to try out this LSD stuff with the Animals, and I am interested but slightly nervous. Coinciding neatly with this and executing the coup de grâce to our fun-filled relationship, Angie is in Chiswick at St. Mary's Hospital, having what is delicately known as a scrape—in other words, an abortion. Whether it's me or some other lucky guy who has planted the seed, I don't know; but as a last-ditch attempt, and with the usual apprehension I have come to experience regarding this girl, I make arrangements to go over and collect her. With a churning stomach, a bunch of roses, and a box of Cadbury's milk flake, I mount the stairs to Ward Six. The day feels like lead.

Like a long white coffin, the ward stretches into infinity. Angie is in the last bed at the far end, or so I think. With a look on my face somewhere between a shit-eating grin and a death's-head rictus, I begin the long-roses-and-chocolates trek. With my Cuban heels clicking like overheated castanets on the stone floor, I wake one or two patients who stare at me with downturned mouths and say, "What's that?" I keep smiling and go forward like a prisoner on the way to the gallows. Eventually I get there and, of course, the bed is vacant. In shock and paranoia that come at me like déjà vu I stare at the ghostly white sheets and ask the ward sister where Ms. Angela King is. This is the bed, isn't it? Or is she actually in another ward?

She looks at me with a Nurse Ratched smile that seems to convey pity, disdain, and chilling contempt for the male of the species.

"She left this morning with someone called Eric Burder—a pop singer or something."

Fuck, the bitch—I should have known—fucking cheated again. And with him—my friend!

I feel a strong urge to lie down and throw up, but I toss the roses on the bed, decide to keep the chocolates for later, spin on my heel, and make the mile-long fandango back down the ward, all eyes on the one-man carnival, fringed leather, girl's hair, eyeliner, and cowboy boots.

Back in Kensington, I kick the wall and throw an LP across the room. It smashes on the floor and I start laughing—this is ridiculous, I am giving her all the power, what about my power, and . . . oh, fuck it all. I lie down on my oversize orange bed, staring at the ceiling. Fuck it . . . what is it with women? . . . or is it just this one? . . . I can't handle her . . . I'm too hung up on her. Just like the Mothers' record is going on about at that very moment: Are you hung up? Do you have any hang-ups? Well, yes, I fucking do—it's this Anglo Indian with the incredible body that I seem to be sharing with about two thousand other people in London. After a while, helped by the spacing effect of the Nepalese, a new peace flows through my mind. It's all in the past, I am free, I am free—bye-bye, have a good life—and the Zappa record grows large and deep in my mind as I drift into a rose-colored sleep.

I wake up around nine-thirty P.M. feeling groggy, hungover, and with a sense of something missing. What—oh yeah—her. I sit on the edge of the bed for a moment and think, *This time it's different . . . that's it . . . victim no more . . . must eat . . . Chinese.* I play a few eleventh chords on my Telecaster—they have the right air of renewed hope, a new beginning—throw on a jacket, grab a book on Zen, and slam the front door to cross the street to the Lingam and Lotus. I plonk down in a dark corner and squint at the menu: sweet and sour shrimp, vegetable fried rice, and crispy seaweed, that should do it. I open my book, sip a beer, and try to make up some Zen koans. Where is your girlfriend when eating rice (on the end of someone's dick)? No, that's no good. . . . Ummm . . . where is God when practicing (having it off with her)? What is your name before you are born—oh, for fuck's sake. This is pathetic. I look at the greasy menu and change my mind—vegetable fried rice, kung pao chi . . . no, Mongolian beef and spring rolls . . . yeah. I stare at my book—"to give your sheep or cow a large spacious meadow is to control him." Christ, what does that mean: give 'em enough rope and they'll hang themselves? I must stop thinking about her, let her/it go, there is peace out there, another world, the guitar—that's right, the guitar—the savior of my soul . . .

I eat, and with the nutrition I start to feel better. The food, the earthy clarity of Zen, the shrouded peaks of Japanese mountains, and the words of Bodhidharma, the twenty-eighth patriarch, crowd into my mind and suddenly I start laughing. A tear forms in my eye and mistily I stare up at the Hokusai print of Mount Fuji on the wall. It's all beautiful: this place is beautiful, the rice is beautiful. I laugh some more—the guitar—ha-ha. Li-chee the waiter comes over. "'S everthin awright?" He smiles anxiously through several gold teeth. "Yeah, great." I smile back. "'Cept could I have some jasmine tea—ta?" I stare down at the tablecloth with its brown stain like a Rorschach test. "Strive on with diligence," I say to myself—the last words of the Buddha—and, placing some pound notes on the chipped white plate and patting the table in thanks, get up and raise my hands in namaste to Li-chee, then exit.

I return to the flat, remembering that tonight we are supposed to take a mind-altering drug, but I feel like practicing and pick up the guitar to play for a while. I feel light and strong, the guitar feels good in my hands, I'm filled with a pleasant new resolve: I am who I am . . . I have leapt over an obstacle . . . what doesn't kill you makes you stronger—yeah, that's it, okay.

I play a beautiful raga scale called "Purvi" that has been taught to me by Nazir Jairazbhoy—it has a mood that is sweet and romantic and I work my way into it, finding variations and centering myself with its structure. After playing for three-quarters of an hour, I hear the sound of voices upstairs and, with my new light but steely resolve in hand, decide to go up to Zoot's to see what is going on. The illuminati are arriving, bottles are being opened, sounds are coming out of the record player, and smoke is drifting upward. By about twelve-thirty A.M., with a nice crowd of fifteen or twenty hanging out amid a smorgasbord of scotch, vodka, wine, and hashish, the fiesta is grooving and convivial with the sounds of Ravi Shankar, the Beatles, Ray Charles, and Tim Hardin in the background. Hilton Valentine and Chas Chandler of the Animals arrive and slide into the well-oiled groove. After a while Hilton comes over and says, "Feel like tripping?" I feel a sliver of apprehension, but all innocence and wanting to be a groovy cat, I smile and say, "Yeah, man—yeah." I don't have a clue about the seriously mind-bending effects of this drug, that it might put you into a psychotic state from which you may never return, that it's akin to being asked to go jump out of a plane with no parachute and told to fly, but I keep smiling. As the clock strikes one, Hilton places a capsule in my hand between the heart and life lines. I swallow it and go on enjoying the party, not feeling anything much other than the nice buzz I already have. But after half an hour Hilton looks at me and says, "I think you're ready." He pulls Timothy Leary's book *The Psychedelic Experience* from his bag, studies my face carefully again, opens the book, and begins to read.

In a low voice he starts intoning the following: "Andy . . . the time has come for you to seek new levels of reality. Your ego and the Andy game are about to cease, you who are about to enter the nameless void—turn off your mind, relax, and float downstream." As he speaks, my mind, my perception, my visual sense somersault into a new hyperkinetic reality—the room in front of me dissolves into an egg-yolk rainbow of bright plastic colors and all that once had dimension and solidity becomes liquid.

"It's a trick," I croak, "a trick," and it comes to me in an instant that my whole life up until this point has been a cosmic joke, a hoax perpetrated on me by everyone else, they are all in on it, they know, but now I am ready for this sacred moment and they are pulling back the veils.

I hear a voice say, "And he's off," and I start down a tunnel of intense kaleidoscopic imagery propelled by the music, which now takes on incredible significance and seems incredibly loud and right inside my head. Alice going down the tunnel into Wonderland, oh yeah, oh yeah, so this is it, and it's scary and exhilarating as hell, but like a returning memory, I know in the way that you can't speak about, this is the hot line. Burroughs, Ginsberg, Watts, Huxley, de Quincey, the Zen masters, Lords of the Realm Within, this is what they are talking about.

I shoot from one brilliant cartoon image to another, barely able to keep up with the speed of my own mind. Now I'm in a brilliantly lit cave of sparkling jewels; now I float down rivers of gold; now I merge with sky-silvered dragonfly wings of shining translucence; now I see the eternal Buddha smile and impossible towers of iridescent blue—this is it! "This is what you have been looking for, the search is over, you are home," I whisper to myself.

As the trip continues I experience extremes of joy with wild swings of intense paranoia. One second I am surfing a rainbow, and the next moment— if I open my eyes—the room appears full of horrible little monkeys staring at me with burning eyes. I try to let the music take me and return to that vast cosmic moment that always has been and always will be, the canopy of space time. Vast infinities illuminate my soaring consciousness, and West Kensington dissolves into the flow of eternity: no birth, no death, just shining mindlessness—inseparable from radiance. A ceaseless transformation of life energy, rhythmic pulsing activity, the molecular dance of infinite change; interconnected, interbeing.

I stagger out into the kitchen and try to eat a piece of cheese. How so normal an activity manages to pierce my Krishna consciousness at this point I'll never know, unless it's the voice of my mum echoing in some deep recess to make sure I eat, but it tastes like cardboard in my mouth and I try to spit it into the rubbish bin. But as I do I notice that the bin is like a box of incredible jewels. Old banana skins, cereal boxes, and cigarette packets are dazzling jewels of incredible energy that appear to me now in either particle or wave form; everything is a dance, a pulsating waltz of the submolecular world—electrons, nuclei, quarks, and hedrons.

And I know. I know in a way that I have never known before—and I know that I know it, and it is familiar in the sense of finally returning home. "It is," I whisper to the used box of sugar-frosted flakes lying on top of the garbage like a handful of quartz crystals. "It . . . is." I become sentient and about a billion years old; I myself—and what or who is that? I snigger at the concept—am nothing more than a complex of energy passing through the infinite spiral. I place my hand on the draining board and watch the atoms that are me happily sink into the dance that is masquerading as a draining board. I stare up at a strange relic from the mechanistic universe, a clock, an artifact of classical physics, the cosmic machine, the *mécanique céleste*. I wave my hand through the air and see it atomize into a fan. Energy packets, photons, quanta, probabilities of interconnections, tendencies to exist, all dancing together in Smith and Gardner-Brown's subatomic kitchen. I cackle like a mad parrot and see my life unfolding as if in a series of corridors like *The Cabinet of Dr. Caligari*.

I float back to the far-off land of the sitting room, examining the corridor wallpaper on the way because now it's alive with exquisite mountains, valleys, and rivers, and I talk to it for a while and then like the Archangel Gabriel arrive by the record player, which shines like an ancient source of energy, with everyone now sprawled out on the floor around it. A few million years later the trip levels out into a steady cosmic plateau and I find that I am able to control the pendulum motions and steer myself toward the beautiful, the beneficent, and the ineffable light. By now I am standing in the center of the room, radiating bliss and God power like a celestial blast furnace, and into the room walks the Betrayer—She, Angela, Kali—and with her, him—Eric, Shiva—but I see them as part of the cosmic fabric and from some remote Tibetan mountain peak I bless and shower them with my radiance. We all love one another; *we all love one another,* says a distant heavenly voice that is mine; and I continue my spiral on through the whirling geometric dance, the fire flow of internal unity.

At this point two things happen as I am standing and reaching upward for the bliss, the ineffable source of all being. I surrender, and like a giant sun of peace, light floods my mind, my soul, my being. Radiant bliss? God? There is no other description, and maybe it is the most singular moment of my life. But on the earthly plane on ironic little event animates this moment, for as I experience this absolute mind with both arms raised overhead, the action causes my pants to fall down around my ankles. Somewhere miles below me there is laughter, but I am elsewhere, I am in the ray of God, the alpha and omega, the peace that passeth all understanding, the Buddha field, the Void, I am bathing, swimming, spiritualizing here, in this eleven-quid-a-month flat in West Ken. This is the Clear White Light, the infallible mind of the pure mystic state, and direct experience and phrases from Buddhism float like ticker tape through the white field of my mind: "Obtain Buddhahood in the realm of the densely packed." "Merge into the heart glow of the

Buddha." And then somewhere far below a flat London voice says, "It's horrible." It's Angela staring at my writhing and reaching with a sick look on her face, but I bless her again and continue to illuminate the wallpaper. Eventually the light fades and I slump back down on the couch full of love and rainbow color. But here, tonight, in this one-bedroom flat in London, I have received the light, I have known.

Sometime around six A.M. I feel myself drifting toward Earth and float off downstairs to my bedroom, but when I get there I feel afraid to be alone in a different place. I stare at my face in the mirror and watch as it goes through a metamorphosis of Hindu princes, princesses, animals, kings, queens, eagles, Cherokee Indians, skulls, and various historical personalities. Obviously they are all the incarnations I have lived through, but it is frightening and I have to turn away from the intensity. Exhausted, I finally crawl between the sheets and attempt sleep as the working day begins. As if in litany, the words of John Dowland pass through my mind: "Come, heavy Sleep, the image of true Death / And close up these my weary weeping eyes," and through the darkness and the blackness of closed eyelids, I observe the final burst of fireworks, the hymn of the universe singing softly in my head—we all love one another, we all love one another. . . .

I wake up at three the next afternoon and, regaining consciousness in the kitchen with a strong cup of Darjeeling, shakily realize that I have just been through what might be termed a life-altering experience. Clearly LSD is not for the fragile; it's risky, dangerous, a journey from which you may not return. But as it comes back to me in floaty shards of memory it connects with psychology, Buddhism, Zen, and quantum physics and verifies the information. My hand disappearing into the draining board, the colors, the white light, the incredible white light, a nonintellectual experience of absolute reality. I stir the spoon in the tea, watching the ripples that float from the center of the cup and think, *That's it, that's the whole of it right there—waveform.* The meeting of spirit and matter. Oneness with everything. I smear some butter onto a piece of toast, and the words of Chang-tzu float into my mind: "The still mind of the sage is a mirror of heaven and earth." That was the white light, but what was the rest of that insane kaleidoscope?

Hilton has left me his copy of *The Psychedelic Experience,* and over the next few days I read through it. Based on the Tibetan Book of the Dead, *The Psychedelic Experience* purports to be a modern reading of the ancient tome. Rather than its being a book of instruction to guide the dead through the forty-nine-day period between death and rebirth according to Tibetan belief, the more esoteric idea is that it is a guide to ego loss, to a state of transcendence that is attained through strict discipline and meditation. Leary, Alpert, and Metzner state in the introduction that in modern times these states can be achieved with chemicals and that they have come to us because we all need to have this experience.

In London we who are not yet international stars had been hearing vague reports about something called tripping but were confused as to whether it's a new form of holiday or stumbling over a log. Now we know. Are the changing times a result of this, or is it the other way around? We are in a state of flux, all is possible, all is permitted, so let's blow our minds. Guitars sing; hair flows; clothes radiate; brown rice, seaweed, and organic vegetables invade our human corporeality with deep nature; and with a Buddha-like smile we extend free love and compassion to all of God's creatures. A deeply muscled man in a loincloth walks to center stage and bangs a gong, and in a shower of ringing silvery frequencies the world morphs from black-and-white into full color. Acid gets you there in about half an hour.

The Beatles by this time are experienced acidheads, and although we haven't yet realized it, their songs reflect this. The words—turn off your mind, relax, and float downstream—are in fact Leary's words, right out of *The Psychedelic Experience*. Now we are in on the joke, we have joined the fraternity, and the code reveals itself.

The Tibetan Book of the Dead describes three stages that you pass through on the inner journey: the first Bardo, the second Bardo, and the third Bardo. The first Bardo is when you are supposed to experience the white light as you let go of all ego and game playing, as Leary puts it; in the second stage you experience intense hallucinations of a karmic nature; and the third is the period of reentry or rebirth.

I stare out the kitchen window at the scruffy garden facing a row of dilapidated terrace houses and try to rethink my experience. I had been through all those stages, including the radiant white light, the paranoid visions, and the final comedown. It was overwhelming, an incredible parallel universe, and yet the memory is still so vivid, so clear, it appears as real as the uneaten toast on the plate before me.

Zoot and I take more trips, and it becomes obvious that we are going in a different direction from the rest of the band: we are heads and they aren't; there's a division, and to me it's growing more painful daily.

One day we have a session booked at Pye Studios near Edgeware Road, where we are halfway through making an album. The session is booked for two o'clock. Zoot and I have been on an all-night acid binge and are about as much use as a chocolate fireplace. A recording session at two in the afternoon is what we probably think of now as some old form of game playing. But we turn up late and find the rest of the band waiting for us. It's hard to take anything seriously, as we are still on the way down from God knows what cosmic peak we've been perched on during the night. But we get to work trying to teach the others a song we have recently written called "I Really Learned How to Cry." With suspicious looks from the rest of the band, it's assuming direction—although slowly because the two of us are hungover and indecisive and break into giggling fits. Somehow we get into putting the song down on tape with an incredible amount of guitar distortion. No one's playing with this amount of fuzz, not even Eric, so I don't know if it's a premonitory look at the future of the guitar or I am just too out of it to make much sense of the studio, but at three o'clock in the afternoon it seems inhumanly brutal and vulgar and the studio engineer, screwing up his face at my guitar, which sounds like a mosquito on steroids, looks at us through the control-room window as if we need straitjackets.

After hearing the playback and feeling somewhat disconsolate, we wander out of the control room and into the corridor. A recording engineer we know is standing there and asks us if we would like to hear a song that the Beatles have just recorded; no one has heard it, as they had been in these studios just a few days before. He ushers Zoot and me into a tiny playback room and rolls the tape. A sound of heaven fills the room; it's them singing "She's Leaving Home." We listen, stunned at the absolute pop perfection of it; to our acid-soaked ears, it sounds like running honey—sweet, poignant, perfect—and, boy, would we like to have done it ourselves. After staring at the carpet and murmuring things like "Christ" and "fuck," we wander back out. But it has the odd effect of inspiring us, and we go back and listen to the track we've just recorded and I find myself digging the distorted guitar. It isn't the Beatles, but with its nasty snarl and bracing headwind, it is something alright.

A few months later we're due to play a BBC show called the *Saturday Club* with Brian Matthews. The night before we have again taken off into the inner realm again with a substantial dose of something called white lightning, and Zoot has lain on his bed without moving for something like fourteen hours. We arrive at the BBC and somehow perform the songs that we are up for, and then it's time for Zoot to be interviewed by Brian. At this time there is a lot of news and bad publicity about LSD in the papers. Once he has got a few of the usual boring questions out of the way, Brian starts asking Zoot his opinion of all these young people who are now illegally taking LSD. The rest of the band is sitting up in the balcony, giggling away like schoolgirls, as Zoot—still coming down from the night before—manages to croak out some righteous and politically correct response to Brian's probe.

But this cannot last and the band begins splitting apart. It comes to a head one night after we've played a show at the A-Go-Go in Newcastle. In the dressing room I have a conversation with Zoot in which I express my views with considerable intensity. I think we are doomed if we carry on in the way we have; something else is happening in music, and we are getting left behind. I believe we should get rid of the saxophones and start writing our own songs, maybe get a light show and be a part of the wave.

The combination of the times, the drugs, and the urge to write our own songs stretches the skin of our band to the breaking point. Within a fairly short time we finish up whatever gigs we have booked and then make the announcement that the Big Roll Band is over. There is a gasp of disbelief in the musical community; people think we are insane, the band is loved, we are in demand, promoters would still book us. It's not a popular move; in fact, you can almost hear the booing, but we do it. Maybe Zoot recognizes some of this, or not; but I will forever feel responsible for the breakup of the Big Roll Band. I pushed for it and it happened. Zoot and I are caught in the fever of psychedelics and maybe we're not thinking straight, but they are a major influence in the decision to move on. We have seen the other side, and it's calling to us. Nick Newall gets a gig elsewhere, Johnny Almond forms his own very successful band with Jon Mark, and Paul Williams goes on to considerable success with his own band Juicy Lucy. Zoot, Colin, and I stay together and, with a new bass player by the name of Pat Donaldson, turn our faces toward the cosmic future.

BRIDGEHAMPTON, AUGUST 18, 1983

Lying flat on my back, I close my eyes and concentrate on my breathing. As if in meditation, I sense the breath rise and fall. As I lie between the sheets, the words "every breath you take" echo out like a mantra across the country. Songwriting is the lifeblood of a band, the scaffolding on which you hang your skills, show them to advantage. Sting is a naturally gifted songwriter. The songs he writes become the catalyst for the Police's instrumental energy. Before the Beatles very few people wrote their own songs, but the Beatles opened the door and set us all on the songwriting path. This idea took hold and developed until the mark of a group became not only how good the songs they play are but how good are the songs they write.

Our new band begins with Zoot and I sitting around late at night on the floor of the flat with two acoustic guitars, trying to write our own songs. Sometimes we read through the daily newspaper, trying to find some incident that will provoke our imagination. After a while we have a fair number of songs under our belt, enough to make a record and enough to go out on the road: "High Flying Bird," "Four Firemen," "Fourpenny Bus Ride," "World War Three!" and our own psychedelic anthem, "Madman Running Through the Fields," which for the next thirty years will remain on the list of all-time great psychedelic pop songs. Eventually the song will be released on Columbia as our first single, becoming an underground hit.

Replete with a track of backward hi-hat cymbal à la "Strawberry Fields Forever," a ringing eleventh chord over the hi-hat in the middle (to rise again to great triumph many years later as the intro to "Walking on the Moon"), and a sweet "c" section that can only be characterized as Bambi tripping through the woods, the song features a breathy flute to conjure up the sylvan setting. Over this—the sylvan bit—the title of the song is breathily intoned by Zoot. The lyrics craftily point to the idea that the madman running through the fields is in fact the individual who is truly free and wise, while we, the slaves of conventional society, are the ones who are truly insane and in chains and yet have the temerity to deem this fellow the one who is mad.

It gets great reviews, one saying it's worth all twenty-three shillings and the best thing we've done. We are rather proud of it, and thinking it a superior piece of pop—that we have captured something rather special—gives some relief about breaking up the Big Roll Band.

In the 1980s it's the kind of music that Spiñal Tap will take the piss out of while I lay on the floor of the Waverly Theater in Greenwich Village howling with laughter. But many of our songs are along these lines, a hopeless mix of misguided sixties idealism and the effects of regularly imbibed hallucinogenics. Love is always in the lyrics, not really personal love of the boy-meets-girl variety or the bitter truths of failed relationships, but rather a love of the universal kind or universal mind, if you prefer—a love that will reach and touch mankind everywhere, bring an end to war, and begin a golden era of world peace. Without a trace of cynicism in sight, this is what we believe. Possibly people our age are undergoing a mass acid psychosis, but a shift in the collective unconscious is happening and we aren't alone with these thoughts, although it's possible that those of us who have undertaken the inner journey are more so.

The Beatles have spearheaded the way, and like the children of Hamelin, we—and just about everyone we know—follow. "All you need is love," we chant. "Love is all you need," we bleat. It feels as though we are surfing the wave of cosmic change and that the future has arrived. Now we make music and write lyrics that are striving for, yearning for, a great spiritual freedom.

Our music becomes open to other influences, and I feel that all the exotic sounds boiling in my head now get a chance to fly. The guitar solos become long and searching, the chord progressions are reduced to modal drones, and

the music starts to have an organic feeling as we jam in a manner that might be described as "free" many years before the idea of a jam band is thought of. This is an era of conceptual unities: painting, music, dance, religion, and science converge or reconvene the way they did in the twenties. Jackson Pollock in the United States has already set the art world on its head with his breakthrough into drip paintings; Coltrane has abandoned the use of chord progressions, replacing conventional solos with incredible sheets of sound over drones and quartral harmonies; Ornette Coleman has come up with free jazz; and the Beatles have arrived writing their own songs, with LSD bubbling to the surface as the chemical key to the spiritual highway.

This is the new zeitgeist, but we don't know what to call ourselves and grope around trying names like Tibet, Karma, Reincarnation, Lord Vishnu's Magic Bus, and Mountains of the Moon, but it all feels vaguely daft. And then we meet Jim Bramble. Jim is working as a publicist in the West End and agrees to help us out, and he comes up with the ludicrous name Dantalian's Chariot. It turns out that Jim, like many people right now, has a fascination with the occult, and from somewhere in his dark and mystical library he finds a reference to Dantalian, lord of the seventh seal or some such hocus-pocus, and in our benumbed state we agree to it.

So we become Dantalian's Chariot, which we quickly refer to as the Dandelion Charabang and always pronounce in a thick Yorkshire accent as if entering a pub on the moors from a night of heavy rain. Maybe we actually get the daftness of our enterprise because trenchant humor never deserts us, but we are inspired and sail on regardless.

To complete the full psychedelic truth we are about to bring to the people, we take a few more radical steps as well as a few more drugs. We paint all our equipment white so that it will fully reveal every nuance of the glorious color we are about to project onto it, the stage, and ourselves; to complement this extravaganza, we wear all-white clothing. With our extended raga-style jams and heady rainbow-hued light show, we are ready to descend to Earth below.

People are interested to see what Zoot is up to with his new band. There has been publicity about the demise of the BRB, and despite the furor, we get bookings. But we hit a wall; apparently, the prevailing spirit has not yet passed the upper reaches of Barnet to the north or Croydon to the south. Although we get gigs and travel around the country, the reception is not

always great and, in fact, more often than not we are greeted by stunned silence. We are delivering an amazing light show and playing what we think
is mind-blowing music, but it seems as if we are too far ahead of the audiences outside of London; East Grinstead is not Haight-Ashbury. They want
the old Zoot and the pounding R&B of Otis Redding and James Brown.
Maybe we have fucked up, but there's no turning back. We have seen the
light and, propelled by the new inner truth, carry on spreading the word.
Maybe the difference is that we have taken acid, but the audience still
thinks that to be some type of coruscating cleaning agent. Their blank ex-
pressions reveal that they are not as one with us. In London at this time, the
real marker—the sign of the real man—is he who has tripped or taken acid,
has been there; but even with this acid spirituality, there is a subtle hierarchy.
Those who have, know; and those who have not, play out the old games,
the old life roles. . . .

In the Roundhouse, the UFO, and the Middle Earth Club in London
everyone seems to get it, and it's as if we are all in on the same joke. Our music expresses the release, the dropping of old conventions, the newly found
freedom—and to play old-style R&B in these places would be distinctly un-
cool. Going onstage at the Middle Earth at midnight or two A.M. and playing in a sea of swirling organic color to a crowd of stoned-out faces covered
in trippy makeup is the moment of truth, the place where it all comes together. In the flow of this seething moment, announcements are abandoned
as we join the songs together in one long reaching set to take the audience on
a ride through the outer reaches of the cosmos. Rather than merely playing,
we now soar. In my guitar solos—rather than the deft and to-the-point
sixteen-bar break in the middle of a pop song—I reach for the spirit and try
to get the Coltrane thing going. Solos that move with the inner mounting
flame are extended indefinitely until the statement is complete, the circle
drawn. Beginning with a ruminative phrase or two, they move into a sentence, a paragraph, and on into a soaring cosmic hymn. After two or three
spins around the godhead, the improvisation slowly spirals back toward terra
firma on wings of burnished gold. Members of the band nod their heads
wisely, and one has the feeling of great spirituality.

Meanwhile, free love has arrived and we cast off what we imagine to be
the constrained moral restraints of our parents. To end up in bed with a

stranger, locked in an embrace both chemical and physical, is considered normal behavior. We are the love generation. After yet another night of helpless rutting, I wake up in some dark recess of London and stare across the sheets at a face that I have seen only in the darkness of a club last night. Wondering what possessed me—and wishing that my brain was located in my head rather than the lowest chakra—I ease out of the sheets and cross a cold hallway to pee and decide not to flush because it might wake the unknown sleeping form that I have just left and then it would get complicated: sex and subterfuge. I close the bedroom door, silently pull up my pants in the freezing hallway, and then creep out of the house, trying not to bang my guitar case against the front door or trip over a milk bottle as I exit.

Spread-eagled on my vast orange bedspread, I read a heady mix of books: Alexandra David-Neel's *Magic and Mystery in Tibet,* Hindu mythology, Camus, Dostoyevsky, Hesse, Koestler, Kerouac, Burroughs, Bowles, and books on macrobiotic cooking. I put them in a row on top of the small upright piano next to the bed and gloat over them like treasure. My LPs are stacked along the windowsill: Ravi Shankar, Vilayat Khan, Hamza el Din, Coltrane, Miles, Mingus, Bach, Messiaen, the Beatles, Frank Zappa. Up on the wall I have some posters from the Fillmore in San Francisco announcing nights with the Grateful Dead, Janis Joplin and Big Brother and the Holding Company.

This room is my universe, and it contains all the information I need. There is no view other than a slimy grey concrete wall and the steps up to Gunterstone Road, but in here I am happy as I listen to music, practice, and take in useless, arcane information. Sitting on the floor with the *Three Pillars of Zen* balanced on my knees and chopsticks flashing, I eat a bowl of brown rice and bonito flakes, Messiaen's "Colors of the Celestial City" clanging away in the background.

But just beyond my front door everything is getting loony, and as an outer manifestation of the great interior change that we all imagine is happening, we dress like circus clowns. I wear shirts made of bright Indian fabrics, little bands of shell appear on my wrists, my hair grows to shoulder length, the bottoms of my trousers balloon to a full eighteen inches, and I become visible from about a mile away. I have a pair of purple velvet pants that I love, and over these I wear a long fringed brown suede jacket, with a scarlet neckerchief and handmade yellow boots—the overall effect being somewhere between a court jester and a Hobbit. I begin having expensive cloaks and trousers made in places like Thea Porter. One of my more memorable pieces is a stunning bell-sleeved wizard's coat in brilliant reds and greens with gold stitching around the cuffs. I play onstage with this beautiful coat, feeling like Merlin. We all want to feel like wizards now, have magical powers, transform and subvert people's minds. The coat helps.

As I move through the scene I now hear conversations about ley lines, mushrooms, ancient stones, configurations in the night sky, magic, vernal equinoxes and summer solstices. In our country it seems natural. We are an island nation and see our green fields bouncing with fairies, wizards, and gnomes; in fact, we like to place ceramic gnomes in our front gardens. We have a heritage of arcadian thought, or at least an English fondness for mind-altering substances as demonstrated in the work of de Quincey, Coleridge, Tolkien, Blake, Lewis Carroll, and the Arthurian legends. I nod groovily at all of these things, as if acknowledging the reality beneath the everyday surface. Like everyone else, I nod in acknowledgment of all of these things but somehow I also hang on to a parallel mind-set and my own little stack of books about Zen and the practice of music that seems the opposite of a ley line or belief in an Arthurian legend. I'm still drawn to Kerouac's equation of hipness, jazz, and the open road.

In my desire to make the sound of the guitar more accurately echo the images currently strobing across our new consciousness, I begin opening up the chords of the songs. I never play a chord as a straight triadic harmony but always add another note or two—a suspension or a minor or major second because it gives the chords an expressionistic and mystical power. A soundtrack to the Himalayas, the sound of deep contemplative solitude combined with the ecstasy of sucking on a pebble and gazing out over the Annapurnas—this is what we are looking for in our music. The standard barre chord of so much pop or rock guitar playing now appears dead to me, lacking even the slightest hint of ambiguity; the barre chord is the sound of a room with all the doors and windows shut. I want harmonies that burst like star clusters, intervals that whip cometlike across the corpus callosum, dissonant open-string clusters that make minor seconds beat against sevenths and ninths and elevenths to create a trembling beauty. ("Beauty is nothing if not convulsive," said Debussy.) Some of these combinations are enough to give a cat a heart attack or make a dog howl. But I find them strangely soothing, and I try to get a mix of koto meets sitar, never playing an E chord as a straight E chord but rather as a cluster of notes, G#, bb, b natural, and whatever else I fancy at the moment—after all, it's all beautiful and this makes the sound of the guitar pungent and strange, like a dish being served with exotic spices. It's not to everyone's taste. Pat Donaldson, our bass player, complains about my playing too many chords with open strings, as if these configurations represent beginner's guitar rather than the expressionistic little beauties they are. I see them as arrows to the edge, an escape from the guitar's imitation of the piano that has dominated since the forties. We are acid rockers, cosmic beings, avatars of the light—and this is our music.

But while I have a path, most guitarists in London are still following Eric down the road to blues heaven. I don't want to join the brown-eyed blues boys, instead, I make solos out of drones, playing one string against another, copying Vilayhat Khan's sitar solos and Indian raga-style phrasing. I have a path, but it will be a few more years before it leads to the right door.

We arrive on a Friday afternoon at Middle Earth to set up our gear and do the sound check for our midnight appearance. On the bill tonight with us is the Graham Bond Organization. Graham is a very talented jazz musician who principally plays organ but also plays alto saxophone and sings in a gravelly world-weary baritone. Graham is also noted for having put out a single of the song "Tammy," which can really be described only as the aural equivalent of kiddie porn as Graham is heard chanting the name Tammy over and over again in his whiskey-sodden voice to the skimpily clad young lass who is cavorting in the cottonwoods. It causes great hilarity in the musical fraternity when it's released. Graham is not the most becoming fellow to look at; fat, unshaven and with a Sicilian-style moustache, his appearance is slightly threatening, and with his raving style of organ playing, the picture is that of a human inferno.

We're doing our run-through and practicing a new piece of cosmic wisdom that we call "A-E-I-O-U" in which we intone the vowel sounds before completing the picture with further loaded imprecation. But as we finish up and climb down from the stage, we are summoned with a worried look from a beaten-looking roadie to Graham's dressing room. He sits cross-legged on a raised dais between two burning candles, his bulk casting a silhouette on the wall behind. "You can't sing that song," he whispers in a gravelly undertone. "It's written you will bring down evil, the dead. The Egyptian Book of the Dead—the instructions—they warn against intoning those sounds. What you're doing is an invocation, an invitation, don't do it." Well, we don't know whether to take him seriously or not. He's a long way into the occult and he might be on to something and he scares us just enough not to perform the song that night. We are not about to risk the wrath of evil spirits or the wrath of Bondy. We don't cross paths again with Graham after that but are saddened a few years later to hear that he has committed suicide by throwing himself in front of a train in Brompton, and it's a great loss to the music world.

BRIDGEHAMPTON, AUGUST 18, 1983

Death is never more than a breath away from the act of playing music. Each note on the guitar represents a small curve: birth, life, and death—and then you start over. To play, to create, to attempt the extraordinary, pushes people to extremes. You go to the edge and stare over; some pull back, some keep going. You feel saddened but ultimately shrug as someone you once knew doesn't make it, and along the way there are many of them. The music remains, and this guitar—at this late point in the career of the Police—has survived through everything: near crashes, dangerous plane flights, subzero temperatures, extreme heat, high humidity, death, birth, and divorce. Although it appears to be a classic Fender Telecaster, it is in fact a half-breed sort of instrument. Someone has pointed out to me that the neck is actually from a Stratocaster, the front pickup is a Gibson humbucker rather than the Fender single coil, and it has been rewired with an overdrive unit inside the body. One-third Les Paul, one-third Stratocaster, and one-third Telecaster, its eclectic character works for me. I am able to produce fantastic tone from its weird pickup combination, and its body size and weight are comfortable.

Guitars begin as trees, float down rivers, get hauled into lumber-yards, are sawed into planks, and then are dried, cured, and left to age. They arrive in the player's hand still with the memory of a tree, atoms and molecules reforming to become a guitar. A history begins; fate is determined; events take shape; someone builds his life around a specific guitar; luck changes, moves forward, or runs out.

The guitar is an instrument that most players become obsessive about. That's the way it is with guitars. You have it in your hands and you restlessly fiddle, twiddle, experiment, run your hands up and down its neck, find new combinations—new pathways. It dominates, rules, monopolizes, and grips your imagination to the point that you are in a lifelong wrestling match. You become bedeviled by thoughts that there is always a better guitar—it goes with the territory. I stare at my Police guitar lying on the white sheets: there is hardly any paint left of its original sunburst finish, raw wood now shows through its scarred surface, but I like the red and yellow solar flare that spreads as if from major to minor across the belly under the strings. Arriving at this guitar was a bit like having several relationships with the wrong women before finding the one you truly love and will spend the rest of your life with. And before it, to go along with our all-white stage show in Dantalian's Chariot, I purchased a white three-humbucker Gibson SG model, which I twirled in the prismatic fantasy of our light show at the club in Covent Garden named after Tolkein's novel.

At the Middle Earth after we've played one night, I'm down on the floor of the club grooving around when I notice a petite, dark-haired, and attractive girl staring at me. Somehow we get into a conversation. Her name is Jenny and she's working in the ticket office of the club; she asks me if I would like to go to a fashion show with her on Monday night, which is a cool way of setting up a trial date without anything obvious—so, yes. She says she will call me with the details, and I give her my phone number. Monday night arrives and we trot off to the show in South Kensington. Afterward we return to her flat in Queens Gardens in Bayswater. We hit it off, and the conversation flows easily. Being a spirit in the material world, I lay my advanced mystical ideas on her, to which she responds with educated skepticism and humor. We smoke some hash and go to bed, where things also go nicely, and it seems that I have found a new girlfriend.

Over the next few weeks I gradually became more immersed in Jenny Fabian's life. In her early twenties, she has two young daughters from an Italian husband she has already divorced. Her flat is a scene of constant comings and goings, and we share the same hairdresser, Gavin at Leonard of London. Jenny astutely remarks that it's a sign of the times when opposite genders meet and find out that they are getting their hair done by the same person.

I continue on playing around the country, trying to cause a cosmic revolution with Dantalian's Chariot, and most nights get dropped off at Jenny's on our way back through London. We talk a lot about the times we are living through, drugs, fashion, books, culture, various wars, countries we would like to visit, our dreams, fantasies. Jenny is clear-eyed and intelligent, not cynical but healthily questioning of the acid-inspired optimism that is surging through the streets of London.

Most of these conversations will be regurgitated a couple of years later when Jenny writes a novel called *Groupie*, which makes her an international literary star for a while. By the time she writes it I am living in California and have a different life altogether, but I am amazed on reading the book because it seems a straightforward account of the time we spent together. She has reproduced our conversations exactly and even a letter I had written to her is unashamedly reproduced. In the book I am given the name Davy, Dantalian's Chariot is renamed the Transfer Project, so on and so forth.

Somewhere in the middle of all of this I get a call from Chas Chandler, the bass player for the Animals. He tells me that he's bringing to London an incredible guitarist he found in New York who is going to sit in next week at Blazes with the Brian Auger Trio. I have never heard of this guitarist, but Chas raves about him and I say I'll be there. A few nights later I walk into the darkness of the club and see an amazing sight. Up on the stage is a black man with a white guitar in his mouth. Sporting an Afro about a foot wide and wearing a buckskin suit with fifteen-inch fringes, he holds a white Stratocaster up to his face and plays it with his teeth. I lean against the back wall and stand there transfixed.

It's shocking, an alien encounter. This is a whole new bag, this is no white boy playing the blues, this is music from another planet. It connects with the gut as if emerging from a deep recess of the African psyche and simultaneously from outer space; it comes through this guitarist as if it knows that he is the vehicle through which it will come to Earth. Standing in the dark among the small tables, the clink of glasses, and inane chatter and faced with this primal noise, I feel very white and inadequate. How does he get that sound, that alpha thing, that siren call, the sound of a fuck? We all have guitars, but ours whisper; his screams. I know I am witnessing the birth of a new animal that will shake the music world to its roots and change the sound of the electric guitar forever. I lean over and ask someone, "Who is this guy?" through a mouthful of rattling ice cubes. I get the answer—Jimi Hendrix.

We are introduced in the dark. He's soft-spoken and shy: the music is something else. Chas quickly forms a band around Jimi consisting of Mitch Mitchell, a very good drummer but an unusual choice with his jazzy style, and Noel Redding, who is essentially chosen for his hair. Within a very short time everyone is talking about Jimi, and the word spreads. He puts out his first single and gets a hit, and the world embraces him.

I see him from time to time for a couple of different reasons. My girlfriend at the time is best friends with Kathy Etchingham, who is Jimi's girlfriend, and there are moments when we end up in a club together because of the women. On a few occasions I end the night in Mike Jeffries's flat, where Jimi lives, and I sit on the bed with him as he speaks softly and gently strums the Strat, which never seems to be out of his hands.

One night Dantalian's Chariot has a show at the Speakeasy, a very popular club in the West End. Generally the crowd at the Speakeasy are hard-core musicians and music-biz types. The club is small and crowded, with a stage about the size of a dog kennel. We are announced and emerge from the dressing room to blow away these music-biz types. Sitting right in front of me, literally no more than four or five feet away, is Jimi with a couple of girls. By now he is probably the most legendary guitarist in the world and I have to perform the entire concert with him right there under my nose, staring at me. It's unnerving, to say the least, and consequently it's probably not

the most career-building playing I will ever do. We finish and I run into him
a few minutes later in the men's room, where we stand side by side relieving
ourselves. "Yeah, man, cool," he says as he pisses away the last three scotch
and Cokes.

Providing our oil-slide light show are Mick and a wild man named Phil.
Mick is tall and very thin and has borrowed the money from his father to provide the equipment. Phil is the artist and the one who does the actual projection. Phil dresses in whatever comes to hand, has a wild and shaggy appearance,
speaks with a BBC voice, and has an enormous appetite for drugs. He swallows
hallucinogenics and other substances by the handful, washes them down with
great gulps of alcohol, and then takes off on binges of three or four days' duration without sleeping. What would have killed most people doesn't seem to
affect him. A Herculean character, Phil is also very entertaining, and sometimes it seems that he is the one who should be onstage rather than us.

We are eventually able to put his unconstrained personality to use when
we arrive at the port of Copenhagen for a Scandinavian tour. To get publicity and create some static, we have decided beforehand that as we arrive, we

will have Phil, dressed only in a bearskin, on the end of a steel collar and chain being led by Mick, who will be wearing a white safari outfit complete with pith helmet. Naturally enough, Phil rises to the occasion; in fact, he rather overdoes it. As we pull into the port, drifting past the Little Mermaid with the strains of "Wonderful Wonderful Copenhagen" filling my ears, Phil smashes his chain into the plank and begins leaping and cavorting about the deck. He rolls across the steerage to the feet of lady passengers with an intimidating leer on his face and then, howling like a wolf, leaps into the lifeboat to perform apelike challenges to the crew by showing them his ass. He rounds this off nicely by dry-humping the mast and simulating orgasm until it becomes quite doubtful as to whether we will be let into Denmark. Later Phil just grins innocently, asking if he went too far, and then swallows something purple.

Our theatrical efforts have, however, interested a gentleman by the name of Sean Murphy. Sean has apparently worked at the National Theatre, done Shakespeare, and comes with a prestigious theater pedigree. We come together because he is supposed to put on a show in Paris that involves pretty much anything of a psychedelic nature. The performance concept is that two groups will play onstage together at the same time to create a duel—a clash of bands. The lucky bands chosen for this visionary idea are us and the Yardbirds, and we have an initial meeting with Sean at our mangy flat. A charming and polished middle-class chap, he describes his ideas to us in a very theatrical way. He talks about prisms, arcs, curves, and sweeping forms, and from this moment on he will be known forever to us as Sweeping Forms Murphy. This is usually expressed with a grandiloquent Shakespearean gesture and a long drawn out "daahling." Now we take great delight in pointing out sweeping forms to one another, noting that in fact the universe is alive with them and may be seen even in something as mundane as a dog turd lying in the street.

Jimmy Page turns up one day to discuss the possible musical interaction between us and his group, the Yardbirds. He is gentle and intelligent, and I remember how he let me borrow his Les Paul Black Beauty to sit in at the Marquee. We hang out in my basement bedroom and he admires my collection of books on Zen and various mystical philosophies. He too has an interest in this area and later starts his own occult bookstore in W8.

The show with the Yardbirds doesn't happen, but Sean gets us to Paris anyway on a great sixties extravaganza called La Fenêtre Rose, an indoor festival of psychedelic music, happenings, dance, film, light shows, and enough drugs to sink the British navy. Something like thirty English rock groups are scheduled to play, and it promises to be an event that will stay in the memory—if memory remains.

Two weeks later on the drab grey platform of Victoria Station among advertisements for Tit bits, Omo, tipped Woodbines, and Cornish Dairy brick ice cream, we—a ragged multihued army of young musicians—come together like a cluster of monarch butterflies milling about in the station, bonding and smiling in recognition of the extraordinary weekend it promises to be. We are all on the same trip and beatific in our assurance that we are the revolution. Robert Wyatt, the drummer of the Soft Machine, approaches me and tells me that he admires my solo on a track we have recorded called "The Mound Moves," that he listened to it on a jukebox in Kent and has always wanted to play with that guitarist. He is funny, and self-deprecating. I'm flattered by his remarks, attracted to him, and immediately become interested in hearing his band.

As the clock strikes the hour, we leave Victoria for Paris—a blue cloud of hashish, twanging guitars, ribald jokes, velvet, caftans, loon pants, and high-heeled boots. It's nine o'clock in the morning.

In Paris we play at Olympia. La Fenêtre Rose is an all-night extravaganza of trippy lighting, wafting clouds of incense, pulsating music, and painted faces. With music, color, light, and the chemical message coming together in a brilliant synesthesia, it's a celebration of throbbing tribal intensity.

I wander in and out of the backstage area and out into the crowd, where the heat of the bodies, the forest of faces painted with whorls and symbols, the thick smell of hashish, and the pulse of the electronic dance combine to make me feel as if I am levitating. Onstage a beautiful woman appears in a flimsy diaphanous tunic and slowly disrobes to the sound of a violin a few feet away. The Soft Machine take the stage. Mike Ratledge pushes his arm into the keyboard to make a large rainbow-colored dissonance and they crash into their set with Robert Wyatt's soulful vocals arching over the angular harmonies.

We play, and the performance passes like a dream, with music, light, bodies, and minds fusing into a synaptic meltdown. We end the set with our strobe lights pulsing like two white suns and float offstage hardly knowing we'd been there. I drift off with a crowd of French hippies and a headful of hashish to lie on the floor of someone's hotel room, Ravi Shankar's sitar droning in my head like a buzz saw.

After playing a show in Cornwall one night, we spend the night in a nearby hotel. A friend of ours—Vic Briggs, the guitarist with Brian Auger—comes to see us, saying that he has something special. Naturally enough, before the adrenaline of the gig wears off, we end up hanging out in someone's room and getting festive. Vic pulls out some acid that he says is especially good, just in from the States; it's called Window Pane and, well, why not? We each swallow a tab, all of us except Vic, who surreptitiously palms his. (And I will always feel suspicious of this cunning move.) While we crawl around the room in a deranged state, he merely observes. The night unfolds with the usual set of extraordinary fantasies, hallucinations, and insane laughter. Vic puts on an Indian film music LP called *Guide,* which apparently is a big hit on the subcontinent. He plays a track called "Piya Tose," a glorious piece of music and arranging with a beautiful Hindi vocal sung by the incomparable Lata Mangeshkar.

This track is so transcendent to me, so utterly joyful, that I ask for it to be played over and over again for what (under the time-stretching effects of Window Pane) seems like hours or even years. The acid takes me to a place somewhere in the South Pacific, where I sit in the prow of a dugout canoe that is being paddled by a team of young and bronzed Tahitian natives. It's a drug hallucination, but so vivid and intensely happy that it is printed deep into my cortex, never to be forgotten. In the distant future I will record that song on an album called *The Golden Wire* with the beautiful Indian singer Najma Akhtar.

The night progresses or, rather, descends, into a prismatic fantasy. After a brief episode of working in a wheat field in late-sixteenth-century Germany, followed by running with wolves in the Arctic Circle, I put myself into the lotus position. With a realization as deep as the ocean, I understand that this, the lotus position, is the ancient key to life. From this revelation I begin to experience birth (maybe I have cramps after sitting in the lotus for a while) but—and this is discussed in the Tibetan Book of the

Dead—I suddenly start going through a process that somehow I know or re-member from before as parturition—birth. In Tibetan terms it is referred to as the birth and death of the ego—two sides of the same coin.

Appearing to us as a place we have occupied before and after the end of time, the room we are crawling about in has, in typical good English taste, floral wallpaper that not only covers the walls but also the doors and ceiling. This creates the effect of having the walls of your brain pasted with flowers, which is heavenly but also really fucks you up. At one point I open what I think is a door to the bathroom but end up stepping into a clothes closet for a piss. Pissing while on acid is an experience all its own. Staring at the pink shriveled thing lying in your hand like a baby carrot, you wonder who it be-longs to and what it is. But whatever, it's cute. If you actually manage to uri-nate, you will observe the golden stream with wonder and see its great beauty arcing forward in an infinite rainbow and the mind of God at work in all his mystery and power. Flushing is probably forgotten but if attempted will be greeted with childlike awe and glee and then repeated as many times as pos-sible until someone gently guides you away. This Cornish night ends with us slumped in great flower-covered armchairs like men who have traveled a vast distance and now, like the flowers themselves, slowly fade and wither.

Toward the end of our sojourn as Dantalian's Chariot we do a minitour of Scotland—two gigs actually. We cross the border slumped in the van in var-ious states of disarray. After a long day's slogging drive from London and with bellies full of fried bread, Heinz baked beans, eggs, and sausage à la transport café, there is a suspiciously sulfurous edge in the air and someone suggests we rename ourselves the Farting Zombies.

At this point we are heading into the Cairngorms and hopefully to a place called Craigellachie, the location of the gig. We study the map and find that apparently it doesn't exist; this, of course, would be par for the course, the ineptitude of an office secretary, a misspelling, tea spilled over the word we are supposed to decipher. No doubt we are meant to be in Cad-diff but naturally we are in Scotland. We can't find it on the heavily creased and misfolded rag that is our map. Like an ancient Celtic code, it is nothing but dark brown patches covered with unpronounceable Scottish names and circles describing the heights of the mountains.

It's getting late. Out on the hillsides kindly old shepherds are herding their flocks back to the farm after a hard day's sheep shagging in the heather, and as the sun begins to sink behind the ancient mountains and we are faced with the sturdy reality of the Scottish hillsides, our garish psychedelic clothing and benumbed state suddenly feel rather ridiculous. A strong pair of brogues, thick kilt, tweed jacket, a pipe maybe, a keen eye for hawks, would feel right, not the bright-red-and-yellow pantaloons, fringed jackets, shoulder-length hair, and mascaraed eyes. Laird of the glen material? I don't think so. The argument over "where the fugawe" continues, and I decide to retire from the bother of it all knowing that surely we will arrive there somehow. I'm in an intense Zen phase, full of koans, satori, and lines from Bashō, and rather smugly I lean back into my seat, trying to savor the moment in all of its cracked perfection.

Fine people, the Scots, I think to myself as I open *The Three Pillars of Zen* by Philip Kapleau and begin to read, "The mind must be like a well-tuned piano string taut but not tight." I sit up straighter in my seat and imagine my mind growing taut and aware just as we narrowly avoid an entire flock of sheep coming unannounced around the narrow bend. "For fuck's sake!" I yell as we swerve and miss death by wool by a mere inch or two. "Shit—very fuckin' taut," I curse to myself. I read on: "Nirvana is the way of life which ensues when clutching at life has come to an end." *Any more near misses like that last one and I'll get this first-fucking-hand,* I think. "To attain Nirvana is also to attain buddhahood." "Yr nae goon tha right wae y shouldna hae com this far— git y se turned aboot." We have skidded to a halt about two inches in front of an abundant hedgerow, and I look out the window to see a small, oddly dressed gnome in a kilt gesticulating with vigor at the road behind us. The next forty-five minutes may be neatly summarized as follows: "to know by seeing, to become cognition, to become truth, to become vision—this is the ideal," "yr no on the right roade, y' shouda turned left by McCocelby's farm," "the supreme form of knowledge is knowledge conforming to *reality*," "git ta fuck," "realization of the voidness, the unbecome, the unborn, the unmade, the unformed implies buddhahood, perfect enlightenment," "can ye lend us a quid, ahm dyin 'for a wee drink,'" "form is no other than emptiness; emptiness is no other than form." And then, "Ye no sayinit right, 'Craigellachie'"; with the fizz of an exploding lightbulb, a Krishna wave of enlightenment passes through the van. Sid, who is driving the van and also our chief inquirer of directions, has been asking the way by leaning out of the driver's window and asking in a thick South London accent, "'Scuse me, mate, know a place called Krajer-latchi?" The Scottish pronunciation that at last we hear correctly is a tight small word that is perfect in form. It is issued like a tight musical phrase from the back of the throat—imagine late Sean Connery. Through ignorance and ineptitude, we have just wasted two hours being lost in the Scottish mountains. "Take a wee right, lads, jes right up the road here and follow tae signs." I put my book down, stretch, and yawn as evening slips into night and we sail into a small Scottish village.

We do play, but it's a case of colliding worlds. The gig is in a small hall overlooking the village green. All rather lovely in a way, but not suitable for droning drug-based rock; it's more of a kilts-and-reels scene. Shattered as we are, we haul our gear out of the van and set up. The village hall is an all-purpose affair that serves as a school, a place for the village council, and a shelter in case the Germans ever get this far north or the Vikings make an unscheduled return. As we set up, a small crowd of interested parties stands around us, some actually in kilts and several small children with lollipops. "Whas that, mister?" "That's a wah wah pedal, son." "Wass a wah wah?" "It's something that scares small children." "Wassat, then?" "That's a banana." "Looks like a guitar." "You made a mistake, didn't you, Rob Roy." "Wass yr ban could?" "Max and the Bruisers from Hell." "Up yr kilt, yr no could tha." "Yes, we are."

Setting up the light show, Phil and Mick have their own group of admirers, especially when they start running images to test the equipment, which is greeted by "och aye the noo" and many other varieties of guttural sounds. The whole procedure has the faint ring of showing a Kalahari Bushman a Polaroid or his own face in a mirror. I am sure that booking us has been a mistake or a perverse joke on the agent's part. They had probably asked for Dan McChallon and his Jiggerty Reelers, or Glen Fiddich and his Tartan Trombones. By the time we have completed the sound check, it feels as if we've done the show.

About an hour later we hit the stage, or rather we wander out of the tea room and climb up the full six inches of scaffolding that is covered with old planks, and off we go. To say that the good people of Craigellachie are gobsmacked would be an understatement of gargantuan proportions. It's as if we are visiting aliens, delivering a strange intergalactic message to a new planet. There is very little applause, mostly just a low Scottish moaning interspersed with a few "och ayes" and grim headshaking. At one point I hear a bleating sound and look over at Zoot, thinking that he might have some new effects pedal that he hasn't told me about, and then a sheep on a leash wanders by the stage, held by a very old lady who looks about ready to croak. This is surreal enough to send me into hysterics, and they think we're strange. To put the icing on the cake, a bearded gentleman with what looks like a stomach full of haggis sidles up to me and says out of the corner of his mouth, "Can ye no play the 'Campbells 'rrr Comin' or summat? Yrrr people rrrr getting a wee bit frustrated the noo." So throwing any last thread of musical integrity down the drain, I nod vigorously, look over at Zoot, say, "The 'Campbells are Comin'," and hear back something like "fuckin right" and launch off into the stirring melody. Zoot, with a look of *ahh, what the fuck,* shrugs his shoulders and joins along with Colin and Pat. There's a loud cheer from the tartan clan in front of us, and to a man they lock arms and begin reelin' and jiggin' around the hall. It's a case of "if you can't beat 'em, join 'em"; we do about ten minutes of "Campbells" and finish to wild applause. This is good, so we carry on with "Loch Lomond," again greeted with wild enthusiasm, then "I Belong to Glasgow" and on and on until we have played everything faintly Scottish we can remember. Eventually we run out of material, but it doesn't matter; everyone is in need of a wee drinkie anyway. The hall manager comes up and thanks us vociferously. "Greet show, lads, ahmm gonny buuk yoo wee yungsters agin, ye kan riily play ah meelody, but ah thynk we can do away wi those silly lights the noo—jes tek a luuk out sie wil ye." We don't know what he is on about but we climb down from the six-inch stage and follow him outside. Out on the green the entire village is standing together and staring up at the sky in awe, where a magnificent display of the Northern Lights is taking place. The Aurora Borealis, more beautiful and psychedelic than anything we have played all night.

Maybe this is where we should have ended our time together as Dantalian's Chariot—under a sky full of light. But as if grinning into the face of the devil, we play on for about another six months; and then as if Dantalian himself has put a curse on us, it all comes to an end one stormy night. . . .

We are driving back from Newcastle, and it's snowing and we have to cross the Yorkshire moors on B roads. There are four of us in the car—me, Phil, Pat Donaldson, and Colin Allen—Zoot having taken alternative transport. We aren't driving fast, as the snow is coming down steadily and head-on, but we are passing around a joint and I do have some apprehension about Colin taking a hit because I think he might get mesmerized by the snow. Maybe he does, maybe he doesn't, but we suddenly go into a slow skid right off the road. The car hits the left-hand ditch and goes into what feels like an eternity of somersaults. As if in a dream, I bounce in slow motion from the roof to the floor to the window and back again, until with a final grind of metal the car crashes to a standstill in the ditch. All is quiet; the snow gently pattering down from the sky seems beneficent and peaceful as if gently whispering, *Fuck you, fuck you.*

The silence is broken by groaning, profanities, and gasps. And then, "Are you alright?" "Yeah—fuck." "I think so." "Fuck." I feel broken in half, smashed and in deep, swamplike pain. Somehow I get out through the trunk of the car into snow and crawl up the embankment to the road. My face feels pummeled, my back broken, and I can't stand up straight. But Colin, Phil, and Pat eventually emerge and, apart from the groans, seem okay. But I don't feel good. I am experiencing some kind of trauma, it's below freezing, and we're in the middle of nowhere in the eye of a blizzard. There's nothing to do except stand there—or in my case, bend—and wait for a car to come along this freezing strip of road and take us to warmth and safety. After twenty minutes I feel the onset of death and mentally begin to compose my own obituary.

But just as I begin making a list of superlatives, lights appear. Thanking God or whoever that we are going to make it, we start imagining warm Yorkshire hospitality, steaming mugs of tea, brandy, warm beds, etc. As our car is upside down in the ditch with its headlight brilliantly lighting the night sky, it's a sure thing that whoever comes by must stop. But with growing anxiety we realize as a car approaches that this fool is not slowing down; we stand there in deep shock as this heartless Yorkshire person simply drives right by us. We warm our shivering bodies for a few paltry moments by hurling nasty epithets after the retreating auto (some of which involve his mother in a rather sordid way) and wait again. The snow continues peacefully, freezing and killing, until about three minutes before my release from the earthly plane, at which time salvation arrives.

Wheezing and coughing with one windscreen wiper not working, our chariot of mercy slides to a halt. A cheery face appears as the window rolls down. "Eh, lads, what y doin out there? Trouble like—berra gerrin." Numb and relieved, we squash into the back of his tiny car, someone croaks out that we need a hospital fast, and we do a greasy U-turn on the icy road and head in the opposite direction. The hospital is in a small town—or village, actually—about twenty miles down the road. When we get there I am in fact dead, but by a miracle I am returned to this life with an incredible, lingering kiss from a ravishing young nurse and then carried into a semiprivate ward in the dark.

The night nurse tells me to wait—and I wonder where she thinks I might be going in this condition   a doctor will come. I'm floating in a vast Sargasso of pain, and the examining doctor tells me I have a badly lacerated back and a broken nose. "Now get some sleep; we'll fix you tomorrow," and then he sticks a foot-long syringe into my arm. As I am about to black out with a quiet version of the "DamBusters March" playing through my head, I remember that I have my contact lenses in and probably should get them out unless I want to add deeply scarred eyeballs to my problems. I feebly ring for the night nurse and explain my predicament. It's difficult to move and get into the correct position to remove the bloody things, but by some Houdini-like contortions we manage the removal with only two or three bloodcurdling screams, and then a blanket of black.

I wake up the next morning hurting all over. *Where am I? Oh yeah— nowhere.* It turns out that the others have all fucked off back to London and left me to tough it out with the Yorkies on my own. *Thanks, boys.*

The medical authorities inform me that I am to be kept in the hospital for about a week to recuperate and that I will never have children, walk, or play the guitar again. *Fuck it,* I think, *back to the dole.* But then my spirit kicks in and I decide to fight this thing, to rise, to be twice the man I was . . . which is not saying a lot.

Three days later I am told that they are going to break my nose. I wonder if I have upset them with my nasty London ways or by ogling the young nurse, but in fact my nose is knitting back together in a way that resembles a gargoyle. They hold a mirror in front of my face and I'm vain enough to agree. "Okay, smash me," I moan.

I am wheeled into an icy operating room and given an armful of vicious-looking black stuff while a gnomelike doctor with an evil grin and a silver hammer stands at the side of the bed ready to bludgeon my face. "Count," he says. "Pardon?" I say, thinking I misheard him "oh, ten . . . niiiiiine," and the last thing I see is the silver weapon of nose destruction raising into the air. An hour later I am rolled back to the ward with a thick wad of plaster of paris circling my head and down my freshly minted proboscis.

I get two inches in the local paper. LONDON POP STAR IN NEAR FATAL CAR CRASH, FAN CONCERNED. I feel like a hero for a full three minutes and then with a sneering attitude reality sets in.

I return to London on the train a few days later with the ghastly mask giving me 200 percent in the humiliation stakes. As we rattle down to London I notice other passengers staring at me, pursing their lips and making comments to their fellow travelers with a strange mix of revulsion and pity on their faces. I try to smile, but it makes me look even more bizarre, so I resort to a stoic stone-faced attitude that doesn't invite comment, at least not directly. I feel like a freak; it's impossible to feel cool with this monstrosity wrapped around my mug—no amount of rainbow clothing and jangling bracelets can disguise the fact that I look like a visitor from *Star Trek*—and everywhere I feel the snickering schadenfreude. I try to turn it into a Buddhist life lesson in humility, but it doesn't really suit me. *I Advance Masked,* a tragedy starring Andy Summers. Hmmm. In the future I will record an album with Robert Fripp with this title; maybe its genesis was in this experience.

Eventually we have to go onstage together, my huge quotient of vanity humbled to the size of a farthing. Naturally I bear the brunt of many pointed remarks: "Zorro" becomes a commonplace; "the Phantom," spoken with a lisp; "the Lone Ranger." I try to bear up but wish that I wasn't so fucking ugly. Sex, of course, is completely out the window unless it is to be with some perv who gets off on plaster of paris.

We appear once again at the Middle Earth with me resembling one of Picasso's early cubist African ripoffs. I stare over the heads of the audience, hoping I look mysterious and threatening rather than merely stupid. What makes matters worse is that by now, in the time-honored fashion, everyone has taken to autographing my mask, so my face more or less resembles the crayon scribblings on a three-year-old, hardly the stuff of rock legend. Robert Wyatt alone remarks on how cool he thinks it is and that he would like to have one too, and then scribbles *R Wyatt* across my forehead.

Somehow the car crash rings the death knell for Dantalian's Chariot. Zoot is shocked at what has happened; by a pure fluke he was not in the car with us. The crash, the lukewarm reception outside of London, and the diminishing list of gigs seem to indicate that we are not on a winning streak— maybe the Dantalian spirit is a bringer of bad luck. Johnny Mac, Ronni's Scottish cousin who has looked after us during this period, remarks that he thought something like a specter was dogging us—a hellhound-on-my-tail job.

We have come to the end of something; we are lost and don't know where to turn. There seems nothing left to do but split up. I have been having conversations with Robert Wyatt, and I get an offer to join the Soft Machine. I take it, leave Gunterstone Road forever, and move out to West Dulwich.

Seven

I move into the home of Honor Wyatt—Robert's mother—where live not only Robert, his girlfriend, Pam, and their baby, Sam, but also Mike Ratledge, the keyboard player of the Soft Machine, and several other clan members. All seem to be related in a mildly incestuous way, but who they all are is so confusing that I can never quite get a handle on the whole thing. The front of the house is painted with a large multicolored spiral which immediately announces the occupants as being of a different disposition than their neighbors.

In the tenor of the times, the household might be described as a commune, as it seems able to accommodate innumerable people who drift in and out at all hours of the day and night. Honor is a slightly eccentric but a sweet, charming, and cultured person who gives talks on the BBC and presides over all. When in the mood, she makes a table full of elaborate dishes, amazing quiches, pies, and savory foods that have little labels describing their contents. The atmosphere in the house is a mix of cultured bohemianism and tribal village. Eating, shagging, smoking, and drinking, and making music are all laced with scathing remarks to one another about diminished intellect.

I have arrived not only in an alien part of London but in a setting that has its own established genealogy, codes, and rites. This crowd has been together for a while and through a lot of different scenes, but they welcome me into the house and make me feel like one of the family. Gradually I get used to it and shake off the feeling of being an interloper. It had been a bold move to uproot myself from the familiarity of West London and the group of people I had been with for the past five years. But here I am in the Soft Machine, where I have essentially replaced Daevid Allen, the original guitarist, an Australian who got stuck in France and was not allowed to return to the United Kingdom for visa reasons.

We begin rehearsing and I fit my guitar into their music. In its best moments the music of the Soft Machine at this time is a swirling rush of dense, washy keyboards, repeated vocal lines, and drum patterns that fall outside any traditional song formats. In the vernacular of the moment, it would be called "trippy." I quickly realize that I am the better musician, something I sense Kevin Ayers, the bass player, comes to resent, and I begin to feel a slight undertow coming from his direction. Robert and Mike are both avid jazz fans, and the more we go in that direction, the more they like it, but this is a test of Kevin's bass playing, which is functional. Kevin has some very droll songs that he intones in a laconic manner and a deep voice à la Noël Coward with a hangover. There are no tours or gigs in sight; we are waiting for a tour of the United States with Jimi Hendrix, which is being handled by Mike Jeffries, so all we do for a few months is rehearse. I have a room upstairs in the front of the house, and here, if not rehearsing, I read, sleep, practice, and wonder if anything is going to happen with this band. Every few days there's a phone call about why a tour is not happening, and weeks turn into months. Despite the cordial company, I miss West London and I feel that I'm treading water. But Robert and I often jam together late at night after smoking hash. The improvisations go off into the weirdest possible tangents as Robert makes up Dadaist lyrics about butchers or the measurements of a room, and most of the time we end up on the floor choking with laughter and tears, unable to play.

In May we finally get the word that a tour of the United States has been arranged and that it will culminate with our joining up with Jimi on his tour. I am excited and relieved; finally I will get to do something with this group and get to America at the same time. Before we leave I attend the glittery wedding of Angela King and Eric Burdon. Being a pop-star wedding, it's a huge media event and I stand in line with the other well-wishers. Feeling as light as air, I grin and shake hands with Eric as he passes with his bride and think, *Good luck*.

When I arrive in Manhattan late at night with Wyatt, Ayers, and Ratledge, the city hits me like a glittering glimpse of the future. I stare up into

the black night and the corona of neon, mesmerized by its scale; flaring energy; dense jungle of jutting slabs, angles, and upward-thrusting concrete;
the mute containers of power, history, and the American Dream. This is it:
New York, USA.

Nothing in England compares with the adrenaline of this city. I lean back in
the cab and laugh as the force enters my bloodstream, and the summer heat
of the city slams us like a blast furnace.

   We're dropped off at the office of Mike Jeffries in the upper Fifties.
"Welcome to the Americas, gentlemen," he says, greeting us at the door. We
stand around in his office for a while and look at pictures of the Jimi Hendrix Experience and the Animals on the wall. Mike suggests that we eat, and
a short while later we drive down to Chinatown for a late dinner. In the confines of a blood-red booth, I wolf down a plate of chow mein and stare
around like a Bushman. I am excited by everything: the Chinese waiter; the
menu; the American accents; the thrum of people milling about in the smelly,
overripe street; the stink of hot tarmac, garbage, and gasoline; the fact that I
am here, alive and breathing in the Big Apple.

   The next afternoon we return to Mike's office and he plays us some of
Jimi's new record, *Axis: Bold as Love*. I sit cross-legged on the tasteful oatmeal
carpet at the base of Mike's desk and let these raw otherworldly sounds enter
my brain. Jimi seems so far ahead now, creating a new language by extracting
sounds that have never been heard before out of his Strat. His touch and
sound have the obliqueness of Picasso in the sense that he is setting a whole
new approach to the electric guitar, as did the Spanish painter with cubism in
the early years of the twentieth century. No one has heard this album yet. We
are the first and we languish in that office in New York, murmuring words of
admiration. The expressionistic use of the whammy bar, the amps, and the
studio create a new model of rock music that will be followed for the next
thirty years, and the only appropriate name for it is Hendrix.

   I lean back in the plush office chair and wonder how he gets those sounds
out of his Strat. The place that Jimi seems to live in is like a dreamscape
where he reigns like a protean wizard. No doubt he is ingesting a fair amount
of acid, but the music comes through as a powerful new truth.

   We leave the next day for Texas to begin our six-week tour. Arriving late in the afternoon, we are met by a friendly Texan in a large hat (which he's wearing not to complete our boyhood ideas of Texans but because of the heat and humidity, which are enough to knock a man to the ground), and even this I find wonderful. We drive toward Houston, and Kevin and I nudge each other as the skyline creeps up over the horizon like something we have seen in a movie, something incomparably glamorous. Despite horrendous CIA activity around the world, the United States still has a fairly untarnished image. We have grown up in an era in which everything we aspire to comes from here, and I stare out at the rippling heat, dirt, sand, and cactus and love it. In the backseat Mike Ratledge moans about being stuck in this godforsaken country again and buries his face in *Remembrance of Things Past*. In Vietnam the Tet Offensive gets under way.

Our first show is at a club called the Cave, a sweatbox on the outskirts of Houston. We perform our set and are greeted with enthusiastic howls by the young Texans, who like us because we are English and weird and therefore cool. But the music of the Soft Machine is more demanding than the average rock bands. In the middle of the set we perform a piece called "We Did It Again," a song that consists of repeating the chant "we did it again" to the rhythm of "You Really Got Me" on two chords for thirty to forty-five minutes' duration. At this time the idea of repetition and transformation of consciousness through music is being performed by people in the avant-garde such as Terry Riley, La Monte Young, and Steve Reich, who have adapted the idea from Indian and African music, but it's not yet being heard in the rock world. The Frug, the Watusi, the Twist, the Mashed Potato, the Monkey, and the Slop are impossible with our fucked-up beat. After the first five minutes people become confused and then angry and start booing, and then something else begins to take place. The rhythm begins to take hold, the chant infiltrates the neural pathways, and the mood rises into a sort of ecstatic trance state. This is the intention at least, and some of the time it works. This song marks the Softs as being different from other groups, but it takes balls to play it in front of an audience who just want to frug.

When we come offstage we are surrounded by Bob, Dave, Ricky, Rob, Karen, Carly, Shannon, and Julietta, who bathe us in light, sweet remarks. Dressed in T-shirts, varsity sweaters, white pants, and sneakers, they seem innocent, fresh-faced, and ten years behind London. But they are fascinated by what we are doing, maybe in the sense of a beautiful woman wanting to have sex with an ugly dwarf—but interest is justified because we're English. "Gee, you guys really go places. Man, where does that music come from? Like wow." There are several attractive girls in the crowd who almost as a dare from their friends are ready to accompany us wherever we want to go, and not wishing to appear churlish, we grab as many as possible.

We have a couple of days off, and our new friends take us to the Gulf of Mexico to swim and hang out on the beach. I bathe in the warm waters of the gulf, float on my back, and stare mindlessly up at the blue skies above while a nubile Texan languorously waits for me on the sand. Everything is perfect until some one yells "Shark!" and I fly to shore like Donald Campbell on the salt flats of Utah. From the beach, with my heart pounding, I stare back at the ocean. Dark sleek forms cruise through the water like bats with black fins breaking the waves. A school of hammerhead sharks is paying a casual visit. "Christ," I choke, "nothing like that in Bournemouth." "Don't worry," says a laconic Texan voice, "they're harmless." I make the sign of the cross and imagine a bloody stump dangling over the strings of my guitar.

In Columbus, Ohio, we take a walk down Main Street. I wear a purple cloak, orange corduroy pants, yellow boots, and the hair of the Savior. By the current sartorial standards of Columbus, we appear alien and threatening, a parade from the cackle house. As we walk along the street we are hissed at and told to go home, along with charming epithets like "limey motherfucker." We enter a store that looks interesting; it turns out to be— lawdy lawd—a sex shop with all the magazines behind little iron-barred windows and only viewable by request. This is amusing, and we wander about, making droll comments about the merchandise. "Ooh, what a lovely dildo." "I've always wanted one of those ring things." "Nice piece of latex." The proprietor behind the counter cannot stand our being in his shop and is visibly twitching with rage, our Gypsy appearance turning him purple. He is a respectable vendor of porn, and we are seriously compromising his position, undermining the standards of the establishment. Nevertheless, we calmly just stand there eyeing the merchandise and quietly remark on the quality of rubber and leather. After ten minutes the poor freak can't take it anymore and hisses at us to get out of his store immediately or he will call the police. We wish him well and leave. Maybe we should be dressed in raincoats or something, and how can you call the police if what you are selling is illegal?

Kevin Ayers and I fancy ourselves macrobiotic, and rather than ingesting nasty American hamburgers and french fries, we cook our own little dishes of rice and fish on a small primus stove on the bedroom floor of whichever Holiday Inn we're stuck in. This often causes trouble, as the maids turn up and see a fire burning with two hippies sitting cross-legged on the floor. Our very being—like a strange new virus—seems to constitute a threat. In the American heartland long hair and nonmilitary clothes intimidate, and we are constantly asked to leave. The soundtrack to this sad picture would be the chorus of boos as we leave the stage. The droning forty-five-minute performance of "We Did It Again" pisses off most of the promoters, as well as the audience. Herman's Hermits we're not.

Despite the booing, I am thrilled to be going around the United States and fill the role of a clear-eyed Candide. Being in the Deep South, playing avant-garde rock, and meeting nubile American girls are a heady combination, and I can't think of a better place to be. We complete three weeks of gigs and then head back to New York to take a brief pause before joining the Hendrix tour. We arrive in the city and hole up at the Chelsea Hotel, where I share a room with Robert. This is when the hotel is its most infamous, housing writers, artists, musicians, émigrés, and philosophers, as well as hustlers, drug pushers, hookers, ex-cons, and several thousand cockroaches.

Shortly after we arrive, Robert tells me with great apology that I will not be continuing on with the group, the reason being that Kevin does not want either me or a guitar in the band. The Soft Machine as he sees it is a trio, and either I go or he does. As Kevin is an original member, the course is clear. I have felt this undercurrent for a while, but still I am pissed off—wounded. My playing was pushing the band in a direction that didn't suit Kevin, and he simply could not keep up with it. The truth is, we never had much more than an uneasy alliance. Although invited, I remained an interloper in Kevin's eyes.

Having finally made it to the States, I don't feel like going back to England with my tail between my legs, so I stay on at the Chelsea Hotel, scraping by on the last few dollars I have, in the hope that something will turn up. But I don't know anyone or how to connect, and nothing much happens except that I get to know the city. I wander around aimlessly, go the Museum of Modern Art, try to meet girls in Central Park, see movies, visit record stores in the Village, and in the late-afternoon heat sit on my bed and practice on an unamplified guitar that I can't hear because of the roaring ancient air conditioner.

In the room next to me is an Eastern European by the name of Piotr. He is a violinist and has escaped Hungary to try his luck in New York, but he too is running out of time and is close to pawning his fiddle and getting some sort of day job. He talks about a dry cleaner's in the East Village, and there is a girl there he likes but he's worried that she's using heroin and he doesn't want trouble. I hear him sometimes at night when the windows are open as he works his way through a repertoire of Strauss waltzes and Bartók. He's good and should be working, but there's a problem with the union.

I spend six weeks at the Chelsea hoping to seize a chance, but nothing comes my way and I begin to think about returning to England. As a final effort I contact Zoot, who is now in Los Angeles playing with the Animals. My call coincides with the band's firing guitarist Vic Briggs. It isn't working out; would I like to join the band? The timing is perfect, California, the Animals. I go west.

Eight

I pick up the Telecaster and play through the chords of "The House of the Rising Sun," then get out of bed and cross to the window. Tentatively I pull back the curtain; the sea-washed light floods into the room, almost blinding me—like the light of California when I first landed, L.A.'s bright incandescent light promising everything.

As the plane touches down on the runway at LAX, the California sun streams through the window and I feel a surge of optimism. A few minutes later as I walk toward the baggage claim, I am greeted by Terry McVey, a craggy bloke from Newcastle whom I have met a few times in London. An old mate of Eric Burdon's—he's the roadie, the voice of sanity, the anchor—he's been with the Animals since they started. As we drive toward Hollywood and Laurel Canyon, he tells me in a thick northern accent that Eric has finally divorced Angie. The marriage is over. Eric had the same problems as I did, and finally he got rid of her for the price of a plane ticket. I stare out at the endless stretch of sun-drenched streets and feel a sudden chill of alienation and am glad to be with someone British.

Eric's house is a hotbed of activity. Girls, bikers, actors, and dope dealers pass through the door at all hours. The party never ends and it's a radical change from where I have been, and I see how quickly you might lose yourself in a scene like this. I have a room that looks out onto the pool below and across the canyon to the hills on the other side, and I take refuge there when I need to. I am still wrapped up in Zen and related subjects and I like to practice, meditate, and study. I cut carrots on the diagonal—macrobiotic style— sauté them in olive oil, add them to short-grain rice and sardines, and then stand on my head. *This is the life,* I say to myself, observing Laurel Canyon through the window from an upside-down position and then intoning the word *Om.*

With its hot sun, dirt, fulminating nature, and warm spontaneous girls, L.A. is seductive. The life of the senses, like a powerful aroma in the head, is fully present. The word is out that there is a new guy in the band and I get checked out by the girls already in attendance to the Animals and receive a couple of letters with requests to be my girlfriend. I am a job to be applied for.

At this time in California the groupies are beautiful butterflies who take time and pride with their looks. With laced-up boots, fluttering sleeves, and brown thighs, they appear like contemporary pre-Raphaelites and more exotic than the girls in London; it's easy to fall under their spell. Girls like this will exist for only a few years and then will evanesce like summer pollen, to be replaced by chicks in leather and lurid makeup who talk tough. But for a while it seems as if there is a code between them, a way of dressing and being, with a knowledge of music that makes them the courtesans of rock.

This new scene is the perfect antidote to my cerebral but disenchanting time with the Soft Machine, and with the scent of oleander and night-blooming jasmine filling my head, a guitar in my hands, and a long-haired girl in my bed, I see my future beckoning with a bejeweled finger.

Sun and lovingness float over us, and mental meltdown occurs almost without noticing. You quickly drift into a lotus-eating state of dyspepsia. Mental rigor is left to bake in the solar rays, and language is reduced to simple utterances of "yeah, man," accompanied by meaningful nods as the babble of utopia and heightened awareness permeate the nooks and crannies of everyday living. California is looser, more open, less claustrophobic than London. Here the revolution is a natural event that envelopes and coddles everyone in a tribe like warmth, a euphoric physicality. It's a wonderful feeling of fraternity, but blinded by the light of good vibes, we don't see the creeping shadow.

Most nights Eric and I climb into his electric-blue Sting Ray and scream down the canyon and up the Strip, past Dino's to the Whiskey. Leaning back in the convertible with a joint between my lips and the warm night air blowing across my face California dream–style, London seems like a far-off greyness. We sit in the back of the club among a bevy of giggling females and listen to Buffalo Springfield, Love, the Byrds, Iron Butterfly, and Canned Heat, and we know that this is it—the heart of the scene, where we are supposed to be. At the end of the night, if not going on to another party, we drive back through the canyon to Eric's house. I'm in the Animals, a world-famous band; we're surrounded by beautiful young girls; most days start with a marijuana joint; most nights begin with a substance called THC that is washed down with alcohol. The drugs make you love everyone and everything: you reach out to strangers . . . you spout little bits of spiritual wisdom and knowingly smile at one another . . . this is the sixties . . . this is our time . . . the lights from the Whiskey swirl across our faces and I feel happy—blissful, stoned. I pull a young girl closer, and Eric turns to me with a scared look on his face and says, "Help me, man, I forgot who I am—you gotta help me." We go outside and sit in the Sting Ray for an hour as I guide him back down from the narcoticized altitude that he is cruising in: no face, no name. We drive back up through the canyon to Eric's house and the dark velvet hills with their soft star-clustered lights, and the houses on stilts with beautiful people exhaling blue clouds and all reach toward me.

We start rehearsing, and with Johnny Weider and I trading between guitar and bass, I quickly integrate into the group. Zoot and I resurrect some of the Dantalian's Chariot material Eric is interested in, and we start to sound like a band.

A few weeks after I take up residence in Laurel Canyon, the Soft Machine turn up at the stub end of the Hendrix tour. There is a concert with the two groups at the Hollywood Bowl. I go see them and am enthralled by Jimi but have mixed feelings about the Softs.

We get the word that Jimi will be recording in Hollywood at a studio called TTG, and we are invited to drop in. After eating at Ah Fongs at the bottom of Laurel Canyon and pondering the significance of a fortune cookie, I drive with Zoot over to the studio on Highland. Jimi is recording in studio A, the big room. We walk into the control room and are greeted by the amazing sight of Hendrix leaning sideways into the glass dividing window with a cigarette dangling from his lips, the hat with the Indian feather on his head, and the white Stratocaster in his arms roaring and snarling out of the speakers overhead. The impression of Jimi in this moment is one of shamanic power, a force of nature that is both sexual and spiritual. Hearing him is like having your guts turned inside out.

Jimi turns and sees us in the control room, and we wave shyly. He smiles, puts his guitar down, and comes into the control room to greet us in his soft-spoken manner. We talk for a few minutes and then I wander out into the studio, where Mitch is jamming with himself. I pick up a guitar that's lying there and start jamming along with Mitch. A few minutes later Jimi comes back out into the studio and picks up a bass and starts jamming along with us. *Christ,* I think, in a hallucinatory flash, *Jimi Hendrix is playing bass with me.* But I don't freak out or stop but just carry on playing. This might be (a) the greatest act of self-confidence of all time, (b) incredible arrogance, (c) my being medicated to the eyeballs, or (d) deafness, but we continue for about ten minutes and then Jimi says, "Hey, man, do you mind if I play guitar for a while?" "Sure," I say, trying to be cool as if this is an everyday occurrence—all musicians are in total awe of Hendrix at this point and I fight against breaking down into a sobbing heap.

We swap instruments and carry on jamming, with me now holding down the low-end chords and choking on the inside. After a number of variations and different directions, the jam turns to a warm glow, cools, and finally turns to ash, at which point we all nod and agree that it was cool, croak outa few "see you later, man" style good-byes, and look for the exit. Zoot and I wander back out onto Highland, shaking our heads in disbelief, while inside Jimi carries on wielding his axe through a new frontier.

That night when I finally lie down, I know I have just passed through a seminal moment in my life. Jimi is having a huge influence on guitarists everywhere: people are mimicking his style, and little Jimis are springing up everywhere. The Hendrix style is very seductive, and at this moment in

the world of rock guitar, it's hard to resist trying to get all his licks and ap-
ing his style. But I wrestle with it because from almost the first moment I
began playing the guitar, the one precept that has consistently come at me,
been hammered into my brain, held up as the sine qua non of playing music, is the idea that you must find your own voice, you must—in the words
of countless musician interviews in the magazines I read as a teenager—
"have something to say." Jimi has something to say, but somehow through
a combination of natural stubbornness, inborn musical instincts, and the
long embrace of the "own voice" idea, the thought of being a Hendrix
clone is anathema to me. I am in a position that many guitarists would
covet, but inside I have a nagging feeling that it is temporary and that I
have not yet found the environment in which I can be the most expressive.
London and the Flamingo seem like a half-remembered dream; other guitarists I started out with—Clapton, Beck, Page, Albert Lee—are well on
their way. Maybe I have been sticking to my own path too rigidly, maybe I
should have taken a more obvious route like everyone else, or maybe my
time hasn't come yet. But like anyone, I need the setting in which it can
take root. At the moment the partners I am seeking are both still at school
in England: one at Millwall in the English west country, the other at St.
Cuthbert's grammar school in Newcastle.

I push my head into the pillow; sleep will help. But just as I lower my
head into the downy softness, the bedroom door bursts open and in charge
two girls and a bolt of lightning known as Keith Moon. "Christ!" I yell, and
sit bolt-upright in bed with a thumping heart, trying to look casual. "Sorry,
man, were you sleeping?" "I was just about—" "Heard you were here—
wanna go out somewhere?" It's approaching five A.M. "No, man, that's alright." But we talk for a few minutes; Mooney is obviously still in high party
mode and wants company. He finally explodes out of the room and I collapse back into the pillow. Where was I? Hendrix, guitar heroes . . .

The Animals eventually get into a studio and make a recording, which in the
spirit of the times is called *Love Is*. I never get paid for playing on this record
but I do get to play one of the longest guitar solos ever recorded until this
point. On our version of Traffic's "Colored Rain" I take it all the way with a
soaring "hymn to ecstasy" style solo that is so long that I find it impossible to

play in a full trance state and still come out at the right place, so Zoot stands in the studio, counting the whole way, and at bar 189 he gives me the cue out. Although I don't hear much at the time, the solo does get a slight legendary reputation and gets mentioned in interviews twenty years later.

We tour across the United States, and even Mexico, with two high points being shows at the New York and San Francisco Fillmores. In New York we top a bill that also features Sly and the Family Stone. They go on before us and are incredible, with eight of them in a row at the front of the stage, thrusting and grinding to a deep funk rhythm that conducts your pulse, drenches you in the sweat and smell of Africa, and feels like a direct message from the Congo. It's an impossible act for five little white boys to follow, particularly as one of their songs is actually called "I'm an Animal," but we clang away on our electric guitars, whip through the catchy hooks of the Animals hits, and just about manage to avoid public humiliation by ending with "The House of the Rising Sun."

Afterward in the dressing room as we bathe in the cool glow of a Pyrrhic victory, the door suddenly bursts open and fifteen or twenty huge black-leathered and shaggy men stomp in. Hells Angels. An odor of sweat, beer, motor oil, leather assails the room, accompanied by a visual display of muscles tattooed with swastikas, skulls, and the word *mother*, and the only response is to grunt, nod in a macho way, and say "fuck" a lot. Although it's not actually articulated, it appears that what they want is to get up-close to an English rock group and see what they're about—like dogs sniffing each other's arses. After about ten minutes there is some grunting and they shove off. The door shuts and we look at one another, grinning like frightened schoolboys. "F-u-u-u-u-ck, that was heavy," someone says in a soprano voice.

The next stop is San Francisco to play the Fillmore. This is the city where the freak flag is raised to its highest point, and I am excited finally to be in what is considered the dead center of it all. Before the hippie movement the city has been a witness to the fifties beat scene and the lights of Ginsberg, Kerouac, Gary Snyder, and Ken Kesey. With its black, white, and Chinese mix, it is a natural fulcrum for alternative culture, and the step from beatnik to hippie is just one of degree. The beat culture of coffeehouses, bebop, poetry, beards, and leftist thinkers has morphed into a tribe of dropouts and acid takers. A crowd that now eschews politics, believing the system to be corrupt, prefers to engage in activity that has no inherent meaning other than being a way of surrendering to the spirit. A great deal of this new agenda is spurred on by Owsley, the rebel chemist who locally manufactures acid hits by the millions. LSD acquires several street names: White Lightning, Sunshine, Mr. Natural, Orange Wedge, Purple Haze, Window Pane.

We visit different parts of the city—North Beach, Berkeley, Golden Gate Park, and Haight-Ashbury. I wander about the Haight but find it disappointing after the huge buildup. Apart from the coffee shops and natural-food restaurants, it's seedy and run-down, with teenage kids on the street looking hungry and homeless. There seems a disparity between the legendary love generation and the street reality, as if the dream is already fading.

The local record-company publicist takes us to the house of a young journalist by the name of Jann Wenner. He shows us some copies of a new music magazine that he's just starting. It's to be called *Rolling Stone*. What do we think about it, do we like the name? We all nod wisely and murmur words like *cool* and *groovy* and wander back out into the Haight.

The next day we go out to Stinson Beach and spend a euphoric day climbing the rocks, diving into the Pacific, and sleeping in the grass. Stretching out on the sun-warmed rocks, I think about Kerouac's book *The Dharma Bums,* with its phrases out of Buddhism and Zen and how it all seems to blend so effortlessly into this California landscape. No doubt the itinerant monkish life would be easier out here. It's a beguiling thought and I imagine wandering off down some dusty trail free of possessions and reciting the Diamond Sutra just like Japhy Ryder. We gaze down onto the lapping sea, our heads filled with the scent of pine and marjoram, the sun arcing across the sky like yellow lead and the heavy air working its somnolent spell on us.

Later in the afternoon we return to the city, reviving with coffee on the way. Tonight is our gig at the Fillmore, and we are in a mood of high anticipation. Before the show we are taken to a party somewhere in the city where we're going to meet Chet Helms. Helms, a counterculture guru, is a well-known figure in San Francisco and leader of the Diggers. We arrive at the party and are greeted by numerous people, all strangers but superfriendly, as people are in these times, for it's an implicit acknowledgment of the fraternity we share—and after all, we are the Animals, groovy English musicians.

Eventually Chet Helms arrives. He enters the room like Jesus, dressed in flowing white robes with a radiant smile on his face. There's a buzz around him, an energy field that may be self-importance or the expectation his followers project. I can't tell because at this point I'm out of my head on a substance called THC. I can no longer feel my feet on the floor, and as a fat girl near me says, "M-a-a-a-n, you are glow-ing," I can't wipe the Buddha smile off my face. I am intensely happy and feel as if I have the universe in the palm of my hand. When I speak, my voice comes out like warm and oily sunshine.

We are introduced to Chet and he offers us a few words of beneficence as even we have our place in the scheme of things. A small thought passes through my mind along the lines of *Oh yeah, and what do you know that I don't know, Mr. Guru?* This is known as a "negative vibe." I see it and drop it like a hot potato and carry on grinning like a Cheshire cat and eventually, after realizing that I am staring at an empty space where Chet once was, float off with the other groovers.

We pile into taxis and head across town to the Fillmore. Even the taxi ride seems cosmic: San Francisco! The Golden Gate Bridge! It's all such a *groove!* In the confines of the filthy taxi I remark on what a beautiful thing it is. "Beautiful cab," I say, and run my hands lovingly over a frayed Marlboro ad pasted on the back of the driver's seat, my voice fuzzy and sonorous with alkaloids and godpower—I am really gone.

We arrive at the Fillmore and it's packed wall-to-wall with heaving bodies. *Maybe that's why it is called the Fillmore,* I giggle to myself. We can't get to the dressing rooms or the stage from the back of the building because somebody has locked the backstage entrance, and despite heavy pounding and more giggling, no one hears us. This leaves us with the ominous prospect of making our way through the crowd to get to the stage. The girl at the entrance actually recognizes us and lets us through, staring at me—the supposed lead guitarist who is being pulled into the steaming crowd like a man with two broken legs. But with a person on either side of me I am shuffle-dragged across the floor, with me smiling beatifically at all, until we get to the dressing-room area and are told that we are due onstage in about fifteen minutes. The Chambers Brothers are already up there and doing a fine job of warming up the crowd for the big act—us.

Someone hands me a wooden thing with bits of wire attached to it and tells me it's a guitar, it's my guitar, a cream-colored Les Paul Junior. I stare at it, fascinated. Black coffee is poured down my throat and I am perambulated around the room like a helpless geriatric and then it's showtime. "Let's do it!" someone yells. What? I croak-smile through a haze of caffeine and cannabis residue and then fall on the floor in a giggling fit, amazed by my own deep humor. A few moments later we hit the stage—or in my case, crawl out from the wings—to a Fillmore roar. Miraculously, instinct and nineteen cups of coffee kick in and I get through the show, the whole thing flickering before me like a dream. A small voice somewhere tells me not to look at my fingers, because if I do, I will get hung up on them—so I don't, and the digits make the connections while my brain drifts over vast cosmic spaces.

BRIDGEHAMPTON, AUGUST 18, 1983

I get out of bed and lay my Telecaster against a chair. Holding my hand up to the light, I study the nails of my right hand. They look too long. Despite being in a rock band, I keep my nails in good shape—a habit left over from my years of obsessive classical guitar playing. I pull a diamond deb file and some fine sandpaper out of my travel bag and begin working on them, carefully holding them against a black T-shirt so that I can see the curve that I'm trying to get.

When Sting and I first began playing together, a point of contact between us was the classical guitar. It turned out that he was quite a fan, and as I could still play a lot of my repertoire, he would ask me to play certain pieces for him, usually Bach or Villa-Lobos. This was a pleasant discovery for me because it is unusual to find someone in the rock world who appreciates this kind of music, and it felt like a surprising but sure confirmation of where I had just landed, a mutual love of a music that despite being from another genre would find its way into our songs. I finish filing my nails into the perfect half-moons that make the thick, sweet sound on a nylon-string guitar and pick up the Fender, in the mood to play something from that time. I drop the bottom string down to a low D and begin playing a piece by the Mexican composer Ponce, "Scherzino Mexicana." I can just about remember it—the bridge with its pattern of changing harmonic movement is tricky, but it comes back, sweetly romantic, from another time, another place, Mexico. . . .

We go to Mexico City and stay in a hotel in the Zona Rosa, an attractive tourist area in the center. I enjoy walking around and seeing a world I wouldn't have dreamed of a few years before. Our promoter is a very likable and crazy Mexican by the name of Mario Olmos. Many years later I play for him again, first with the Police but more notably on my own at the Teatra Angelo Peralta, where together we will enjoy a splendid riot with armed Mexican police and the night ending with Mario handing me a brown paper bag of pesos in payment as he slides dead drunk under the table.

One morning I drive down Laurel Canyon to our manager's office on Sunset Boulevard. I walk in and ask for David, manager of the Animals. A strange look passes across the secretary's face and she tells me that he will not be in that day because his best friend has been killed the night before, has in fact been murdered. His name was Jay Sebring.

This is the first time I hear about the Manson murders, although it isn't called that until later when the whole story begins to emerge. But gradually it takes over the news and the press, and there is a feeling of shock and disbelief. It feels as though a crack has appeared in the dream. How could this be? In the center of this grooving, loving scene, a grotesque distortion has surfaced; Manson, with his Christ-like appearance, hippie followers, and brutal acts of murder, has shattered all illusions.

In the days following as I talk to friends on the telephone, it's obvious that this horror has deeply shaken many people and some decide to get out of L.A. Wrapped in tie-dye and batik, they sit cross-legged and gaze out across Lookout Mountain while dipping their hand into a bag of Acapulco gold, rolling a joint, and saying, "Heavy trip, man—heavy trip." In Laurel Canyon the horror is palpable, a cold black shadow crawling across the hills. Hippies and flower children become figures of suspicion. It's hard to think in quite the same way about a bearded man buying a bag of lentils or a long-haired girl getting her short-grain rice at the country store halfway down the canyon. As the word spreads it's frightening how many people around the

Strip have connections to Manson and his gang. David, our manager, might also have been there that night.

About this time we play a festival somewhere near L.A., and backstage I meet a very beautiful girl by the name of Cathy James. We eye each other up and soon get talking; within a week or so, I move in with her.

Cathy is eighteen and has been on the scene since she was fourteen. She has a baby by Denny Laine, who is now in Paul McCartney's Wings, but it hasn't worked out between them and she's returned to L.A. and a bevy of admirers. Often these Cathy fans turn up late at night, and I see a parade of famous people pass through her small apartment on Bronson Avenue. One of her most ardent fans is Tiny Tim, who arrives one night fluttering and quivering like a butterfly. It appears that the tremulous female personality isn't fake. All nerves and high-pitched voice, he sits at the end of the bed and sings to Cathy, accompanying himself on his ukulele. It's an extraordinary moment, but at the end of the song something freaks him out and he starts screaming and flapping his arms and says he has to run and literally bolts out the front door like a deer. We pursue him down the street for a while, trying to get him back as he vanishes into the night, screaming and waving his uke in the air.

But after about three weeks with Cathy it seems that despite the physical attraction, we don't really have any chemistry. We both recognize it and agree to split. I miss the riotous scene at Eric's house anyway. I call him up and move back in.

A tour of Japan has been on the books for a while, and finally we fly to Tokyo. This is a place I have fantasized about for a long time, and I am filled with excitement to investigate it firsthand. I indulge in vague thoughts about leaving the group to enter a monastery, take the Zen path to satori, and leave this mundane world behind—even if it means giving up the guitar—but it all turns out rather differently.

We arrive at Narita Airport and are greeted in the lounge by a large mob of screaming schoolgirls who wave, scream, laugh, and cover their mouths at precisely the same moment. It's strange but it's a positive reception, and any-way this is the Far East. But on the right-hand side a shadow appears in the form of an argument between David and the promoters, who have turned up to welcome us, or at least make sure we are there to honor the contract. David never says much—he's a pretty introverted type anyway—but there is a problem about contracts and money, and despite the continuous bowing and smiling, it appears we are in conflict.

We do the usual round of press interviews and stay at the Princess Hotel, where young girls gather in the lobby each day hoping for a glimpse of our pale English faces. I look high and low for signs of Zen or the odd stray koan but, to my disappointment, find nothing. The spiritual otherworldly Japan that I revere seems to have disappeared, to be replaced by a country obsessed with cameras, cars, American TV, and weird sex.

We always begin playing our shows at 6:30 P.M. sharp, a time that is set in stone for concerts in Japan. We're done by seven-thirty and then wonder what to do for the rest of the night. Apparently it's forbidden for young Japanese to get excited, stand up, or express enthusiasm, and the audience—mostly young girls—sit like statues and applaud politely as if on cue at the end of the songs. The clapping starts and stops with split-second timing, as if their hands are wired together or it has been repeatedly rehearsed—like a school of fish who all turn to the left together with an unseen telepathic communication. This is followed by a graveyard silence before we begin the next song. Announcing the songs is like reading an obituary. The whole thing is unnerving and the polar opposite of the raucous audiences in the United States. Here it's akin to lying in a coffin: eyes wide open, about to be buried, the scream locked in your throat.

It becomes obvious that the strain between David and the promoters is unresolved. Eric knows something about it, but he doesn't let on. But after a gig one night we are taken to a place in Shinjuku, the red-light district of Tokyo, a place that might be called a brothel/restaurant. We go down some steps into a basement room that is filled with yellow-blossom trees, running water, and a fake backdrop of Mount Fuji. Flitting through this ersatz Japan are several girls dressed as geishas. We plonk down in a row opposite our promoters, and they offer us all a whiskey. While the whiskeys are being delivered we get surrounded by a bevy of giggling faux geisha girls. They shove themselves into the table with us, giggling and making suggestive sounds. One of us gets his pants unzipped by a hostess and his penis is pulled out. This causes great hilarity, but right then the seven glasses of whiskey arrive on the table—six full and one empty except for a few cubes of ice. As we raise our glasses one of the henchmen leans over to David and whispers something to him with a leer on his face and then removes a pistol from inside his jacket and empties the chamber of 9mm bullets into the empty whiskey glass. At this point of samurai symbolism Eric gets up and storms out. Sitting at the table, the rest of us are frozen. "I'll be with you in cherry-blossom time," I whisper to the little mound of rice on my plate.

Above a seedy-looking joint located on a noisy street, a small sign with THE ANIMALS spelled out in dirty white plastic followed by a row of Japanese characters hangs in defeat. Our dismay at this booking is expressed in terse but poetic phrases like "what the fuck are we doing here?" and "fuck this for a sixpence." In truth it doesn't add up. We are the *Animals*—one of the world's most famous groups; this doesn't make sense and basically—really— what the fuck are we doing in this place?

The inside of the club is the usual small-time fare that can be found anywhere in the world. Dark and gloomy with an advertisement for Suntory on one wall and Asahi on the other. The clientele is mostly greasy-looking Japanese in suits who are already three sheets to the wind. As we enter, in an uncanny act of timing, so do our promoters. Several waiters bow extremely low in their direction, and you don't have to be Sherlock Holmes to know that beneath the veils of Eastern passivity lies Oriental duplicity. Terry McVey is with us, but David is nowhere to be seen. This is strange; normally he is with us at all times. We try to delay going onstage until our manager arrives, with Zoot in particular trying to hold us back as if he knows something we don't. But it gets later and later and eventually we haul out of the tiny dressing room and up onto the stage.

As we do the show feeling like a third-rate variety act, it's hard not to be suspicious of this audience. There are no teenyboppers in sight but mostly middle-aged men in suits and mouths full of gold teeth accompanied by sultry-looking women who look suspiciously like working girls. It comes to me that the whole setting is like something out of a forties film noir, with clichéd Orientals, mysterious women, and either large amounts of opium or missing priceless artifacts. *I may never be seen again,* I think as I twang through the folksy chords of "The House of the Rising Sun": a minor—mysterious death in the Far East; C—out like a candle; D—the good die young; F—a brief intense flame; E7—may his spirit continue. The irony of playing a song with that title in this place suddenly cracks me up and I have a strong urge to pee. But we finish the show and there's still no sign of David, and we begin to feel like a baby without its mother. But we guess that he must be doing business or something, so after a few drinks we decide to head back to the hotel. We have to leave at nine A.M. the next morning for Hiroshima.

Everyone leaves except me. Typically, I have met a girl in the club, a nice-looking American girl from L.A., and am hoping to spend some extracurricular time with her. The boys return to the hotel and I go off to spend the night discussing Proust with this girl at her hotel. By a small miracle I manage to wake up early enough to make it back by taxi to the Princess Hotel in time to leave with everyone else. As I get ready to slouch out of the room, my new friend lifts her raven locks from the pillow to ask, "Where are you going?" to which I reply, "Hiroshima, mon amour."

I arrive at the hotel to find my room vacated and my bags gone. I start knocking on other doors, only to find that there is no one around—they have left without me. I go into a cowardly funk, and the word *mummy* silently crosses my lips. I am alone in the Far East: no money, no credit card, no passport, and no courage.

I run down to the lobby to inquire in fluent Japanese as to the whereabouts of my distinguished colleagues, the scumbags. As I enter the lobby Mick Watts, our erstwhile roadie, comes bursting through the entrance to the foyer. "Quick," he says breathlessly, "ger airpor nah." "Whaaa the—," I reply suavely, not thinking that anything is really amiss but that I have just fucked up. On the way to the airport Mick gasps out the story.

Apparently our promoters are part of the Yakuza—the Japanese mafia. They had captured David last night and taken him at gunpoint to a filthy hole somewhere in the bowels of Tokyo. In this dark spot they threatened to cut off one of his fingers unless he signed security notes to the tune of $250,000 and added that they also might kill one of the band, probably the lead guitarist; in fact, they have actually named me as the demisee. David—cool as a cucumber on a December day and flipping my paltry life in the air like a dime—cleverly surmises that they don't understand the queen's English and writes out the checks and a note stating that at the moment of writing he is being threatened at gunpoint by knaves of the Orient and that if he ever gets out of here, he will see them in the international courts. Luckily for David, none of the villains can read English (or Japanese, for that matter) and they seem satisfied, but they say we all have to leave Japan the next day and add that they have lost a lot of money because the original tour has been canceled and rebooked too many times.

I lean back in the cab in disbelief. This is bloody impossible and very disappointing—it just feels like more shit, and life-threatening at that. Do I really want this anymore? There must be another way. Meanwhile, our equipment—including my guitars and particularly a little cream-colored Les Paul Junior that I am starting to befriend—are en route to Hiroshima. I never get them back. The loss of my guitars cuts deep, and if I resent our "promoters" for anything, it's this even more than the threat of death at a young age.

At the airport, as Mick has warned me, our former thug employers are present, sitting in a row together and watching the band like predators; they are going to make sure that we leave and never return.

The good news is that David has made a decision that we should go stay in Honolulu for a few days to get over this nasty experience. It will also give him an opportunity to go to the bank and cancel all the checks he wrote. A week later an article is written in the *International Herald Tribune* giving details of the incident.

We stay in a hotel right on Waikiki Beach and sink with relief into the thick-scented air of Hawaii. For a moment it is seductive, as if this island paradise is the final reward for all the dreaming and striving. But I lift a cup of tea from the tray and stare out of the window at the white surf and the happy people below and feel a wave of sadness. With this failure in Japan, it feels as if something has just broken. I pick up my new guitar and strum a few chords while my bare feet make circles in the blue shag. I will be twenty-three on my next birthday, and then what? Everything feels like a great self-conscious effort; I feel as if I am peeling out of a skin, losing something; the years stretch on ahead like an endless maze—how am I supposed to fill them up? I suddenly experience fragility: I want something to hold on to, something to shore up this feeling of pointlessness. A sadness fills me—Eric is going to break up the band, I can feel it coming. What a drag. Maybe Zoot and I have been overpowering him onstage and it's put him off. That plus the squalid little drama we've just been through—he's tired of this scene. I run a few chords and stare at my guitar, a little plywood thing from downtown Honolulu with a palm tree silhouetted against a red sunset and the words *Waikiki dreams* just above the sound hole. Music—yeah, music. Just as I am about to become the victim of my own melodrama, I hear Mick's voice through the walls, shouting out in a flat East London voice, " 'Ere, John, this 'Ead and Shoulders— beautiful shampoo, innit?" I laugh out loud, and with Mick's Zen master proclamation, everything clears. I hit the beach and then fuck around for two weeks in Hawaii on my own.

Nine

I return to L.A. and the house in Laurel Canyon, where Zoot gives me the news that Eric is ending the Animals or the New Animals, as it's sometimes known. In the time-honored tradition of all who arrive in Hollywood, he now wants to be a film director. So that's it, my intuition was right, but I'm not ready to leave California. Having finally made it this far, I am intent on staying, but it's close to December and in a somewhat confused state I return to England for Christmas, with the vague idea of coming back.

In early January, not quite sure what to do, I go up to London. I have nowhere to stay but after a couple of calls get invited to crash at the Blossom Toes house in Lots Road, Chelsea.

I turn up in a night of pouring rain like a waif in a Dickens story. The group is away on tour, but I have been told that I can stay there until they come back. I am greeted at the door by a tall American girl who says I can share a bed with Rene. Well, as it turns out, Rene is not half bad and I slip into bed with a total stranger. Naturally, we become a humpbacked beast within—what?—five minutes. Small, dark-haired, with a pretty face, she shags like a minx, and between the sheets I bless the Blossom Toes and wish them a top ten hit. In fact, it turns out that there are a few girls in the house and I become—how should one put it?—wanted by all, a household sex pet. I enjoy this situation for a while but I have the light of the blue Pacific in my eyes and want to return. So, at the end of a cold and bitter

January I turn my back on the sobs of women in distress and board a plane back to L.A.

I have some reasons for returning. David has told me that he will manage me, that he will put a group around me, that I will be financed, and that maybe I can make a solo album; in other words, stardom is but a breath away. Los Angeles is still lingering in my head like a perfume, and these tenuous but thrilling possibilities are enough to lure me back. For a few months I carry on, intoxicated with the L.A. scene and living in a big house at the top of the canyon. I spend weeks at Sunset Sound, making a solo record, and people are interested in me. For a while I am able to maintain the illusion that returning to L.A. was the right move. But David's interest is now elsewhere. His heart is not really in management—it was fun to manage the Animals, but faced with the real job of building a career, his enthusiasm dies.

I spiral down, money runs out, David's enthusiasm fades away, and after a few short months of being on the West Coast, I start to worry about money. I start counting change, figuring out how long I can make a bag of brown rice last, and begin using a set of guitar strings a lot longer than I used to. I am about to hit bottom, and as I do, it opens like the mouth of a whale to become an abyss.

Before my little Fiat Spider gets repo'd I decide to take a trip with my girlfriend, Della, to Palm Desert to see Henry, a friend I made while in the Animals. We leave around nine P.M. and I drive the whole way with the top down, enjoying the beautiful California evening. When we get to Palm Desert I have to locate Henry's house, which is somewhere off the main road. I have to find it by the number painted along the curbside, so I start swinging the car from one side of the road to the other. Suddenly—and practically scaring me through the roof of the car—a loud amplified voice cracks through the air, commanding me to stop right where I am. I turn around and there's a cop car right behind me, its headlights scorching my little convertible with a blaze of white light. I pull over, feeling scared because sitting between me and Della on the floor is a bag of marijuana. I lean down, pick it up, and stuff it into my pocket. This is a mistake. The cop walks up to the car with a gun aimed in our direction and tells us to get out of the car.

We climb out and he asks me why I leaned down, and after I mumble some incoherent answer, with his gun aimed at my head, he pats my left pocket and pulls out the dope—which is his big mistake. "You are under arrest for a federal offense," he barks like a rottweiler, then handcuffs me and tells me to get in the back of his car. In the middle of all of this, poor old Henry has come out into the street and watches dumbfounded as the arrest takes place. The cop, excited that he has hippie scum in his grasp, forgets about Della, slams the door, and takes off with me in the back as Henry and Della stare in disbelief at the disappearing taillight. In the backseat, handcuffed and seated behind the barred screen between us, I feel my heart beat like an exhausted rabbit. I ask the cop why he's arresting me—"Can't you let me go?" I plead. "You have commited a federal offense," he snaps back. Outside, the sky is refulgent with starlight, the air filled with the aroma of date palms, desert flowers, and sage brush. Behind a thick meshed window I slump against the backseat with anguish flooding through me like a black river.

We arrive at the Indio county jail ten minutes later. Towering in the front office like something out of a Dickens tale is an oversize pulpitlike desk that might have come from a film set. Its monstrous girth is like a surreal hallucination and adds to my state of confusion as I stand below it—a skinny, frightened white kid with blue eyes, long blond hair, and silver handcuffs. My details are entered with icy cold detachment by the night sergeant, and then I'm hustled into the drunk tank.

This part of California—near the Salton Sea—is rough and weird, a magnet for those who live on the fringe. I have entered an alien world and I sit on the cold iron bench of the cell, shaking and staring at the iron bars between me and what already seems like my former life. I feel as though I am disappearing down the gullet of a large black beast, Jonah in the whale; I feel sick inside and a very long way from home. I am in possession of marijuana—fm7b5—a federal offense—Bb7b9—I could be here for years—ebm9. . . .

At five A.M. a silent cop takes me to what they call the day cell, where they keep the real cons. Men who are in for rape, violence, murder, or crimes committed at gunpoint. As I am marched along the corridor toward the cell I hear a chorus of wolf whistles. I have a somewhat androgynous face, and no doubt to those who have been missing female company for a while, I look tasty. My heart sinks as I imagine all the worst jail-movie clichés. The door to the steel cage is unlocked and they push me, now a common criminal, inside.

Various brutes are sitting around and they look at me with interest, like vultures circling over a fresh piece of carrion. In an effort to become invisible I move into a corner, a place from which I don't intend to move. I have made the one allowed call—to David, who groans as I desperately explain the situation. Luckily for me he has a house in Palm Springs and is there this weekend. He promises to bail me out, but it sounds as though he doesn't really want the bother. I offer up a prayer to make it a reality. I notice another kid who is about my age. We start up a conversation: like me, he's in for pot, but it's been months and he hasn't been able to get out. I panic. Is this to be my fate? How will I explain this to my mum? Letter from jail: Dear Mum, Having a lovely time—behind bars in America, food so-so. . . . I stare at the wall, and a wave of nausea passes through me—I long for my guitar, the sweet open air, girls, the life that was out there, anything but this nightmare.

At nine A.M. another humiliation is delivered as we are marched at gunpoint out into the prison yard for an inspection. This consists of standing in line naked while a prison doctor passes in front of us and feels our testicles with his rubber-gloved hand, at which time we are supposed to cough. Personally I feel like choking at this outrage, want to call the British embassy. What a pathetic cliché, but here I am—naked, vulnerable, with someone's nasty mitt on my balls, manhood stripped. Eventually we are passed fit and miserably troop back to our steel cage.

The longest day of my life passes in torturous increments, and I feel as if I should be on my knees, praying, but then I probably would be the recipient of a rearguard action. My imagination goes into overtime as I contemplate a life inside. I wonder if it would be possible to escape; I imagine trying to saw through several tons of concrete with a nail file (probably be dead of old age before the task is completed), starting a riot but then going down in a hail of bullets or becoming impaled on barbed wire, finding the sewer tunnel and getting flushed out into the desert covered in shit and piss to die of a disease in the baking sand.

As I am thinking up these fantastic scenarios David finally shows up to bail me out, and it's almost with a sobbing relief that a few minutes later I pass through the gate to freedom. As we walk toward the car, the smell of hot tarmac fills my head like perfume, the key turning in the car door lock sings a sweet melody of freedom in my ear, the engine hums a Bach chorale, and as we pull out onto the road for Palm Springs, the sweet air and high desert sky combine in a moment of blessed reprieve. Driving back to David's place, I look out across the desert at the late-afternoon shadows and think, *Yeah, whatever doesn't kill you . . .* Sixteen gut-wrenching hours. I wind down the window and spit in the sand.

Back in L.A. I try to stay out of trouble while my circumstances crumble. A few weeks after the arrest the case gets dismissed for illegal search and seizure—stupid cop—and I can breathe again. I stare out across Laurel Canyon and begin to feel isolated. I'm not in a band, David has disappeared, and within a week I will be in a foreign country with nowhere to live.

One house up from me lives a tough-guy actor. No one around here likes him. Middle-aged with a paunch and a surly demeanor, he yells at the mailman and seems to be permanently pissed off, probably doesn't get enough parts. He confronts me out on the dirt one day and snarls, "You play guitar?" "Yeah," I say, watching a blue jay out of the corner of my eye. "Whydonya come over and teach me." "Okay." "How much?" "Five dollars." "Come up in half an hour," he says. The blue jay disappears through a window into my house. Half an hour later I trot up to his front porch and ring the bell. We spend an hour together: I teach him a few beginner's chords as he frets about my putting an orange juice down without a coaster. He's an asshole, but I take the five dollars and am glad to get it. A day later I meet a girl who is a friend of Della's, a gifted songwriter by the name of Robin Lane. Robin has sung with Neil Young and Stephen Stills, and her dad, Ken Lane, is the piano player for Dean Martin and the Rat Pack. He is also the composer of Dino's greatest hit, "Everybody Loves Somebody." I start hanging out with Robin, seduced by the songs that seem to pour out of her. I meet her friends, and the two of us become embroiled.

Within a week of my getting a new girlfriend, my house is taken away, the car gets repossessed, and I bury the blue jay. I move in with Robin and her mother and, almost without realizing it, I am in the San Fernando Valley and another life. I sink into the California sunlight, the smell of oranges, and the sound of guitars. Robin's friends crowd around me, and everything is about music. I don't leave L.A., go home, or return to the grey, rainy streets of London, the moldy basement flat, the gas fire, the bands, pubs, bars, and guitar shops of my former life.

The heat of the sun penetrates the surface of my skin, papaya juice trickles down my throat, the scent of exotic night flowers fills my head, the proximity of Mexico puts a spell on me, and under this glow the call of safety and security fades. I don't feel compelled to return to the familiar, to pick up where I left off, or struggle on up the ladder. I am out west.

But after a successful five years in London, culminating with the period in the Animals, I have plummeted to rock bottom. I have no money, no car, and nowhere to live except the house of my girlfriend's mother. And this begins my forty days in the desert, which turns into five years in about five minutes.

The bluntness of this situation is softened by having a girlfriend and being surrounded by people who are all possessed by music. Something inside me has snapped, but though I feel compelled to withdraw from the world of bands, to do something else, I can't stay away from music, which remains the force in my life. As if staying faithful to a faint signal—like a man rowing to a distant shore guided by a star—I make one decision. I know that music is the way and that I have to go deeper with it, to study and play in private without the distraction of being in a band. I marry Robin, enroll in college, begin studying classical guitar, take in all the music I can, and scrape by with some minimum-wage teaching gigs. These conditions don't make for much of a marriage, and within two years Robin and I separate. I continue on in college and for a while enjoy it, but I question academia.

I survive on sixty to a hundred dollars a month and don't care much, as I have no responsibilities other than practicing the guitar. I survive by teaching when I can at a little guitar shop out at the west end of the valley. Most of the time it is excruciating, with only the odd student sparking my interest. Some of them know that I was in the Animals, but I tend to keep quiet about it. At four in the afternoon, with a heavy sense of irony and long shadows dogging my steps, I walk over the road to the Robin's Nest, where I drink some tea, read a book, and try to remember who I am.

Three years pass and I begin to feel like I'm living on borrowed time. My life is without momentum, and the only time I feel forward motion is when I'm practicing. I begin to feel sick inside. I don't belong here but, driven to finish what I started, I slog on. I drive an ancient Cadillac with retread tires and no windows, buy gas for twenty-two cents a gallon, move to a new house every few months, and use fake names to get a telephone account. For a while I live in a small apartment building under the Hollywood sign. At night it strobes through the window as if taunting me while I practice Bach. This apartment building is seething with marijuana plants—all the occupants have them growing in their apartments. The landlord is a grumpy old guy of about seventy who knocks fiercely on your apartment door and demands his monthly rent as he steps across the threshold. Somehow he misses the giant green plants that, like "Audrey II" in *Little Shop of Horrors,* grace every cheesy apartment.

My interest in Buddhism, and Zen in particular, continues and I begin getting up at four-thirty every morning to go to a zendo, where I sit in meditation for a few hours and grapple with a koan. This period of my life is akin to the training of a monk, enduring poverty and surviving on almost nothing but rice. Practicing is everything, and I work up to ten hours a day. Despite the rigors of this existence, I retain a sense about myself, not one of cheery confidence but the grim inner conviction that the path is leading in the right direction even though I can barely see it.

Although Robin and I have split, I continue to interact with the crowd of musicians I first got to know through her. In this crowd and also on the brink of a failed marriage is a stunning girl by the name of Kate, who has recently returned to Los Angeles. I met her before and was immediately attracted to her, but she was married and so was I. But now within the parameters of the incestuous set and her fading marriage, we fall in together.

For a while we have an empathetic relationship, and for the first time I experience the feeling of being with someone I believe I could spend the rest of my life with. She is the one. We lie in bed and talk all night about every possible subject while I covertly record everything on a cassette tape recorder and then play it back in the car the next day, much to her cringing embarrassment. Somehow we swing into a zone that feels as if it has always been there. Kate is not bothered by my material poverty, and for a moment I also forget it as we groove together. But there is a shadow in the form of her husband, who is still around and *pressure* is on her to make her marriage work. It reaches a point where she feels it necessary to give it one more try.

On New Year's Eve, the night of my birthday, knowing that she is returning to her husband, we are at a friend's house as if for the last time to-gether. We drink champagne and toast each other; she leans over a kitchen counter to pull a cracker apart with me; our eyes meet and, knowing that I'm losing her, it feels like a knife is slicing through my gut. It's over and it seems to symbolize the end of everything in L.A. for me. The evening comes to an end and, feeling suicidal and slightly drunk, I return to Hancock Park, where I live in a stable at the back of Fatty Arbuckle's old Hollywood villa. As the clock strikes midnight I stare at an empty bed and, like a ghost, open a letter from my mother.

In the morning I get up and make a small cup of green tea on the single-ring gas burner and stare through the window across the vast expanse of lawn to the white Mediterranean-style villa. At the other end of the grass the owners lean back in their chairs, laugh, and clink glasses to the New Year. A girl student knocks at the door. She is here for a lesson. We sit down and in some sort defiant and desperate attempt to have spirit, I give her the best possible guitar lesson I can. She is a sweet girl and she raises her head from the guitar at the end of our session and says, "You're great." At that point I find it hard to contain myself—her remark like a candle flame in a cave mirrors my fragility and I feel like wailing like a baby who has lost his mother. She leaves—I pick up my guitar, hit a chord, and put it down. Kate's gone, four years have passed since I arrived here, and now like a page in a book on Zen, I am a brushmarked circle, a zero.

I begin to experience an unshakable depression, an emotional landscape that becomes so black that I can find literally no reason to get out of bed in the morning. The will to survive—to push forward—becomes a thin thread, a few remaining routines that I pass through as if wearing a blindfold.

A few weeks later one of my few students brings an old guitar to a lesson and offers to sell it to me. It's a battered '61 Fender Telecaster. I don't really want one but when I start to play it something stirs within me, comes back like a memory as if reminding me of a self I had forgotten. It shakes me and I ask him to leave it with me. That night I take it home to try it out for a few hours and find that I can't stop playing it; this guitar sparks something in me and I have to have it. I call the kid the next morning and tell him it's a deal. I start practicing, and something comes back, begins again, pushes toward the world. This new energy is sustained a few weeks later when I get the chance to join a local band. I start playing guitar solos again, look forward to the group sessions, begin thinking up guitar parts. This activity has the effect of renewal; the old Telecaster has a fantastic tone, and I play like a man possessed.

Through a friend of Kate's I still see from time to time, I meet up with Tim Rose, a well-known singer who has had a hit with a song called "Morning Dew." Tim is also down on his luck, but we hit it off and he uses the band I have just joined as his backing group. We start playing around L.A., and within a short while I am back into the group thing.

One night we go to see a band at the Troubadour, and after the show I leave on my own. As I cross the road I see an orange VW. I recognize it as Kate's car. I feel a jolt and decide to wait for her, leaning on the car and staring across the street at the neon sign of the Troubadour. A few minutes later she exits the club. With a big smile on my face, I watch her cross the street and wait for her to come up to me and throw her arms around me, but instead she walks right past me, unlocks the door, and tells me to please get off the car. Typical of her otherworldly sense of spatial perception, this is par for the course. "Kate, it's me," I sigh, and laugh. She stares myopically through the L.A. mist—the last scene in *Casablanca.* "Oh, my God," she murmurs, and comes over. We embrace, and somewhere violins play.

From that dime-size moment everything begins to unfold as if by magic. The attempt to repair her marriage has failed, she is free, and this time there doesn't seem to be any question that we will be together. I want to scream, "I love this woman!" She makes me strong and I am ready to take the bullet between my teeth.

I begin living with Kate in her little house in Echo Park. With three rooms and a roof like a Japanese temple, it is a romantic setting; every night we lie in bed listening to the scrabbling sound of raccoons as they climb across the roof. I get a Saturday-night gig playing in East L.A. at the El Dorado bar and compound that with my other new band, more gigs, and college. Everything begins

to move forward again. The only ironic little shadow in all of this is that yet another admirer of Kate's now begins to threaten me. We begin getting phone calls from him in which he describes the weapons he has and how he is waiting where I can't see him.

And then I know that I am done with this part of my life and that it is time to return to the U.K. I have the guitar, the girl, a gun aimed at my head, and a future like a freshly wiped plate. We finish up our do-it-yourself divorces, Kate sitting on the steps of City Hall at eight A.M. with a typewriter on her knees minutes before we both go in front of the judge to get divorced from partners with identical first names. I pack up my stuff—which takes nearly three minutes—and with a loan from my dad book two seats on British Air. I am twenty-nine.

BOOK TWO

Ten

On a pissing cold day in November 1973 we lurch across a runway at Heathrow Airport. My family, whom I haven't seen in five years, all turn up to meet us. It's a loving, hugging moment, although I notice that in the intervening years everyone seems to have shrunk. We have decided in advance to spend the first two weeks in England with them in Bournemouth while we get oriented. As we drive south from Heathrow with the watery sun softly illuminating the ploughed fields and rolling green of Hampshire, I am excited to be back even though the road ahead looks like a screen with no movie. I have been away from London for what has amounted to one-twentieth of a century: no letters, no message in a bottle, no birds with words concealed in rings. *Hello, remember me, the guitarist? Yes, still playing. . . . I was wondering . . .* I'm entering the unknown with a secondhand guitar and a flaxen-haired muse at my side; the architecture of the future, like a ripped Polaroid, will have to be pieced together with fragments of old relationships and whatever guitar skills I have.

The reality of stepping into the adult world begins to pervade my musician's mind. I feel the weight of it, and my excitement turns into anxiety, pushing me farther down into the backseat of the car. Then I hear my mum telling Kate that the wooded area we are now passing through—so familiar to me—is the New Forest, although in fact it was planted a thousand years ago by William the Conqueror, and that she and my dad have not been abroad since the war because they've been too busy, and what sandwiches does she like? I hoot like a maniac in the backseat: England—bloody England.

We spend a week or so with them, getting used to the idea of being in Britain. My first impression after California is that England is bleak, sunless, and drowning in the black-and-white reality of the tabloids. But after a couple of weeks of sitting around, I know that somehow I have to move forward, return to London and try to revive old connections. Maybe there is a destiny, maybe I have an intuition, maybe I just have missed my own country—but the fact is that I am here, and there is no turning back.

January 1974. Kate and I arrive in a dark, wintery London, a city that because of an electricians' strike has lights only three days a week. The country is also riven with a miners' strike, and it seems to rain twenty-five hours a day. I have a distant cousin living in Muswell Hill who agrees to let us stay with her for a couple of weeks while we get our bearings. She has a large Victorian flat and a couple of kids: a pouting seventeen-year-old girl and a funny but obnoxious boy of about twelve with an advanced sense of sarcasm.

I begin the arduous process of reentering the scene by calling my old bandmate Zoot Money to see if there are any bands I can get into, sessions, gigs—anything. He gives me a few numbers to call and wishes me luck. I start calling around and begin having conversations that involve a fair amount of silver-tongued lying on my part as I cough up stories about a glorious career in the United States, but here we are, back in London, might be nice to do something. But it's thin on the ground and difficult because musicians tend to be paranoid and protective of their turf; they're not really interested in other people's problems. In my corner it's best to exude an attitude of positive confidence, but the truth is that I have sold everything to pay for the flight home and don't even own a guitar amp, my Fender Twin now with some kid in the San Fernando Valley, sold for a rock-bottom price.

After a couple of weeks at my cousin's flat it feels as if we've outstayed our welcome, and with thanks we decide to move on. Kate has landed a job at the new Gap jeans store; between that and the pocketful of change I have left, we have just enough to rent a ground-floor flat in Shepherds Bush.

Eighteen Woodstock Grove is like a nightmare out of *Macbeth* or a hellish joke from the Outer Hebrides: the whole place is decorated in what appears to be a kilt. A garish plaid fitted carpet covers the floors, and drunken tartan wallpaper reels up the walls in every direction; but at four quid a week it's the only thing we can afford and we take it. It does, however, provide a nice line in Scottish jokes. Everything becomes "Mc" for a while—McBed, McPaper, McEgg, McPhone, McYou, McMe—and I begin answering the telephone with a soft Scottish burr and throwing "och ayes" into my everyday conversation. As I reconnect with a few old friends we describe our flat and ask them over to see our plaid. I think about wearing a kilt while we endure this Highlands nightmare but worry that if I do, I might disappear—sucked into the vortex of tartan wallpaper.

In the basement flat, one floor down from us, there lives a very meanlooking skinhead replete with tattoos, chains, and a nasty habit of playing violent music at a decibel level that's enough to rearrange your internal organs. Since I'm someone who prefers his space inviolate, this repeated assault sends me into paroxysms of fury until finally I think, *Right*—or more probably, *okay—you fucking asshole, it's payback time.* One morning he starts up and I leap into action by putting my own speakers facedown on the floor, cranking the volume to eleven, and artfully covering them with every cushion and blanket available; this aims the sound like a bomb straight down through the ceiling and into his shaved skull. I put on Led Zep's "Whole Lotta Love" and let it rip for an hour or so and return to *The Magus*. Later I realize that I have probably risked a premature death with this mad act of retaliation, but oddly enough we never hear another whisper from him. The only time I ever see him again is in the Shepherds Bush market, where he is bending over and patting a small dog; he sees me and gives a shy smile.

A few blocks from Oxford Circus the Speakeasy is still throbbing and packed wall-to-wall every night with the London rock fraternity. Zoot advises me to hang out down there because that's where everybody congregates. "Put yourself about," he says. I begin leaving Kate at around eleven-thirty every night and drag myself to the Speakeasy for the grim task of networking. I don't enjoy this process very much, because at that moment I'm down and in the position of asking for a job, but it's what I have to do and I do it. Kate understands what I am going through, and is supportive. However, as I drift around in the twilight zone of this hell, trying to act cool and uninterested, I am surprised by how many people remember me.

Five years wasn't so long after all, but still it doesn't help with the employment situation. Behind the "yeah, mans" and "eh, where y bin, good to see yas," you witness them almost visibly back away if they think you might be about to steal their gig. It's depressing. The scene at the Speakeasy is a small-minded hierarchy: players from different groups act superior to one another, depending on who has a hit, who doesn't, who has played in the U.S., or who's hot or has appeared in the *New Musical Express* this week—and you seem to get allotted a good or shit table accordingly.

I have no table; I can barely afford the price of a beer and I wander through this crowd of rock snobs with a fake smile, hoping for the casual encounter that will lead to work. And I'm painfully aware of the currently successful pop stars slouching over tables that only they can get while I wander around in the club, the mantra "only connect" echoing in my head in time to the thumping din of the PA system. I return home night after night frustrated and empty-handed after fruitless time-wasting conversations and three hours of nursing half a pint of lager. Stinking of beer and secondhand smoke, I slide back into bed around three A.M. to give a brief whispered account of what happened tonight and tell whether there is anything promising.

My luck changes when I run into Robert Fripp, an old friend who is now very successful with his band, King Crimson. He's there at a table with some friends one night, and someone suggests that I go over and speak to him. I sit down and talk with him for a while. He's different. More intelligent and more aware than the average rocker or most people, he gets it. He suggests that I speak with the drummer Mike Giles, who is now touring with Neil Sedaka and is involved with many things on the London music scene. Mike and I had once been in the Boy Scouts together. Robert gives me his number and I walk the four miles home from the Speakeasy, a fingernail of hope illuminating the darkness.

I call Mike the next day and he tells me that it's unlikely he can get me the Sedaka gig but that he'll put a word in. But miraculously the phone rings one night later and it is Neil's wife, Lema, who says simply that Mike has recommended me as the guitarist for the upcoming tour but that they can pay me only thirty-five pounds a night. Thirty-five quid a night! I try to remain calm and avoid choking as this fabulous sum reverberates through my skull, and answer, "Well, s-u-u-u-re, I will probably have to cancel some other engagements, but it would be fun to play with Neil for a while, and when were you thinking of starting?" Lema asks me if I can come to the Inn on the Park to meet Neil, and I have to hold back from screaming, "I'll come right now!" so I tell her I am in the studio all day tomorrow and might I pop by the following day? We agree, and putting the phone down, I collapse into the red-and-purple plaid on the floor below me. Neil is a big star in the U.K.; he has a hit single with "Laughter in the Rain," is always on TV, and plays places like the Royal Festival Hall. I let go of my higher aesthetic ambitions and begin making a vicious curry.

Two days later I catch a bus from Shepherds Bush to Hyde Park Corner and walk over to the Inn on the Park to meet Neil. He has a large pastel-shaded suite facing the park that matches his star status. When I arrive he's in the bedroom, writing something; he gives me a large smile and a hi as I enter and tells me to sit down on the bed next to him. "Mike tells me that you are a great guitarist." He smiles, and I smile back with a self-deprecating w-e-ell, thinking, *Good old Mike,* who hasn't heard me play in years. We chat for a while, and it appears that I have the job without actually playing a single note. I also get the idea that Neil rather likes me. Now comes the delicate part: I have an electric guitar but no amplifier, and smiling as casually as possible, I ask Neil if he might advance me three hundred pounds so that I can go out and get one—my gear is still on the way over from the U.S. and unfortunately hasn't reached the U.K. at the present time. No problem, and Neil—God bless 'im—giving me the hugest benefit of the doubt, throwing me a lifeline, giving me a cigarette and a brandy, reaches into his pocket and fishes out the three hundred. There is a slight twinkle in his eye as he does so, but I guess the universe is with me that day because he never asks for it back, doesn't call my bluff, only tells me that I have nice hair and that he looks forward to seeing me for the first rehearsal with the Royal Philharmonic Orchestra at London's Royal Festival Hall.

I depart his suite dazed and full of the warmest possible vibes; I love this man. I stagger out of the hotel, trying to appear insouciant but with a gulp and one more wave and one more ingratiating smile—at the hotel itself—I walk toward the underground in the pouring rain, laughing all the way, happy to be the living embodiment of the Sedaka hit "Laughter in the Rain." Hanging from the strap in the tube, I can't wait to burst into the tartan towers to tell Kate the news. We're going to eat, I have the rent, we can go to the movies—as long as I don't blow it on the first gig. We celebrate by going to the Standard, an Indian restaurant in Bayswater, and to hell with the expense. The next day I hit the nearest music store and buy a Fender Twin, get it home, and plug in the old Telecaster that I've managed to bring back with me from L.A.

The Royal Festival Hall, the Royal Philharmonic Orchestra. This is deep for a reentry shot, my first gig back in the U.K. I hope that my sight reading is up to it and that I can keep up with hard-core London pros. It's a start, but as I struggle across the wet pavement, step in dog shit, and grimace at the voice of pissed-off cabdrivers, the luminous reality of the Santa Monica Mountains, the hummingbirds, the sweet murmur of Spanish, and the scent of magnolia fade like a dream. I stare down at a small cream-colored bandstand and a pile of tricky orchestral arrangements with a surge of remorse.

We rehearse and I am filled with the tension of pretending that this is just a knockoff for me. But with only a small amount of faking, and returning a big smile to the glances in my direction, I get through it. The Royal Festival Hall gig comes, and although it's unnerving to play along with the Royal Philharmonic, I don't blow it and even manage a couple of saucy solos. I get to know the rest of the band. The bass player, Dave Winters, and I hit it off and there is a general appeal to everyone about having a Summers and a Winters in the ensemble—in any case, it doesn't hurt.

We begin the tour and I feel relief at having gotten at least a start back in the United Kingdom. Playing with Neil turns out to be a great time. He proves to be not only more popular than the queen of England but a very entertaining guy who likes to enjoy himself. He has had several hit records in his career, including the classic "Oh Carol," and we play around the country to sold-out shows. Most nights we have a massive banquet before the show at which we all eat and drink to the point of stupor—Sedaka often becoming the most inebriated—and by the time we manage to find the stage, we are in a very loose state. Backstage before the shows Neil slumps over the piano, rips through Chopin, and regales us with ribald stories about him and Carole King as teenagers; then, falling over one another, we carry him to the stage. But the truth is that behind all the merriment, Neil is a great pop song composer and a musician of real talent.

He takes a great liking to Kate, and the three of us go to the movies together. One night after dining together in Notting Hill, happily waving bye to us, he walks out into the road and would have been hit by an oncoming car if Kate hadn't seen it coming, made a near miraculous dive, and dragged him out of its path. We do two riotous tours, and then it comes to an end when he decides to take some time off.

Back in Shepherds Bush, Kate and I are in better shape. I now possess an actual bank account and we are able to buy a car—a Dyane 6—and move out of the plaid pad to a larger basement flat a little farther down the street. The new place is nicer by virtue of being slightly less depressing, the one drawback being the train line at the end of the garden. Each time a train passes, the flat rocks as if experiencing a mild earthquake—just like L.A. after all. . . .

One afternoon in the summer of 1974 I go to a concert in Hyde Park. There are a number of performers on the bill, including a rotund teddy bear of a man by the name of Kevin Coyne. I'm amused by his acid wit, self-deprecating presentation, and edgy lyrics; he sounds like no one else. A couple of weeks later I hear that he is looking for a new guitarist. I find out where the audition is and go down with the Telecaster and the Fender Twin. We play through some of Kevin's songs—"Marjory Razorblade," "Eastbourne Ladies," "Mona, Where's My Trousers?" We hit it off, and I enter the realm of Coyne.

Kevin has a brilliant ability to freely improvise amazing lyrics with views of people and life that are poignant, funny, and painful. A gifted and original artist, he is the Brendan Behan of the rock world, and I'm happy to get onstage with him. Once we start rehearsing, one of the first things I learn is that in this band I will be required to drink large amounts of alcohol on account of Kev's heavy reliance on the brew to get him in the right frame of mind. The ability to suck up beer seems as important as the ability to play. As long as the pub is open, that is where we will be—the term *pub rock* takes on a very real meaning.

Originally from Derbyshire, Kevin is intense and passionate and wears a slight air of psychosis but is also very funny, and through a fog of lager and cigarette smoke, he entertains us with endless stories of inmates and madness at the asylum he used to work at. Through this blur I see a fusion between Coyne and his background, and it's hard to tell where one ends and the other begins. But in the Rose and Crown as we work our way through the brown stuff, the atmosphere of derangement grows and expands until these pub sessions often turn into bitter and rancorous diatribes, with Kevin pissed out of his mind and psychoanalyzing each one of us in turn. Any cherished notions we might have about ourselves are shredded, pissed on, and trampled underfoot; usually it boils down to a slurred "you're no fuckin' good—you can't play, you're fuckin' useless." After the first gig I ever do with him—in Oxford—he abuses me so much on the way back that, not yet realizing this is a Kevin ritual, I finally tell him to fuck off and find another guitarist. Slamming the van door, I huff off down my dark basement steps, guitar case banging against the mossy wall, brain full of fury and insults, and slip inside to peace and further unemployment.

But he calls me the next day full of apologies, and with a shrug we resume. As I get to know him I realize that I love this man and have great respect for him because under the raw-nerve personality, he is full of humanity, compassion, and music. But often, after hours of Carlsberg, abuse, and exhausting verbal swordplay, personal perspective goes and I return home ready to get out. I don't leave, because the band—with Kevin banging a wooden chair up and down on the stage and giving fantastic maniac performances—is great. The band is rough and bluesy (akin to the current style of pub rock), and we become more and more popular, with Kevin getting recognition as a British original.

This is London 1975, a music scene full of old hippie bands, vinyl albums, gatefold sleeves, collectors, record shops, glam rock, progressive rock, art rock, ambient music, *The Old Grey Whistle Test,* and the dregs of the sixties. In this framework I feel as if I've returned to almost exactly the same place I left a few years ago. I put everything into the music but wonder where this is leading. This is the life of the gigging musician, the hired gun. In a way it's fun to be back in a band, with its banter and bullshit; but like an echo of my first incarnation with bands in London, it isn't quite enough.

In private I write music, tape endless demos of songs for my own imaginary albums, keep journals, and grip the bars of the cage that helps us survive but keeps me from breaking into a larger space.

In the midst of my private distractions, my star seems to be rising in the London scene anyway. I've now had several favorable reviews about my playing, been singled out as a possibility to join the Rolling Stones, and had a large photo essay in *Melody Maker*. But despite all of this, nothing much has changed. Did I make a mistake by leaving for five years; is it too late? How long can I do this? Kate and I have married, and although I am not looking for a bourgeois existence, the idea of a kid of our own is appealing—but not on this pittance.

Kevin begins to get a lot of notice on the London scene, and it's not long before Virgin Records decides to sign him. As Kevin likes his mates around, we all go along with him to witness his signing. Afterward we cross the road to the pub to celebrate this good fortune, and as usual with Kevin, we start to drink—and drink and drink. In a overly convivial mood I manage to down four vodkas, a beer, and a lager, which turns me into a drooling and mindless puppet. I can no longer walk or talk except in a garbled idiom somewhere between Chechen and Urdu, so it's thought best to drag me up the road to Richard Branson's house. We arrive at his front door and ring the bell. Richard opens the door with an inquiring smile as I lean forward and spew with great violence about fifteen feet down his rather nice Persian rug, to a great chorus of oohs and aahs, with poor Branson whipping back against the wall to avoid death by vomit. I'm then laid down gently on a couch and left to sleep it off. I wake up around two in the morning feeling like a piece of dog shit and shamefully creep out of the house, find the Dyane 6, and make it back to Shepherds Bush.

Despite this shabby rock-and-roll start, I begin to hang out at the Virgin offices on Portobello Road. This is still the early days of Virgin, and at least on the surface there is a loose hippie feeling to everything. I am able to wander around the buildings, getting to know a number of people in the offices: Jumbo, Simon, and Al Clark, a former journalist and now the head of publicity. Doors are literally open in this company, a mark of sharing and openness.

A few short years before the corporate and MTV-ridden age begins, Virgin feels like the last holdout of the sixties. Mike Oldfield's hugely popular "Tubular Bells"—a cunning weave of Irish jig, dancing elves, goblin music, and all instruments played by Mike—is a phenomenon. It stays at an unassailable number one position for two years and basically finances the incipient Virgin empire. There are bands like Hatfield and the North, Matching Mole, Caravan, and Gong, all of whom have a wonderful English quirkiness and occupy a late-hippie world. For a moment there is a softness to everything, a placid surface, a lull while something new and aggressive stirs in the substrata.

Most afternoons I climb up the basement steps with a sense of déjà vu and slump into the back of the van with the rest of the Coyne band. We greet one another with sardonic remarks, to the effect that we'll all be dead soon anyway, and then head off for the ferry to Holland, Germany, or Belgium or for the MI up to Birmingham. We play at the Paradiso or the Melkweg in Amsterdam, sleep at the top of crooked little guest houses, eat boiled eggs and hard yellow cheese, drink beer and stare at the hashish dealers who sit in a little room with plastic packets of ginger and brown dope lined up like turds on a counter. Kevin screams, bangs his wooden chair about, and wacks at his open tuning, and I whip a brass slide up and down the neck of my Tele. We adopt facial tics, weird mannerisms, and accents; mock our landlady, who complains that the streets of Amsterdam are too lumpy; and retire into various paperbacks: we are a band. We have a great drummer, a little guy named Peter Wolf, and I love playing with him. Zoot even joins the band, and it feels as if everything has come full circle.

In the confines of the van Kevin continues to regale us for hours with further tales of lunatics, manic depressives, pyromaniacs, dipsomaniacs, and schizophrenics. Every ten minutes he will sing out the name Doreen, a reference to a running joke that seems to sum it all up with the line "Doreen, Doreen, arch your back—gentlemen's balls are on cold lino." These tales of madness permeate everything until it feels as if we are no more than a mental ward on wheels. I compound this by reading *Nausea* by Jean-Paul Sartre, getting carsick, and feeling a strong urge to hurl myself into the nearest Dutch canal. At night through the thin walls of whatever cheap accommodation we are in, our leader can be heard in his room, howling at the walls and moaning away to himself—some of this no doubt due to the effect of the extremely large amounts of alcohol downed prior to bedtime. But astonishingly, like a wind-up doll, he always makes it down to breakfast. He sits there like some creature that has been invented the night before in the lab of a mad scientist and always orders the same thing: a boiled egg and toast cut into soldiers. Like a man a hundred years old, he feebly swings at it with his spoon, trying to take the top off but missing by a few inches. He sighs deeply and buries his head in his hands. Maybe he's acting with brilliance, but it's hilarious and we have to stifle our laughter so as not to upset him. But maybe that's what he is after.

Sadly, the band comes to an end after a grueling eight-week tour of the Continent. This one was simply too much, and by the time we arrive back in England, we are frayed and suffering from temporary brain damage. The word comes a few days later from Kevin's manager, Steve Lewis, that Kevin is breaking up the band. He's had enough—never wants to tour again. I think it's a terrible decision on his part. The band is great—one of the best in the U.K. now—and I know that he will relax for a couple of weeks and then regret it, which he does.

Later I think I should have called him up and tried to talk him out of it. I don't, because another opportunity arises at almost exactly the same time. My old nemesis Kevin Ayers, the bass player from the Soft Machine, is putting a new band together. I am given his phone number and told by Al Clark to call him. It turns out that he is living on a houseboat in Little Venice with his American girlfriend, whom he has stolen from Richard Branson. Kevin is friendly and suggests in silky Noël Coward tones that I come over to see him at the cocktail hour. I have some mixed feelings but I am not really in a position to be choosy, so I agree to go. The appointed hour comes, and we sling back a couple of vodka martinis and with a warm glow put our less-than-successful history behind us. The next afternoon I am at a rehearsal with the rest of the band. In the intervening years Kevin has become an indolent sort of pop star in his own right, having some European success with the albums *The Confessions of Dr. Dream and Other Stories* and *Yes, We Have No Mañanas.* The Ayers band has Charlie and Rob, the bass player and drummer from the original Kevin Coyne Band, plus Zoot again. I have no trouble fitting in, but now it's beginning to feel like a repeated joke, the bandleaders even sharing the same first name. I spend yet another year on the road in the Kevin Ayers Band, and although lacking the trenchant genius of Kevin Coyne, the year is full of daft adventures.

We are returning to England from Bremerhaven, Germany, via the ferryboat, and as we drive on we notice some equestrian types boarding with a horse trailer, and with them . . . the royal personage of Princess Anne. After several ooohs and aaahs and a few typical musician remarks, we park our grotty van in the bowels of the ship and go in search of the bar. Later that night as we are making the crossing it turns out that we passengers will all be dining together. The supper is a generous-looking buffet served in a small dining room on the upper deck, and all passengers—should they wish an evening meal— will eventually arrive here. We crowd into the small room just as Princess Anne and entourage arrive and we delicately press back into the wall to let her pass by. Pressing back with our disheveled ensemble is a Scottish roadie by the name of Soapy, a man deeply appreciated for his perverse and ill-timed sense of humor. The princess begins to make her way around the buffet table with her lady-in-waiting. As they pick daintily at the food, they are followed closely by Soapy in his filthy T-shirt asking them questions about the items on display, a look of pure innocence on his face. As the responses from HRH and her lady-in-waiting become more and more tight-lipped, the rest of us sit in the corner of the room quietly cackling to ourselves. Shortly after the buffet it's time for the ship dance. Like some weird throwback to colonial England, it's held on a postage-stamp-sized floor, and all are invited. This is asking for it, and naturally the moment HRH gets out onto the floor to do the twist, Soapy and I follow and start in with a drunken shambles of a boogaloo right next to her. After a few minutes of serious getting down, a thuggish-looking and oversize military type appears at our side with the advice to get off the dance floor pronto if we know what is good for us. He looks nasty, and with Zoot right behind us, we hop to the edge of the floor, spy the exit door, and stagger up the stairs. As we hit the upper deck, the tilt of the ship and the icy wind blasting from the fjords of Norway seem to worsen our crapulous condition, our grip of reality becoming a greasy blur. Zoot and Soapy, both laughing like Zen monks, think it will help me recover if they hold me upside down over the side of the ship. Bevied to the eyeballs, they somehow manage to pull me out from behind the life jackets and dangle me by the ankles over the rail, where I stare glassy-eyed and giggling down at the black and icy waters fifty feet below, where giant waves pound the hull; a drunken slip of the fingers would mean certain death. Finally they haul me back onto the slippery deck and we slide off in three different directions. I try to go back to my cabin but get hopelessly lost in the labyrinth of swaying metal corridors and fall into Kevin's cabin, where he is canoodling with his girlfriend. I immediately throw up spectacularly on the nearest bunk, sending Kevin and beauty shooting out the door in search of another cabin and leaving me to moan incomprehensibly at the rivets in the cabin wall for the rest of the night.

As we dock at seven the next morning to begin the long drive back to London, I feel full of remorse, horribly fucked-up, and more ill than at any other time in my life. I finally collapse on the couch about midday, feeling like a victim of Crohn's disease, and pass out watching *Emmerdale Farm.*

One Saturday afternoon Kate and I return home to find that we have been robbed. Things are thrown about the steps that lead to our flat as if the burglar left in a hurry. In shock we walk through the place and note everything that has been taken, including valuable heirloom jewelry of Kate's. Oddly and symbolically, my Telecaster has not been taken but has in fact been played. It's propped up next to the little Fender Princeton amp, which hums quietly to itself, its red power light glowing like a watchful eye. I pick it up and play a couple of chords; it seems alright, but the word *cunt* fills my head anyway.

Soon after this event, having finally scraped enough money together, Kate and I move to a more spacious flat in Putney. Kate now works at Young & Rubicam as a copywriter and has written an award-winning ad for Smirnoff vodka, something along the lines of "Smirnoff won't make me an overnight sensation—that's alright, I'm busy tomorrow."

I sleep until eleven every morning, at which time Kate calls me and we exchange a few sweet words. Through Virgin, which seems to be our epicenter for everything, we make many friends and move in a crowd of like-minded people, in particular Martine and Anthony Moore from the band Slapp Happy. We become Tai Chi fanatics and go to the house of Master

Chu three times a week, practicing "wave hands like clouds, single whip, needle at bottom of sea." Kate begins sessions with a Jungian analyst, and a few months later I follow; our conversations become laced with references to the shadow, archetypes, anima, animus.

We sink into London life and like most young couples gaze into the future, hoping for the best. Although some months it is a desperate struggle to get the mortgage payment, put up with the pissing rain, and struggle through dense traffic, it's okay because we are in the hub of the scene, surviving and surrounded by friends. We go on a package holiday to Tunisia and walk up and down the beach outside of Hammamet, talking about the future we want to share. But first I have to make it, break beyond this hired-gun-playing-in-bands mode. But it seems impossible. We walk back toward the hotel, kicking through waves and expanding our dreams.

A small burnoose-covered man approaches us, insisting that we buy his carpet, and we get into a huge wrangling match full of jokes that neither side understands. "You are sheepstich man," he keeps telling me. Eventually we buy his carpet and he goes off, smiling and waving, and we go back to the hotel dance for tourists. The whole place is so weird; we get drunk and perversely dance with as many goofy holiday packagers as we can rather than with each other and then spend the rest of the night in our bedroom, howling with laughter and spluttering, "Sheepstich man," as we pass out.

Back in London, I importune people at Virgin to make solo albums, continue to cut tracks on my own, keep writing songs. But getting all the way over is proving difficult, and I feel a strong urge to scream—I hate the business of music.

By the mid-seventies England is in full recession, with unemployment reaching its highest figure since the 1940s and the standard of living crumbling. The "English way of life" is under attack; there are muggings, letter bombs, and public-sector strikes; and the country as a whole becomes masochistic and ripe for chaos. Beneath the hippie surface of Virgin and the dribbling end of the sixties, something is turning a corner. London suburbia is a place of cynicism and boredom, and with it comes the state that gives rise to expression of actual violence and the tendency to fall to the political right. A new generation has emerged, and some of them—already in pub rock bands—are against the music scene of the early seventies with its expensive producers, East Lake studios, and records swollen with ego and overdubs. The pub rockers are a new breed who have returned to a more rootsy rhythm-and-blues-based sound. Performed to rowdy pub audiences around London, this music is gaining ground with bands like Bees Make Honey, Kilburn and the High-Roads, Dr. Feelgood, and Joe Strummer's 101'ers. They are the precursor, the pre-echo of a howl that will go around the world.

Around this time an old word with a new connotation is beginning to be heard in London. The word is *punk,* and the genesis of its new meaning is a shop in the Kings Road by the name of Sex—a place that I have walked by many times, never suspecting that it is the crucible of a new movement and something that will change the world, for a while anyway. I occasionally run into the guitarist Chris Spedding and he tells me that he's involved with a group called the Sex Pistols and that they are great and are really going to shake things up—the guitarist really has something.

By the end of 1975, after the Sex Pistols have appeared on the nationally televised Bill Grundy show and called him a fucking rotter, punk has exploded onto the national consciousness and is emerging fast to shake the music industry to the ground. The Union Jack rises upside down to the top of the mast, and the kids of England become rotten. But this year, in which North and South Vietnam reunite, Mao Tse-tung dies, Jimmy Carter becomes president, and on television we watch *Rising Damp, Porridge,* and the *Rise and Fall of Reginald Perrin,* punk bands proliferate like a swarm of locusts. We hear the names of the Clash, the Damned, Siouxsie and the Banshees, Generation X, the Slits and X-Ray Spex. Toward the end of the year a club called the Roxy opens and becomes the place to see and hear punk. It lasts for about three months and then is replaced by the Vortex. Playing around Europe with Kevin Ayers and out of the country half of the time, punk feels like only a slight threat, a roar in the distance.

In this brief mid-seventies moment, punk, prog rock, pub rock, glam rock, and disco all coexist. In New York the Ramones, Television, Blondie, the Talking Heads, and Patti Smith are playing at CBGB's. In London in the stifling summer of 1976 punk fashion is everywhere, and sweeps through the city with spiked hair, ripped T-shirts, black leather, pogo'ing, and sulfate amphetamines. The Sex Pistols and their manager, Malcom McClaren, are at the front of the new dispossessed as they storm the gates and attempt cultural access. McClaren, with his art school background, clothes design, and partnership with Vivian Westwood, has constructed this new scenario partly as a way to sell his (or rather Vivian Westwood's) clothing designs, partly out of his "political interest" in the Situationist International, and partly because he is a born entrepreneur/snake oil salesman. Inspired by the New York Dolls—as was the pre-glam David Bowie—McClaren had seen them on a trip to New York and attempted to manage them but after a series of mishaps they disintegrated and he returned to the rag trade until the arrival at Sex of Steve Jones, who gets him interested to try again. I had seen the Dolls at the Whiskey in L.A. just before returning to the United Kingdom and thought they were fantastic and definitely the progenitors of a new scene—or at least the latest version of punk, which has its own precedents in the United States with the Stooges and the MC5, the Velvet Underground, and Devo and writers like William S. Burroughs and Jack Kerouac.

At first the whole thing, with its gobbing, violence, and nihilism, seems faintly repellent to me. Coming from another era and still foolishly embracing bourgeois values like wanting to be able to play your fucking instrument, I think it's just the latest model of rage and fury that signifies nothing, looseness mistaken for a political concept. But this new movement hasn't come out of a vacuum. The peace and love of the previous generation did not accomplish any real change: corruption and capitalist propaganda continue, and a lot of kids feel it. What is there to do but get numb and stay numb or rage and spit against the machine? There is a part of me that identifies with them because I also have a tendency to mouth "Fuck you" when faced with any kind of authority. We all want the power to shake the world and despite being one generation earlier, I think they are doing what youth always does—it's just wearing bondage gear this time. But then I have another problem because I have a whole other set of musical values that are foreign to the punk credo, and joining the ranks is not an option. As I have always held the core belief that music is a spiritual force, an agent for change no matter how angry or aggressive, spitting on it is counterintuitive. But rage and aggression can be the elements of productive

tension. As nice as Virgin and the soporific "Tubular Bells" are, music needs a hefty kick in the ass—and these bands, clawing their way into the public imagination, are doing it. This is rock and roll.

In October 1976, at the opposite end of the spectrum, Virgin Records asks me if I would like to play the guitar in a performance of "Tubular Bells" with the Newcastle Symphony Orchestra—Mike Oldfield can't make it on the appointed night. His album is still dominating the charts, so despite misgivings about "Tubercular Balls," I agree. Standing in the middle of the orchestra and playing all the famous guitar parts under the baton of David Bedford turns out to be fun, and for an hour or so I have the spotlight. There is an intermission spot that will be filled by a local band called Last Exit, a jazz fusion group. They have a bass player named Sting and are supposed to be quite good, so I decide to watch them. I stand at the back of the hall and watch for about five minutes and then wander off for a cheese roll and a cup of tea.

Eleven

Two weeks later I am back in Newcastle again, this time with the Kevin Ayers Band. After our gig we return to the Drogenheyer Hotel, where it turns out that the group Curved Air is also staying. In short order we end up in someone's room, sharing the usual drinks, smokes, and musician bull. I sit on the floor and get into an intense conversation with a young American: his name is Stewart Copeland. He is engaging, friendly, and intense—a nonstop talker—and he gives me a long rap on how there is a guitar factory not far from Newcastle and how he has been in there and has hustled them into giving him a free guitar, even though he is the drummer in the group, and recommends that I do the same—it's easy. *Easy, I think, with a mouth like that: they probably gave him the bloody guitar just to get him to shut up and go away!* But I like him immensely and wonder vaguely if I will ever see him again.

At this time I retain a loose connection with the Soft Machine/Gong/ Virgin crowd. The reigning queen of this set is a woman known as Lady June. Occasionally there are parties at her large flat in Maida Vale, and at one of these I run into Mike Howlett, the former bass player of Gong, who as a group have now called it a day. We get into a conversation and he tells me that he's seen me playing around London and is complimentary, asking me if I would like to be in a group that he's putting together as a special project for the Gong reunion in Paris. The event will be an eight-hour concert in which each former member of Gong will bring his own new group, the culmination being Gong themselves playing together again. I express mild interest and Mike tells me that he has a bass player from Newcastle named Sting whom he wants to use. He's in a punk band called the Police, and maybe we could use their drummer, and he—Mike—will also play bass. It sounds odd—two basses?—but I shrug and agree to meet again.

A few days later in Shepherds Bush, Mike plays me the material, some songs of his and some by this Sting bloke. I tell him that I'm not all that impressed but think the songs are okay; we can make them work for this project.

He arranges a session for a few days later at a studio in Swiss Cottage called Virtual Earth. I make the trek across London from Putney and get up there around eleven A.M. The bass player and drummer are already there; they seem like just a couple of musicians, and I have no recollection of having met them before. The one with the bass says nothing but saw me a few years earlier in Newcastle playing with Zoot, so to him I am a well-known London musician—someone who, although scratching and clawing to survive, has already made it. We get into the rehearsal, and as it's his gig, Mike leads the way. The atmosphere is affable as we feel out one another's playing and learn some of Mike's material. But things suddenly come alive when we start a song by the bass player called "Visions of the Night." With a furious forward drive and a punk edge, this song pulls me out of a pleasant, if slightly somnolent, state to a fully galvanized awareness and I start playing with renewed energy.

We take a break and the drummer enthusiastically tells me of their activities as the Police, how they are out on the road with a singer from New York called Cherry Vanilla, backing her up for fifteen quid a night and then doing their own set. He speaks volubly of the punk scene, how great it is, how alive —that this is what's happening—and I find it hard not to get caught up in his enthusiasm. He then reminds me that his name is Stewart Copeland and that in fact we met three months earlier at the Drogenheyer Hotel. It comes back to me like an old black-and-white photograph—lying on the stale carpet of a hotel bedroom in a haze of beer and cigarette smoke, Stewart's words flying past my ears like arrows. And then the bass player, Sting, points out that the two of us have also sort of collided, as he was the bass player for Last Exit, the support group for the "Tubular Bells" concert. "Now I remember you," I say (or rather, lie), but the three of us are in a room together and the wheel of fortune clicks forward.

I drive back through the dense London traffic with a feeling that is different. Playing along with the kinetic fury of Stewart's drumming and Sting's soulful voice and bass playing was raw but powerful. Staring out across the standstill traffic and blare of Capitol Radio, I intuit something but try to put it to the side: this is a one-off project, not a real group; they have a guitarist and are out gigging with him; they are a band. My natural enthusiasm tends to pull me into difficulties because I find it hard to play with the necessary emotion and remain detached at the same time, but something is getting to me.

A few days later Mike gives me a cassette of the songs we recorded, and it's a letdown. Rushing and charging along with no finesse, it's the sound of a train wreck; maybe it's punk, but it doesn't sound like a band, isn't yet cohesive enough to be powerful. But despite the crudeness of the tape, there is a provocation that comes through and I decide to reserve judgment and carry on for a while. We continue rehearsing and by degrees get deeper into one another's skin as we work our way through the songs for the Paris show. This is a potent period because I am replacing Henri Padovani, their guitarist, for a while and a new bond is being formed. But underneath the groundswell of rhythm, bass lines, and chords and the conversational banter being tossed back and forth, another agenda is forming. Sting, who doesn't always verbalize his feelings, is already brooding about Henri's lack of ability, is frustrated by it; it's limiting him and his own considerable songwriting abilities. I stumble into this fragile scenario and we play; we interact; and not holding anything back, I demand more, push for musical excellence even if it's for a one-night show. Sting says nothing but sees a new set of possibilities, and the seeds are sown.

We play the show at the Hippodrome in Paris to a large crowd of Gong devotees as a group called Strontium 90. We go over well enough, but I am somewhat ambivalent about it. The two-bass thing seems wrong—unbalanced—but the idea of a knockout power trio begins to take shape.

We part company the next day, as I have to get to Colmar to play with Kevin Ayers. But after the intensity of being with Sting and Stewart—the three of us playing together stays with me—being back in the Kevin Ayers Band suddenly feels too comfortable, too tame, the old world.

Back in London Mike has set up a few gigs for us as the Elevators, the name he chooses to replace Strontium 90. We play a couple of shows, one at the Nashville and one at Dingwalls, but from a musical perspective both gigs feel strange. It's okay but it's not quite coming off, the two electric basses distorting the focus of the band. The other problem is that we all like Mike but he's the odd man out. Compared with the three of us, he is mellow—relaxed—and we are all intense and edgy, as if from the same mold. After a few furtive phone conversations we decide to go on without him. He is disappointed but not devastated. But there's another problem: I am not actually in the band, but somehow I'm half in the Elevators and half in the Police, which is frustrating. But this fuzzy move to continue without Mike seems to imply that together we have made a decision, a commitment that somewhere in the future we will be a group.

The energy from Paris subsides and I am left feeling let down. Nothing seems clear. Despite all the talk, Stewart wants to carry on being the Police with Henri playing guitar, as he fits the punk image Stewart has in mind for the band. But there is a potent disabler in the form of his bass player/singer, who is wrestling with his dissatisfaction. I begin returning to the thought that it's a lost cause, but a few days later, as if not quite willing to part company yet, Sting and I have a long talk on the phone. Maybe we are reaching out toward each other, propelled by some faintly felt vision of the future, but in the grey light of an April morning it boils down to the fact that, yeah, we should play together—there's a natural musical affinity. The conversation goes along the lines of my joining the band. But what about Henri? How would we deal with that?

Neither of us knows quite how to get around it, but at this point in my life I don't want to play in a band with another guitarist. I feel selfish about my skills, don't want them diluted by playing with another guitar or having to drop my language down to a simplistic level. Unfortunately, Henri has been playing for only a few months and would not be the guitarist I would choose should we go that route. It's a difficult moment, but I feel clear that I am in if it's a trio. That will have to be their decision. We both feel the circumstance, its pain, lack of resolution, potential. Sting says he'll call Stewart later, and maybe we'll speak again tomorrow. I put the phone down, my head churning. I was just about to let go of this, the idea of being in this band—and now?

A short while later I take the tube from Putney into central London. Sitting in the train, I stare up at the posters advertising holidays in Majorca and promises of a golden future if you save with the Halifax Building Society. My outlook, more like pitted brass, is uncertain. I stare at the filthy floor of the carriage, the dirt molecules of grime, dust particles, ticket stubs, the crap of people's shoes, and think, *Fuck it, I've got to get past this.* The past three years in London have been good, but I'm running on empty. I need the right setting to push it all the way. In my head I have written that script and acted the whole thing out, although I still don't know if it's here, staring me in the face. On a gut level I am excited by this group, but rationally there's not much to go on. How am I to know as I rattle along on the Central Line that this band will be responsible for my biggest high and my biggest crash? No one has heard of the Police; if I join them, I might be throwing myself down yet another black hole.

The train jerks to a halt, and as I get out at Oxford Circus, Stewart gets out with me. We look at each other, laugh, and make the standard remark about it being a small world. But this is the brilliant collision: one train later and it might have all turned out differently. Imagine: Sting eventually becomes disillusioned, returns to Newcastle, takes up teaching, and plays music only on the weekends in a pub; Stewart realizes his true calling and joins the diplomatic corps and at the moment is heavily engaged in the Middle East. But I have been on the train brooding about my own future, a situation now exacerbated by the talk with Sting an hour earlier, so I suggest to Stewart that we go get a coffee somewhere. We sit down with cappuccinos and begin a jocular conversation about our recent shared exploits: Paris, Mike Howlett, the gigs. But I am cooking on the inside; the dialogue with Sting is fresh in my head, pushing itself forward like a nagging pain. I tell Stewart that Sting and I have spoken and that there seem to be some unresolved issues.

Clearly something happens when we play together. Sting feels it, I feel it; the bass player thinks I should be in the band, it's obvious. I'm ready, but it will have to be on my terms—in other words, one guitar. "But that," I say, "is your decision," and take another slug of cappuccino. Instead of being cool, I probably put this over with too much intensity because what's in my head suddenly feels out of control, as if it's pushing me to seize the moment before it fades. I want to play in a trio, and here it is. But instead of embracing what I think is apparent, Stewart counters all of this with replies that I couldn't possibly want to be in the band because it wouldn't suit a musician like me. I would have to lug equipment, and what about Henri?

There are undercurrents to Stewart's simple protest, because he knows and I sense that Sting is fed up with Henri's limited guitar abilities and might leave if things don't change. The future of the band is at risk, but Stewart is loyal to Henri (or so I imagine). With a certain amount of emphatic enthusiasm, he states that Henri is authentic—a real punk (although Henri had cut off waist-length hippie hair to join the band). The look seems more important to Stewart than the quality of the music. He is the one who hired Henri in the first place, and having me come in would be a shift of power. The shadow side to this little scenario in the future legend about my replacing Henri, of course, is that I am supposed to have callously pushed him out and, as Stewart puts it, bludgeoned my way in—a parallel to the Ringo Starr/Pete Best story of the Beatles.

But there is a subtext to this tale. As the Police, Stewart and Sting have toured England by joining forces onstage with the guitarist and keyboard player that Cherry Vanilla has brought with her from New York. In the context of gigs and sound checks, they jam with these two musicians: Louis Lepore on guitar and Zecca on piano. Louis is a very good guitarist who can also play jazz and some classical guitar, and the jams have a different quality from what they are doing in the official Police trio. One night before a show in London, Stewart, Sting, and Louis go out to a little café before the gig. Stewart leans across the table and says brightly to Louis, "Okay, I've got the new band—you on guitar, Sting on bass, and me on drums." Louis is taken aback and, somewhat confused, tells Stewart that he can't—he's with Cherry and in fact is her boyfriend: it wouldn't work. And besides, the Police at this stage are absolutely nowhere—they're not an authentic punk group and they have no songs worth mentioning—so there is very little appeal for Louis. But as if to further compound Sting's unrest, one night Louis goes over to Sting's flat, where sits a small music stand with some classical guitar music on it. Sting asks Louis if he can play anything like that, and Louis sits down and sight-reads the page in front of him, thus pushing Sting's frustration one step further. As Stewart and I talk the situation through, I know nothing of this and so can't use it as proof that a change needs to be made—and anyway, I wouldn't bother. But as if foreshadowing my arrival with this early attempt to replace Henri with Louis, Stewart has underscored that maybe the guitarist isn't right yet. For years I have to deal with asshole journalists who like to bring out this story and then vaguely paste me with the image of a cruel bastard who pushed Henri out of the group, as if everyone else were innocent. But this is the stuff from which groups are made: conflict, desire, betrayal, and strategies that Machiavelli would be proud of.

Stewart really wants to be the Clash or the Damned, but it's a pretense because it's not where Sting is at all—in fact, it annoys him—so there's a fragility to the existing structure, with a crack appearing that has been made wider with my involvement. They have already had a conversation about my replacing Henri but haven't yet reached that uncomfortable decision.

Sting and Stewart are in the battlefield with a guy whose sword can't give them the cutting edge they really need. While Stewart identifies with the uniform, Sting is looking for the weapon. With that in place, they would have a locked unit that could become a fighting machine on all levels. In a way Sting's emotion mirrors mine. He's been writing songs for years and instinctively knows how good he is but, like most of us, isn't sure of how to push it to the top. He needs a catalyst and so do I, and maybe we have both intuitively recognized it in each other. But the demands of just trying to stay alive usually outweigh the luxury of taking a risk. The situation is compounded by the scene now in London, a moment when if you aren't gelled, spiked, and ripped, you might just as well go home and forget it. Being punk means that you might at least get a couple of gigs, so in a sense Stewart, who has leapt from the ultimate hippie band into the Police, has made what appears to be a smart move. But it is undermined by there being no real credentials for striking this pose, and the audience out there knows it.

Over the past three weeks my playing with them has put things into perspective for Sting. Something has to happen, or he is going to take off. He is in London—away from his hometown, with a baby and a wife to support—and it's a strain. He is already thinking of taking a gig with Billy Ocean for ninety pounds a week. Stewart talks him out of it, but my appearance acts as another trigger. Sting wants the dream and is prepared to be ruthless to get it. The something that has to happen is that the right guitarist has to appear.

Unaware of any of these undercurrents, I stare out across the crowded West End cafe with the doleful impression of a sad chord twanging in my gut, the sense of an effort wasted. Despite the various subplots and—to Stewart's credit—for being loyal to Henri, we don't agree on anything more than maybe we'll try it with two guitars. A weak compromise.

Stewart's cartoon version of this story will be that I absolutely demanded to be in the band, wouldn't take no for an answer. But with no idea of the sub-rosa machinations—the early attempt to replace Henri with Louis Lepore—I wrestle with a weird mix of intuition and pain, knowing that I would be pushing someone out of a job. But, on the other hand, what exactly is it that I am doing? Pushing someone out of a band that right now is nothing? Although I might glimpse the potential of this group, it is not exactly a paying gig. But it is the natural resolution of converging desire and it happens, and the subsequent history justifies it so that even Henri will agree that it was right; to pretend otherwise would be blind.

But first we try a couple of gigs with the Police as a foursome, the first one at the Music Machine. Henri and I arrive at choruses and verses at different times with different chords; it feels like a disaster and I don't see much hope in this, but we try to make light of it, as if it will work out.

Our second gig is in a bullring at the Mont-de-Marsan Punk Festival in France on August 5, 1977. We travel all the way to the South of France in a clapped-out old banger of a bus with Eddie and the Hot Rods, the Clash, the Damned, the Jam, and the Maniacs. Low on the bill, we are up against bands that are already famous and have a strong following; but we go on, determined to compete. Even though it feels clumsy with two guitars, we pull off a short but intense set and acquit ourselves. After the show Sting, Stewart, and I go into the town and find a cheap café, and when I make some acid remarks about the waiter serving us, Stewart laughingly remarks, "Oh, so it's going to be that sort of a band is it?" It seems like a nod toward acceptance and I feel the possibility of fraternity.

On the way back to Paris in the bus the "punk" bands are generally trying to outdo one another by lighting farts and spitting in one another's mouths while Stewart and I trade sardonic remarks aimed in their direction. Sting reads a book, and Stewart is mortified by this defiant act; no one is supposed to read in the punk world. Paul Simonon of the Clash sits down next to Sting and asks him about bass playing. Underneath the sneer of punkdom, it appears that he actually loves his instrument and wants to play better. As we pull into Paris, Sting, Henri, and I are all seated together in the back of the bus, Henri enthusing about the new possibilities of the group while Sting and I catch each other's eye and feel the poignancy of the moment because we sense where things are going.

In Paris we're put up for the night in a filthy hole of a hotel fit only for rats. The four of us are directed to one room at the top of the hotel. As we enter the room with moans of "Sacre bleu," we see that there are only three beds in the garret. Stewart and Henri immediately lie down on two of them while Sting and I are left to share the remaining queen. Wearily, Sting and I climb in between the sheets with remarks like "Oh well, if this is what it takes," "No farting," and "Boy bands are coming back."

There is one last thing with Henri, a session at Pathway Studios with John Cale producing. This is supposed to be a good idea by someone who imagines that working with John Cale is going to give us a hit or make something magical happen. But it's an ill-conceived idea; Cale has no more idea than the three of us and isn't really attuned to the London punk scene. He arrives at the session late and drunk, which pisses us off, and none of his suggestions seem to be in accord with the direction in which we are headed. Maybe this is the moment when the three of us first stand shoulder-to-shoulder and act with a group mind. We are getting nowhere with Cale, and although it's unspoken, we are all frustrated and angry. Maybe it has something to do with a problem with authority—someone telling us what to do, the idea that this guy is going to teach us something. The truth is, we are more serious than he is and we simply don't need him. This situation is compounded by the fact that Henri and I are klutzing about, trying to get a sound between two guitars. It's not working and I'm frustrated because it doesn't seem to be right. It finally comes to a head when, taking the piss, I play an old Led Zep riff and Cale jumps on it and screams, "That's it—let's record that." That does it—we pack up and go home. That night Stewart reluctantly makes the call to Henri to tell him that he is no longer in the band. A painful conversation and one that none of us looked forward to, but Henri exits a band that is still nothing, still nowhere.

August 1977 and now I am the guitarist in the band, but I have a hollow feeling inside and the smell of burning bridges in my head. At home Kate is encouraging; we talk in the kitchen, discuss it in the bath, lie in bed and consider the possibilities. She sees the potential and backs me in the decision even though it leaves us with literally no income, as I have walked out on the penurious retainer I was getting to play with Kevin Ayers.

London is now a maelstrom of Mohawks, Union Jacks, bovver boots, latex, fetish gear, and amphetamine-driven music. *Street credibility* is the PC watchword, and the Police have none. Because so much of punk is about throwing over the old guard, it is better in this moment—if you want to survive—to have no background in music. As Martin Amis puts it, "punk is the celebration of the talentless," and maybe that is the point. By this standard we are fake, transparently so. But so is a lot of this mad, churning scene, with some of its leading lights being people whose background is something more than the gritty stations that punk is supposed to come from. But none of this matters, because it is fabulous anyway. This is what is supposed to happen, and it's happening in a fantastic way that only Britain could produce. As well as being a nation with a long history of readiness to go to war, Britain also has a lengthy charter of protest movements: it's in the blood. Put simply, we like a bit of aggro. The youth of Britain who see the country as being nothing more than a dystopia controlled by an oligarchy produce Sturm und Drang on a regular basis: the Fabians, the Suffragettes, trade unions, teddy boys, mods, rockers, Aldermaston marchers, hippies, and punk. The British also have a knack of translating this into music, often taking American music and reproducing it in an even gutsier way than the original, e.g., the Beatles, the Stones, the Who, Cream, Led Zeppelin. What is rock if not a howl? In this late-seventies moment—though I don't identify with the current outer manifestation of English rage, punk—I love the energy and aggression and the fact that punk is a dynamite blast through a music industry that has gotten fat and complacent. Overnight it creates havoc and puts a lot of fat slobs out of business.

I have thrown my lot in with Sting and Stewart, but now, having to face the hard-core scene, the moment of truth is upon us. With the music we have in hand and the way we play, I feel as if I am smiling into a severe hailstorm with my aggression in place but my musical values at the bottom of a deep black ocean. The songs that make up our set are terrible. Stewart has knocked out tunes in a valiant but rapid attempt to give the band a punk edge, but there's nothing original-sounding, no true songwriting voice that is genuine enough to capture an audience. What we have is a fast, furious row more like three brats misbehaving, more the sound of a fashion statement than a musical message—and it's worthless. In a nutshell, we suck.

On the day Elvis dies we do a gig at Rebecca's in Birmingham. The prevailing style is easily described. It's very fast, very loud, and features heavily garbled shouting noises usually accompanied by large mouthfuls of spit. We go onstage in the small, dark club and whip through our entire set, accomplishing all the above values, and are done in about twelve minutes. We are supposed to play for an hour. I look over at Sting and Stewart in near disbelief: we have just played fifteen songs in twelve minutes as if going for a new land-speed record. Maybe this is the way Dizzy and Charlie Parker felt back in the forties when they started playing bebop tunes at breakneck speed so that the whites couldn't dance to it. I would laugh, but it's pitiful; even the audience is looking at us drop-jawed. If nothing else, at least we're the fastest band around. We are so intent on being viewed as punk that we miss the music entirely; the idea seems to be that if you are seen as authentic, then you will be successful—content is secondary. It's a suspect stance, and it can't be sustained for long. We are a band, but to me it feels like one in name only. Even Miles, Stewart's brother who is heavily involved in the new scene, doesn't think much of us at this point because he too thinks we are fake. Stewart calls it reverse nepotism. Miles has a problem with me in particular because I have gone onstage at the Music Machine wearing trousers that are half an inch wider than regulation punk.

We play the Marquee at the height of the gobbing syndrome, and it is ugly. Gobbing on the band has become de rigueur at punk gigs and probably represents an all-time low in the British music scene. One of the reasons that gobbing becomes so rampant is possibly that amphetamine sulfate causes a large amount of saliva in the mouth—and where better to get rid of it than on the band you have just paid to see? As we attempt to get through our set, phlegm flies at us like evil rain from the mob below. It lands on the neck of my Telecaster, splatters on my face and hair, and drips down my shirt. This is a moment when I feel an intense loathing for those we are playing to. Feelings of violence well up in me that make me feel sick and I can only think, *Fuck it, it's not worth it.*

Now I am in the middle of the inferno, but it's like being hurled about at a party you haven't been invited to and I hang on to my guitar like a cork raft. Once again youth is revolting, another generation countering the established order; but like the hippie scene, it too will pass, leaving a residue in the world, its trappings becoming those of the museum with punks with Mohawks and Union Jacks posing for tourists in the Kings Road. Steve Jones's comment—we aren't into music, we're into chaos—sounds remarkably like Jim Morrison's remark ten years earlier when he said he was interested in revolt, disorder, chaos, and any activity that has no meaning. But with punk's fashion and aggression, it's easy to see how kids become caught up in it, although the truth is that most of them are unaware of the politics and the fact that in London the scene has been at least partially engineered by a fashion entrepreneur with a view to selling clothes. I am forced to fall back on my defense—the guitar, the axe—with a basic attitude of "fuck it, I can play any of these wankers under the table."

Somewhere in the middle of our first few weeks as a trio, Stewart turns up at Sting's flat in Bayswater with a big grin on his face and his hair dyed a shocking platinum blond. Sting and I stagger back at this flamboyant move, thinking that Stewart has lost his marbles. But as serendipity will have it, a few days later Sting gets a call to do a Wrigley's chewing gum commercial. They want him to appear with a punk band, all of whom have to have blond hair. It's a chance to make a little bit of side money, which we desperately need, so in short order Sting and I also become blond or blonder. Maybe this is the original message in a bottle, because once the dye is set, so is our future.

In a sea of sarcasm about old tarts and with my head stuck in a bowl, Kate helps me dye mine on Wednesday night, but instead of a Marilyn-like platinum, it comes out a shade of ghastly orange more like Coco the Clown. The next morning I look in the bathroom mirror and a haggard streetwalker stares back. With horror I realize that this apparition is me, and whispering the words "Faustian pact" into the mirror, I get back into bed, hoping that I am just having a bad dream. I get up again, I am still orange, and I decide to wear a beret for a while until my head stops looking as if a UFO has just landed on it.

But I get it blonder, and it turns out that our three blond heads work like a charm. It unifies us and gives us a strong identity—the bleach boys—and we begin noticing more blond heads in our pitiful little gatherings. We have a short list of fast, aggressive songs—"Landlord," "Nothing Achieving," "Truth Hits Everybody," "Dead End Job," "Fallout"—all reflecting the current flavor of angst. They're enough to get us through a gig but will not turn a record company's head or give us a career. We continue to play gigs around London, trying to hold it together, but are always mired in difficulties like hiring a cheap PA and a crappy van to get to the gig. Usually the bloody van breaks down and the PA costs so much that we end the night dividing up five quid between us and then start into the task of pushing the van back through the West End, where the lights of restaurants glow like an invitation from the other side.

We get a gig at the Hope and Anchor; it's supposed to be important, a step up. We are excited and revved-up for it, desperately thinking that this pub gig will change our fortunes. We have a small coterie of fans and our wives— Kate, Sonja, and Frances—so we are never entirely alone. Between us and the audience we can count on a good solid crowd of about fifteen or so. The big night arrives; the audience is in place. We crouch in a very small dressing room at the side of the stage. It's time to start and we are ready to go on, but as we walk through the door and directly out onto the stage, the headstock of my guitar bangs against the door frame—"Oh fuck," I say, but don't check the tuning. We get a tiny cheer like a mouse fart from the audience, which is still mostly our wives, babies, and a few drunks, and then launch into a fast and furious version of "Truth Hits Everybody." My guitar is so far

out of tune that I want to scream, but we can't stop because (as usual) we are going like a fucking express train. I'm somewhere between c# minor and E major—although you could hardly call the sound I am making those sweetly harmonic appellations, more like Arnold Schoenberg on acid or a cat being stabbed to death—and I try within the confines of a nanosecond to reach for the machine heads, but no such luck. The 9:02 is out of the station and shooting down the track like a bat out of hell, and when I attempt to move my hand from the chord toward the tuning peg, it merely looks as if I am creating a new style of guitar playing or possibly having an epileptic seizure. We roar through the whole song while I have the experience of a drowning man, reviewing the entirety of my life in about two and a half minutes flat, making the most horrendous atonal din, and deciding that it really is time for me to get out of the music business. We finish and Sting looks over at me with an arched eyebrow that says it all. I look back sheepishly and say, "Mind if I tune up?"

On nights off, which are most nights, we are in the habit of going out and spraying our name on the walls of various buildings around the West End, which is what all the best people do. It's called spraying your way to the top, but in its own criminal way it's thrilling because you're out there with your spray guns and paint, daubing THE POLICE on a wall, watching out for the real thing in case you have to make a fast getaway. POLICE GET ARRESTED would be an interesting headline. But we are scrabbling, trying to stay alive, and graffitiing our own name on various walls around London seems like just another fingernail hanging on to the ledge of survival. My bridges are charred beyond recognition, and I stare through a veil of angst as I spray our band name across a nice stretch of unsullied wall. It's not looking good, the road ahead; it isn't even the luxury of selling out, as there's no money on the horizon, not even a faint whiff. At that moment the Police are not even a real p—k band, and in the eyes of the old guard, I have jumped on the bandwagon, faintly disguised as some rare breed of orangutan, orange hair blowing in the roar of my Marshall stacks. I have a number of friends who think that I have finally lost my marbles by joining a band called the Police and it begins to feel lonely, but I have to hold on to my original instinct about Sting and Stewart, the music I think we will make.

Through an accountant by the name of Keith Moore, whom Stewart was involved with during his days with Curved Air, we are approached by a couple of Iranian gentlemen with huge ambitions in the entertainment industry, Alex Riahi and his sidekick, the long-suffering Tony. Alex thinks we might have something, and there is talk of his paying us a retainer of sixty pounds a week if we sign up with him as a manager for five years but give him the publishing rights to all the songs. We are in a vulnerable position; it's tempting; we couldn't get much lower and we sure could use the money. But we agree to rehearse over at his studio in Pimlico and see how it goes for a while before we make a heavy commitment. This is probably the sanest decision we ever make. Maybe we are invoking our own future or acting on intuition, but to a man we are fiercely protective about not giving up our publishing rights for sixty pounds a week.

We start practicing in Pimlico and quickly find out that Alex is intense, to the point of being obnoxious. Most days he roars into the garage of the studio in his Mercedes convertible, leaps out, and start haranguing us. These diatribes usually take the form of "Why can't you be more like the News?"—

another group he's managing who have a minor hit at the time. He holds them up to us as a shining example and tells us that they are going to be the biggest group in the world within two years. We hate them, their stupid music, and their bald-headed singer, but Alex says, "The News, the News." "Bad fucking news," we mutter behind his back.

Tony, his partner, is a gentle soul who comes down when we are rehearsing to ask how we were getting on. But if Alex turns up when Tony is present, he storms into the room, gold chains swinging around his neck, turns, and barks, "Tony—coffee, now," and poor old Tony slinks away like a beaten dog to get the filthy brew. And then in another flurry of gilt medallion, Alex spins back to tell us how it's going to be, what we should do, and do we want to have Rolls-Royces, Lear jets, expensive women, and marble floors, or what? It all sounds like an Iranian nightmare, and our only response is to stare at the floor in a silent embarrassment while he raves on until he leaps back into the Mercedes, guns the engine, and roars out of there at warp speed. The best thing about all of this is that for a while we have a free place to rehearse. It's a strange moment when we seem to stand still: we have made a slightly false move and maybe we know it, but at least we haven't signed anything; there's still a way out.

In the afternoons we walk around the corner to a small coffee bar and get a cup of tea and a sausage roll and morosely discuss our somewhat clouded future and the tunes we are rehearsing. In this phase we don't yet have the songs that will make us famous. Sting has a few ideas, but we are groping, as if trying to fit a key in the dark. The pressure of writing "punk songs" just to keep going doesn't come easily. Sting has a natural talent for writing melodic and harmonic material, so we fall between two poles and come up with nothing satisfying. We need a catalyst. I find it discouraging because to be without gigs is one thing, but to be without music is another. We even try to play a blues, but it doesn't work and I begin to seriously question whether I have made the right decision and return home, moaning to Kate that these guys can't play. We seem to be in a dead zone: no gigs, shit management, nothing. But we walk back through the rain and cold and carry on working at songs, trying to improve, trying to survive on a diet of music and hope.

Prior to throwing in my lot with Sting and Stewart, I have had an on-and-off gig in Germany with a conductor by the name of Eberhard Schoener. I have one commitment left with him, and conveniently it falls at the tail end of a few days' playing in Holland and France with the Damned. But there are problems because there is no way for us to get our equipment to Rotterdam, and as I have the only car with an engine that starts (or maybe the only car with an engine), we have to risk it in that. If we actually get there, we can borrow amps from the Damned, maybe.

We pass a few queasy hours on the ferry from Ipswich to Holland, eating cheese sandwiches and staring out at the dismal puke-colored Channel, which churns below like vomit going down the toilet. We hit the grey shores of Holland and drive into the bowels of the Netherlands, praying that the bloody car won't give up the ghost—it's already wheezing like an old asthmatic. A few hours later, after driving around most of Holland and Germany and skirting the Russian border, we end up somewhere that can only be described as somewhere. We play that night in a dark, smoky hall in a Flemish field full of Flemish punks and Flemish puking. The Damned are the big stars, and we the poor side attraction, but they are decent enough to lend us their gear without putting us through total humiliation. Brian James, the guitarist, lets me use his amps and I am grateful.

After the gig and a night spent in a Belgian hostelry suffused with the sharp tang of animal urine and spilled beer, we set off for Paris in my cancerous auto, lurching toward la Belle France like a sausage sliding across the surface of a greasy omelet. We arrive in Paris the day before the show, and although we are excited to be in the French capital, we don't know what to do with ourselves. But we find somewhere to stay in the sixth arrondissement for the exacting sum of roughly a quid a night for a smelly matchbox of a room at the top of the building. It isn't worth even half that, and because there is no room to stand, we lie down and make remarks out of the side of our mouths about feeling romantic and gay. As usual, we have no money to do anything except play the gig, but Stewart and I scrape just enough together to see the afternoon showing of *Star Wars* with French subtitles in St.-Michel. As we sit there in the dark, watching Darth Vader and making comments about the line "May the force be with you," Sting is wandering around the streets of Pigalle, observing the beautiful prostitutes.

The next night, after grinding through morning and afternoon like something out of Nausea, we go to le gig. It turns out to be a basement room below a restaurant somewhere near Les Halles. When we get there, the place is empty and the Damned are nowhere to be seen because the gig has been canceled. A Johnny Hallyday wannabe with a Gauloise hanging from his lips tells us that the Damned haven't sold enough tickets. "Ze Damned, no one knows whoza fuck she is," and "Ze Polis, don'mek mi larf." With a deep sense of failure and an "ah, fuck it all" attitude, we slink away in the direction of our Parisian shithole—but not without one more adventure.

Being good tourists, we're interested in seeing the sights and decide to make a detour back to the hotel over the famous Pont Neuf. We pull up in the middle of the bridge and get out to stare over the expanse of the Seine below. Paris and the Seine, such beauty, such history. We are silent for a moment, then awed by the weight of it all, inspired to poetic commentary: "I wonder how many dead prostitutes have ended up in there?" "It's full of piss, and that's where they get their drinking water from, froggy cesspool." "Brigittey Bardot Bardot." Having gotten that out of our system, we go into a mutually supportive eulogy about our own future. If we can survive this, we can do anything; it's just a question of time, obviously, isn't it? We become quiet and, staring across the river, fall into a dazed reverie—Sting generating a lyric for "Roxanne," me imagining weird chord inversions, Stewart hearing snare hits on unorthodox beats, the future unfolding like a path, like the river itself.

We turn back to the car for a contemplative drive back through the streets of Paris, but naturally the fucking Dyane has had a mid-bridge seizure and now won't even start despite my furious cursing, kicking, and twisting of the ignition key. To playfully compound the situation, it begins to rain—well, not rain, but piss down with a vengeance so mean-spirited that it feels like we need an ark, not a piece-of-shit French thing.

With more remarks like "I've pushed cars off better bridges than this, French turd," and out-of-tune whistlings of "La Marseillaise," we start heaving the waste of money off the Pont Neuf in the direction of the sixth arrondissement. Shortly after getting off the mighty bridge, we are stopped by the gendarmes, who want to see our passports (which by some bizarre piece of fortune we all have). Then ensues a long page-one Berlitz conversation about how we aren't actually stealing this French car but how in fact one of us, so admiring of French ingenuity, has actually purchased it and what a great little thing this French car is and what bad luck to have run out of petrol on a night like this, but, oh well, regret *rien* and *c'est la vie,* constable. After much Gallic shrugging of shoulders and lip curling and probably not knowing what to do with us, the gendarmes climb back into their nice warm little van, light up some Gitanes, and take off in a haze of warm blue smoke while we stand like sodden sponges in the Niagra of water that is destroying all of Paris. With aching limbs and purple lips, we push on through the flood all the way back to the hotel with a desperate feeling in our stomachs about the morning.

Daylight arrives and in the streets below, well-heeled and chic Parisians with a *petit déjeuner* and strong French coffee in their stomachs go about their lives with smiling faces, thinking of a satisfying morning's work and a long delicious lunch of seafood crêpes accompanied by something dry and white from the Loire Valley. Above their well-groomed and healthy bodies we drag ourselves out of our stinky little pallets, knowing that the first thing we have to do is find ze bloody garage. After a confused conversation at the front desk, it turns out that in fact there is one close by and, even better, it is downhill the whole way. With a dangerous combination of pushing, running, and braking amid filthy French insults, we skid into the auto repair in less than five minutes. After the mechanics look under the bonnet with disdain and clouds of Gauloise, we get the sage advice that they, French auto masters, could get the car going, but if the engine is ever turned off or if it stops, it will never start again—ever.

The horrible task of getting this wretched heap of metal back to Blighty falls to Sting, who has not been hired for the Eberhard Schoener gig in Germany. This is a Herculean task: he has to get the car onto the boat and keep the engine running all the way across the Channel. But he makes some remark that he is born for the job, and one can only admire his steely resolve and think that it was with men like him that the empire was built. Stewart and I luckily have been advised by Eberhard to hire a vehicle on his dime and drive to Munich, and we cheerily wave Sting off from the garage as he sets forth on his long journey back to the Emerald Isle. Maybe there is a hint of schadenfreude from Stewart and me, but in my case it's mixed because it's my car and I'll probably never see it again. There are murmurings of "poor fucker," "bastard," "he's had it coming for a long time now"—you know the sort of thing.

Having waved Sting off in the dying Dyanne, Stewart and I busy ourselves with the task of getting to Munich. Now that we are spending someone else's money, everything takes on a new brightness. We rent a nice new VW van at the appointed place, fuss a bit about the color, make sure the tank is full, and make an executive decision that we need a good meal before we set off on the long drive. We accomplish this in a rather expensive restaurant and then sleepily and contentedly set off for Munich and a paying gig. On the way there I relate to Stewart the story of the man we are about to share our fate with.

Eberhard is notorious in the German classical music scene because he's pulled off stunts like bringing an entire Balinese gamelan orchestra to Germany, combining them with an orchestra and electronics, and taking them on tour. I was introduced to him by Jon Lord, the keyboard player of Deep Purple, who asked me to come to Munich to play on a classical-rock album he was making there, with Eberhard conducting. I had run into Jon one night at the Speakeasy and he asked me if I would like to do it because he needed a guitarist who could read music and maybe play classical as well.

I arrived in Munich a few days later at the Hilton, where the sessions were taking place in the basement, now converted into a recording studio. Here I met Eberhard, a tall, thin German with a wild artistic shock of hair. With many stories to tell, he was very pleasant and fun to be with; we hit it off, not knowing how intertwined we would become in the future. The sessions, although difficult, went well as we worked through the day with the orchestra—all Hungarian refugees, with an entire village to themselves somewhere outside of Munich. Problems arose because we (the rock band) were on a stage at one end of a large hall and they (the orchestra) were stuck at the far end, so when we all tried to play together a tremendous time lag made it very difficult to arrive at the beginning of a bar together, never mind the orchestra's very legato phrasing, which dragged horribly against the rock band's pushing beat. But over the course of a day we managed to solve the problems by having Eberhard in the middle of the hall, waving his arms about like an epileptic rag doll. Somehow it worked, and the end of the day is rosy with many Germanic murmurings of "zumzing new, I tink, zumzing new, ya—gut."

Eberhard and I must have bonded in some way because shortly after I returned to London he called to ask if I would mind returning to Munich to do some more guitar overdubs for him. Naturally enough, I went back, as I was on the verge of selling my guitar, but from then on I regularly returned to Munich to do guitar stuff for Eberhard. I always stayed with him and his family in his beautiful apartment in Schwabing, a high-end quarter of Munich. A great raconteur, he was fun to be around and usually let me play whatever I want.

As the relationship progressed Eberhard gave me free rein until we reached the point where I would turn up at the studio, open the place up, start the tape machines rolling, and record myself. The studio was at the side of an old hall called the Burgerbrau, infamous as one of the places where Hitler had made early speeches on his way to power and in fact the scene of an assassination attempt on his life. One of his enemies had packed the place with dynamite, intending to blow him to kingdom come while making his speech, but unfortunately Hitler finished early and left, and so history unfolded in the way we know. Each day as I wandered in with my guitar I would stare up at that stage and try to feel the evil vibes coming from the spot where he stood, but actually I didn't feel anything much. Outside, though, it was different. There was a café attached to the building; sitting at the tables were many men in their sixties or seventies, all wearing dark glasses and all in competition for the number one Dr. Strangelove look-alike. They would sit there silently in the pale Bavarian sunlight, staring off into the distance, perhaps dreaming of the former cruelty and power they had once enjoyed.

Occasionally you would see them smirking to themselves as they raised yet another cup of bitter German *kaffe* to their thin lips or speared a hapless bratwurst, the other black-gloved hand desperately gripping a chain attached to the panting throats of a Rottweiler, Alsatian, or other weird breed of Bavarian killer dog. There was no question that beneath the thin veneer of respectability, they were Nazis. I made a few discreet inquiries and, sure enough, there were places around town where they had secret meetings and paid homage to the swastika. It hadn't gone away but had merely gone underground, presumably until the Führer rose once again. I would sit there alone at lunchtime, forking up a plate of sauerkraut, feeling a strange mix of a giggle fit and fearful humor.

My story told, Stewart and I drive all the way across France, studying the map and rambling on about our possible future. We arrive in Munich in the early evening, make our confused way to Schwabing, and are greeted warmly by Eberhard. Over dinner we tell him about our terrific bass player Sting—what about him? Can we include him? In an expansive mood, Eberhard agrees that maybe we should have him along as well. We call Sting in London—apart from the small matter of abandoning my car in Dover, he has gotten there fine—and tell him to get the first plane out in the morning. Two nights later we are in a circus tent in the center of Munich. This gig with an opera singer, electronic keyboards, and an acrobat (plus a rock band) has a Fellini aspect to it. *Well,* I think, *I dreamed of running away with the circus, but this is ridiculous.* Sting sings some stuff for Eberhard, who is very impressed and immediately uses his voice in the show. He asks me about Sting: where did he come from? Wonderful voice, but he's like a child—so quiet, so mysterious. Clearly Eberhard is fascinated by this wunderkind. We form a relationship with Eberhard and quickly establish ourselves as German circus performers.

Returning from the Fatherland, having actually worked and gotten paid for it, we go back to Pimlico feeling more confident and quickly realize that Alex Riahi is achieving nothing at all for us and that we are losing time. A few afternoons later, almost on cue, we look at one another and say fuck it, pack up, and leave. Although we have nothing else, we feel better, as if we have taken our power back. We never hear another word from the Iranian pop king.

We carry on practicing and like rats pass through a series of sewers that are laughingly called rehearsal rooms, each one more like the Black Hole of Calcutta than the last. Smelling of shit, piss, and vomit, they're all painted from floor to ceiling with black paint and filthy graffiti. If you make the mistake of looking up at the ceiling, you will see a huge asshole graffitied taking a shit in your direction. But there is a rose in Spanish Harlem, and from the wound grows the flower, and somehow in the gloom of these caves we move toward the light, groping our way toward the music that is a hidden seam in this subterranean gloom.

In the middle of this intensive practice period Sting gets left on his own for a few days when his wife, Frances, goes home to Ireland; Kate and I offer to let him stay with us in the interim and make sure he gets fed. Sting sleeps in the living room, and one night as Kate and I are finally disappearing off to bed we hear a softly strummed nylon-string guitar and a song about a girl named Roxanne. It's pretty and I like the chord sequence, but Kate immediately picks up on it and, turning to me in bed, says, "This is great, this is really interesting."

The experience in Paris has been turned into a song—in fact, a perfect pop song with a gritty lyric and interesting harmony. We lie in bed and listen to "Roxanne" for the first time. This song will one day take the world by storm, put us on the map, and change our lives irrevocably. We roll over and drift off to sleep as the germinating seed of "you don't have to put on the red light" caresses the last embers of consciousness and makes a lullaby for the baby that grows in Kate's belly.

A few days later Sting, Stewart, and I are in the half-constructed basement of a gay hairdresser's flat up on Finchley Road in North London morosely banging about and not really having a good time. The room is damp and the air thick with the stink of plaster, concrete, and paint. We are about to chuck it in when either Sting or I suggests that maybe we try out his new song "Roxanne." At the moment it's a bossa nova, which is a problem—not because it doesn't work that way but because in the prevailing climate it would be suicidal to go Brazilian, and we already have enough problems. So, how should we play it? We have to heavy it up and give it an edge. We decide to try it with a reggae rhythm, at which point Stewart starts to play a sort of backward hi-hat and tells Sting where to put the bass hits. Once the bass and drums are in place, the right counterpoint for me to play is the four in the bar rhythm part. Now we have three separate parts, and with the vocal line over the top, it starts to sound like music. We are all pleased with it but have no idea just how important this song will become for us. Smelling of powdered cement, sand, wet concrete, and oil-based paint, we emerge onto the High Street in Finchley at the end of the afternoon feeling good; we have a song called "Roxanne."

Christmas arrives, and other than our rehearsals, we still have nothing happening. It's a bleak end to the year, and Kate and I go the U.S. to see her parents while Sting and Stewart stay in London. While I'm away Sting has a party and Stewart lends him some of his Bob Marley records for the event, with the result that he starts picking up on the bass lines of the reggae grooves. After I return we still have nothing to do but rehearse, and we find an upstairs room on Jeddo Road in Shepherds Bush, one of the few not painted black—which makes it hard to adjust to.

One day Sting brings in a new song he has written called "Can't Stand Losing You." He picks up my guitar and plays it to us. Stewart and I are both knocked out; this is good, a real pop song. We work it out, playing it over and over. It acts as a guide to the territory that we have been looking for, and almost magically we seem to change gears and pick up momentum. "So Lonely" comes a short while later, and this too gets the treatment and becomes a song with our signature. Something is starting to happen. Under the influence of Bob Marley and the groove of reggae, the bass parts move away from the thumping eighth-note pattern into a sexy, loping line that is as much about notes not played as those struck. Over the top of these patterns I begin playing high, cloudy chords that are colored by echo and delay, and Stewart counters this with back-to-front patterns on the hi-hat and snare. From a dense in-your-face frontal assault, the songs now become filled with air and light. This is gratifying; material is now appearing that I can really bring something to. Sting is emerging as a songwriter, or at least that's what we think; the truth is that he has been writing songs for years, and some of the songs we imagine he has just written this week have in fact been knocking around for quite a long time. But it doesn't matter, because with this material and the way the three of us play it, we are moving into an identity of our own.

Sting incorporates more reggae into his writing, and we flow with it. I find that I can play exotic chord voicings behind his vocals and it doesn't throw him at all—in fact, he likes it. The minute we hit anything that we agree to be a cliché, we throw it out. We have long diatribes that now, as if faintly glimpsing the possibility of a future, extend past the music and into a group manifesto: the way we look, what kind of gigs we should do, record releases—we dream together and basically are as one, tossing out anything that sounds like the past or another band.

We rehearse for a while at Manos on the Kings Road in Chelsea. The guy who runs the place tells us one night as we are packing up that there is something about us that's different from the other bands. "You boys are going to be famous," he says. For some reason this remark is almost enough to make me cry, as if we are being tossed a very small bone. I drive back up the Kings Road with a tiny glimmer of hope.

Stripping away the conventions of standard electric rock also means dropping guitar solos. As a lot of the new bands are incapable of delivering a guitar solo, its absence in the current climate has become an arrogant hallmark, the extended virtuoso solo now being regarded as a symbol of the old guard and people like Eric Clapton. So, any solos are brief, which is irritating when you've spent most of your life trying to be good at them. But there are other ways to make the guitar parts effective, and this is what I turn my hand to.

I get hold of an old Echoplex, which is basically a device to create echo by using a piece of quarter-inch tape that revolves in a spool around two tape heads. You can speed up or slow down the number of repeats by sliding a little metal arrow up and down the length of a metal bar that runs along the top of the spool. It's crude but it works and adds a rich harmonic sound to the guitar and a spatial dimension to the group sound that sets us apart. I begin to use it all the time and create a churning double-rhythm effect with it—in other words, I can play a rhythm in eighth notes against the drums and get a sixteenth-note pattern, which, colored by dissonant harmonies and accented syncopation, results in a guitar sound that becomes huge and prismatic, like a rainbow arcing over the band.

The use of this device is seminal in changing and pushing the group into a unique direction. Creating a curtain of space, it appears to act as a catalyst to set us free. Sting is able to wail and vocalize over the ambience as if he is Miles Davis brooding his way through a solo—and with Miles being a major influence, it's a natural result. Against these jams the reggae bass line is held in place, while Stewart inverts the rhythm, and I add biting little dissonances that are not standard rock. Suddenly a set of natural responses converge to bring about a sound that no trio in rock has possessed before, but we are too buried in it to hear it ourselves. Strangely enough, other people recognize it before we do. But eventually we raise our heads and begin to see the territory we have arrived in and recognize it as if we have known it all along. With this information in place, we are able to codify it to the point where we can take almost any song and, as we say, "policify" it—even a piece of material by Noël Coward or a folk song from the Scottish Isles. From an instinctive and unself-conscious journey, we discover a sound for which there is no previous formula, a space jam meets reggae meets Bartók collage with blue-eyed soul vocals.

After a few months we wonder if we can rise to the almighty task of making an album, but as usual we have no money to pay for a studio and no record company to get us one. At this point Stewart's big brother Miles steps into the picture and gets us into a studio a few miles south of London. It's called Surrey Sound and is in a town called Leatherhead. Miles makes a funky deal with the owner, a local M.D. with aspirations to be a record producer. His name is Nigel Gray.

Twelve

In January 1978 we start going out to Surrey Sound whenever the studio has an afternoon free, or if some important rock stars like Godley & Crème cancel their session. We begin with the material we have in hand, but as we listen back in the new environment of the studio, we recognize flaws and imperfections and begin the process of abandoning songs and writing new ones. Gradually we find our feet in the studio. Though arguments are a feature of our sessions, they are always about how a song should go down on tape; this friction is a contributing factor to the tension that is part of the Police sound—it might be described as the sound of tight compromise.

Over a period of about six months, borrowing days and jumping in when other people's sessions are canceled, we cobble together an album that ultimately is the distillation of about three albums' worth of material. Miles pays an occasional visit to see how we are progressing, but most of his remarks are of a caustic nature. Although visionary, he is not loaded with small talk (or tact, for that matter), and often we are afraid of playing for him what we have recorded because we know in advance what he is going to say. Like Stewart, Miles too has the punk light in his eyes and can't really hear anything else at this point, or so in our paranoia we think.

One night he turns up wanting to hear what we have been doing, and as usual we play him the fast and furious stuff, thinking that's what he wants to hear. Finally after he offers a series of grunting responses but no enthusiasm, we play him a new song we have recorded that day. We are scared to play it because we are certain that he will hate it; for all intents and purposes, it's a ballad and about a million miles from the current party line. The track plays and the three of us stare off into the distance as if slightly embarrassed. The song ends and for a few seconds there is a pregnant silence, which seems to confirm our worst suspicions. And then Miles stands up, smiling. "That is fucking great—I'm taking it to A and M tomorrow, gimme a tape." We're stunned. He loves it. We were sure he would hate a ballad, but Miles—like one of the old-time kings of Tin Pan Alley—hears it, smells money, and begins plotting. The song is "Roxanne."

We drive back through the night into London, jabbering away at one another like maniacs, very excited that one of our tracks is actually going to make into the office of A and bloody M, a real record label. It's fucking miraculous. Feeling expansive, we celebrate our vision of the future by dropping in at the Happy Eater for a sausage sandwich and a cup of tea.

A&M are enthusiastic, and "Roxanne" is released in early April '78. It gets reviewed by John Pidgeon in *Melody Maker*. The general consensus is that we are a band to watch. It's a great track but it's not a hit, and our excitement fizzles like a dying party balloon. We have indulged in dreams of glory, but right now "Roxanne" isn't going to give us the ladder we thought she would.

We read the reviews. The critics think we are good, but it seems that we are still suspect; despite the classic pop brilliance of "Roxanne," the myopic party-line concerns of the hacks override the ability to hear the incisive edge and ultimate staying power of the song. However, one of the side effects of getting a single released by A&M is that we get into a relationship with the office on the Kings Road. It turns out that our timing is propitious, as A&M has just recovered from a nasty and highly publicized moment with the Sex Pistols. Like everyone else, the label has tried to jump on the punk bandwagon and has managed to get its hands on the Pistols, who are signed to great fanfare outside Buckingham Palace. Unfortunately, one week later the group went into the Kings Road office and terrorized the entire place by pissing on the furniture, ripping gold records off the walls, and overturning desks in a lurid moment colorfully illustrating the punk credo. Derek Green, the head of A&M UK, immediately tore up their contract, and that was the end of the deal.

Shortly after the Sex Pistols debacle we arrive like good little boys able to engage in a more reasonable discourse. We are struggling, and having a single out with a major record company means a lot to us. We want a situation in which we can develop, actually have albums released and be a band. "Roxanne" hasn't made it, but after what it has just been through, A&M breathes a metaphorical sigh of relief and gives us an unusual amount of latitude. We begin to develop enough of a relationship to get a second shot with another single, "Can't Stand Losing You."

An interesting situation develops with this song. The record company thinks that it's a great track but that it needs remixing—and they know how to do it. There is a slight attitude of "let the professionals take over now, boys, we'll get this right for you." We are slightly miffed, but there isn't a lot we can do: they are the almighty label, and we need them more than they need us. They disappear with the track for three weeks but eventually come back to us looking mildly embarrassed, saying that they have tried five different mixes but can't get it better than ours, which is honest at least. This is a minor triumph for us and establishes a precedent that proves of considerable worth over the next few years because from this moment on, A&M never interferes with our recording process again.

Between March and August we have very few gigs to sustain a belief in our own future. But we get a few opportunities as a support group—a couple of appearances with the American group Spirit, another with the reggae group Steel Pulse at the Roundhouse in London, and another in Germany with Eberhard on his Laser Theater tour. Finally on August 14 "Can't Stand Losing You" is released and gets to forty-two on the British charts. We are so elated by this small success that it's as if we have actually gone to number one. Unfortunately, the BBC won't play it because it's about suicide. Although it's tongue-in-cheek, they believe it might cause a rash of suicides and cannot take the responsibility. Besides, the cover has Stewart standing on a melting block of ice with a rope around his neck. So, without the power of the BBC behind us, we get stuck at forty-two and our hopes fade again. But still, we have a hit (even if a small one); as a result, A&M agrees to release our album in October, which feels like eons away. But it is going to happen.

We drag our way through the summer, managing only two shows as a support act for Chelsea and one on our own at the Rock Garden in Covent Garden. We are not exactly a roaring success. Every time we play on our own, no one comes and we end the night dividing two pounds between the three of us and then usually start pushing the van back down the street. Stewart alone keeps the spirit with calls to go out and graffiti our name up on a wall somewhere, but I get depressed. The long summer evenings drag on with a buttery glow, the TV flickers on and off with cricket test matches, and happy people go to the pub. For me this summer is turning into a test of faith. Like a permanent solar eclipse, this—the summer of '78—is the thinnest, the most tenuous, point of our existence.

In September things take a slight upward turn when we play gigs at the Nashville Room and the Marquee. We get a substantial turnout at both gigs, and it seems that maybe things are progressing slightly. These events are capped by an appearance on October 2 (Sting's birthday) on *The Old Grey Whistle Test,* a very popular television pop music program. Anne Nightingale, the host, announces us as an exciting new group who look like angels, and then we play "Can't Stand Losing You." This event should be a big break for us but is slightly marred by Sting's having had a can of hair spray explode in his face just before appearing on camera. By incredible luck there is an eye hospital right around the corner from the studio, and they manage to wash all the chemicals from his eyes. This takes time and by the skin of our teeth we just make it onto the show, with Sting wearing a large pair of dark sunglasses. Two weeks after this we leave for a three-week tour of the U.S., Miles having decided a few weeks earlier that we have to do something to save the band. If we can't really break through in the U.K., maybe we'll have better luck over there. Miles is always espousing the opinion that if you make it in America, the rest will follow—and he turns out to be right.

In '78 there is a company by the name of Laker Airways that has been conceived and masterminded by the redoubtable Freddie Laker, who in rebellious opposition to the mega-airlines has set up a cheap and fair-minded airline. On the Laker Skytrain it's possible to get a round trip to New York and back for sixty dollars.

Ian Copeland, the brother of Miles and Stewart, is an agent working out

of Macon, Georgia, with Capricorn/Paragon Production and he books us into a series of clubs on the East Coast, starting with CBGB's in New York's Bowery, which is already the legendary mecca of punk and New Wave. Ian and Miles work out the finances: with the small fees we will get paid for the gigs, we can do a three-week tour and just about break even. It's a bleak financial scenario but it represents a chance. CBGB's—the beating heart of the new music—is the coolest place to be. By so doing, we would naturally acquire a few more points of street cred, something we are not seen as having back home. But for me it's risky because Kate is now eight months pregnant, and I am going to disappear as the baby is about due. We talk about it and agree that it is the path we're on, that I should go, and that as long as we stay close, we can deal with the situation.

To help us with this tour we have hired a former drummer by the name of Kim Turner. Kim played in a group called Cat Iron that Stewart worked for as road manager a few years back before deciding at a young age that he would rather be on the management side of rock. Kim becomes almost a fourth member of the group.

On October 20, 1978, Sting and I fly to New York; Stewart is already there, visiting his father. We arrive at around 10:30 P.M. and are supposed to be on stage at midnight. Kim meets us at Kennedy and we drive hell for leather into the city and straight into the Bowery. As we drive into Manhattan I have a slight sense of déjà vu.

CBGB's is surrounded mostly by industrial buildings and places known in the United States as flophouses. The exterior atmosphere around the club is one of seediness and violence. In this part of New York the streets contain many derelict and homeless people; mugging—or jack rolling, as it's known—is commonplace. Started in 1974, CBGB's actually means country, bluegrass and blues, which was the favorite music of the owner, Hilly Kristal; but by the time of our appearance in 1978, it has become the shrine to punk and New Wave—a melting pot and laboratory to try out new music. With bands like Television, Blondie, the Talking Heads, Richard Hell and the Voidoids, the Heartbreakers, Patti Smith, and the Ramones, it has become a club with a pedigree. But physically, just like the clubs in London, it's not much more than a filthy hole. With graffiti everywhere, nowhere to change, a dressing room with no door and practically in the toilet, it's what we are used to and we start setting up our gear. I am renting Marshall cabinets for this tour but have brought along my Echoplex. We do a quick rough sound check in front of the audience and then are ready to go. No one there knows who we are, or have ever heard of us—we have to prove our worth, and knowing this makes us all the more determined to blow the audience away. We're tired from the long plane trip, but somehow New York comes in off the street to fill us with adrenaline and we play a hard and edgy set that rivets the audience, who haven't heard anything like it before. The Echoplex-reggae jams and Sting's high vocals cut through the tawdry atmosphere like a knife, and by the end of the first set the audience is on its feet and literally howling along with us. Despite the small numbers, it feels like a raging success.

We come offstage and disappear into the dressing room to wrestle our sweat-sodden clothes to the floor; as there's no door, most of the audience walk right in too. We're asked a lot of questions about our style: "Where d'you get that from?" "How you doin' that?" "You guys rock—yeah." This is very different from the London scene—these people really seem to like us for the music we are making and don't seem bothered about punk credibility. Less hung-up on fashion and more musical, they catch on to the music as it organically happens onstage. As time goes on I realize that the U.S. audiences are my favorite because they have the most natural appreciation of the music. They get it on a gut level. Maybe in the dark gloom of CBGB's they are more receptive to us. They know nothing about us—we stand or fall on the music alone, a clean shot without the "proto-hippes on the other side of punk" smear courtesy of *Sounds* magazine back in England.

Our second set at CBGB's starts at about two-thirty in the morning, and we repeat the first one with almost no variation. We are so short of material that we don't have much choice except to jam and extend all the instrumental sections in the middle of the songs. This lack of material becomes an important factor in the creation of our style because it means we have to extract as much as possible from each song just to play the required time. Although we have rehearsed a lot in London, playing in front of an audience every night for three weeks will be a different experience. The energy of an audience gives us the power to take our jams all the way out. We start meshing and pushing toward a new edge in our playing that simply doesn't happen in a rehearsal room, proving the axiom that one gig in front of an audience is worth ten days of practice.

Some people refer to our music as space jams. We are able to hit a place where with a combination of tape delay, Trenchtown beats, dissonant harmony, and Sting's soaring tenor over the top, we start sounding like a punk version of Weather Report. But with no formal agreements or rigid arrangements up-front, the playing develops naturally and we find our way by pushing, pulling, and reacting to one another. From a tight little repertoire of six or seven songs—"Landlord," "Roxanne," "Can't Stand Losing You," "Nothing Achieving," "Next to You," "Truth Hits Everybody," "Hole in My Life"—we are forced into a new freedom and a way of playing that becomes our style. We leave CBGB's that night with the sound of the crowd in our ears and a sweat-soaked sense of renewal.

We work our way up the East Coast, playing places like Willimantic, Philadelphia, Syracuse, Rochester, and Buffalo. One night we turn up in a town called Poughkeepsie to play at a venue aptly called the Last Chance Saloon. It is bitterly cold and we unload our gear from the van into deep snow. It looks like a decent place, but obviously tonight we are not going to get an audience. There are four people. These are hardy or insane souls who have braved the bone-numbing cold to see an unknown English punk band called the Police. Four? For a moment we feel a sense of doom—maybe we are fated to go under, even in this country, and suddenly the success of CBGB's feels a long way behind us. But we set up our gear and after getting something to eat are recovered enough to say, "Oh fuck it, let's play, we need the practice and at least we'll keep warm." And we hit the stage in front of our almost invisible ticketholders and give a full-on show, leaping about like maniacs, strutting, parading, and jamming our asses off. The four recipients of this mayhem respond in kind with vociferous applause, and in a perverse way we have enjoyed ourselves—there's a nice fuck-you about it, a raising of one finger to the gods. After the show everyone joins us in the dressing room and tells us how much they dug it. The manager tells us he was blown away by the performance and would love to have us back despite the pitiful turnout. We return to the motel feeling rather pleased with ourselves.

In Boston we have a booking for four nights at the Rat club, a cellar with a German theme in the middle of the city. A&M US, despite initial protestations to Miles not to bring us to America, is now getting interested. Just because we are signed to the U.K. label doesn't mean A&M US wants to get involved or put up any money. But now, after having seen us play and how we are received by U.S. audiences, they do an about-face and turn up at the Rat wearing cop outfits and sheriff's badges and handing out all manner of police items like handcuffs, rubber truncheons, whistles, and badges. This is the start of cop shop as we think of it, a pathetically literal translation of our stupid group name. It will go on for a couple of years with some of the most inane Police promotions imaginable, until we finally put our collective boot down and tell them we won't be appearing if they pull anymore of that Police shit. Along with this, of course, we have to put up with endless review headlines like IT's A FAIR COP, ARRESTING PERFORMANCE, COPS BLOW THE WHISTLE TO THE POINT OF DESPAIR.

Boston has a radio station, WBCN, whose most popular deejay is a guy by the name of Oedipus. Oedipus is playing "Roxanne" in rotation; in other words, it will be heard at least once an hour. The song, which is also being picked up by other radio stations, is becoming a hit in Boston. We're thrilled to hear this, and when we get a request from A&M to do several interviews on different stations in the area, we are ready to go. Because of the Sex

Pistols furor, the U.S. media are aware that there is something called punk or New Wave going on in Britain but have found it difficult to embrace in the form of the Sex Pistols, who were too raw, too British, and didn't have a song that they felt could be played on the radio. We fill the slot perfectly. We have a great song, they think we are a punk band, we can articulate the new scene, and we don't destroy offices or insult people—at least not to their faces.

We sell out four nights at the Rat and suddenly feel that we are on the way again, although there is no tangible success other than the audience applause each night. At this point "Roxanne" is being played only as an import and is not an official release, but now seeing the potential, A&M changes its mind about us and decides to release the album in America. Despite the rigor of travel, vans, and icy conditions, I find myself excited by our transformation from a raw nothing into something. Maybe I'm finally in the right band. I can't afford it, but I stand in a freezing motel hallway each day and call back to London to talk to Kate, to check on her and let her know how it's going with the tour. She is stoic, calm, and encouraging. She's the one with the guts, not me.

We drive out to the Midwest and into Cleveland, where we have a show at the Pirates Cove. It's late October and we pull up to the stage door in gloom and cold. Inside, the crepuscular ambience of the club is suffused with the faint smell of beer and cigarettes, the vestige of loneliness accented by the garish posters on the wall. There is a small stage at one end where we will try to take it to the people. Just as we are setting up, four or five guys who look like roadies march in and ask what the fuck do we think we are doing, and who the fuck are we. We let them know: the fucking support group. They grunt at one another and tell us that they are here to set up for Raven-Slaughter, the local headliner, and need to set up first. "Okay Okay, whatever," we say, letting them have their little power play, and take off up to the dressing room, where we piss ourselves with laughter. RavenSlaughter—Christ, in this day and age.

The group themselves eventually turn up, and we are not disappointed. In black leather, biblical hair, eyeliner, and metal studs, they look like fugitives from a Dracula film. They give us the cold shoulder—we are nothing, they are RavenSlaughter—and we try to keep a straight face, but it's difficult. The lead guitarist is called Killer and he keeps swigging straight from a bottle of tequila. In our tiny corner of the dressing room we quietly make remarks like "'Ard, ever so 'ard," and continue reading our paperbacks. After the show, their having brilliantly fulfilled all our expectations with songs about the coming darkness, Satan, werewolves, and such, we watch gently as poor old Killer heaves his guts out at the side of the dressing room—a night's work complete.

We finish the tour with another gig at CBGB's. With three weeks of playing we have gelled, and we finish with an aggressive in-your-face show with me pushing it as hard as I can because I am desperate to get back home to Kate and the imminent birth of our daughter. After lying on the floor of a fan's apartment for about an hour after the gig, staring like a zombie at a Jimi Hendrix poster, I get a Yellow Cab to Kennedy for the flight that leaves at six A.M., praying that I will make it in time. The fare uses up the last bit of money I have made from the tour, and I briefly wonder how I will get from Heathrow to Putney.

Thirteen

Kate breathes an audible sigh of relief as I enter the flat, and I echo it. She is stretched to the point of bursting, having hung on by sheer willpower until my return. A few hours later as we finish up a Chinese takeout and crawl into bed, she begins having contractions. The roles reverse: she is serene and I am a riot of nerves, walking up and down the hallway until she tells me to just relax—it will be alright. The contractions go on all night, with me calling the hospital every five minutes, wondering if we should go in yet, with about half a clue, and trying to answer weird questions like "Is she dilated?" I sit in the kitchen and eat the rest of the Chinese and wonder if I am coming down with the flu. But eventually a midwife arrives and says it's time to go, and very gingerly we get down three flights of stairs, out into the London mist, and into the newly fixed never-say-die Dyane 6 to drive about three miles an hour to St. Mary's in Chiswick.

In the hospital everything is routine and they take over without batting an eye. Kate is wheeled into the delivery room and starts giving birth immediately. I hover uselessly in one corner like a sparrow on one leg, feebly crying out, "Push," along with everyone else, but the baby doesn't come—something is wrong. After what seems like hours of effort to no avail, the doctors realize that the baby's umbilical cord is wrapped around its neck and that the incessant pushing is merely strangling the baby. They produce a medieval-looking pair of shears and yell out that they are going to cut the cord. They do it, and like a cork blowing out of a champagne bottle, my daughter enters the world. There is another tense moment of silence as she is carried over to a small table and then routinely smacked on the behind, which produces a hearty cry from the baby and a flood of tears from me, followed by insane laughter as I hug Kate and we slobber over each other. We stare at our daughter wonderingly, a life, a being, a miracle. I go home later that day overjoyed and wiped out from the experience. I call my parents, friends, and relations; tell them the news; and then, feeling fragile, pass out for about sixteen hours.

The next few days are nothing but hospital visits and getting used to the new world of parenthood we now inhabit. Stewart is sweet enough to drop by with a big bunch of flowers and kindly asks Kate, "The baby—is she mobile yet?" In a few days we have to take over, bring the baby home, and go it alone. It is a terrifying prospect; touring America is nothing compared to this. It's raining with a torrid vengeance the afternoon I pick Kate and baby Layla up from the hospital. Half numb with fear lest anything happen on the way back and mildly pissed off that the windscreen wiper works about only once every ten minutes, I drive so slowly with Kate and the baby back to Putney that I cause the traffic to back up on Hammersmith Bridge. But I don't care. "New baby, mate," I yell back to the raised fingers that are proffered from cars swerving past us.

Back in the flat we have a special room for the baby, with a cot ready to go and a tiny plastic speaker thing that I bought in Marks & Spencer to monitor the baby's breathing. We hardly sleep the first night, nudging each other all the time and nervously asking, "Can you hear her?" "I'm not sure—better take a look." And we go on like new parents the world over, agonizing and rejoicing, but meanwhile there is the small matter of a rock band with its own hungry mouth.

Miles has arranged a tour for us as the support group for the Albertos y Los Trios Paranoias. The Albertos are a comedy rock band with about eight members who enjoy great popularity on the college circuit. The pay is fifty pounds a night, and we are happy to get it, a small handout that will let us continue the fantasy for a while.

The first gig is at Bath University. Without rehearsing, we drive down from London in the late December afternoon, happy to be back together and not really knowing what to expect from this tour. It doesn't sound like our crowd—but then, we don't have a crowd. We set up our gear onstage in front of the Albertos. Though we are the support, at least we are getting paid and we are looking forward to playing in front of a packed auditorium. The hall looks as if it can hold about a thousand people, ten times larger than the matchbox-size holes we usually play in. Showtime comes and we dutifully trot out to warm the crowd up for the Albertos. As we arrive in front of our amps and drums the hall erupts into chaos. A rushing tide of black leather, spiked hair, and ripped T-shirts charge and push up against the stage as if this is the last band they will ever see. For a minute we are shocked; what the hell is going on? Is this the Albertos' crowd? But in the heat of the moment we can't stop to analyze but instead react and begin churning through our set, responding to the wave of adrenaline as if this will be our final gig. It's pandemonium; we can hardly hear ourselves, but inspired by the force in front of us, we pull off a killer show and leave the stage to a mob of scream-ing, hysterical girls calling out after us.

The poor Albertos stand on the side of the stage in shock, their faces chalky white. As we fall into the wings their drummer, Bruce, remarks with a bemused look on his face, "So that's your game, is it?" We're so blown away by what has just happened that we feel almost apologetic as if we have pulled a dirty trick; it wasn't really cricket, and we were obviously going to be a very hard act to follow. The Albertos realize that they might have made a wee bit of a mistake, but back in the dressing room we are practically bouncing off the walls. How could this be? In London we get iced, but here—here, on the outskirts of Bath we are gods.

After some casual questioning, it turns out that "Roxanne" and "Can't Stand Losing You" have both become legendary outside of London. Tonight we have witnessed the manifestation of their success. We leave through a heavy mob scene, with girls sobbing and throwing themselves at us, and this will be repeated every night of the twenty-date tour. We drive back to London that night howling with glee like winning a fight for the first time and sure that we can do it again. Arriving back in Putney about two A.M., my head spinning from the previous few hours, I open the door to the flat, trip over the baby monitor wire, curse, recover, and with barked shins creep into the bedroom—the world of mother and daughter. Kate is awake, breast-feeding the baby. I whisper in the dark, "How are you two? You're not going to believe this. . . ."

The Albertos tour comes to an end three weeks later with us feeling cocky and triumphant. For the first time in months the scenery stops moving, and instead of pacing the few feet between thrashing drums and howling audience, I unwrap Christmas presents, watch the telly, and cuddle up with Kate and our new daughter. The aroma of baby smell acts like a strange new soporific, and for a moment I relax into a becalmed state, but I know it is only a temporary lull in the proceedings. We are heading back to Germany right after Christmas to work with Eberhard again. Our relationship with him is undergoing a change. It is fast becoming evident that we are a hot new band, and working with Eberhard feels like something we don't have time for, yet we still need the money. We have agreed to do the tour. We like him, and without him we may have been forced to go our own separate ways, so on January 9 we fly back to Germany.

We do the tour of twenty dates, cruising from one German town to another and enjoying the fact that we are working and making some money, even if putting our own career on hold somewhat. But this time around, having more muscle, we insist on opening the show with four of our own songs, which are in distinct contrast to the rest of the night with its string quartet and synthesizer sounds.

One of the highlights of this show is a song called "Code Word Elvis" in which I play classical guitar with a string quartet for the opening part of the song and then race across stage at midpoint to pick up the Telecaster and whip out an electric solo. I have to put the classical guitar down quickly but carefully, extricate myself from behind the music stand, remember not to trip on my footstool, and then hurl myself across twelve feet of stage, skid into position by the amp, whip on the Telecaster, and launch into a burning solo as Eberhard raises his left eyebrow and baton, all of which is performed to the snickering attention of the German audience, waiting for me to blow it. Finishing the solo, I race back to the string quartet as a four-bar drum break takes place and recompose myself into a classical-musician demeanor to strike up some sweet arpeggios with the quartet. It is a tricky little feat, to say the least, but it goes down well with the audience every night as they place bets as to whether or not I will crash into the lead violinist.

Returning to petroleum-colored England in February 1979, we are lifted by an intense media focus that appears to dispel all doubts about our future. Although most of the world still doesn't know us, England is suddenly right behind us, with journalists pounding on the door and offers coming in from everywhere. A&M now realizes our potential and becomes eager for us to get on with the second album. There are murmurings of "don't you want to use a big studio in London, have a famous producer?"—as if that would be insurance to get the hits they want—but they don't see that the magic formula is already in place. We opt to carry on at Surrey Sound. We resolutely do not want a producer or anyone telling us what to do; we have three producers in the band. We like Nigel and the funky low-key quality of the studio in Leatherhead that provides the creative atmosphere we need, and we return.

Recording this time around feels different, for we are flooded with a new wine, the dark energy of CBGB's, the visceral energy of the stage, the tense improvisations, and the needle-stabbing surge of the crowd. Filled with this brew, we reenter the studio as if we already own it. We still have to make the record, but it comes faster this time because now we are in possession of an identity, a signature sound and style that is the music of the Police. Sting has established himself as the main songwriter and brings in new songs, a couple of which, "Message in a Bottle" and "Bring On the Night," are gems. We have a process of getting to know the song and then rearranging it to give it the Police sound, which means moving it into a place where the sound is tight, lean, and spare, the meat close to the bone. "Message in a Bottle," "The Bed's Too Big Without You," "Walking on the Moon," and "Bring on the Night" are all great songs, and we argue and fight our way into tracks that remain the tight compromise between our ideas.

As we record this time, we are fueled by the wave of excitement and ex-pectation. We have gelled as a band, and driven by the rush of playing to-gether, we are determined to push our nascent success further. Our engineer Nigel referees and nudges us along in the right general direction but lets us try out our ideas, so the atmosphere is creative, daring, in flux. In the spirit of opening up the sound of a three-piece band, I experiment with a variety of different effects pedals. Under my foot now I have a flanger, a phaser, a compressor, a fuzz box, all of which I send through the Echoplex. I rarely try any other guitar than the Telecaster because it seems to work on just about everything. We make our extended onstage jam from "Can't Stand Losing You" into the instrumental title song—"Regatta de Blanc"—of the album. With guitar harmonics and ricocheting snare drum hits from Stew-art, this piece sounds like no one else. "Deathwish," a new song of Sting's, is treated with a Bo Diddley rhythm and given a modern edge by using the Echoplex. For the intro to "Walking on the Moon," I play a big shining d minor eleventh chord that acts like fanfare to the subsequent get-under-your-skin melody. "Bring on the Night" has a beautiful classical guitar arpeggio and a pungent stabbing bass line accompanying the vocal line. "Message in a Bottle" is a masterpiece of pop song writing by Sting, and will always remain a favorite of mine. Somehow in this moment we are able to take the energy of punk and combine it with a more melodic and har-monic approach so that the result has the required edge and hipness, doesn't have the complacency or the bloated quality of earlier seventies rock. It's an unquantifiable moment, when the right three people come to-gether under the right circumstances at the right time. There is no formula for this—and we simply make it up as we go along, but always with the intention of arriving at something that has inner tension. We fight about the music but are a locked unit. Later many musicians approach us with a somewhat wry expression and mention that they wished they had thought of it. But it would never have been so, the music of the Police could have been made only by the three of us. Recording *Regatta de Blanc* is a moment that remains as one of the best in our history.

Dale and Mike, the boys from A&M, come out one night, and it is gratifying to see their spontaneous smiles as we play them "Message in a Bottle." Within two weeks we have the album in place. We can do this because we record as a performing band, with the studio almost another gig. We don't need much help other than with the engineering, and despite the banter and the sarcastic tone we take with one another, the truth is that we know where we want to go. We become a sealed unit, hermetic, impossible to penetrate. A&M sees this and leaves us to get on with it.

At this time in Britain there is a popular television show called *Rock Goes to College*. Each week a college somewhere in the country is picked as the venue for a current rock band to perform. We don't feel big enough yet to get this kind of exposure but are thrilled when we are asked to do it. We are given a date at Hatfield Polytechnic, yet another so-called important step because it is national exposure and will help propel us upward.

At home I try to be fully attentive to Kate and Layla, but I find it difficult to be as present as I should be, the success of the band tending to wash through everything, be everything, eat everything. I sense that I am walking a tightrope. The phone rings off the hook, the baby cries, the press beat on the door, the monster begins rising from the dark of the lake, and we set out on the path of success and mutually assured destruction.

On February 21 we drive up the M4 motorway, past the sign that says Hatfield and the North, a sign that groups know as a constant reminder that once again they are about to travel away from home locked in a grimy van with a pile of drums and amps. Oddly, no one to our knowledge has ever seen or been to Hatfield, and the general belief among bands is that it does not actually exist. But today we are in high dudgeon because, as if visiting the ancient ruins of Ephesus, we are actually going to see Hatfield—or at least the college.

NEXT TO YOU
SO LONELY
WALKING ON THE MOON
HOLE IN MY LIFE
DEATH WISH
FALL OUT
TRUTH HITS
BRING ON THE NIGHT
VISIONS OF " " " "
MESSAGE IN A BOTTLE
BEDS TOO BIG
PEANUTS
ROXANNE

CAN'T STAND LOSING YOU

After getting over the wonders of Hatfield, we perform in the evening to a raucous college crowd. We play "Message in a Bottle," "So Lonely," and "Can't Stand Losing You," and they roar with approval. We are nervous because this show seems to represent a chance to break through, but now fueled by the tours on the East Coast and the Albertos, we manage to stay loose enough to get through it with enough fire and conviction to deliver a strong set. Stewart and I also add backing vocals even though it's not our forte; the parts we play are too complicated for a lot of oohing and aahing, but we do it anyway. Kate has come to the show and brought along Layla, now three months old. We return to London in the A&M bus, sitting in the back. Stunned by all that is going on, I stare out at the M4, which I have traversed constantly in my life, and think, *Maybe this time . . .* I turn to Kate in the dark; the baby is asleep, but Kate whispers, "I think she might be in shock—the volume . . ."

We have two weeks off and then as if we never left, we return to the United States. We have made enough noise on our first "save the band" tour to warrant a second shot and because now we are also officially on the A&M US label. Leaving Kate and a three-month-old baby behind in London, I ride in a cab to Heathrow full of mixed feelings. This flight is to Los Angeles.

Fourteen

Beneath the plane a jeweled megalopolis spreads its wings out through the Santa Monica Mountains like a giant butterfly. We hit the runway and a feeling of entrapment floods my head, sweetened only by the assessment that maybe it was neccessary; this is where I saved myself, retooled for the future, found a mate, prepared the ground for whatever this new thing turns out to be. I stare out the window at LAX. We have three nights booked at the Whiskey.

The Tropicana Motel, with its smell of shag carpet, cleaning fluids, and chlorine from the swimming pool, is a sharp reminder of shabby Hollywood and the torpor of failure in bright sun. I wake up to the incandescent glow of California breaking through the half-torn blinds, and for a second I am filled with a sense of futility and familiar depression. I lie between the sheets for a moment to let it pass before finally pulling myself up to remember that Dukes coffee shop is part of the hotel; you never know who you might run into there.

Like a seedy joint out of a Bukowski novel, Dukes has been the hangout for many legendary writers, rockers, and assorted characters, including the Doors. I am excited to be back as part of this band but I have to shake the harsh overlit memories that beat through my brain as if to accent my nothingness, as if to remind me that while the rest of the city rolled in money, fame, and celebrity, at twenty-six I already couldn't think of a reason to crawl out from between the sheets.

Stewart and I have breakfast together. There is no one of note in the diner, and we decide to walk up the Strip to see if our name is on the Whiskey marquee. After the London winter the fizzing brightness and tremor of L.A. pour into the bloodstream like champagne, and suddenly it is intoxicating. Our name hovers over the Strip and we walk up the street laughing because it feels so good. I note the irony of being back at the Whiskey; it has hardly changed over the years, but this time around it feels different, like an enchanted portal, a point on the compass that we must pass through, and for us it's the equal of the Hollywood Bowl.

The Whiskey is sold out and we play to a hot, sweaty room. I have been on this stage before, but this is It. A&M personnel are in attendance every night, and even Jerry Moss—the M of A&M—comes to check us out. Here, away from the judiciary of London, we have credibility. No one cares about our past, only about the music we are making now. It feels just. We can succeed or fail as a band and no longer have to apologize for having picked up a guitar before the punk era.

We play tough, overdriven sets every night, blasting and improvising our way through "Roxanne," "Message," and "The Bed's Too Big," and come offstage drenched in sweat and high from the adrenaline that pumps from the audience. After the final roar of drums, bass, and guitar, we rush upstairs to the dressing room, where we collapse in a heap on the ratty sofa and chairs, dazed but triumphant. Within five minutes people begin pounding on the door, and with towels around our necks, we let them in. "You guys were great, wow, I really like your music, supercool, where do you get that sound?" The litany that is becoming familiar begins again. The dressing room rapidly gets packed wall-to-wall with fans, well-wishers, piranhas, vampires, and predators who hustle us with silky tones of persuasion, who make offers of sex and drugs—whatever it takes to get on the inside. The high buzz of animated conversation and sexual energy floods this small room over the Strip, and it feels as if the real gig is taking place in the dressing room after the show. I see someone who once threatened to kill me with a gun; he stares at me, then turns and walks away. Old friends turn up to see me, amazed but happy that I am now in this group that appears to be heading like a rocket for the big time. Adulation rolls over us in a warm wave like a strange new sun. It takes getting used to, and as faces appear and recede, I feel as if I'm standing in a hall of distorted mirrors. People are relating to us in a different way, as if we are already on a pedestal, have a power that sets us apart, and they stare at us with the milky look of adoration.

After the show we walk up the Strip and crowd into Ben Franks to sit with key lime pie and hot chocolate or scrambled eggs and hash browns while at tables around us half the audience sit and slurp on straws embedded in tall foamy-looking drinks. They pretend not to be aware of us, but it is a farce. "Our first stalkers," says Stewart. "Get used to it," says Kim, blowing a perfect smoke ring toward one of the tables.

We leave L.A. and begin zigzagging our way across the country. Faced with endless miles of black road and not enough time to get were we are going, we slump in the car stuffed with flu remedies and vitamin C in an attempt to stay well enough to perform. Austin, Houston, Dallas, Chicago: we suck up the distance, spit out the tarmac. It's March and we drive on and on and on, through endless rain and snow, great turrets of storm clouds and crackling radio static. Sleeping and snuffling, we stare though slitted eyes at the prairie, the plains, the cumulus-shrouded mountains in hopes of seeing a buffalo or an Indian reservation. We pull into rough-looking truck stops to eat hamburgers, tuna melts, and french fries in the company of large tough-looking men who could pulverize us with one hand. Beside them we look pale and effete. We get strange looks and usually don't hang around too long but rush through the gift shop on the way out, grabbing postcards, kachina dolls, and snack packs of tortilla chips. The truck stops are an all-American universe of monster trucks, engines, oversize wheelbases, CB radio, country music, and men who will fight for the US of A.

In the late afternoon as the small-town neon begins pulsing in the last streak of sunlight, we pull into a parking lot of a small concrete building. This is where we are playing; we know because our name is on a black-and-white plastic thing in front, but they have missed the *the* and it just says PO ICE—uncapitalized, the L on the ground somewhere. Someone says, "Fucking L," and we all give a weary laugh. Sitting there in his Camaro is a middle-aged man with a long grey ponytail who pulls a Marlboro out of his mouth and grins over at us. "Stingstewartandy," he drawls. "Good to meetcha a, aaam Rick. Plice eh naas recid boise ok lesgo." He is enthusiastic, and wearily we pile into the back of his Camaro to rush off to the record store where we are scheduled to make an appearance and sign albums. These in-stores, as they are called, are mob scenes where we sign not only our records but parts of anatomy and anything else that gets pushed in the direction of our Magic Markers. On the walls oversize posters in lurid colors have our faces and names, details of competitions organized through the local radio stations, and the names of the tracks on our first record.

We know nothing of these things in advance and, like drunks staring into a mirror, we are amazed to see ourselves in these places—Austin, Dallas, Chicago, Pittsburgh. Like Hollywood movie stars we hover over bins filled with Black Sabbath, Neil Young, Joni Mitchell, the Beatles, and it is thrilling because suddenly it feels that we are really a part of the music scene, like professional recording artists, and yet we've barely started. Girls push and tussle among themselves to get close to us and pull down their tops to have *Sting, Andy,* or *Stewart* written across their cleavage, giggling nervously as the Magic Marker penetrates their skin. Sex is part of the equation, sex is rock ard roll, sex rings the cash register.

Back in the Camaro, Rick points to the various turquoise-and-silver bracelets that cover his wrists and, turning down the booming reverb-laden voice of the deejay on the local radio station who is announcing our performance tonight as if it's the Second Coming, tells us that they are Navajo symbols. Dragging on the stub of his cigarette, and staring out the windscreen as if in search of rain, he describes what some of them mean—the myths, the sun climbing across the sky, the Native American conception of the world—and then, exhaling a cloud of blue smoke into the air and simultaneously revving the engine, tells us his mother was a Navajo, and we roar out of the parking lot.

At the radio station we talk "live on air" to the local deejay, Redbeard, about our exploits, what we are doing in the country, where the tour is going, where "Roxanne" came from, why the Police. There is a competitive edge in these interviews because each one of us wants to do the talking, but Stewart, who is extremely verbose, makes it hard for either Sting or I to get a word in anywhere. In the future we will do interviews separately so that we

each get our own space. Exhausted by all of this, we finally go back to the
venue, get through a sloppy sound check, and slump into a backstage corner
among beer cases, a pool table, and a set of broken chairs and pass out until
the first set. These interviews, signings, and shows are a period of intense
hard work fueled by adrenaline and willpower, but we don't complain because we are fighting to make it and maybe we enjoy a good fight. In the
United States the radio stations play only safe, formulaic music that is
proven and prescribed, that fits in with the advertisers' idea of inoffensive
middle-ground pabulum. Our music is not play-list material, and we have to
battle this convention by accepting all the radio interviews we can and pros-
elytizing for the new music scene.

We stay in low-level motels like the Days Inn and buildings with no
name other than *motel* and are constantly ill with colds, viruses, and sore
throats that pass between us like a game of Ping-Pong. It doesn't occur to
us that maybe we should ease off a fraction. We try to sleep in the car during the ride to the next gig by taking over-the-counter sedatives and wake
up a few hundred miles later hungover and groggy from the sleep that is
not sleep. American highways stretch on like a blacked-out dream, and the
motel rooms, with their weird chemical residue and mind-numbing same-
ness, must have been made by one person. With your ears roaring and
your head spinning, you think that room number from two nights back is
your number tonight as you stand in front of a tarnished-gilt seven or
nine, moronically wondering why the key won't go in, until the mental
roulette wheel rolls forward and another number clicks into place and you
feel sorry that you cursed the proprietor, the country, the promoter.
"Compassion, compassion," you murmur as you step into an eight-by-
eight room with a candlewick bedspread, the stench of Pine-Sol, and a picture of Jesus on the wall.

We travel on through a series of repeating scenes as we bounce from the
adrenaline charge of the show to the struggle to refind our motel on the outskirts of town to the early-morning call to get back in the van for the next
slogging drive. But even at this early stage people are waiting for us as we arrive to set up our gear. They extend their hands through the biting midwest-
ern chill, holding out our LP or the "Roxanne" single or a small pink

autograph book. They are polite and address each one of us as "sir." We are from England, and by most standards outside of New York or L.A., we—with our dyed blond hair, bomber suits, and narrow black pants—look as if we have arrived at the wrong party. The local bands, with their long hair, denims, and cowboy boots, give off a vibration of heavy boogie and blues and rock-and-roll machismo. We appear as martian drag queens.

This second tour of the U.S. again ends back in New York at CBGB's. It is still black and depressing but, like an old coat, is beginning to have the comfort of the familiar. New York is a rush; the electricity of the city pushes into the music. We get animal in the performance and don't fuck around. It is 1979, and though we don't have America by the balls yet, we have the knife out.

Fifteen

I lie between the sheets next to Kate and baby Layla, my ears hissing, the sensation of a helicopter whirring through my head. The familiar bed, scent of females, breast milk, fragility and nurturing the soft end of the pendulum swing, the gentle opposer to the scrape of distance, stench of tarmac, phantom highway, tedium, and death at the end of a pool cue. Swaddled in the animal comfort of touch, the low murmur of endearments, luminous swell of dreams, and the comfort of our history, I'm home. Half asleep, I burrow into the sheets as Buffalo, Chicago, New York strobe across my brain, red in a field of black.

Now that we are back in England, A&M re-releases "Roxanne"—and this time it goes into the Top Twenty. It is a moment of triumph edged with grim satisfaction, and it is hard not to indulge in a slice of "I told you so." The BBC has graciously lifted the ban on our pop song, and we are allowed to appear on *Top of the Pops*. So we give it our best with a piss-taking sort of performance, Sting singing into the camera and casually waving the mike about two feet from his head.

We cap this brief two weeks back home with a performance at the Nashville in West Kensington. This time, unlike the hollow loneliness of the year before, the place is absolute pandemonium, with lines around the block and rabid fans desperately trying to stuff themselves through the window.

Inside it is packed like an overheated jail, and I find it hard to wipe the grin off my face, as it seems only five minutes ago that we couldn't even get a gig here. Among the crowd are many fully paid-up punks who sing along with us. The barriers are down.

We leave for the U.S. once again. I am excited to get back onstage and continue our push in North America, but again I feel conflicted about leaving my family behind. It seems as if I am going off to have fun and adventure while Kate—going along with the situation in her own sweet and intelligent way—is being left alone to cope with a new baby and the poison of postnatal depression. The band and the family pull in opposite directions. It becomes like a Zen koan: "New baby, new band, where is the heart?" But I can hardly walk out of this situation; this is the shot; the arrow has finally penetrated the target; and now, with its double-edged aspect, it arrives quivering like Jekyll and Hyde. I feel like a man hanging over the edge of a cliff with a pistol at his head. In the surging maleness of it all, the band, the success, the money, power, is everything—and little thought is given to marriages, babies, or fragile situations. We have to conquer America, eat the world.

With this brew of emotion, I return to begin a tour in the southern states with Sting, Stewart, and Kim Turner, who is with us all the time now. Miles repeats the mantra that if we break the States, the rest of the world will follow. Grueling touring is still the process that works. Miles is right, but it will take three albums, three million miles, and three marriages.

After dates on the East Coast we arrive in Atlanta for a gig at the Agora Ballroom. One of the first things we are confronted with is a "Roxanne" contest. This has been organized without our knowledge by a local radio station, and when told about this event, we are mildly disturbed—as we are to be the judges. We feel that we have to take a stand about women being treated like cattle, but we are in a double bind because the radio station that has been promoting us heavily thinks we'll love it and so we have to zip our mouths shut. The girls, on the other hand, are loving it and there is no end of willing contestants. The idea is that each girl will try to become the very embodiment of Roxanne, an impoverished prostitute.

After we have ripped our way through the show and toweled off, we reappear on the stage, this time in a judging capacity, and the contest is announced. Our steely nonchauvinist resolve goes out the window as fifty scantily clad girls troop out onto the stage in front of a whistling and cheering audience. Dressed in all manner of sexy underwear and fetish garments, many of the girls are stunning, along with a few assorted insane ones whom only the demented would purchase from the flesh market. But even for these poor creatures this is a moment of glory; you have to admire their ingenuity at least as they imaginatively show their affinity with the strumpet, the tart, the trollop, the whore, the sister of mercy. "Okay, so we're sexist pigs," we say to one another as we stroll up and down in front of the line of giggling girls, our eyes roving over the Roxanne wannabe flesh. "Now look what you've started," I say, nudging Sting. "I didn't mean this to happen," says Sting, pausing in front of a pulchritudinous young beauty in stockings, garter belt, and a cute little pair of furlined fuck-me boots.

You make a song and if you are lucky, it lives, enters the world, is sung, whistled, purchased, memorized, becomes the soundtrack—the witness to the unfolding union, is remembered with joy or bitterness, a smile, a sighing stare into the mirror, and uninvited crawls between the sheets to stay with you forever. It seems only a blur since the three of us were in Paris, Stewart and I watching *Star Wars,* mouthing "May the force be with you" back at the screen, and Sting wandering around Pigalle and observing the demimondaines, the seeds of "Roxanne" sprouting in his mind.

On the stage of the Agora it is tempting to pick one of the short fat girls because she is courageous and beautiful on the inside, but in the end a sexy dark-haired girl in corsets is led to the front, and with Sting raising her hand-cuffed wrist above her head and the lust-filled drunken mob below slurring out the chorus of "Roxanne," with half-embarrassed, half-libidinous looks on our faces, we proclaim her—She.

We head out of Atlanta and into the Bible Belt, playing through Louisiana and Florida and then up into Oklahoma, Colorado, and Arizona. There is no time for sightseeing but just the hamburger, fries, and coffee grind, the I-90s, the I-65s, overpass, underpass, the turnoff for Baton Rouge, the detour outside of Denver. But despite the grueling hours, the experience is like a torch to the blood. The arching skies of the West stretch over our heads like an infinite canopy, a powder-blue canvas as we barrel, a boatload of Vikings, toward the next town. Each night, despite the hours and the miles traveled, we work and push to galvanize the audience into heated response, beat them into submission, bend them to our will, seduce, collude, conspire, transform. We don't leave the stage until we have won.

"Roxanne" is now a hit, and the crowd sings it with us every night. We leave each town with a tinge of sadness because it was so good there. *Why leave?* you wonder, the traces of last night's adrenaline hanging off the side of your brain, until one of the others tells you to get over it, Phoenix tonight. We are like sailors constantly sailing off to the next port, leaving behind scattered fragments of promises: call me, write us, yeah next time, back in a few months, yeah you too—a dirt path of expectancy, the faint optimism of a future shared. We meet hip, savvy people who want to befriend us, talk to us, and take us to their homes. They give us books, paintings, thick joints of sinsemillia, red wine, and offers of beds, food, comfort, and succor. There always is a friendly fat guy with a beard who wants to carry our gear and hang with the band.

Every night there is also an offer to p-a-r-t-y. You pile into a Firebird or a Chevy with a bunch of kids, a tape goes into the deck, and "Roxanne" is played at high volume while a joint is passed around, followed by a bottle of tequila; everyone screams, "You don't have to put on the red light," and as we skid into an American suburb the stars in lush cluster against the deep dome of Colorado sky are broken only by the golden arches of McDonald's.

Across the lawn and into the house we go, trying not to trip on the sprinklers. "Don't piss off the neighbors," someone giggles. The TV in the front room is on with Reagan's withered mug moving silently in a black-and-white pantomime. More music goes on. "What are you into, man?" "I dunno—anything." "Yeah, cool—how about some Marley?" Outside someone retches violently into a bush and then begins laughing and says, "Fuck, man, my fuckin' shoes." A red guitar appears from nowhere. We look at the record collection: Zeppelin, Sabbath, Marley, Velvet Underground, the Stooges, Bowie, the Police. We lean back into the couch, sprawling like live bait—we have been captured. We stare at fluffy animals on top of the TV set, and I think of James Mason as Humbert Humbert when he turns up at Lolita's house at the end of the film and asks her to leave with him. "This is America," I say to no one in particular, and I can't decide if I love it or hate it.

I begin going into the guitar stores in these towns, on the lookout for the odd vintage beauty that can sometimes be found at a bargain price, and I come up with a red '62 Stratocaster, a killer blond 1958 ES 175, a Martin D28. The George Gruhn store in Nashville sends an emissary at eight A.M. one morning as we are leaving the motel to drive to Arizona. With my breath freezing in the air, I climb into the van and hand over five hundred dollars for a tangerine-colored Gretsch Chet Atkins. Most of these guitars are paid for by Kim Turner, who makes a careful note of how much is paid out on my behalf. He always shakes his head in disapproval, asks me if I can afford it—wife and baby at home—then hands over the money. Despite our burgeoning success, we are still existing off the gig money; actual recording royalties will not turn up for another two years after going through the meat grinder of the record-company accounting department. But I am thrilled finally to have the finances to buy guitars, remembering when I was reduced to just one battered old nylon string a few years earlier.

Reinforced by the emphatic response each night, we reach a new confidence in our stage performance. The shows become a conduit to chance and we push out toward the edge. The instrumental break of "Roxanne" gets extended to epic proportions, and within it we find new licks, new territory, new grooves, so that the improvisation becomes a piece unto itself. "The Bed's Too Big Without You" gets a jazzy reverbed-out treatment full of iteration, repercussive snare, and springing bass lines: punk jazz. "Can't Stand Losing You," with its added high-drama key change (F major to B major) and interchange between us and the crowd, brings the set to a climactic ending every night and leaves them hanging from the rafters.

I get to know Ian Copeland, our agent and Stewart's other brother, a little better, as he is often at our gigs. I ask him about his agency who else is on

the roster, etc. He replies that his number two band after us is Robin Lane &
the Chartbusters. My former wife. I pull another Bud Light out of the crate.

One night in Boston in a surreal out-of-body experience, I get it—our
thing, whatever it is they like about us. We have been going so fast that
about all we have time for is brief sweaty thanks that whatever it is we are
doing is working and then we're gone. Halfway through "Can't Stand Losing You" at the Paradise, in what must be something like an endorphin high,
my head zooms offstage and I see us from the audience viewpoint; for a second I see it—it's cool. But I don't want this information; it'll fuck me up; I
stomp another box on the stage.

Now that we are achieving minor fame, a rotund smiling Hispanic man visits
us from time to time. An executive at A&M, his name is Bob Garcia. He
drops out of the sky like a visiting angel into the maelstrom. We are always
glad to see him, for it is as if the cavalry or our fairy godmother has arrived
and for a moment the shabby motel, the stinking van, lighten like a distant
memory and we get the perfume of the real world again, the place that has
been obliterated by the surge and grind of touring. Bob has a wit and an acid
humor that key in nicely with ours, and for a few days it is like having a gen-
erous uncle around as he takes us out to eat, buys us VapoRub, and checks us
in to the Bates Motel. With plenty of gossip and an encyclopedic knowledge
of books and movies, he entertains and mothers us for a few gigs before getting back on the plane to Hollywood to make a report. He will stay the course
with us.

Toward the end of the tour we play in Cleveland again. We are interviewed on local TV before we get to the hotel. We mention having been
in Cleveland before and our good mates RavenSlaughter—good eggs,
those boys—and then go on to the local legendary rock-and-roll hotel
Swingos. When we get there RavenSlaughter are all waiting in the lobby
for us and want to have a drink, go to the bar, chat about old times. They
saw our interview and are very grateful for the mention, so we have
drinks.

The after-show scenes at the gigs begin to take on a sycophantic quality.
There is a subtle undertow to the dialogue now; need, desire, possession,
flow beneath the surface, the dolorous chord that is not about music but

about power, heat, control. And with glossy words and eyes fizzing like carbonated water, they try to fold us in meshes of silk. "Hi . . . I'm Julie, why don't you let me show you around? I have some excellent grass; do you like champagne?" You realize what is happening and erect a psychic shield that will stay in place for the next several years if not forever.

Sixteen

After the exotic climate of the Deep South and the wide skies of the western states, London 1979 is like a pie in the face, and for a minute we experience culture shock in our own home. We have a week off before we begin a tour of the U.K., for the first time as headliners, but we are too wiped out even to speak to one another, knowing that before we've even rolled over in bed we will be thrashing it out onstage again.

I stare out the window in Putney at dark rain and rivulets of water streaming into the drains with LCC embossed on their iron grids. Befuddled and jet-lagged, I'm confused by the way England seems to have shrunk in size while I was away. Kate and I go to the local Chinese restaurant with the baby, who sits in a high chair in front of the lazy Susan, throws rice on the floor, and then begins crying inconsolably. The TV drones in the living room with the sound of BBC voices while we make pasta, open a bottle of Beaujolais nouveau, and try to get back to where we were.

We walk across Putney Green to the river, where we push Layla in a baby stroller along the path at the side of the Thames. Kate wears a bright red coat, and the streaming gold of her hair floats out in the wind as we talk and make cooing sounds to our daughter. I stare at my wife as if seeing her for the first time, the slender form, the Botticelli face, the grey-green eyes, the soul. "I'm lucky," I croak into the wind, and put my arm around her. A young couple come toward us on the path. "My God," says the man, "aren't

you"—he says my name—"love your band. Do you mind?" Paper and pen
are struggled for, found, and proffered in the freezing wind that comes off
the river. I take off a glove and scrawl my name, our moment gone.

Our popularity in Britain having now reached a point where we can be
deemed headliners, we finally have the pulling power and are to begin in
Scotland.

The stage at the Glasgow Apollo slopes downward to a drop of about
twelve feet. The edge disappears into blackness, and in the heat of the moment it would be easy to dance off it. We pogo about on this incline, with
the Scottish audience chanting and screaming. The balcony sways, bending
up and down as if it is about to shatter, but oblivious to the fragility beneath,
the fans jump up and down as if tempting fate. This is our first gig as headliners in the U.K., and with a crowd surrounding the hotel and waiting outside the Apollo, it's already out of control. I hit my pedals, leap in the air,
run around the stage, and pray that we are not about to witness a tragedy.
Toward the end of the show we do a song called "Be My Girl—Sally" which
after the initial chorus has a monologue from me about a hapless individual's
love affair with a blow-up doll. I always deliver this ditty in a Yorkshire accent, as it seems to give it the right tone, and even this unlikely piece gets
chanted along with, and we all rise to a crescendo with "And I only have to
worry in case my girl wears thin."

Back in the dressing room, drenched in sweat and sitting among piles of little tartan-wrapped presents, we remark about the bouncing balcony, amazed
that the whole thing didn't collapse. Later we find out that the Apollo has been
condemned.

We leave the Apollo thinking we are going to walk to a nearby club, but
there is a mob of teenage girls yelling our names and coloring them with
their sweet Scottish brogue and we have to run, with the girls in hot pursuit.
We run past redbrick walls, off licenses, pubs, a couple of people passed out
in the gutter. As I run I hum the melody of "I Belong to Glasgow" and
think of Hank Marvin. We end up in front of Charlie Parker's, the local hip
nightclub where we are expecting a warm welcome and a bit of special treatment, having just played the Apollo, but typically the bruiser on the door
won't let us in because, as he grimly points out, we are too casually dressed.

"Yeer tuee cazshally driised," he slurs, leaning his gorilla-size torso against the lintel as if to say "go on, fuck with me, why doncha." "Let's go," I say, "*Planet of the Apes* is on the telly." We get into the limo, which has finally caught up with us. I go off into paroxysms about Scottish peasants, Charlie Parker jazz, and the fucking Apollo. Back in the hotel bedroom I open the minibar and end the night with a Schweppes Bitter Lemon and a packet of shortbread biscuits.

An American group called the Cramps is on tour with us. They are on Miles's label, Illegal, and by conventional standards they are weird. Their guitarist is intentionally nasty to look at, with one side of his head shaved, a pockmarked face, and half of his hair bleached white; the singer is Lux Interior, who creeps about the stage, chanting and moaning, while his pretty girlfriend, Poison Ivy Rorschach, stands there as if catatonic. They call their music psychobilly. The audience hates them, but I like them, for at least they are attempting to do something different. But after a while their act palls. What they are selling is an attitude; what you are supposed to come away with is uncertain. It is like watching or listening to a B horror movie (which is probably the intended effect), but is that what you want from music? Compared with them we are normal, and a number of the British rock press try to make a meal out of this, preferring to cast their lot with no-chance weirdness than with anyone who tries to put an honest song across—and we are criticized for playing too well.

We are on a fast upward swing, and you can hear the knives being sharpened. Our presence appears to be a challenge to some of the press, who attempt to deride us because we have good songs, can play our instruments, and have a flash and bravado that have already engendered a fanatical following. One critic attempts to put us down as old-fashioned rock; I wonder, then, if our music with its unique sound and diverse sources is old-fashioned, what, then, is the new fashion? Is it punk? That lasted for all of five minutes.

Despite all of this, *Melody Maker* has sent a journalist to Glasgow to write a big story on us. He has us in convulsions when he tells us that a few nights back he looked down the sheets and noticed the size of the feet of the woman with whom he was sleeping, realizing with a shock that he has been in love with a transsexual and on inquiry the next morning finds out that she had once been a he. And what was that you were saying about the Cramps being weird? The truth is that the Cramps, once you get past the mask, turn out to be rather nice, normal people.

We finish the tour in London at the Lyceum Ballroom, with fans in the front whom we now see at every show, their white arms stretching up toward us like the necks of hungry swans.

In Holland we play the Pink Pop Festival, a gigantic open-air festival that takes place every June. We hit the stage in the early afternoon to play to a crowd of several thousand Dutch rock fans. We start the set at a frantic pace and I look over at Stewart with a snarl, telling him to fucking slow down, but we roar on in the heat of the afternoon and I feel as if I am swimming through the air as the sun beats down, the music wails, the crowd surges, and blistering white light erases the little red signals on my pedal board. When I hit the buttons I can't tell if they are on or off. I don't know what I am doing; I feel blind and deaf but by instinct make it through to the end of the set. The crowd howls and John Peel, the British deejay par excellence, intones something salutary over the PA, and in a moment of sweaty inspiration we leap fully clothed from the high backstage edge into a swimming pool below as a phalanx of press cameras snap like guns. The next day we are all over the papers, grinning, triumphant, arrogant, and wet. John Peel has endorsed us, and in our mind this is as good as winning an award. In the U.K., once you raise your head above the crowd, the media is a beast that you either ignore or slay. With John Peel's stamp, we feel we have at least slipped some poison into its throat. The tour continues with twelve more shows in the England and then back into Europe. We arrive in Amsterdam to play at the Paradiso. We are there a day ahead, and what better to do than go shopping for things we don't need? I go looking for something nice for Kate and a toy for Layla but end up buying a pair of fancy-looking red ankle boots with big studded soles. I think they look supercool and decide to wear them onstage that night. As we begin the show and I stomp on my pedal board to make a tricky but required effects change, nothing happens and I think, *Oh fuck, now what?* then realize that the studs on my showoff boots are hitting the flat surface of the board and still leaving a gap, which stops me from being able to press the switch down.

I keep missing things and my sparkling guitar sound is reduced to a flat buzz. This isn't good, and cursing and sweating, I begin a peculiar crouching motion, trying to smack the fucking switches down with the side of my foot. These antics are definitely not those of a guitar hero; Sting and Stewart look over at me with bemused looks as I curse the bastard who made these nasty red things that are now crippling me. After the show I toss the boots into a trash can and write a new rule for guitarists: never wear new shoes onstage, especially if they are red with spiked soles.

Sting is fast becoming a media star. With his Slavic good looks, tenor voice, and moody arrogance, he is perfect fodder for the starmaker machinery. Stewart makes comments to the press about how he created Sting, realizing at even this early date that this is how it's going to be, but he also makes some more PC comments about how the singer always gets singled out and how lucky that the face of the band—our face—is Sting's. We have a publicist by the name of Keith Altham, a cheery bloke who carries the atmosphere of fifties London, skulking Soho, and glossy eight-by-ten photographs. Yet he is the publicist for many stars, including the Who, and is used to wheeling and dealing with the press. He has quickly seen Sting's potential and has fed him to the press like goldfish food. When he bursts into the dressing room of the Brighton Dome one night to tell us gleefully about some publicity stunt for Sting, the writing is on the wall. Although at the time Stewart and I try to raise a "What about us?" argument, Keith—looking hurt and pained—explains that not just Sting but all of us, all three of us, are going to be stars, megastars, not one but the whole group. In the end we all get more than our fair share of press, almost to the point of nausea. Sting also realizes he is perfect fantasy material for the hungry maw of the tabloids, and he doesn't deny them. The truth is that this attention to our singer rather than causing friction only powers us further, although underneath there is the lingering shadow that maybe he will, in the time-honored phrase, "go solo," that Sting will become STING, with the band having been a fantastically successful launching pad for him, the rock from which he will push off into his own career. He'll make comments to the effect that ambition is stronger than friendship—"I'm out for myself and they know it"—but right now, in the summer of '79, there's no sign of that. Only a fool would walk away from this kind of success.

As the summer approaches things heat up even more with all the noise surrounding the film *Quadrophenia,* in which Sting has a small part playing one of the mods, the Ace Face. But the media play it up as if he has the starring role and he overshadows little Phil Daniels, the central character of the movie. Pictures of our singer now appear in the British tabloids with frequency, and it appears that the band is moving into the center of British life.

The film premiers at the Gaumont in Leicester Square, and we arrive in black limos to walk up a red carpet in a hail of light. Dazed and smiling, you walk up the crimson strip like a grinning zombie, all eyes on you as cameras flash like white lightning. You have seen it on the telly, and here you are, a wave of vertigo creasing your brain as somewhere far below a crowd waves at you and you float like a moth into the soft twilight of the foyer. This glittering ball-gowny parade seems a long way from standing on a small, sweaty stage in Des Moines or Buffalo, another reality that is like an end result too early in the game. As we trip down the aisle among the buzz of glittering conversation, I remember that at the back of the Gaumont there is a spot of redbrick wall where we graffitied our name less than two years ago. It's probably still there, unless the rain has washed it off.

With *Quadrophenia* our name is everywhere and we surge forward like a Viking ship, with Sting as the bowsprit. This tide of energy now seems unstoppable, and we bring it to a peak by topping the bill at the Reading Festival on August 24, 1979.

Held at the height of summer each year, Reading is the number one rock festival in Britain, and to headline it is a clear stamp of success. We arrive in the late afternoon to the sprawling festival site. There is a crowd of thirty thousand out in the muddy field beyond the stage. Backstage we sit in a tent with our feet on planks of wood because of the mud. The smell of mud and canvas mixes with the crowd's buzzing noise in the field, and I remember sitting on a hard wooden bench beneath the big top of Billy Smart's Circus between my parents, terrified as they laughed out loud at lurid clown antics, ice cream dripping down my woolly sweater and pee running down my legs.

We can't sound check because of the vast army of fans out front, but smiling faces keep appearing around the tent flap to wish us well and check on our well-being. Various luminaries from A&M drop in to see us. "Alright, boys? Good show," they say. Miles and Kim poke their head through the canvas flap and give appraising professional stares.

I have Kate and Layla with me; Sting has his son, Joe, and wife, Frances; and tonight it feels as if we are attending our own coronation. Outside the tent we hear the grind and thrum of Lemmy's Motörhead, the roar of the crowd—can we follow that? A small moment of paranoia—that guitarist sounds to . . . we have to go out there and blow the crowd away . . . be the best band . . . this is *Reading*, the tension like a tightly wound E string.

Weird—this mix of confidence and vulnerability, like thick cream in the gut. Is it time to reinforce with a quick toot? We have to go out there and do it—don't want to let the side down. Some people call this the willies, or stage fright, but it's more like a flesh-eating spider crawling through your liver. But wait, we're— The moment of madness and self-doubt passes, and with nothing more than a couple of sips of pinot grigio, we exit the tent.

In the already chill evening we mount the stairs to climb from the dark into the light, and a roar like a crashing wave rolls across the stage, drums explode, and we rocket into the first song.

This is the biggest crowd we have played to, and it's like trying to take control of a writhing beast. But we are intense, furious, tenacious. Sting takes command of the crowd, and they are willing conspirators who sing, chant, and clap along until we finish with a roaring "Can't Stand Losing You." It's a moment of triumph, and as I descend the steps to the backstage area Lemmy is standing there and he leans forward and whispers into my ear, "Who smells of roses, then?"

The evening is now topped off backstage with a little ceremony as A&M presents us with gold records for *Outlandos d'Amor*, but as we stand there with big smiles and popping flashes, a dissolute arbiter of punk, Mark P of *Sniffin' Glue*, staggers into the scene, drunk and yelling epithets about betrayal and bullshit. Our success is like the ultimate letdown of punk, the signifier of its ultimate failure. From his perspective we are the destroyers of the dream, and he staggers about, clumsily knocking down a child. At this point Stewart strides over and tells him to fuck off and he is hustled away, sobbing. It is a moment shot with pain and embarrassment and I feel for him as I stand in the mud, gripping my first gold record with press cameras flashing. For him the shining beacon of punk has been pissed on by barbarians. We didn't carry out his agenda, but that was never in the cards.

Two weeks after the Reading Festival, our first single from our second album is released. "Message in a Bottle" enters the charts at number eight and rises to number one in its second week. We set out on another tour of the U.K. as the headlining act again. The tour is an intense rush of hysteria and pandemonium. Somehow we have morphed into a band that girls adore, and trying to leave the venue each night, we run a gauntlet of desperate sobbing females and a waving forest of records, photos, and autograph books, hands, arms, and the occasional bared breast. This state of affairs is interrupted rudely one night when we play a gig at the New Theatre in Oxford. Halfway through the show, the doors at the back of the theater burst open and a gang of about thirty skinheads in black leather, bovver boots, and a host of swastika tattoos march in. They come to the front of the theater and stand in a line below us. After a few minutes they begin chanting, "Sieg heil, sieg heil," up at us. By now the auditorium is crackling with tension. Sting takes his life—our lives—in his hands and invites them up. All thirty of them mount the steps and come onto the stage with us. Meanwhile, we have never stopped playing. The Skins begin pogo'ing all over the stage and turn it into a mosh pit. The curtains close, so now it's just us and them in a small enclosed space. The violence as they smash into one another and crash into the drums and amps is intense. But Sting is from Newcastle and has seen plenty of this stuff before. He takes control of the situation, lets one of them sing into the mic and then basically tells them to fuck off. He's faced them down; they seem to accept it and now, having done their bit, leave the theater to make a problem somewhere else. The curtains open and we finish the show to those of the audience that are left. The promoter of this show is a very tough guy from the East End of London. The following week he visits Oxford with a few friends and delivers divine retribution. "They're not gonna fuck up my shows," he says.

We finish our headlining tour and return to the U.S. Our first gig is three nights at the Diplomat Hotel. For the past two tours of the U.K. we had a guy named Dave driving the gear from gig to gig and helping set up the equipment. Besides Kim Turner, he is our only roadie. He is a truck driver from the West Country of England. A lovely guy who is the salt of the earth, we all really appreciate his efforts and fondly always call him "Doive" in homage to his rural accent. On the third day of the gigs at the Diplomat Hotel, Kim by chance gets into the hotel elevator with Dave and asks where he is going. Dave with a sad look on his face tells Kim that he is going to the airport and follows that with "Oim leavin' the band—can't take it no more." He tells Kim that the pressure is too great and that he is now drinking an entire bottle of scotch a day to handle it, and heads off to Kennedy Airport. That night a new guy turns up—Danny Quatrochi, a guitar player from New Jersey. He pulls in his friend Jeff Seitz, a drummer from New Jersey. Both are very good musicians who agree to do this only on a temporary basis—but in fact they stay right through to the end and even beyond. Doive goes back to England and becomes a legend in the annals of the band. Eventually, T-shirts are made with his passport photo on the front, we start a religion of Doive, and it goes on and on and on. Becoming simpatico with our new New Jersey crew, Sting, Stewart, and I acquire Hoboken accents and become versed in the ways of Jersey subculture.

In October *Regatta de Blanc* is released and enters the U.K. charts at number one. But instead of capitalizing on our British success and enjoying this moment of glory, we perversely go back to the U.S. to play in kennel-size clubs with undersize audiences who have never heard of us. America is so vast that all we can do is hope to invade it like a virus or expand in it like the mitosis of a cell. It might take years, or the rest of our lives. As we bask in the number one spot three thousand miles across the Atlantic, we ignominiously head down a set of sunless steps in Virginia Beach to play in a gloomy cellar filled with beer drinkers. We are merely the evening's entertainment, our name in white chalk on a board behind the bar; tomorrow, Bret and the Falcons. It is a bitter pill to swallow, but encouraged by Miles, we try to keep the pioneer spirit going as we work our way through a new frontier, despite the fact that in our own country we are kings.

Seventeen

Staring across the dark at a cobweb-decorated bar serving Budweisers and Coors Light, I feel as though we are in someone else's movie; but with faltering resolve, we announce to the frat boys that tonight's entertainment—us— are actually number one in the United Kingdom right now. The response is not the roar of Reading, but the strangled sound of voices giving a half-hearted "yeah" through a can of slurped Bud.

After a restless night with the sound of the Atlantic a few feet from the window deliberately mocking our plight, I decide to elevate my hungover mood by shopping at the local Woolworth's. It's situated on the promenade overlooking the beach, and I wander in from the brightly lit scene of photo kiosks, weight scales, and slot machines as the gusting wind blows the smell of candy floss in my face and the gulls overhead screech and dive for scraps of hot-dog bun in the trash cans. Inside the store the salt smell of the ocean blows in and fine grains of sand cover the wooden floorboards, so they constantly need sweeping. I trudge around, desultorily picking my way through the goods. Maybe I can find something for Layla—a shoe scraper, tooth-powder, a thing for deboning salmon, a never-fail corkscrew, assorted buttons in a box. After ten minutes, feeling bored, I get a pair of baseball boots and a can of pink paint. I pay and go over to the soda fountain, slide onto the chrome-rimmed red leatherette and lean across the shiny Formica to read down the list of malteds, root beers, and shakes. I order a giant shake with ice cream, banana, and peach called a Virgin Explosion from a middle-aged blond, a Shelley Winters look-alike who says, "What'll it be, hon?" her ruby-colored lips exuding the word *hon* as if she is chewing a stick of gum. "I'd like a Virgin," I say. She stares at me for a second and then, without batting an eye, says, "You can keep your hands offs me, limey," and bursts into convulsive laughter at her own joke as she slings the ingredients into a glass. I laugh too, and briefly wonder what it would be like to have sex with her, but move on quickly from that vision. I chug the Virgin down and a few minutes later, feeling sick and wasted, return to the motel with the boots and pink paint to collapse on the bed opposite the open window.

After half an hour the effects of several pounds of white sugar have been partially nullified by enzymes, and apart from a mild feeling of having been assaulted by a herd of enraged cows, I am fit enough to undertake the task of boot painting. I gingerly open the can of paint with a quarter and place it on the bedspread beside me. As I lean forward to pick up the boots, the can gently tips sideways to create a nice pink lake in the middle of the bed. "Damn, shit, fuck!", I cry to the Andrew Wyeth print on the wall, and leap off the bed like a scalded cat. I have to do something, get the pink paint from hell off the bed, but I need it for the boot job and I pull the dripping bedspread from the bed and upend it over the can on the floor, hoping desperately to get some of it back into the can. A meager amount oozes back in, while the rest just stays there or throws itself into the shag to smirk at me in triumph.

I rush into the tiny bathroom with the bedspread and try to stuff the whole thing into the sink with the tap running. Nothing moves and I quickly conclude that Woolworth's paint is made out of horse glue. Now the washbasin has a thick coating of pink. Almost in tears, I quietly close the door on the carnage with a feeling of bitter remorse. I hate Virginia Beach, hate it. I try not to drip pink on the tobacco brown shag as I cover the boots in a lurid rose. It occurs to me that Layla, who is still less than a year old, would probably like this color and would probably drag these boots across the bedroom and chew the laces. I need to call Kate, who is back there bobbing like a lone cork on the ocean, and I feel pain. Great as all of this is—touring the hamlets of the U.S., playing to tiny audiences, with somewhere at the back of your mind the idea that with the winnings you'll be able to provide for a family—it's tough to be away from those you love. I pull out a photograph and stare at a picture of a beautifully smiling Kate with our baby in her arms, then look up at the tawdry room I'm in and think, *Christ, we've got to pull this off.*

The boots are wet and the paint seems to have shrunk them one size smaller, but there is just enough left to do the laces. I lift them up onto the windowsill and quickly whip the paint onto the laces, and it all goes well enough except for a few pink streaks running down the exterior wall of the motel. *Shit job,* I say to myself in the mirror over the bright pink bathroom sink. *Why don't you fuck off?* replies the mirror. *Okay,* I say to the reflection, wiping a dollop of pink into my hair, *fuck you too.* Holding my suitcase in one hand and the boots in the other, I pass through the lobby quickly to meet the others outside in the pale watery light of Virginia Beach. "What happened to your hands?" asks Kim. "Oh, nothing," I say, trying to look unconcerned about my hands, which now look as if they have been painted for an exotic ritual. "It's calamine lotion, you know—those bloody mosquitoes." I hold up the boots inside the van for all to admire. "Please, I haven't had lunch yet," says Sting. "You offering those to the Tate?" says Stewart. I will wear these boots for the next few years as they get photographed on different stages around the world. I hang them out the window, where they jiggle and bounce, roses in the Virginia sun; inside we pass out and dream of the glory two weeks past.

BRIDGEHAMPTON, AUGUST 18, 1983

I stare at my open Samsonite. The fabled pink boots sit on top of everything like two small exotic birds. By now they gave been around the world three times, photographed by Leica, Nikon, Canon, Minolta, and Pentax cameras; stomped on the pedal board; trekked from endless dressing room to endless stages; emerged icy from cargo holds; wrapped my feet in the familiar; flashed in the faces of the front row; witnessed fights, arguments, and bad jokes; and acquired their own very distinct smell. But the pink is wearing thin. . . .

We get to Tennessee and Kim, Stewart, and I pull into a weird-looking diner with a giant yellow chicken on the roof, the bird above presumably signifying the meal below. There are not many people in the place except for three guys who look like extras from the movie *Deliverance*. A very bad feeling emanates from their table, and almost on cue they begin snarling and spitting in our direction, warning us to get out or they will kill us. They don't like our hair; they don't like our clothes; and did one hear the word *faggot*, or is that something on the menu? Stewart Copeland, my hero, gets up and in so many words tells them to prove it or fuck off. Stewart is big, lean, and threatening, and they zip their mean little mouths shut and stare at their food like whipped dogs. We carry on eating but don't stick around for too long, just in case they have reinforcements, but we pass their table on the way out with an attitude noting the smell and the spittle that greases the tabletop.

In the middle of this American leg (*leg* always being the term used, to the point where you feel that rather than playing music, you are having intercourse with a centipede), we arrive at Cape Canaveral. The reason we are here, apart from playing a gig at nearby Miami, is to film a video for "Walking on the Moon," which is to be our next single release. We have a special pass to see the rockets and spaceships of the 1960s, and we clamber about this old technology that has actually been into space and I think about Dan Dare and the Mekon and *Journey into Space*. We begin the daft process of illustrating the song by miming the lyrics and larking about on giant fins and retro-boosters, etc. This is a couple of years before MTV and the era of solipsistic video. Handheld super 8 and 16mm with introspective victim attitudes are still a thing of the future. We are still in the Beatles era of happy, larking-about personality video, and our efforts are based mostly on this alone: our job on camera is to shine.

Before we leave the bright sun and yet weirdly unpleasant atmosphere of Florida, we have one more show—at Disney World. This turns out to be strange even by our standards. We are doing it for the money, a mighty eight thousand dollars, which seems astronomical. We feel uneasy about it, as if we have let down our guard. It's not good for street credibility, but it sure will help with the expenses.

Like ghosts in the Floridian sunlight, we arrive at Magic Kingdom and are greeted by a tanned and smiling automaton who leads us through the labyrinth of underground corridors that stretch for miles in every direction. We pass Disney personnel who walk with giant badges of Mickey or Pluto and wear fixed smiles like the Stepford wives. It's chilling. We realize that we have made a mistake, but the contract has been signed and we have to play or be exterminated. We are led to a small concrete bunker, where we are told to sit and wait for further instructions. Someone makes a remark about Eva Braun, and raising a plastic Donald Duck cup to my mouth, I cackle. At zero 1500 hours automaton 60001 70034 reappears at the door to lead us to our place of duty. We trudge back through the underground labyrinth, the Disbot says, "In there," and we see a room set up with our amps and drums. "But it's underground, no one wills see us," bleats one of us pitifully. "It goes up," says Disbot. "Play when I tell you." We take up our positions, and a few moments later a red light comes on. "Now," says Disbot with a final dazzling smile. "Roxanne," wails Sting, and we ascend upward to Disney World, feeling like Daniel in the lions' den.

Staring over the perimeter at us in wonderment are the good folk of the Midwest, who gaze down at us with a blank expression as we surface like a noisy German U-boat. For the next five or six minutes we play to mums, dads, grandmas, and sticky little kids all full of McDonald's. With the spinning rides of Disney World proving a greater attraction, they wander off, leaving us with a slender crowd of punky-looking kids who in the garish neon of D World appear like frail little aliens. We find out later that we have been playing on the Tomorrowland Terrace, but to us it felt like Sunday night at the London Palladium—with the final humiliation being our exit on the downward-spiraling stage, still playing, our voices and instruments growing smaller and smaller, like canaries in a coal mine.

As a reward for enduring the Disney experience, Miles decides that we should now go to prison (or rather, go to a prison and play for the inmates), as it will help keep up our gritty street image—POLICE PLAY IN PRISON, COPS BEHIND BARS, that sort of thing. In fact, we have a gig booked at the Terminal Island prison in San Pedro, Los Angeles County.

We drive at night to the prison from Hollywood, where we are staying at the Chateau Marmont. We are not sure what to expect: a riot, gunfire, searchlights, or mere indifference. Someone makes a joke about cutting out a couple of bars and tries to throw the stub of a joint out onto the road, but the confluence of speeding car and wind blow it back in and we spend five minutes leaping about like idiots, trying to extinguish the renegade sparks.

My mind races through various prison scenes: *Riot in Cell Block 11, Jail-house Rock, White Heat, Cool Hand Luke, Caged Heat, I Am a Fugitive from a Chain Gang.* This will be my second time in a California prison. The irony of my visiting as a Policeman this time is not lost on me.

We arrive in San Pedro, a small coastal town, and it's like something out of an old Bogart movie. Like monstrous shadows, the ships look as if they might have come from the Far East, might contain vast quantities of heroin or falcons from Malta. We find the prison and, after a complicated ritual at the gate, drive into the yard, ready to entertain the inmates as "the Police." The truth is that in this prison they have a music program but are very short of instruments, so as well as thrilling the detainees with our sounds, we are also donating five thousand dollars toward buying them some—music being the medium that soothes the savage beast. We are led into what appears to be a holding room; the gear has already been set up on the stage for us by the crew in the afternoon. We stare at the walls of bare concrete. A life inside is a chilling thought, and when I think that I almost . . .

It's time to hit the stage, and we shuffle forward. "Take no prisoners," says Miles with a smirk. This is different: rather than arriving onstage to thrill the audience with our very presence, we troop out onto a stage that is at one end of a dingy room and it feels more like being on the gallows. There's no applause. Out beyond the stage, small groups of men stand huddled together as if in the middle of a drug deal. This is a situation in which it's difficult to be positive, get people smiling, or tell them to cheer up. These men are doing time, some of them for crimes of a violent nature; they aren't moved by three white guys, aren't going to have a sudden revelation and see where they have gone wrong on life's path. So, we do our set without saying an awful lot and try to at least play decently, but the pogo'ing and leaping about the small stage all feel painfully artificial when faced with the reality of a darker caste. In the end we slink off stage, mumbling platitudes like good luck, see you next time, etc.

We spend the rest of November crisscrossing the country like a game of snakes and ladders, tours always being planned to be as circuitous and phys-ically demanding as possible so that the artiste only ever performs in a con-dition of shell shock.

Houston, Dallas, Tulsa, Lawrence, St. Paul, Chicago, Detroit, Milwaukee. Again it all turns into a kaleidoscopic journey of freeways, truck stops, invitations to party, motel rooms, discarded paperbacks, high pressure fronts, altostratus, cirrocumulus, urban whiteout, dew, frost, low clouds, and solar flares—the central motif being the shows and the familiar backstage aroma of beer and marijuana and the taste of jack cheddar stuck on a wheat thin. We are winning, but it's inch by inch by inch.

Back in Europe we continue straight on by touring in Germany as if it's another U.S. state, and on the autobahn to Aachen someone remarks, "Surely that must be Detroit just ahead." As we travel up and down the Ruhr Valley, "Walking on the Moon" is released and enters the British charts at number one. It feels good to be back in Europe and we decide to cap the year off with a double gig in Hammersmith on December 18, the end of another U.K. tour.

Miles sets up both the Hammersmith Odeon and the Hammersmith Palais just half a mile down the road. We will start at the Odeon and then travel slowly by a heavy armored military vehicle in full public view to the Palais. It will be a brilliant publicity stunt—a night full of glitter—and the tickets will probably sell out in a few hours. This is one more crafty underlining of the word *Police,* which Miles never seems to tire of. As he was brought up in military circumstances, anything paramilitary seems to get him going, and for much of our existence we are presented in dominant male power terms, almost to the point of parody.

The night arrives and is a spectacular success, with all sorts of well-wishers and celebrities turning up backstage before the show, the Police gig now being the place to be. We play to an audience that just can't get enough. One of the regular features of our U.K. performances now is the attendance of the St. John Ambulance Brigade, as we have large numbers of girls passing out and getting removed on stretchers by the men in blue. It reaches almost absurd proportions, and there is a nonstop chain of stretchers going by the stage for the duration of the show. Some of the girls are faking their swooning just so they can get to the front of the stage, and they grin up at us as they pass below us. We get to know the faces of the men and eventually can just call down: "Evenin', Sid. Everything alright?" The St. John Ambulance men add a nice touch of normalcy to the proceedings, which is sometimes absent in other countries. They are usually at the sound check, scoping out the venue for possible mishaps, and we talk to them about their job, and our job, and over communal cups of tea agree that we are all in it together. "Nice lads, those p'lice," you hear them murmur.

After the show, with cameras flashing like a snowstorm, we pile out of the Odeon and climb into the half-track army vehicle to make the journey up the street to the second show of the night, at the Hammersmith Palais. As we cruise up the street with three or four thousand cheering fans surrounding the vehicle, it's like Moses parting the Red Sea and feels like a great joke that we and our fans are in on together. It is absurd but great rock-and-roll theater, a splash of surrealism in the drab English winter; as we grin out across the camouflage paint of the half-track, we see nothing but smiling, cheering faces giving us the hero's welcome home. They do love a parade in Blighty.

1979. Thatcher is in power, the Ayatollah is back in Iran, the Yorkshire Ripper has run riot, Saddam Hussein has become president of Iraq, the Soviets have invaded Afghanistan, and the British public has bought a band called "the Police." We are a pop success. With two number one records and a huge number of shows performed, we deserve a long rest. We get two weeks.

Eighteen

I stare across the room to where my guitar leans against the wall with the light still glinting off the strings. It's worth a shot. I get out of bed and pull a Nikon FE from my camera bag and start photographing the collision of light and strings from several angles, being careful to expose for the detail in the shadows. The second time we arrived in New York I went to B&H Photo on Thirty-fourth Street with a rock photographer who offered to advise me and then took pictures while I made the purchase of a Nikon FE and a 24mm lens.

I begin photographing everything around me and quickly learn to hate the distortion of the wide-angle lens. Realizing I have been given bad advice, I move to a standard 50mm lens and began getting better results. I love the feel of a camera in my hand—it feels like a gun: I shoot the world. Inspired by Walker Evans, Diane Arbus, Henri Cartier-Bresson, Lee Friedlander, and Ralph Gibson, I begin wandering around at night trying to photograph in the dark with fast film and no flash. Everything in America seems like a photograph, and as my head becomes crammed with black-and-white imagery, my hands are always around a camera. As the heat grows around the band it becomes a private world I can retreat to, one in which I am alone.

Gradually the road, the hotels, the groups of fans, the long lines of a limo in the Arizona night, become constructs of seeing; my relationship to touring shifts, now not only playing music but dreaming through the camera.

Nineteen-eighty. The year begins with a quick visit to Hamburg for a TV show that we barely notice: we are about to set off for a world tour that will take in thirty-seven cities and nineteen countries, including Hong Kong, Japan, India, and Egypt. We have a film crew that will travel everywhere with us to capture our exploits, eventually to be released as a video called *Police Around the World*. But before we get to the more exotic countries, we have to take yet another pass through the U.S. just in case we could have possibly overlooked a hamlet or two. We arrive in Buffalo to play at Clark Gym. Outside, the ground is covered in deep snow and the temperature is below zero, and with the Niagara roaring in the background, we enter another round of the American Dream. Arriving back in the U.S. always feels like a comedown after the mayhem back in Europe, but Clark Gym is packed and we melt the snow surrounding the building.

Buffalo, Cleveland, Ann Arbor, Madison, St. Louis, Memphis. Being rock historians, we know that Elvis was born just down the road from Memphis in Tupelo, Mississippi, and we have to pay homage. We rent a car and

drive south to Tupelo. As you enter the small township, it is as if you have come to a weird religious site. Signs, pictures, and messages line the side of the road with the kind of devotion to El that normally is reserved for Jesus. Naturally, there are also more commercial messages that encourage a fine dining experience at the Elvis Inn or to get your Elvis T-shirt at Arnie's. There are arrows pointing to the birthplace of the King just down the road apiece, and in three minutes flat we are outside the miniscule shack where he was born. Surprisingly, you just walk up to it and knock on the door, which we do. The door is opened by a very, very old lady who might have been El's mother (except that she is dead, as we all know). It is a tiny shack not much more than ten feet square. It can truly be described as humble, but knowing that from this small patch arose greatness, we are reverent. Like visiting Magi, we stand in silence for a few minutes and feel the vibes—my mind drifts back to the shag rug of Carl Hollings's mum, the fake coal fire, and the King crooning "Teddy Bear"—there's a lot of love in the shack. Sighing, we leave and begin the drive back into Memphis without speaking, just pulling over once to get a burger or six in honor of the King.

New Orleans, Oklahoma City, Denver, Salt Lake. We arrive on an afternoon flight and after we have checked in I take a walk because I want to see how peculiar the city really is. I am always interested in photographing these places anyway. Dominated by its massive tabernacle, the city sits in a valley surrounded by mountains and salt flats. Salt is one of those things that people and cities get turned into when they raise the wrath of God, and like a warning sign, there is plenty of it around here. Here in underground vaults the Mormons keep the records of everyone who has ever lived (according to them). One of the richest organizations in the world, they sent preachers to Africa, where they were able to get plenty of practice in the missionary position. All this leads one to speculate on how the gig will go tonight. Will there be a protest at our profanity? An arrest by the sheriff's department, or what? But we come offstage a few hours later, having just played to one of the wildest, most out-of-control crowds of the tour, the local girls coming up to us with wads of gum in their mouth and blowing large pink bubbles in our faces, the message implicit.

Seattle, Vancouver, Portland, Honolulu, and on to Narita Airport in

Japan, where a flood of memories come rushing back. What if those guys are still around? What if they want to settle an old debt? What if? I decide to let it go and hope that the new promoter has the wherewithal to protect his investment. Before we are actually let into the country, we get a rigorous checking by small grim-faced Japanese men with sniffing dogs that conduct searches of our bodies, equipment, suitcases, guitars, and amplifiers. Clearly disappointed and slightly mystified to have come up with nothing, they finally let us go and we wearily climb onto the bus to make the excruciating three-hour drive to Tokyo.

We are working for the Udo Organization, and Mr. Udo himself, a rotund and charming middle-aged man with a gentle manner, meets us in the lobby of the hotel. He speaks English and has an urbane manner but runs his organization with a fist of steel. As usual with the Japanese, it is difficult to tell what is actually going on—emotions tend to be hidden behind an impassive mask—but with us Udo is never less than cordial. Accompanying him at all times in all shapes and sizes are his boys, who have names like Moony, Snake, Bullseye, and Tommy, who seems to be the leader. There are several of them, and all double as bodyguards and roadies wearing dark blue bomber jackets with UDO ORG in large white letters on the back. Carrying little walkie-talkies that they mutter into in rapid-fire Japanese, they communicate nonstop with one another from positions of scout and rearguard. Wherever we are, they are too; and if they think we are going somewhere, one will be there ahead of us. When we retire for the night, one stands guard outside until you wake in the morning. On rising for breakfast, you are greeted at the door with a bow from Snake, who politely asks you where you are headed. "Breakfast," you yawn, "ground floor." He immediately communicates this information downstairs to Moony, who will stand outside the breakfast room while you eat. It is faintly claustrophobic but also flattering, as if we are some sort of precious cargo. The truth is that Mr. Udo is protecting his investment, and we perambulate down well-marked corridors.

Outside the breakfast room, watching us eat, is a mob of schoolgirls who, whenever you cast a look in their direction, burst into giggles, cover their mouth, and take a step back. It is amusing and it turns into a little piece of theater as you stare down at your cornflakes and then suddenly looking up with milk and cornflakes falling out of your mouth. This drives them insane, and they fall back again as if on a set of invisible threads.

After these intellectual diversions it is time to go shopping in Tokyo with our photographer friend Watal Asanuma. He takes us down to the Yodobashi camera store, the band and about a hundred schoolgirls trailing behind us like a navy blue cloud. Yodobashi has five floors of photographic equipment, audio devices, and every gadget that the Japanese mind can invent, it's half the price and twice as small, stuff you don't see anywhere else. And for half an hour we become rabid consumers, buying things we don't need just because they are so small. As we walk around the store we are assaulted about every five minutes by a very loud track coming through the PA system. It is a song about Yodobashi cameras sung to the tune of "John Brown's Body"; it is incredibly irritating and irresistibly funny, and becomes a theme song for the rest of the tour.

The tour in Japan turns out to be more fun and less lonely than some of our stateside touring. Anne Nightingale of BBC fame joins us, and we go around in a large entourage with the film crew, our stage crew, Mr. Udo and his boys, and an ever growing mob of schoolgirls. We travel on the bullet train, stare out the window at Mount Fuji and visit the Zen gardens and temples of Kyoto. We create out-of-control hysteria for Mr. Udo everywhere, and honor is satisfied. But we like to leave the stage at the end of the show with its bursting-to-the-roof audience and apologize to Mr. Udo for not doing better business, and we'll try again tomorrow night. Udo greets this with a faint Buddha-like smile.

The culmination of this trip to Japan is when I agree to a fight to the death with a champion sumo wrestler in a house on the outskirts of Tokyo. We drive out on a cold January morning to the sumo hostel; it turns out that they all live together (at least when in training). We pull up in an anonymous-looking suburb, I make the sign of the cross, and we enter. After five minutes of mutual bowing and smiling, we are led into an anteroom and I meet my adversary. Imagine Captain Ahab up-close with Moby Dick the great white whale. A vast sea of blubber confronts me in all directions; I

slowly raise my eyes, and looking down with a beneficent smile is Yaki San, my opponent. "He doesn't stand a chance," I say, my voice muffled by the folds of his flesh.

Because there is a spiritual side to the art of sumo wrestling, we have to sit down and eat together as a bonding ritual. We will acknowledge the eternal spirit in each other before trying to beat each other's brains out. I notice that while I take up one space at the table, Yaki takes up twelve. I try not to let this deter me but keep a mean look on my face. I have by this time been dressed to appropriate sumo standards, which means tying my hair in a knot and wearing a skimpy loincloth. I look like a wimp ver-sion of Tarzan. The house is freezing, as central heating is not part of the sumo credo, and I sit slurping noodles through chattering teeth. As I suck down the noodles I recycle samurai flicks through my head, desperately trying to remember Toshiro Mifune's greatest movies, *The Seven Samurai, Yojimbo, Rashōmoan,* a black-and-white pastiche of flashing swords and grunting soundtrack, but it is to no avail—this is flesh and bone, unarmed combat, and I will probably have to finish him off with my secret ar-madillo lizard lock.

The moment of truth comes and we are led into another concrete room with a circle marked out in chalk. After another seventeen or eighteen bows it is time. We snarl at each other, I perceive a small look of fear pass over his face, and then we're across the ring and at each other's throats. Dazed and confused, I pick myself up about five minutes later on the far side of the room, wondering how I got there. I stare across the concrete: he is still there with a large Jackie Chan grin lighting up his mug and pity in his eyes. *Right,* I think, and shoot like a bullet across the ring, to be rolled up like a rag doll in the arms of a giant and gently placed upside down at the side of the ring. We go at it again in a flurry of grunts and slippery moves. Sting, Stewart, and Miles stand ringside, and their shadowy forms merge into the smirking mums and dads at Summerbee school as the Welsh boy Evans pummels me into a near coma. I stagger up from the concrete and bury my head like an ant in the folds of Yaki's vast gut, to be repelled like a pebble from a catapult. One thing I notice as I continue to be tossed like a cork on a rough sea is how sweet he smells. My face is squashed time and time again into his big soft chest, and a sweet perfume wafts over me that is intoxicating and otherworldly. With a voluptuous resignation, I feel myself falling in love with him even as he smashes me back and forth on the concrete. I have no other explanation for this other than the thought that I may be a latent masochist or that in fact I like boys. It finally comes to an end and I grumpily cede the victory on points; meanwhile, in the freezing temperature I have caught the flu.

We fly to Hong Kong to play at Today's World disco. The reason we are playing in a disco is that it is the only gig we can get at this time in Hong Kong and it fits in with our scheme about playing around the world. I have a temperature hovering around 102—the actual Hong Kong flu in Hong Kong, which is rather pleasing. But overriding health concerns is my burning desire to get a suit made; I have been told that in this city you can get a suit knocked up in a few hours, and we decide to put it to the test. We arrive at a funky-looking tailor's shop and go in to order our suits. With a great deal of confusion on the tailor's part, I describe a powder blue number with zips from hell, across the lapels, on the pockets, up the arms, until it looks like a Vivian Westwood creation on steroids. The tailor is babbling away in Mandarin, not understanding this latest fashion from the West until a faint glimmer appears on his face and he finally twigs that it might be a joke.

I am still running a temperature when we turn up to play the disco. I feel quite ill but I get a B_{12} shot and I make it through on that and adrenaline;

strangely, after the performance I feel a whole lot better, as if I have just sweated out the virus. A group of young men are led into the dressing room wearing uniforms with the word POLICE emblazoned across the chest; it turns out that they are British cadets from the Hong Kong police academy, and we all agree to swap T-shirts. We get theirs and they get ours: a very satisfying exchange. After the show Anne Nightingale presents us with some awards for Best New British band and Best Album. The ceremony is televised by satellite live to England, and like martians, we all wave from the disco across the globe to those back in Blighty. I imagine my mum and dad sitting on the couch with cups of tea, smiling as they nudge each other, and Mum murmuring, "Be careful, love." I wonder if Kate and Layla are watching; with the vast time difference, we haven't talked lately.

Driving into Bombay for the first time is an assault. Trapped between the past and the future, the city is a disordered emblem of two competing civilizations. Each time the car stops at a traffic light (if it stops at all), beggars begin clawing and shouting at the window. Other than a piece of rag around the waist, they are naked; many of them have a limb missing. Hands are outstretched for alms, and mothers of fourteen or fifteen years old extend their palms with a look of ancient sorrow. I sit in the back of the car with all sense of what I had previously called reality blown away because nothing prepares you for this. We are here to entertain, which seems incongruous in this first confrontation with Bombay. Billboards stare down onto the masses below encouraging them to brush with fluoride toothpaste and to eat chocolate, as if all can suddenly drop the sham of poverty and go home laughing at their little bit of playacting. After what seems like a torturous and circuitous route designed to say "this is India," we pull up in front of the Taj Intercontinental. Compared with what we have just passed through, the Taj, with its luxurious Western version of India, is a haven of peace and security. Passing through its regal lobby to the main lounge the dichotomy is visceral. Outside, chaos, pressure, disease, and white glaring heat: inside, American Express, room service, and sparkling mineral water. The idea to play in these countries was originally mine, and Miles has flown to Bombay with no previous contact to see if he can set up some sort of concert. He has made contact with an organization called the Time and Talents Club, a committee of middle-aged Indian ladies who work for charity and occasionally put on concerts to raise money. They are charmed by Miles, and as the word gets out about the Police pop group, the gig changes from a small club to a crumbling auditorium that holds three thousand people.

We are taken to a lunch by the river to meet the ladies of the Time and Talents Club. They are excited to meet us, and in their multicolored saris they chatter and flutter about like exotic birds. These ladies all speak in posh English accents and are a different type of Indian altogether from those outside on the streets of Bombay. They are Parsis and hold a religious belief that belongs to Zoroastrianism, which originated in Persia about 1500 B.C. with its prophet Zarathustra. One of the tenets of the Parsi faith is that the elements earth, water, fire, and air are sacred and must not be polluted by human waste. Therefore, when they die Parsis are left in concentric concrete structures—the Towers of Silence—to be picked apart by vultures. As coffee and cake are proffered and announcements are made in voices that echo the Raj, it is hard to keep your mind off the fact that the bones of these sweet enthusiastic ladies—our promoters—will one day be ripped apart by scavenger birds. We are introduced to their president of the box office, a tiny and shrunken woman who must be at least 120 years old, but she has her infant-size fist on the money with a glint in her eyes that says "don't fuck with me, bub."

We have a couple of days before the concert and we go out into the streets of the city to pass through the swarming streets of Bombay. A simple word to describe it would be fucking insane. As you struggle through the crowds with the babble of Hindi penetrating your eardrums, you are confronted by sadhus with gouged limbs who endure horrific acts of penance, merchants leaning across every stall with imploring eyes, naked children, honking taxicabs, and giant billboards showing the latest Bollywood extravaganza in lurid colors. It is a steaming and ancient poverty-ridden version of New York, India style. With nine million people, and more like the movie *Blade Runner* than a city of antiquity, Bombay remains a magnet for all of India. We stop for a moment and watch a mongoose rip the head off a snake. *So much for Rikki-tikki-tavi,* I think as we stagger off into the heat. Life here is so locked in time and tradition that people seem to accept this grinding reality as normal. At night in the stultifying heat, people sleep in heaps in the streets and squares as if just falling down wherever they happen to be. Later we find out that they do so because it beats the other choice—the crowded and disease-ridden horror of the tenement buildings.

In the cosseted security of the Taj Mahal Intercontinental we pop stars lark about for the movie cameras, camping it up in Indian costumes and fighting with swords. We sit around the tearoom and play sitar, tamboura, and tablas, coming up with a warped raga version of "Walking on the Moon." The English press have come out for this show, including Paul Morley, a cutting-edge pop music journalist and arbiter of taste for *New Musical Express.* At twenty-three years old, he is a star writer for *NME* and writes well although mostly with a morbid narcissism. As he is notorious for cutting musicians to pieces, we imagine that he must hate us and our music, so we are not sure what to make of his appearance other than the fact that if he has been flown at great expense to India, he will be nice to us if he wants to live. There is no place for stars in the Paul Morley universe, but when he returns to England he writes a self-obsessed piece about his love of Sting, how Sting is a supercool star, and how stars like him are necessary. This happens because Sting deliberately sets out to get him, make the kid fall in love with him. "Love is the ultimate cruelty," Sting says later.

The concert at the Rang Bhavan auditorium is sold out, with a crowd of 3,500. We turn up late in the afternoon to sound check in a scene of mild chaos. This is India and nothing really works. All things eventually succumb to the heat and rot. We have anxieties about the electrical power: Will we get electrocuted? Will we play in darkness? Should we go acoustic? But after lots of shouting, hand waving, and invocations of various Hindu deities, everything comes to life as if waking from the afternoon slumber. I am excited; to be playing music in India seems like the achievement of at least one life ambition, and I gaze out over the rows of folding metal chairs, smiling on the inside. The night arrives with its mosquitoes, arc lights, and soft greenness, and we wait in the wings to go onstage. Before we go on, an excruciatingly long speech is made about politics, the Time and Talents Club, the officials themselves, what a historic occasion this is, and the hopes and dreams of India. This takes so long that, decimated by the heat, we are almost ready to call it a night and go back to the hotel. Finally the colonial tones of the Time and Talent president announces, "And now without further ado, the Police," and we charge (or rather, exhausted by humidity and lassitude, flop like fish) onto the stage. The entire audience explodes to surge forward like a herd of wildebeests and presses up against the stage in crazed abandon, with rolling eyeballs and upward thrusting arms.

Unfortunately, the first two or three rows, which have been carefully roped off for the city's elderly officials and a night of genteel entertainment, are now totally annihilated by the seething mob and we never see them again. We hear later that one of them ended up in the hospital, and we send along flowers and a letter of regretful condolences. The concert is mayhem from beginning to end, with clouds of insects swarming against the glare of light, heat bursting through the floorboards, and a wall of screaming faces a few feet away. It's hard not to laugh out loud because you feel as though you're surfing a giant wave or in the middle of a riot in the madhouse. We finish with possibly the best live "Can't Stand Losing You" that we ever perform, and it feels more like an uprising than a concert of pop music.

Afterward we are taken along with two of Bombay's top models, Indian beauties hovering around the six-foot-one mark, to a small room above a record store in the center of the city. This is the Police party, and in the suffocating heat of a fifteen-by-twenty oven one flight up from the pustulating street we mill about with the buzz from the concert and the smell of rice and chapati fusing with the glasses of vodka that are rapidly placed in our hands. Indian gentlemen in dhotis and turbans come up to us one after another to pronounce that "we are going to play the bloody hell out of your record." One kind soul by the name of Raji Singh tells me that we will sell fifty thousand records in India and that we have a great future on the subcontinent. I swallow a piece of chapati and tell him that I have always loved the place. Through a haze of Smirnoff and curry, I stare out across the room and think of the Four Noble Truths, suffering, attachment, liberation, the Eightfold Path—just like being in this band—and then sign another album with a Bic.

Two days after Bombay we arrive in blast-furnace heat at the Holiday Inn in Giza, Egypt. The only hotel of its kind in the world, with a view of the Great Pyramid, it is slightly unnerving to gaze out of a bedroom window and there, like a relic from an old Peter O'Toole film, is the four-sided triangular tomb erected by a million slaves, or possibly extraterrestrials. The restaurant, with its potted palms and slow-moving ceiling fans, needs only Sydney Greenstreet to complete the picture. We order lunch: *eesh baladi, ta'miyya, babagahannuugh.* We have no idea what we will get but offer up a prayer. The service moves at about the speed of building a pyramid. We wonder if it wouldn't be quicker to nip back to England for lunch, and when it does arrive, it is terrible as if it has been pulled out of the refrigerator where it has been sitting since the time of the pharaohs, mostly just small brown things sitting on a white plate like camel dung.

We are in Egypt to play at the University of Cairo as part of our around-the-world jaunt. But already we have a problem. We have sent our gear by freight because it is considerably cheaper than excess baggage. But because it arrives on Friday, which is the Arab Sabbath, no one is on duty in the air freight section. Our gear is locked up and cannot leave the airport. This is a disaster because we have a concert on Saturday, and lockup is until the following Monday. At first there is a great deal of arguing with upraised chests and waving arms in the volcanic heat of the Cairo airport. Miles and Ian Copeland, who has joined us for the Egyptian gig, seem to be in their natural element as they go at it with the airport officials, the main theme of the dialogue being "I am fuck off, no you are fuck off." This deep command of language and culture gets us nowhere until Miles finally cuts the Gordian knot by making a call to a high-up government official, Colonel Hasan Tuhani, the deputy prime minister of Egypt, and a special government agent turns to open the doors on a holy day and retrieve our gear.

The afternoon before the concert is spent filming, with the three of us galloping through the sand past the Pyramids on horseback, doing our best Lawrence of Arabia imitations. With the sun drifting below the Pyramids, we return to the hotel and as I enter the lobby a small smiling Egyptian in a red fez, white dinner jacket, and bow tie presses a silver tray toward me. On the glinting surface is a small cream-colored envelope with a small ibis embossed in the upper-left-hand corner. Inside on a single ivory sheet are a few freshly typed lines—"Mrs. Summers and your daughter are in room 137. Cordially"—and a flourish of fountain pen signifying the hotel manager's name. I open the door and see Layla lying on the bed asleep and Kate standing there smiling; she raises a finger to her lips and points at the small sleeping form on the bed: don't wake her. I point to the bathroom—let's go in there. We go into the bathroom to kiss and reunite with passion, and as we do so, the entire ceiling in a great cloud of cement and plaster falls in on us, leaving a gaping hole through to the room above. We fall in convulsions on the floor—either it is the power of love or the skills that once engineered the Pyramids have grown rusty. Either way, the baby does not wake up.

The University of Cairo has been thrown into chaos by our arrival; a large group has already filled the hall, and the electrical power that runs all the way from the Aswan Dam underneath date palms, camel arses, screaming children, women in burkas, the Great Pyramid, the khamsin sandstorm, circumcision ceremonies, and the tomb of Nefertiti is not reaching the stage. We are without juice, powerless.

"I hope abortions are legal in this country, because you are about to witness one tonight," says Danny Quatrochi as he struggles with the PA, which has been flown in from Greece but turns out not to possess enough power to get our sound past the edge of the stage. Along with this mess, the Egyptians have scrounged around and come up with six spotlights for the stage, but with only one bulb—clearly this is not the time of the pharaohs. Sting, Stewart, and I sit backstage with our families and wait, slightly relishing the situation with useful remarks like "I want my mummy," "I think they're in de-Nile," "Fez up, it's a fuckup," and helpfully whistle "The Sheik of Araby." Eventually we get out onto the stage with a barely adequate situation of half lighting and intermittent power, but Ramses III smiles down upon us and we get through the whole show without anyone getting electrocuted, although it occurs to me that if one were to die on a Egyptian stage, would you get mummified?

Somewhere in the middle of the show Sting sees what he thinks is a cop having a go at a kid in the front and tells him to fuck off. It turns out that the bouncer is in fact the chief of police, and a difficult situation arises later with Sting refusing to apologize. We all risk incarceration until Miles finally manages to calm the chief down by apologizing on Sting's behalf: honor is served and Anglo-Egyptian relations remain intact.

A day later we arrive in the cool Hellenic air of Athens, and it suddenly feels a relief to be back in the West. We are the first rock group to play here since the Stones in 1969, when the military took over the country and rock concerts in Greece came to an end. When we arrive in our large blue bus there is a huge crowd already surrounding the building and a phalanx of the police trying to control things. There are so many kids on the street that we can't get through, and with its engine running, the bus comes to a stop in the middle of the crowd. Knowing we are inside, they surround the bus and begin banging on its sides. The situation becomes impossible and frightening—clearly Socratic discourse isn't going to work this time; emotions are running high. But the real police get to the bus and make a pretty little corridor of truncheons, through which we are able to exit the bus and get successfully into the stadium. I carry Layla in my arms underneath the raised batons and sing to her, "We're off to see the wizard. . . ."

We leave Athens and tour on through the rest of Europe; the shows become marked more by chaos, disorder, and uproar. In Italy we end the night trapped in the dressing room with a riot—police, tear gas, and burning cars—outside. This is the rock circus supreme. Like a force of nature, we whirl through each port, leaving emotional and physical wreckage in our wake. The three of us sit in the eye of the maelstrom, with a half awareness of what is happening on the outer fringes, the things that are kept from us, lies, collusion, emotional agendas. Distortion is creeping in, and we can regard it only with a sorry shrug, see it as theater. If we try to fix every little hurt, every little wound, we will get sucked into our own whirlpool. In the middle of this inferno we are the still point and in some ways the least damaged, but sitting backstage with my guitar and friends and inhaling the golden poppy of success, it's a drag to know that for some, the Police experience is less than life-affirming.

We perform and make the records, but already it's turned from a trio of unknown hopefuls into a machine that impassively chews people up and spits them back out. We hear reports of people who have been hired. They come into the operation of touring and running a successful band with smiling faces and then later—emotionally wrecked—leave sobbing and vowing never to do anything like that again. Beneath the crowing voice of triumph there is a shadow of power plays, hierarchy, and machismo; as we march forward, the

operation balloons into a swollen monster—a queen bee surrounded by workers guarding the source of the eggs—and in a dreamlike moment, with a few
songs giving the power to destroy, create, get you anything and with our faces
staring out from lurid posters above teenage beds, we grow to an entourage of
seventy-five.

Nineteen

In June our accountant, whose every word we now abide by but who will sadly go to prison in a few short years, tells us that we must get out of the country, must become tax exiles. We take him at his word. Sting and I search around, wondering where to go, as if we don't already have enough to deal with. Stewart, being an American, can stay in England. A few weeks later we both move to Ireland, Sting to the northwest and I with my family to a dot on the map called Aughavanah.

There is no telephone in the house and to make a call I have to walk a mile up the road to a box that sits at the junction of two country lanes. You pick up the phone and the local operator comes on to ask you if your havin' a nice day so far and you reply with something like "ay, a grand day, alright. So, what'll you be wantin then, Mr. Summers," for she knows—as they all know around here—who the new people up the road are. "It'll be a call to London, here's the number." "That's going to be expensive—are you sure now?" "Sure enough," I reply, staring at the blackberries that are just coming to fruit. There is a whirling and dialing somewhere down the line and eventually the call goes through to the twentieth century. I know that the operator listens to the whole thing and makes a formal report to the village. This new life stands in stark contrast to the life I thought I was in, and now I wonder if I have hallucinated the whole thing.

After a few weeks of this, Kate and I decide to try our luck farther south and end up buying an old Georgian house overlooking the harbor at Kinsale, a village south of Cork. It is romantic but drafty, damp, and too big. Living in rural Ireland is a serious change of pace after the action we are used to in London. There is literally nothing to do except walk along the cliffs and gaze at the wild beauty of Ireland, exchange pleasantries with the horsey farming set, and discuss the weather. I'm not really ready for this yet, and despite the warmth and closeness of family, without the band and the rush of touring, I'm left like a junkie going through cold turkey.

I stand with Kate in the McLaughlins' store in Kinsale and stare at the shrunken row of brown things that pass for vegetables in Ireland. It is becoming an act of vivid imagination to come up with a decent dinner every night. In the mornings, with the biting wind cutting through my clothes, I remove the nails that have been placed under my car tires and wash the graffiti off our wall, with its taunts about the Police and being British. I am uncomfortable and it will not be long before Sting actually gets death threats; eventually we both have to leave Ireland.

I wave at Mrs. Keohane across the narrow street and rush back inside to struggle with coal and wood in the grate and wonder if the flue is open as smoke billows into the room. Living in Ireland suddenly feels like a booby prize; instead of the sybaritic pleasure of popular success, we are faced with the harsh reality of grey weather; bone-chilling, damp, biting wind; and bad food—all to beat the taxman. Life here seems to be about the ability to make it through to the next day, keep the damp out of your bone marrow, pass the long grey hours. We try to be a family and embrace the new situation, but it is a strain. I can feel that my head is elsewhere, out there on the road; the unfamiliarity of Ireland, the cold, and the quietness of village life don't suit me. Kate and I begin a slow slide into estrangement. My attitude and the continual glare of the spotlight and the relentless press are beginning to wear on Kate, who did not move to England with me to be deserted.

In our new tax-exile status, Sting and I go with Stewart to Holland to begin recording our third album. The expectation of another hit album is enormous, the pressure not to disappoint with us all the time. In what seems like a flash we have reached a stage where a large number of people are dependent on us: we are their living, their future, their survival. Everyone holds his breath and offers a silent prayer that we pull off another number one. It is as if we have became like a racehorse that has become a surefire bet; as much as we and everyone else enjoy it, it is a situation of inherent fragility.

I have wondered ever since we completed *Regatta de Blanc* how long Sting would play this game, because it doesn't seem natural to him. He is not a team player, doesn't really want to share credit, and makes comments in the press to that effect, as if foreshadowing the ultimate event. I understand, and it feels like a small interior abrasion that is quiescent at the moment but may one day become a wound that will hold the residual pain of being deserted by someone you love. In the classic distortion that always happens with bands, we might already be reaching the point where we think we don't need one another, can go it alone, pull apart like the Beatles. It seems that each one of us really would like to run the whole show or be out on his own. Stewart, brash and outspoken, bulldozes his way through things, Copeland-style, but achieves his goals. If left to our own devices, Sting and I would probably get too subtle, too esoteric; Stewart counters all that and gives things a fuck-you rock-and-roll edge. There is no doubt that Miles is effective as a manager, but sometimes the style grates and is embarrassing as if we are winning through intimidation. But, I reason to myself, we are lucky to have such a character because that is what it takes; subtlety and politeness don't cut it in the rock music world. We have an alliance, but it's uneasy.

We enter the studio at Wisselord with Nigel Gray again in charge of engineering. We notice that Nigel has changed. He has morphed from the local M.D. in Leatherhead to a rock star. His hair is now shoulder length; he wears cowboy boots and a long fringed leather jacket. We have been given a month to make the album, which—considering how much is riding on it—is an incredibly short time. Amazingly enough, this month gets shortened to three weeks when we are informed that in the middle of recording we will spend a week playing Milton Keynes in England and Leixlip Castle in Ireland.

Things are changing fast now that we are a "big" rock band. It appears to be the moment for other people to ply us with as many drugs as possible. But in this situation it makes us anxious because we are here to work, not take drugs; we need this third album. One of the problems of sniffing coke in the studio is that, apart from the illusion it creates whereby you think everything you do is just "absolutely fuckin' great," it affects your hearing, with the result that the more stoned you become, the more you turn up the high frequencies in the mix. The end result often becomes something that would make a dog howl.

Large piles of white stuff are placed in front of us, but we don't want to do this—we are short of time, need this album, can't fuck around. Further compounding this problem are Nigel's disappearances to the red-light district in Amsterdam, and he wants us to go with him. We are pissed off by all of this because we have to get this album recorded, and the process is being jeopardized. It feels as if we have switched roles and are now merely providing the soundtrack to a rock-and-roll party that other people are enjoying. This will become a hallmark of the next few years, a place where boundaries are often blurred as the line between work and being high as a kite softens.

We get on with the music. Sting has brought in a few good songs to provide the meat of the album, "Don't Stand So Close to Me," "De Do Do Do, De Da Da Da," "Driven to Tears," "When the World Is Running Down, You Make the Best of What's Still Around." We get the basics of the songs in the studio and begin the process of giving them Police-style arrangements, and this time I introduce a Roland guitar synthesizer into the sound of the band. Gradually something like an album emerges, but we are short of material. I have an instrumental tune I want to do, a quirky piece with a sort of haunted Middle Eastern theme called "Behind My Camel." There is some resistance to this. Granted, it's not A-list pop song material, but it's interesting. Sting refuses to play on it, which is a drag, but Stewart is willing, so I put down the backing track with me playing bass and later I add the guitar parts. Somewhere in the middle of this action Sting—half joking, half serious—hides the tape in the garden at the back of the studio. I get what's going on and a day later manage to dig up the tape, and the song ends up on the album. We carry on, still warming to this new place, but just as we are hitting our stride, we are pulled out of the studio. We have the two big concerts, the first one in England at Milton Keynes. They are calling it Regatta de Bowl.

The Milton Keynes concert is another marker on our climb. As we arrive in the late afternoon the excitement cuts through the air like a buzz saw. This is the biggest concert we have played so far in the U.K., but ironically, having now attained tax-exile status, we cannot be paid and our fee goes to charity. By the time we hit the stage the outdoor arena is a sea of mud and hysteria. Miles manages to compound things by trying to make the press photographers sign a three-page contract guaranteeing a percentage of the sale of photographs to the band. Sitting in our protective cocoon, we don't find out about this until much later. But it is distressing to discover that Miles and others have begun making decisions on our behalf that we feel don't represent us. It comes with a slight feeling that we are babies incapable of dealing with such realities. We should just be left alone with our music. There is a nasty backlash to Miles's imprecations, with an attitude of "we made you on the way up and now you're trying to charge us for it, well fuck you." *Funny, I think, the press hated us on the way up and now in their normal parasitical way, they are coming to feed.*

The best thing about the Milton Keynes show is that I acquire my own-roadie, a little Scot by the name of Tam Faigrieve. I notice how fast and efficient he is onstage, how all of my guitar leads, etc., seem much more orderly; nothing phases him. We hire him that night. He also stays the course.

From Milton Keynes we fly over to Ireland to play the big festival held on the grounds of Leixlip Castle, the home of the Guinness family. When we arrive at the castle in the afternoon there is a line of people standing in front of the gates to greet us. It is the Guinness clan, along with several retainers. To my amazement, standing with them is none other than Jenny Fabian, whom I have not seen since before she wrote *Groupie*. We don't play that night but sit by the fire in the dining room, sipping expensive brandy and enjoying the hospitality of Desmond Guinness and his family. Jenny and I catch up with each other's lives and laugh about the strangeness of meeting here. She has left London and now lives in Ireland, breeding greyhounds, and is as charming and down-to-earth as ever. The next afternoon we perform on the castle grounds in front of 35,000 people. We get a great reception, marred only by a group of vicious-looking kids who work their way to the front and scream abuse at us for being British and eventually hurl a bottle at the stage, which hits Stewart—the only non-British member of the group—and we have to fix him up before we can continue and finish the concert.

We return to Holland and the stark naked fact that we have a week left to finish our all-important third album. On the last day before we leave on a European tour, we come to the conclusion that the mixes aren't right and on a kamikaze mission remix the entire album in one night. This is like rolling the dice blindfolded, accompanied by the queasy feeling that you might be blowing your future. But this is how it is; everything we do seems crammed into a tight space. Nevertheless, we wind it up at six A.M., and *Zenyatta Mondatta* is ready to go out into the world.

The summer tour is of the north and south coasts of France, and I will re-member it as being the most fun of any Police tour. We travel in a large bus, a laughing and carousing entourage. We have the band XTC along as the support group, and with me I have Kate and Layla.

We pull up in front of the Atlantic Hotel—Biarritz's finest—and Kate, Layla, and I are shown into a beautiful suite that hangs precipitously over the pounding waves of the Atlantic. With a four-poster bed and a pink marble bathroom, the setting is ultraromantic, and Kate and I lie together on the bed as our two-year-old buzzes around the suite like a hummingbird. We or-der champagne, and I hold Layla up to the window to watch the waves below pound onto the rocks. On the beach a kid in a red swimsuit performs som-ersaults for his laughing parents. Thick waves crash on the sand like cello chords, and I remember sleeping on that same beach when I was seventeen and hitchhiking into Spain. The gold of the late afternoon creeps through the shutters, and I slip my arm around Kate's waist; it is a moment when we can reset our course and divert the razor edge of fame.

The next set of events we have to confront is the release of our new album and another tour of the United States to back it up. "Don't Stand So Close to Me" is to be the first single, and we make a silly video at a dance school in Clapham in which we prance about in black gowns and mortarboards in the already dated conventions of pop song videos. I find these video shoots frustrating because they seem a too literal translation of the songs. Why, I wonder, can't we make a different kind of video, something that has some level of ambiguity, a hint of darkness? Something more fucked up— particularly on this song, with its subtext of sex with a minor. But the record company doesn't like this sort of thing yet. They like us to be pre-sented as cheerful, outgoing, nonthreatening, innocuous—something for the mums and dads. I am thinking, what about Godard, Truffaut, Bergman, Kubrick's *Lolita*—am I the only one who has seen these films? But it's too early—that will not be for another ten years—so we keep grinning and prancing.

The single and the album both enter the U.K. chart at number one, but the press give it a good slagging anyway. It seems as if our ongoing success gets right up the nose of some critics. A journalist by the name of Lynden Barber gives us a grade D failure in his book; another writes a protracted piece of shit full of convoluted phrases and nonsense but mentions that Leonard Bernstein, in a letter to *The New York Times,* has proclaimed us better than the Beatles. Julie Burchill, with her histrionic screech, declares us the worst band of all time. But Derek Jewell, on the other hand, reviews a live concert and eulogizes about the brilliant weaving of jazz, reggae, and pop; the beautiful harmonies; the rhythmic interplay.

I begin giving interviews to guitar magazines on almost a daily basis. This one about the song "Shadows in the Rain":

The way we are playing it live now is turning it into a seminal piece of Police music. A lot of people are being pulled up short by it. I found the guitar part after we recorded it. We started more or less from scratch in the studio. Sting had this old jazzy rhythm, nothing like the version on Zenyatta *and we tried a lot of things, I put on two guitars which complemented each other and made a weird reggae rhythm which we decided was an improvement, being slower and more funky. Then I went in and laid the pseudo-psychedelic tape echo part all the way across, and everybody liked that. I did it by playing through an Echoplex with Stewart moving the tape speed up and down so it sounded like it was bubbling, twisting, and turning the whole way. Obviously I couldn't do that live, so I started working out this more orchestral part; chords with the echo and repeat wound all the way up so that when you hit the guitar the original sound isn't heard. All you hear is the echo, and I swell that up with the volume control, shhhhhhhhh, and it's like a string section coming in.*

You've got to hit it just before the beat so that you don't hear the repeat of the echo, you only hear that great cloud of sound emerging. Combined with that, I fragment all the chords. The chord structure is fairly basic, but I play them all in flattened ninths and invert them so that it all sounds much more modern.

I mean, the riff at the end when Sting sings "shadows in the rain" over and over is a basic a minor, but I actually use a strange inversion of an a minor sixth chord. It's high up on the neck, and as it starts to feedback I hit a high harmonic on the top string, which echoes against the feedback, and then you start to get this whole new effect. You enter another world. I really like the dark brooding quality of it. I think it's a good way for us to go.

The fans, who simply like the music, make us number one on both charts. Meanwhile, in the Far West—Colorado, Idaho, Montana, and California—we have work to do, and with unerring accuracy, and once again leaving our wives and children behind, we fly to Canada.

Twenty

Winnipeg sits in the infinite plains of Saskatchewan, and with synchronic winks coming from the wings, we bump down on the runway as if we have slung ourselves into the void. Who are we going to play to, wheat farmers? I imagine rosy-cheeked girls with legs like young oaks, farmers with checked shirts and combine harvesters, great sheaves of wheat on every corner.

We whip through Winnipeg, Regina, Calgary, and Edmonton, playing to about eight thousand a night; then go down the West Coast, missing Los Angeles this time for tactical reasons; and in a blur fall into Mexico City.

We are one of the first New Wave bands to arrive in the country, and the ticket price is high: a rather shocking (for 1980) forty dollars. We are pissed off about the entry fee because we think this ticket price would be out of the reach of our fans, but the show seems to be set up for the Mexico City elite and their girlfriends.

We are greeted by Mario Olmos, a hard-drinking, cheery Mexican promoter who comes up to me with "Andy, Mario," and embraces me—"don't you remember? The Animals . . . Eric . . . I put on your concert. . . . You don't remember?" "Oh, sí, M-A-R-I-O. *Recuerdo.¿ Como está usted, amigo?*" A vague memory like a blue haze of marijuana smoke drifts back and suddenly it's "yeah, Mexico, I love this country," and I do. In a "let's get a drink and pick up right where we left off" mood, we head toward the hotel bar.

The site of our gig is a half-constructed high-rise with two floors, the ground floor and the fortieth, but an elevator has kindly been installed to get you up to the death trap that lurks in the sky above. On the fortieth floor there is a hastily constructed stage that seems like a metaphor for the gallows as we thunder away for the Mexico City glitterati, anxiously wondering if all of us, band and audience, will go crashing down through thirty-nine floors. But this is Mexico: they celebrate the Day of the Dead here, they have magazines dedicated to pictures of victims of car accidents, and death is part of the fabric. So . . . would one be dead before hitting the concrete? Would you splatter bits of limb and crushed skull across half-used bags of cement powder? Would— Can't stand losing youooooo . . .

Those who cannot afford the price of the concert surround our hotel for the next three days and scream a lot. I make a photograph of a toilet roll unfurled from a bedroom door with the word *help* scrawled on it in black ink and then, under armed guard and behind heavy black sunglasses, leave by the hotel kitchen to look at the pyramids of the moon, the jaguar murals, and the Temple of Quetzalcóatl in the ancient city of Teotihuacán.

Mexico is a country where surrealism is normal. André Breton arrived in Mexico City in 1939 to escape the rigors of Paris. He set up house in the city and decided to have some furniture made for his house. He wanted a table for his dining room, so he hired a carpenter and drew up the design in perspective, with the front end of the table naturally appearing wider in the drawing than the far end. Two weeks later the table arrived as per the drawing, with one end wide and the other end narrowing down to a few inches. "I have nothing to teach these people," sighed Breton hopelessly, and immediately returned to Paris.

After the rain god Tlaloc, coyotes with feathered headdresses, and the thrill of playing in Mexican semiconstruction, we reenter the touring mindset and head north to play Chicago, Madison, Minneapolis, Detroit; up to Canada; back to the Midwest; and then down to the southern states. Now we fly by commercial airlines, which most of the time means that we slump around, half asleep, and play callous tricks on one another whenever possible. Flying is about half a degree better than traveling by road.

We emerge from the Sunset Theatre in Fort Lauderdale one night to hear the gut-wrenching news that John Lennon has been murdered. It is sickening and beyond belief. Lennon gone? It feels like a deep wound and yet another nail in the coffin of the fading sixties dream. John: the Beatle we all loved the most, with his acid humor and rebel persona—an anarchist from the inside. We get interviewed many times over the next few days about this, and it is difficult to talk about our new album or say anything about our group in the shadow of this tragedy.

We arrive in Argentina; it is the time of the dirty war, the time of the generals. People are disappearing, abducted in green falcon cars on the side streets of Buenos Aires, *los Desaparecidos*: the disappeared. Mothers are marching in the Avenida de Mayo and holding up pictures of their missing children. There is fear in the city and silent outrage about what is happening in Argentina; people are afraid to speak out, because to do so means that you too will "disappear."

Military gangs called *la patota* operate at night, arriving at their victims' homes to abduct, torture, and finally execute them. Victims are buried in unmarked graves; thrown into the sea, weighed down with concrete blocks; or burned in collective graves. Some human rights organizations estimate that thirty thousand people disappeared between 1976 and 1978. Not only have all the country's political institutions disappeared, but in authoritarian fashion so has all the free exchange of ideas or their expression. Like the final echo of fascist Germany, Argentina is under the rule of the last of the believers.

With only a very vague notion of what is really going on, we are incarcerated—for reasons that later appear obvious—in a Hilton on the outskirts of the city. This gives us no ability to walk out of the hotel and into Buenos Aires itself, the reason being that there is too much tension on the streets and the promoters don't want trouble. So, rather than taking in the culture, we lie around by the stupid pool, trapped in a "little piece of the U.S.A. in Argentina." By the end of the day as showtime approaches, we are all feeling somewhat pent up and need to let off steam.

Around seven-thirty, we start drifting into the lobby to go over to the venue. Somehow the locals have found out that we are in this hotel, which results in a large group of fans also being in the lobby. We sign autographs as we assemble there to leave. I notice one young girl who is very emotional and has tears running down her face while we sign her photographs; it's hard not to empathize with her and the others who crowd around. Something is coming from these kids that is different from England or the U.S., a reaching out, a desire for flight; with our guitars like weapons in our hands, we are men who run wild, and it cuts the air like an electric current.

At the concert there is a heavy police presence (no pun intended); the fans are not allowed to stand up or get out of their seats, and the hall is filled with fat, ugly cops who walk around prodding people with truncheons. The fans express their enthusiasm but with reservation because there is a tension that burns like a slow fuse. It seems as if the cops are just looking for the slightest excuse to get heavy. Our appearance here at this time is like the collision of two worlds: their thick wooden clubs versus our shining guitars and drums. As the concert heats up and we do our best to give the audience a good time, things begin to unravel. A few fans have the guts to leave their seats and come to the stage, including the young girl who was in the hotel lobby. She stands right in front of me, swaying to the music. This isn't to the cops' liking and within seconds there's a big fat 'n' ugly at her side, prodding her with his heavy stick and motioning her to sit down. I feel rage flood through me. Lost in the moment with a face full of rapture, my teenage Madonna doesn't move. The cop keeps prodding and it's me that's being prodded, and I feel anger rising like a bat into my throat. I come to the edge of the stage, put my foot on his shoulder, and give him a heavy shove. This gets a huge cheer from the audience, who clearly hate these oppressors. We continue on, but a few minutes later I think, *Oh, Christ,* because now, at the side of the hall, there is a huddle of cops looking at me, pointing at me. I nervously bang out the intro to "Roxanne," gm, dm, E♭, Sting bounces across the stage with a big grin on his face and says, "They're gonna arrest you. . . ."

Roxanne, what the fuck are they going to do to me? Roxanne, victim 06732. Roxanne, what are prisons like in Argentina? Roxanne, how will I explain this to Kate? We hit the last chord and run to the side of the stage, where we usually wait a couple of minutes before returning for the encore.

Miles is standing there, looking stricken. "Start thinking fast" he says. "They are going to arrest you; we've sent for a lawyer and an interpreter." Jesus! I think. We go back out onstage as I reset my Echoplex, grin at the audience, and begin the churning sixteenth-note rhythm of "Can't Stand Losing You." I have a deep sick feeling in the pit of my stomach, and I know that I've blown it—it will be Christmas in prison in fascist Argentina—and the sour metal taste of fear fills my mouth.

We come offstage and go into the dressing room. Sting and Stewart make ribald remarks about getting Henri Padovani back in the band, or maybe they will continue on as a duo. Would I send them a postcard? I am nervous; what the hell am I going to say to these brutes? Miles comes in with two Argentines, the lawyer and the interpreter. With a nice sense of occasion, Stewart climbs onto the top of a cupboard with his super 8 to film the whole event. After a few minutes there is a sharp rap on the door and in stride the cop and a couple of plainclothes guys. With the needle of the bullshit meter firmly in the red, I go straight over to macho man and shake his hand vigorously, smiling and asking him if he's okay. Phew! Did that fan hurt you? I gaze with a beseeching look into his bovine almond-

colored eyes. "Wow, it was crazy out there, but I guess we made it through—you and me, yep—we're alright now. What a beautiful country this is. Thank God you officers were there to protect us from those brutal fans—how is your mother?"

The interpreter keeps up with me in rapid-fire Argentinian Spanish, the *yo* becoming the hard-edged Argentinean *jo*. A look of confusion passes across his face as I hold on to his pudgy meat cleaver of a hand, but then a faint smile—as if he had just farted in his sleep—creeps onto his mug. He says something to the other two heavies, and they all grunt like the pigs in *Animal Farm*. It seems that honor had been satisfied: they remain strong and powerful, and I the mewing kitten ready to be crushed under the jackboot of fascism. The door closes and I am bathed in a gentle sea of piss-taking sarcasm, courtesy of my friends and colleagues.

But while we are on the subject of Argentina, let us take a digression to the side—which is where most of the action takes place anyway—away from the relentless push forward to the tail end of this story. The Falkland Islands debacle, Galtieri's little tactical diversion to take the country's mind off what is has just been through, unfortunately proves to be a further humbling experience for Argentina.

I will return to Argentina a few years later, this time to play some acoustic guitar concerts with my friend John Etheridge, another British guitarist. We arrive in Buenos Aires after playing some shows in Brazil, and on the first afternoon there is a press conference in the hotel. I am being interviewed by several newspapers and magazines. One thing I notice is that at the end of each interview all the writers ask me about the cop-kicking incident; I am amazed by this, as it is now quite a few years later, but it seems that this incident has been recorded as a great rock moment in the annals of Argentina's history. At that moment in time, when the country was so repressed, any gesture of rebellion was seen as a waving flag. So, after this has been brought up several times I tell them that I now want a statue on Avenida Julio to mark my greatness, which they all think is pretty funny.

As we tour around Argentina, I notice that for the type of gig and the kind of music we were playing, there is an unusual amount of fervor: in La Plata we are given the keys to the city by the mayor in a gentle and touching ceremony backstage, and in Buenos Aires there is a virtual mob scene after the show that, considering we were playing jazz on acoustic guitars, feels a bit unwarranted. During this fervid scene I have the remarkable experience of being asked to bless a baby, and I begin to see what music and free expression mean in this country. The rest of the tour is not without incident either. In La Rosa, a small town deep in the pampas, we are onstage playing in a beautiful old theater when a bat somehow gets in and dive-bombs the audience for several minutes before using its radar to escape out the window. The effect is electrifying; for a moment all attention is on the creature as it whips over the heads of the audience—the bat becomes the show, and John and I merely the accompanists.

Afterward as we sign autographs there are a lot of signs of the cross being made and murmurings about vampires. *"Vampira, vampira,"* they say in shocked whispers as they proffer small floral autograph books and ticket stubs. "Welcome to the pampas," says one slightly less rural journalist type, grinning over the bobbing heads. It occurs to me that we should make the bat a permanent feature, give the show a nice Ozzy Osbourne touch; does it have an agent?

This Nosferatu theme is echoed a couple of years later when I turn up in Slovenia for a gig. In my imagination before going to Slovenia, I see a beautiful old Eastern European town with a lovely old art deco theater, food, wine, and adoring women. We drive over the border from Trieste in Italy. Immediately the sky seems to darken, and the trees, like in a spooky children's story appear to grasp at us with long, sinister claws. We pull over to a building that's like something out of a sixties Hammer film and discover with an inward grimace that this is our hotel. It is Gothic, to say the least, and might be better described as a Transylvanian flophouse. The rooms are dark and tawdry, with filthy sheets on the beds, and I wonder if by morning I will have metamorphosed into a giant cockroach. Should I hang garlic over the door? Wear a crucifix? Michael Shrieve and Jerry Watts leave before I do to check bass and drums, respectively, and then about an hour later I get picked up for the drive to the venue—wherever it is. The two guys who collect me are tall and gaunt with stringy shoulder-length hair and speak almost no English. I climb into the back of what might be a Russian car, and we hit the road like a bat out of hell.

The roads are unlit; the towns are dark menacing shapes with no sign of the living; and the fields are black but probably full of black demonic troglodytes. "Highway to Hell" plays on the car stereo at stomach-wrenching volume, and I think that I will almost certainly go to the grave with the sounds of AC/DC ringing in my ears. I feel very sick. Amazingly, we make it—that is, we pull up in a field that has a small concrete building and a neon sign on the side blinking intermittently with the word KLUB. This is it: gone the beautiful old Transylvanian theater, gone the red wine of the Baltic States, gone the adoring women and the encores between plush red velvet curtains.

I step out of the car into about nine inches of mud and drag myself to the mouth of this hellhole. It is dark and icy with a small stage at one end, no *salon des artistes,* no genial promoter. Jerry and Michael are on the stage, looking desperate and defeated. I make one or two ironic remarks about showbiz and then spot the bar—there is only one way to put up with this. I order not one but two lemon vodkas and drink them fast. This takes the edge off, and suddenly it seems like just another amusing moment in the ever changing tableau. "As long as we don't get killed," I say encouragingly to the boys, but there seems to be a good chance that we will. The few youths around the place are looking at us in an ugly sort of way; only the blood-heating vodka gives me the strength to smile wanly in their direction. One of the tall-and-gaunts manages to garble out something about food, and we follow him back out into the field and around to the other side of the building, where there is a garishly lit room with a bar. "Sit," we are told. "Food come." The war with Bosnia is just a few miles down the road, and my smiling drunk-and-happy falling about does not go down too well with the locals crowded in the bunker; there is a vibe.

We sit at our table and all eyes are on us as we quaff the red wine that appears—I would like to say brought by the landlord's buxom daughter, but instead it is a brutish-looking thing with a scrappy beard and a mouthful of broken teeth who surely must answer to the name of Igor. The food is a huge pile of red meat on a tray; there is nothing else—no vegetables, no sauce, no condiments, nothing—and it's dumped down before us as if in challenge. But like vampires, we lean forward and suck it up.

Now we have to entertain. We go back to the stage, burping and belch-ing, and clamber up onto the wooden boards, where we have to change on a set of stairs at the side of the stage in full view of the audience. It is all point-less but we do it anyway, turning it into a sort of strip show. They are not amused. The crowd in the dark below us is 90 percent male, with a haunted look of extreme discontent, the look of the undead. The music coming over the PA is of the furious death-metal kind and is what they are expecting; this feels like a suicide mission. We get out on the stage and I open with "Hack-ensack" by Monk. This doesn't go over too well. Someone yells out, "Metal!" and I briefly consider doing "Wade in the Water" but think better of it and carry on with something of my own. It is a grim moment in which I have never felt so unwanted. We churn on for a while, hoping we will break through, but they want metal and that's it. Their country is at war, they are depressed, it's a bleak moment, they need a soundtrack to mirror the rage they are feeling—and I am not providing it. I cut the set short, sign no auto-graphs, and head back through the black night to the inn of misery, which features a very raunchy live porno show until six A.M.

Back in Argentina, the tour ends in the city of Córdoba, somewhere in the middle of the country. After the final concert we have a day to pack up and then catch the evening flight out of there. In the afternoon everyone but me disappears to the airport to check on the flight and make sure that the gear gets on, etc. My passport has been taken to show that we are who we say we are. I decide to walk around the depressing little town and take photographs with my Leica, a habit I have practiced for several years. I spend about two or three hours shooting and am finally returning to the hotel when a window catches my eye: the sunlight is falling on it in an interesting way, illuminating a piece of rolled-up paper with flies all over it. I bend down, raise the Leica, begin photographing from several oblique angles, until I feel a tap on my shoulder.

Thinking it's a fan or something, I ignore it. *"Señor,"* comes the voice again, this time with more urgency, *"identificación, por favor."* I turn around and, horror of horrors, it's the bloody cop again—or if it isn't him, it's his twin brother. My gut turns to ice. Now what? *"Identificación, identificación,"* he demands, holding out five sausages and a steak masquerading as his hand. I feel stupid—I have nothing except a driver's license and a couple of credit cards, which I proffer with a hopeful smile. He is not impressed by American Express and asks again for ID. I gulp and try a few feeble attempts in Spanish, to no avail—he isn't budging. *"Viene,"* he barks, and gripping me by the arm, we march off down the street. *"Estación,"* he grunts, and grips me tighter. I get the idea that he taking me to the police station and feel the familiar hollow in my stomach again—now bloody what? We pace across a dusty yard off the street and into a set of bleak concrete buildings that apparently constitute the station.

Inside Hermann Göring (or his double) is sitting at a desk. The cop says something in rapid-fire Spanish to Hermann, and I am shuffled off into an adjacent office and motioned to sit down. I desperately think about making a run for it and then also imagine the spray of bullets penetrating my body as I pitch headlong into the hot dust, which no doubt would make for good rock legend. But how am I going to explain it to my building society manager?

I am in the shit again—it doesn't feel very good—the ceiling fan turns like a dying pulse above my head, flies buzz around the room, the temperature pushes over a hundred. A feeling of panic begins to fill me as I realize that this is deadly serious: I have no *identificación,* no one here speaks English, and I am alone. The guys will return from the airport and I will simply have vanished, become one of *los desaparecidos.* A tall man with cropped hair enters the room, his piercing blue eyes staring at me through steel-rim spectacles. Whoever the costume designer is for this lot is doing a splendid job. He proceeds to interrogate me. *"Soy musico, concierto anoche."* I even resort to using "The Police, Sting," in the vain hope that it might bring a vague hint of recognition, but no, it means nothing to him—nada. A butterfly suddenly flutters into view through a small window high up on the wall; its dancing down like an alien creature in this office seems to me a small beacon of hope. It flutters low and in front of Göring's face; without taking his eyes off me, he lashes out, grabs the butterfly and crushes it with one hand, and then says, *"Claro,"* picks up the phone, barks into it, and motions for me to get up—I am being moved. I get the idea that I am to be taken somewhere else. I start to write my obituary—dead in an Argentinian jail, disappeared in South America, lost to the world, gone—it would be a glamorous ending to a misspent life and would look good on the front page of the *Guardian,* but I don't feel quite ready for it.

I am hustled outside into the yard again, and we frog-march to the front gate. I am being moved to the main station. As I stand flanked by heavies, the ice forming in my heart, another man crosses the yard, someone I haven't seen before. He stares at me in a peculiar way and then tells me that he speaks English and asks what is going on. With a huge sigh of relief, I tell him that I was merely taking photographs like a tourist—just having a good time, I played last night, etc. He asks me if I have any identification, I hand him my driver's license, he takes it and turns his back to me. I imagine he's having a good laugh at my expense or thinking about which fingernail to rip out first when he turns back to me and asks "Are you Andy Summers of the Police?" My heart sinks—they are going to get me this time, they haven't forgotten the incident a few years ago—but yes, I nod vigorously, yes. His face breaks into a radiant smile. "I am big rock fan—I love Police—nice to meet you." I practically break down and weep but manage to croak out, "Why am I here? What did I do?" "Oh," he says, "you were taking photographs of the bank window; we thought that you were probably part of a gang and were casing the joint." I would have laughed but I felt too distraught—and what is the point of going into a long explanation about art photography and the aesthetics of Cartier-Bresson? He smiles, warns me not to take pictures of the bank in the future, and says, "Alright, you can go." I shake his hand one more time and walk up the street to the hotel like a man reprieved seconds before going to the chair.

Twenty-One

After the Buenos Aires balls-up we hit Rio for a few days and then close out the year with the masterstroke of playing a tent on Tooting Bec Common. Someone has had the bright idea of "playing in a tent for Christmas"—nice for the kids. So, we leave the white sand of Ipanema, Sugarloaf Mountain, the swaying dental-floss bikinis of Rio, the softly throbbing pulse of the bossa nova; get into the Concorde; drop by Senegal; catch another flight in Paris; and end up, ten thousand miles later, in a sea of mud and biting December wind on Tooting Bec Common.

I have just enough time to meet and reunite with Kate and Layla before being driven over to Tooting. It is with a wave of emotion that I walk through the door, pick up the baby, and kiss her and Kate together; in the warmth of their embrace, the plane flights, giant crowds, and the fascist regime of Argentina melt away like spring snow. But Kate and I always need a period of readjustment. I return full of adrenaline—having been with the band, having been with men, talking bullshit—and expect everything to bend to my will. Kate returns to the relationship from a soft world of motherhood, having been alone with an infant, and with her own set of ideas about marriage. We reach for each other, but the fabric of our partnership is wearing thin and I have to leave again.

The show is sold out. The gigantic tent holds five thousand, and already there are about ten thousand mud-spattered fans pushing and shoving to get inside. In the Christmas spirit we have had the clever notion to have Tommy Cooper open the show. Tommy is a well-loved TV star in England, an English institution, and we think the crowd will love him. It's a disaster. Most of the kids in the audience have no idea who he is, and they ruin the show by screaming out for the Police all through Tommy's act. As if he has just been stoned, Tommy comes offstage white and shaking, vowing never to do that again. We feel very embarrassed and upset that we have put him, one of our heroes, through such a wringer—good intentions gone wrong.

Finally we get on and it's the usual bloody riot, but this time with dangerous overcrowding and stifling air inside the tent. A large number of fans get carried out by the redoubtable men of the St. John Ambulance Brigade, only now they don't appear to be faking it. Naturally, the next day in the press we get slagged for having the arrogance of putting our fans through such an ordeal and endangering their lives—who do we think we are?—the usual predictable small-minded and boring crap that the English tabloids come up with on a daily basis.

Two nights later, as the capper to the year, we have a big bash at the Holiday Inn Chelsea. This party—our celebration—is the hottest party in London. I sit with Kate at a long table and grin and smile and grip her hand as we display ourselves for the interminable lines of people and paparazzi waiting to meet us. But beneath the hallucinatory party fever I feel the tension of trying to reconnect with Kate and at the same time trying to keep up the requisite rock-and-roll persona. She is a private person—the glaring spotlight of publicity is not to her taste—and beneath the strobe of white light she feels the reality of a relationship that is becoming more difficult despite efforts on both sides. Layla is at home with a babysitter we have never used before, which doesn't help either, and halfway through the evening Kate decides to go home to make sure that everything is okay. I get a car for her and we kiss and she murmurs in my ear, "Do your thing, darlin."

I return to the fray, throw myself into the intoxicating whirl, and after several glasses of champagne decide there is only one thing to do: jump fully clothed into the pool. Someone shoves one of the A&M guys in first, and with cameras flashing in a feeding frenzy, we all follow. The next day it's all over the papers with a tabloidesque "rich and spoiled pop stars cavorting while the world suffers" story line. We have to justify our newfound financial status; we have started a charity organization and are giving all our English earnings away, liking throwing a bone to a rabid dog in the hope that it won't tear your throat out.

After Christmas—as if we never left—we return to North America for a show at the Forum in Montreal on January 7, 1981, as a warm-up for Madison Square Garden, which we will play three days later. Preceded by its own legend, the Garden is one of the premier venues in the world, a gig beyond our wildest dreams, but we sell it out in three hours. I am excited to be back in New York, as it always feels that we have returned to the dead center of the world. As we walk out onto the stage the energy of an already fever-pitch audience is galvanizing. Now they hold up pictures of us, placards with scrawled messages and our names, with sassy comments at the side, and it's difficult to feel anything other than thrilled by the energy.

Our best playing now is during the sound checks, when we can still cut loose and play all kinds of music with almost nothing from the show, and it's during these jams when we come up with ideas for new riffs and rhythmic concepts that are the lifeblood of our music. In the actual shows now as we move through the worked-out set list—the songs the audience expect—I feel frustrated. Although it is fun to do all the textural and harmonics stuff I have developed for the band, I actually want to let rip with some off-the-wall solos and feel as if we are really playing together, creating in the moment rather than performing verses and choruses in the correct order. When I do cut loose there is a strong audience reaction to the moment of release. But there is a problem. At this point Sting doesn't like to be overshadowed onstage; when I take a guitar solo, he wants it over with quickly—as it takes him out of the spotlight. The punk credo of "no solos" is held in place, but it diminishes the range of the group. I get it—I don't like it but, in the interest of keeping the status quo intact, reluctantly temper my own impulses; we have enough problems already. Sting says that he doesn't like guitar solos, and he will stand by this in the future. But in private I practice incessantly anyway, as if preparing for a different future, and listen to music that is markedly different from the Police. I travel down arcane alleys in search of little-known composers, hidden geniuses, music from Mali or southern India, the new jazz of ECM. I often get asked what I am listening to, and instead of being able to give some bright rock-and-roll response and list of a few rock groups, I mutter about Gavin Bryars or Ramón Montoya or Coltrane's Crescent, a Bulgarian State women's choir, wishing that they hadn't asked me.

The show at the Garden is a euphoric success and is marred only by someone slinging a vodka bottle that goes through Stewart's bass drumhead, at which point we have to stop the show and ad-lib while it gets replaced. Most groups would leave the stage, but we just stand there and try to keep twenty-five thousand people giggling. Andy Warhol comes backstage afterward and we have our picture taken with him and he gives me a copy of *Interview* magazine with the inscription "To Andy, from Andy." The next day I turn up at the Factory, off Union Square, and he takes my picture. It takes about fifteen minutes from start to finish.

We land back in L.A. for two shows. The first is downtown at the Variety Arts Theatre, where we pull a stunt called Blondes over L.A.—the idea being that you cannot get into the show unless you have blond hair, or at least a blond wig. To his credit, Miles can still dream up the odd piece of rock-and-roll surrealism, and this is just another lark to make us something different. But backstage there is tension as Sting does not want to go onstage wearing a silly wig. He is pissed off about the whole thing; he is moving away from the band, and I see that from his point of view, this piece of silliness just pushes him back into the collective, subdues his personality, and goes against his grain. But eventually he relents and we hit the stage wearing big black wigs, but by the end of the first song Sting has tossed his onto the stage, joke over.

We play at the L.A. Sports Arena and before the show we hoover up some of Bolivia's finest and play a tight fast set brimming with powdered energy. Stevie Nicks stands at the side of the stage and watches the whole show. As I come offstage I get a note from her asking to meet her later at the Rainbow, a sleazy rock joint on the Strip that everyone fights to get into—unless you are a celeb, in which case you walk in with a cool swagger, superior and more important than the proles who hang around outside. L.A., Hollywood—it suddenly seems like a sewer and I miss New York.

This is the eighties, the era of money and excess. Reagan is king and will triple the national debt, support apartheid, back Saddam Hussein, fantasize about Star Wars, support Central American death squads, and trade arms for hostages. Cocaine use rages like a white blizzard, and to avoid it, you would need a Band-Aid over your mouth and nose. Wherever we are now, drug dealers leap like genies from the wallpaper. We have power now, fame; and like a magnet, it sucks in everyone from celebrities to pushers, all hoping to rub up against the illusion. Everyone does coke: lawyers, bankers, athletes, accountants, office workers, roadies, technicians, limo drivers, and hotel maids. From the straightest to the worst party animals, its use is epidemic, and all activities seemed to be accompanied by a line or two through the rolled-up dollar bill.

In a flash moment one night Kim Turner decides to use a hundred-dollar bill as the snorting funnel. There are several stray people in the party, and an attractive girl on the end of the line pockets Kim's bill and, having made her money for the night, disappears. A few years from now many of these people will have deviated septums and ruined lives. They crowd around us, imploring us to do drugs with them. They want to get stoned with the Police and later brag about it. Some are very smooth and insinuate themselves into the ranks without being seen. They smell money, power, the edge; they're hungry and come at us with drooling mouths.

Every time we are in L.A., a Latino guy with slicked-back hair and a sharp suit appears as if by magic, and his message is always the same: he can get us anything we want, he just wants to be our friend, he's just here to help, what do we need, he just loves the music. *Yeah, right,* we think, and sometimes I wonder if there is a breakdown in the mental processes of these people. Their assumption is that we are a band and therefore must be party monsters, fucked up twenty-four hours a day, and yet creating and making music without a care in the world. We have to be discreet and develop a sixth sense for those who might suck us into the vortex, realizing where too much powder can take you and watching out for one another. Most of the stuff seems cut with crap and dumps you in an ugly wasteland the next day.

The atmosphere around the band is becoming even more excessive, more hedonistic. The party never ends, and with a shrug we enjoy the festivities. Extraordinary demands are placed on us and we simply would not be able to deliver these intense shows without the occasional rocket fuel.

In this moment it is as if we are passing through a danger zone full of tests and enemies before we get to the castle. We are on the threshold of even bigger success, the ultimate prize, and it would be very easy to blow it now. We are swimming with serpents, but the group is our raft—the music our life support.

Twenty-Two

On we go through Hawaii, Japan, and New Zealand to end the tour in Perth. I should return straight home to Kate and Layla, but dazed and confused, I stupidly decide to spend another three weeks photographing in Asia. This is poor judgment on my part, as Kate is suffering alone without help and I know that I should be there. Yet I am compelled to stay on the road, not wanting the illusion to stop for a minute. With this decision, I exchange my marriage for forty rolls of film.

Stewart and I have ourselves delivered to the Oberoi Hilton in Kuta Beach, a fabulous setup where you stay in ultradeluxe Balinese thatched cottages. We spend a couple of days recovering from the rigors of touring by hanging around the pool, and we meet the actor/comedian John Belushi. John is a big star in the United States; his skits on *Saturday Night Live,* the movie *The Blues Brothers,* wild behavior and hard living have made him famous.

Drinks in hand, we meet at the pool and immediately hit it off; no doubt we find a camaraderie through having arrived in the spotlight at roughly the same time and our similar tastes for most things that are off the dial. In five minutes we mutually discover that nearby in Kuta village there is a café that sells magic mushroom omelets. The magic mushrooms weirdly enough are called *Copelandia*; they grow in cow shit and apparently are mighty powerful—in fact, they have the highest concentration of alkaloids found in hallucinogenic mushrooms anywhere in the world. We look at one another

for a full nanosecond and, deciding that we have to get ourselves some of these dang things, head out to get lunch.

The restaurant is a small, rickety building constructed of bamboo poles and thatched palm fronds. At the entrance on a chalkboard is a menu on which is plainly written in English the dish of the day: "magic mushroom omelet." We order from the young Balinese serving girl. She disappears into the kitchen and we hear a lot of giggling. We look at one another. No doubt the Balinese are planning to fuck us up bad. John raises his left eyebrow in the way that he is famous for, and that says it all. The omelets arrive and are in fact delicious, and only a scientific palate would detect the chemical key to paradise. So we enjoy our lunch and then make plans to cross the island to see the famous sunken temple.

We decide to go in my rented jeep. It's an old banger, heavily rented and dented, but it's enough to get us around the island. One of the problems with the jeep is that the canvas convertible roof is broken on the right corner because the snap is missing. It's difficult to get into place, and the only way to secure it is with a rusty nail that is kindly supplied by the rental office with an enigmatic smile.

We climb into the rent-a-crock and start out, the first obstacle being the circumnavigation of downtown Denpasar, which is about twenty-five minutes away. We drive toward the city, waiting for the mushrooms to take effect, looking at one another every few minutes, and murmuring, "I'm not feeling anything yet"; meanwhile, down in the pancreas the mushrooms are setting up shop, chemistry is taking place, and little fungus wizards are waving their wands about. We arrive on the outskirts of Denpasar and realize that we have to get onto the one-way circular road before breaking off onto the road to the sunken temple, the objective of our trip. We pull up at the edge—it's total madness, an absolute roaring chaos of trucks and mad, grinning Balinese on scooters. This unstoppable swarm of people on scooters, which is everywhere, is one of the worst features of Asian city life. We are confronted with it just as the mushrooms take effect and we sit for several minutes in a trance, gazing at this spectacle because now it all seems so groovy, and then as if arriving together on another plane we all wake up.

"Okay, les go," says John, as if making the decision to go into battle. "Yeah," I drawl back, forgetting that I am the driver. "Well, go on," says Stewart. "Oh, right," I say, and pump the gas, and we slide out into the onslaught of a thousand Asian Vespas. Insane and exhilarating, it's like being in the middle of a race against time. The Balinese men on wheels thrive on this madness, and we laugh like hyenas as I weave and dodge and do everything I can to avoid ending up a red stain at the side of the road. The noise is horrendous, like being locked up in an aircraft hangar with a jet revving all its engines, but somehow—in a weird combination of total concentration and dreaminess as the mushrooms kick in even deeper—we hold our course through the storm.

We whip on for a few more miles until we see a large sign for the sunken temple and, yelling and screaming, swerve across the road to the exit. As we do this the sky, like a mouth emitting a giant belch, lets rip with a tropical downpour so thick and intense that you can barely see your hand in front of your eyes. It isn't rain, but Armageddon, an end-of-the-world apocalyptic number. The raindrops in Indonesia are not pretty little rainbow-filled things but rather, being about six inches long and three inches wide, lethal smart bombs of H_2O capable of causing a nasty concussion.

"Get the roof up," we all yell together. We screech over into the dirt at the side of the road, and Belushi and I leap out to secure the roof. With Niagra Falls beating us into an early grave and 'shroomed out of our minds, we heave and tug at the recalcitrant canvas roof that is folded up at the back of the rear seat. Eventually we pull it free and, gasping hysterically, try to fit it in place. Of course, I have forgotten about the broken corner and the bloody rusty nail to fix it, which has gone missing, and suddenly the significance of the enigmatic smile comes to me—bastards! Somewhere in the middle of this mayhem, laughing like hyenas, we realize that we are trying to fix the roof to keep from getting wet when we're already like drowned rats. With this brilliant insight, we just fall down into the road and roll about in the newly formed puddles like deranged children. A couple of Balinese walk by with donkeys and carts and smile, probably recognizing the effects of their local vegetable.

We get back into the jeep and begin driving along little country roads in the direction of the sunken temple. Everything now appears in a wondrous state after the downpour: steaming, fecund, and primeval. Little prismatic rainbows spring up from every leaf and branch, which seem to be growing right in front of our eyes. All along the road Balinese families bathe in the stream at the edge, waving and smiling at us, and I feel intensely happy.

John says, "They don't call it the rain forest for nothing." This strikes a deep chord and we go into hysterics again. As we are going through this new fit of insanity, a truck pulls right in front of us and sits there. On the back of the truck is a huge colored picture with the words TARZAN THE APE MAN, which finishes us off; now we need straitjackets. The truck is advertising an old film that is to be shown in a local village, but because the picture merges so perfectly with the landscape we are in, it's like a trick of the eye—and in our confused state we lose the last vestige of reality. Fully expecting to see Tarzan, we sit on the tail of the truck like children waiting for an ice cream.

We pull out into an open area with a meadow and a huge banyan tree, where a team of white-shirted soccer players are kicking a ball across the field below. John and I get out to watch them. We stand at the side of the field as interested spectators of the game, and then the ball suddenly rolls to our feet. John gives the ball a hefty kick back out into the field and receives a small round of applause. It comes back, and this time I lob it back. That's it, we race out into the field for a full-on game with the Balinese—only it's not a game in the strict sense of the word, but two deranged lunatics laughing and screaming and smacking the ball all over the place in an effort to beat the eleven Balinese players. Expending a furious amount of fungus-fueled

energy, we throw in rugby tackles and headers, run with the ball in our hands, toss it over the heads of the Balinese, until we score six or seven goals and trot off the field to friendly waves, a small round of applause, and looks of disbelief. I turn to John and say in my best Etonian accent, "I think the white man reigns supreme."

We carry on with the rest of our journey, mesmerized by rice paddies, longhorned oxen, more banyan trees, and golden-skinned Balinese kids playing in the ditches, until we reach the sunken temple site, where we spend the rest of the afternoon gazing out at the ocean as the fly agaric runs its course. Finally, after what seems like years of golden dreaming and as the sun slips beneath the silhouette of the sunken temple, we arrive at the idea of returning to the hotel. We climb back into the jeep, and with a glint in his eye, Belushi takes the wheel and floors it. The speedometer hovers around ninety as we yell at one another about great movies, hold on to the sides of the jeep with a white-knuckled grip, and scream as we ricochet out of another pothole. Miraculously, we reach the hotel unscathed.

The next day we opt for another adventure, renting a beautiful motor launch complete with crew, the object being to make it to Nusa Penida, a small island off the coast of Bali. Nusa Penida at that time is inhabited by only one village of primitive Indonesians, most of whom have had very little contact with white people. We each take a healthy dose of chemical omelet again and haul anchor. The ocean and islands we sail through seem like emeralds dropped into a cobalt soup, and as the sacred vegetables take effect we become mute, silenced by the sea, the sky, and the string of green-jewel islands we pass by. The action of the mushrooms intensifies and brings us to a point where we become paranoid and can't look at one another, can't speak. I try to look at the clouds, but they turn into stone to become hostile faces, so I look down and try to concentrate on details of the launch, waiting for this moment to pass. I feel nauseous and go up to the stern of the boat to vomit, and watch fascinated as my spew drifts off into the ocean behind.

Finally we reach the island, and as the internal storm smoothes out we drop anchor and look across the water at the shoreline: a white-sand beach with a dense backdrop of rain forest. A small brown figure emerges, and we wave. The figure waves back. We wave again, the figure waves again until all we are doing is waving at each other like flags in a breeze. It feels splendid and we grin at one another, delighted with our waving. More people emerge from the trees and then more and more until it appears that the entire village is out to greet us. In the magical continuum we now inhabit, this moment is imbued with the feeling of a first encounter, alien beings greeting one another, lost souls reestablishing contact. Gazing out across the Indian Ocean, I feel like Captain Cook arriving on the shores of Hawaii.

We are all waving like mad now and on impulse we dive over the side of the boat and into the water, and then they dive in and begin swimming out to us. Within minutes we are surrounded by brown-skinned people, laughing, smiling, and greeting us like old friends. It's a feeling of intense joy and happiness that somehow is simple and ancient; no barriers, no preconceptions, no fear, just beings greeting one another in celebration. We can't understand one another, but we get the idea that they want to show us their village. Like a school of dolphins, we swim to the shore and follow them on a path through the rain forest to their village, which is inside a staked compound. They have large thatched huts and we go inside one of them and sit on the floor while they show us clay pots, knives, fabrics, the artifacts of their daily existence. Words are grunted out to signify each item, and we grunt back with encouraging sounds. It feels as though we are in an enchanted zone, and all concerns

about records and tours and movies lose meaning as we experience this moment
as if it is the only reality we know or have ever known. The visit finally comes to
an end and we trip back along the trail through a tapestry of thick verdant rain
forest, trilling birdsong, prismatic butterflies, and the sweet smell of fecund nature until we arrive back on the sparkling white sand, where we part company
with sweet smiles and nods, swim back to the boat, and set sail for Bali.

A few days later we go our separate ways. I promise to hook up with
Belushi in a few weeks in New York. I arrive in Bangkok and immediately
fall in with a group of young Thai royalty who have been waiting for me.
For a few days we wander in and out of palaces, float up and down canals,
walk through the underbelly of Bangkok while I photograph and smoke
Thai stick. I call Kate. She sounds distressed and in need of my support. She
puts Layla on the phone, who chirps out, "Dadda." A rush of remorse cuts

through me, and yet I hear myself merely promising to be home soon, as soon as I've been through India and Nepal.

The grinding penury of Calcutta smacks me in the face as I drive into the city in a shrunken cab that's not much bigger than my suitcase. People everywhere huddle together and contort their bodies into little holes in the walls of decaying buildings along the side streets, with nothing but small votive candles to add a pathetic light to the pervading gloom. Calcutta seems even more sunk in decrepitude than Bombay, and I wonder what it is that compels me to visit these places. At the hotel I am met by a suave young Indian who has been contacted ahead of time by one of the Thai set. He tells me that I am his welcome guest and promises to show me around. But the next day, ignoring the warnings not to visit these areas, I hit the back streets of Calcutta alone and—now having developed furtive techniques to disguise the act of taking pictures—manage to shoot several rolls of film without getting killed in the process. In the evenings I join up with a crowd of forward-thinking young Calcuttans who argue vehemently with one another about everything. They are verbal, cerebral, and intense in a way that is a characteristic of the people in this part of India.

Flying into Tribhuvan Airport is not without hazard, as collisions between birds and aircraft occur frequently—a documented fact—but as we lurch down toward the runway, I am full of expectation. The city of Katmandu was the fabled end of the hippie trail in late-sixties London, and the road east was the requisite adventure. As I gazed up through the murky window of my West Kensington basement flat and played over the drone of a dropped D tuning, it hovered in my imagination like a dawn sun, the word *Katmandu,* like the word *Shangri-la,* conjuring up a feeling of ultimate spiritual destination. As I struggle through the airport with my guitar, cameras, suitcase, and dozens of little Nepalese kids holding out their hands and yelling, "Monee," *This,* I think, *is it.*

Checking into the Yak and Yeti hotel, I am slightly disappointed by how modern in 1981 this place already seems to be—a little too Westernized maybe. But excited, I drop my things in the room and set out for Durbar

Square in the center of the city. As I pass through alleyways, *chowks,* stupas, pagodas, and *shikara* temples, I begin to fall under a spell. Katmandu—with its crazy mix of Hinduism, Buddhism, Shamanism, and Islamic beliefs and languages—impresses me as a city where all of mystical Asia merges. In Durbar Square I meet some French kids and get into a conversation with them, and before long we have climbed to the top of a building to lie out in the afternoon sun, smoke some hash, and gaze out over the city. The alkaloids take effect, and the warm heat of the sun makes me sleepy as I stretch out on the tiles. I laugh, thinking that this is completely daft but I had to do it sometime, I suppose, and follow that up with the sacred mantra—*om mani padme hum* (hail to the jewel in the lotus)—and then let my mind drift out across the rooftops into the soft blur of the eastern sky.

A couple of hours later we collectively grunt and begin to move. One of my new friends, Jean-François, offers to show me where they are staying, just off the legendary Freak Street. Located in the heart of old Katmandu, Freak Street was the place you had to go in the sixties and seventies. As I walk through it in the late afternoon I realize what it must have once been, with its resident hippies, the sounds of Hendrix, cheap dope, and fast-track spirituality, but already it seems to have faded. We arrive in a shabby little hotel where my friends are all camped out in a couple of rooms with sleeping bags.

The next day, being a good tourist, I decide to visit a beautiful and revered old Buddhist shrine on the outskirts of the city, the Swayambhunath Temple. A small black taxi drops me off at the bottom of a very steep hill with a shrine at the top, and looking upward, I see the white temple glowing in the afternoon light with its Buddhist pendants fluttering in the breeze. I sling the camera bag over my shoulder and begin the long hike up the eastern stairway to the shrine. It's a warm, hazy afternoon and a small breeze brushes my face as I climb past the figures of Ganesh and Kumar. I feel happy as Katmandu, Nepal, interconnectedness, interbeing, fill my head in a sweet and drowsy brew. Then thoughts about my girls back in London intrude and I feel something else—selfishness, perhaps—but in the soft blur of the moment I promise to make everything alright and send them love from this hill.

Halfway up, as if hallucinating in the afternoon breeze, I hear one of our songs—"Voices Inside My Head." It doesn't seem possible. This is Nepal, the land of a thousand Buddhas, but as I get closer to the top of the hill, it grows louder until there is no mistaking it.

I pull up level with a small tin hut close to the shrine. Sitting there in the dirt is a shrunken old man with a tiny transistor radio, the track blasting out through the plastic grid into the dirt of Nepal at his naked feet. I smile at him and with advanced linguistics try to make him understand—me play . . . you radio . . . good. He looks up at me without comprehension and offers me a Coca-Cola from the crate he has at his side as he extends the other open palm for payment, obviously not realizing that a rock god stands before him. I smile at him with compassion and move up to the shrine to spin a few prayer wheels.

As I stare across the holy Bagmati River at the cremation ghats the next morning, the pungent odors of smoke and flowers fill my head as sensual memento moris of the death and mortality that face you every few feet in Katmandu. The small stupas here each contain a lingam of Shiva, the phallic symbol that represents his procreative powers. A little farther up the river I come to the Bachhareshwar Temple, full of painted skeletons and erotic scenes. I stare at them, thinking that everywhere you turn here there seems to be an illustration of some sort of embrace of life/death, a yearning toward the spiritual, the rising above human complication. In this kaleidoscope of sex, death, karma, and samsara, thoughts of record companies, American tours, and the next hit shrink away—at least until I get back to the hotel and pick up my guitar again. The immediacy of the instrument and traversing of frets and strings wash away these morbid scenes.

On the morning before I leave the Yak and Yeti to fly to India I sit in my room, practicing. For some reason I get into improvising on an old Charlie Parker tune, "Scrapple from the Apple." The door is halfway open and the Nepalese cleaning lady passes by. I hear a murmur of approval and then another one as I riff away on my own. Her face appears with a shy smile around the doorway, and it's obvious that she is digging it. I momentarily raise a finger and beckon her in. She enters and I keep on playing over the Parker changes as she sits quietly on the floor and closes her eyes, listening intently. It is akin to playing to a deer in the forest, a tremulous moment when you might easily scare the creature away. I keep playing and think, *My God, Parker comes to Katmandu*, then she gets up and makes the namaste sign and goes back out into the corridor, presumably to do her work. I pack away the little Gibson acoustic with a smile and think, *Is there anything actually better than music?*

In Delhi I spend the evening with Mr. Hakim Ghosh, who owns a stall in an underground market. I wandered by in the early evening and got into conversation with him, now he insists on taking me to dinner. We sit in a beautiful restaurant and he talks nonstop about his family, the future of India, and his father, who worked under the British. He has a brother with a family now living in Bethnal Green in London. I tell him that is where my mother was born, and we smile at each other in fraternity as we dip into a bit more prawn marsalsa. We finally part company with promises to write and stay in touch, and then having no other option, I spend the rest of the night in a squalid lodge across the road from the airport, waiting for a flight to London that is scheduled to leave at seven A.M. The room, illuminated by a single bare bulb dangling from the ceiling, is filthy and worn with light-green-colored paint flaking off its walls. I lie on the bed, keeping all my clothes on and my suitcase under my feet. At five A.M. sleepless, I wearily roll off the bed, go outside, and get a taxi to the airport, which is a nightmare scene of bodies lying in heaps everywhere on the floor as if dead. In the insufferable heat I join the interminable line for the flight, praying that I am going to get on. The plane takes off about eight A.M., and I let out a great breath, having made it through all of that.

I arrive back to the creeping cold and grey of Ireland and a partner who by now is alienated. This time it's difficult to get back to where we were; I feel I am straddling two worlds but somehow don't quite take it in, thinking that the estrangement due to the demands of showbiz couldn't possibly happen to us. This new feeling of distance between us is compounded by the bone-numbing damp and quiet of an Irish village—particularly in my head after the glamour and excitement of so many exotic cultures.

Although we now have some friends in the area, I find it hard to settle into any kind of social scene. I have a need—like a drug—to keep the illusion, the constant high, going all the time, but it seems impossible here in this tax-exile life I have returned to. I need to repair the damage I have done to our relationship with my prolonged and self-indulgent absence. But it's difficult to feel good here, where most of the time we are just coping with the cold and the lack of resources or anything to do except wander along the freezing and wild cliffs. It is a sad moment: the intimacy, love, and humor of just two years earlier seem to be slipping away, knocked out by the rush of the new world I am embroiled in.

I try but cannot fit into this scene that consists of going to the pub every night, drinking beer, and playing darts. I laugh and swallow brown ale in a haze of thick tobacco smoke, but I'm choking on the inside. As I raise my hand to chuck a dart at the board on the wall, I scream to be in New York or back onstage with a guitar. But I try to trick myself into believing that this is really the life, and in an effort to be like the locals, I go out on a sailing boat one day but feel so sick and hungover that I spend the whole time with my eyes closed on a bunk and Ireland passes through my head in a collage of thick, furrowed dirt, crashing salt water, black rubber boots, and endless pints of strong brown tea. In this village I'm regarded as a rock and roller, with all that the phrase implies.

In an effort to keep the insidious chill out, I dress in thick woolen clothes and leave the rainbow robes of rock and roll in a suitcase, where they lie like flags of a past life. The band begins to feel like a dream I once had, and as I toil with the coal fire and stare numbly at the dying flames, I fail to grasp what is happening to me, fail to see the disintegration of our marriage, cannot grasp what this beautiful woman with our child has sacrificed for me, ignore the widening gap between us, and am inadequate in repairing the damage. To compound this situation, I set up a studio in the basement that has one small window to let in the grey light. It's like a cell and I write songs obsessively for hours on end while my wife and child are elsewhere. Occasionally journalists visit to interview me, and it feels like a reprieve as I regain my persona for a few hours until they leave and I return to my song demos and the gunmetal skies of southwest Ireland.

One afternoon Kate comes into the basement with two-year-old Layla in her arms. There is a nasty gash on the baby's forehead. "Your daughter," she says, and drops her in my arms and then leaves the room. It says everything. I feel gutted. I try to make things better but I am like a man straddling two islands that are drifting apart, and the next two months pass with my feeling like a bright pink doll dropped in a field of grey, the fire of our marriage turning to ash.

Twenty-Three

In contrast to this bleak environment, our fourth album is to be recorded in the month of June 1981 at AIR Studios on the Caribbean island of Montserrat. This is the dream; this is the Beatles—a myth we are happy to embrace. We are sure that we will sell millions of the next album, and recording on a Caribbean island is a luxury we can afford. This time we can relax, take our time, get it right. In fact, we are scheduled for six weeks on the island, which by future standards will seem very short, although we never seem to need more than ten days.

After leaving Kate and Layla in Ireland with what I hope is a soulful departure, I head off to Montserrat by way of New York. I arrive in Manhattan around one A.M. and call Belushi. He screams my name into the phone and wants to hit the town immediately, but having just arrived on a long, arduous flight, I decline and say, "How about tomorrow night?" and pass out. At almost six in the morning there's a rapping on my door and I stagger out of bed to see who the hell it is. It's Belushi, with a big grin on his face. "Okay, man, let's go," he says, and walks over to the dresser and lays out twelve lines of coke and just smiles at me as he rolls a bill. "Okay, whaathefuck," I say, and we bend our heads over enough powder to fell a Peruvian llama and do the lot. Like Speedy González and his twin brother, we hit the streets of Manhattan at six A.M. in search of a party. Whooping, yelling, and numb, we whip around to several locations, banging on doors as John calls out names. But

there ain't much goin' on and despite the blizzard that's raging in our heads, there's nothing to do and by about nine A.M., feeling very wasted, we give up and John says, "Gotta sleep, man. See you tonight." "Yeah, right," I croak. He disappears and sleeps for three days, by which time I'm in Montserrat.

A funky island without the usual tourist glitz Montserrat has a beauty all its own topped off by a volcano that will eventually render two-thirds of the island uninhabitable. We check into the studio and get assigned our own private bungalows for the duration. The heat and lush, verdant topicality of the island drop you like a stone into a state of grooving relaxation, and within a couple of hours you go native. It feels good and it's hard not to laugh out loud at the fortune of all of this as we slip into a luxurious new life of swimming in the mornings, cruising the island, and gathering in the studio after lunch. The other families are here, but Kate has decided not to come; I feel the shadow of her absence under the bright Caribbean light. As I get to know the island I see with a heavy sense of irony that some of the places have Irish names. One village is even called Kinsale.

One of the first things we have to deal with is the fact that Sting has invited a Canadian keyboard player to join us on this album. Stewart and I are incensed, as nothing has been said to us. I feel adamant about not turning our guitar trio into some overproduced, overlayered band with keyboards. But within a day he turns up, a heavily built guy with an oversize ego to match his bulk. He has bamboozled Sting into flying him down from Canada after Sting did a bit of demo recording with him up in Montreal. He is a good player but he's added something like twelve layers of keyboards and synthesizers to one of Sting's songs, "Every Little Thing She Does Is Magic." It's a difficult situation and it's hard for Stewart and me to talk Sting out of it, so we go into the studio with the keyboards. But here the intruder signs his own death warrant because he smothers everything we play with dense keyboard parts so that we end up sounding like Yes on a bad day. He compounds the problem by leaning over his synthesizer every few minutes and playing us one of his riffs and exclaiming, "Listen to that—boy, if I heard that, I'd love to have it on my album." It's painful. He lasts three days and then even Sting wearies of him and sends him on his way.

After this little debacle we get down to the business of making a real Police record. We begin the process of working our way into the new record by tentatively playing one another our song demos, a painful and difficult moment because each one of us would like to have all his songs recorded. But Sting doesn't want to sing anything unless he has written it, and most of my songwriting in Ireland comes to nothing. I have some good songs that will not get recorded, and I resent it. I have to deal with my own bad feeling and try to come out positive, but I can't help thinking that this time one or two of Sting's songs are not as good as mine. Maybe my writing is too close to his or too Police-like for him to feel comfortable. But in the interest of keeping the ship afloat, I go along with it. Sting remarks to Vic Garbarini, a journalist friend of ours, that "Andy is good, too good maybe," and it hurts. We end up recording some songs that in my mind are filler.

However, "Spirits in the Material World," "Invisible Sun," "Secret Journey," and "Every Little Thing She Does Is Magic" are all standout songs, and we get to work on them. "Magic" is a problem because we use Sting's expensive demo as the actual track; Stewart and I just have to try and fit ourselves into it. Strangely enough and despite the fact that it's a great song, it never sounds like a true Police track to me and after the recording we rarely play it in concert. "Spirits in the Material World" is a great new original song inspired by George Harrison. We argue a bit about this one because again

Sting has worked it out on a keyboard and wants it on the instrument he wrote it on. The line under the vocal starts with a beautiful extended minor ninth chord. Sting grumbles that it's a bit tricky for the guitar, but I point out to him that in fact I can play the whole part standing on my head if need be—no problem. But he won't budge and we end up with a sort of generic sound that is a mix of guitar and keyboards. Again, it somewhat lacks the true Police sound. "Demolition Man" is a tough rocker that also puts us though a little bit of a power play. I pull off a ripping solo on the outro of the song that should be played loud and clear, but when it comes to mix time it gets played too low and, much to my chagrin, gets lost. Clearly things are starting to move in a weirder direction and it's becoming a fight to keep up the camaraderie. But despite these internal frictions, the truth that Stewart and I have to acknowledge privately is that without Sting's songwriting talent, it wouldn't happen—and this gives him power over the two of us. On the other hand, where would he be without the two of us? It always comes back to the indivisible sum, and in the all-pervasive group life, lines like this become an interior monologue. But in this moment and put crudely, it becomes either Sting's way or no way; almost all ideas are carried out on a confrontational basis, and the idea of a group democracy fades. However, one of my songs does make it onto the album. It's called "Omega Man," and in the end Sting somewhat resentfully agrees to sing it even though it's clear that he doesn't really want to. Later Miles plays it at the first A&M meeting about *Ghost in the Machine*, and they want to release it as the first single, but Sting puts his foot down and will not let it happen—so it doesn't. When I hear about it, it feels like a knife in the back.

This time the studio feels more like a canvas for dirty fighting. The stakes have been raised, and instead of rejoicing in the unbelievable success we have created together, we lose sight of the big picture and go on in emotional disorder, each one of us battling for his own territory. In the deeper recesses of our collective soul there is a bond between us, but it's getting veiled by the arm wrestling, the internecine battling and striving, the pushy maleness of it all. There are arguments in the studio in which each one of us wants his instrument slightly louder than the others, wants his songs recorded, will not be less than anyone else. It is a combative process, with the poor engineer trying to arbitrate as three sets of hands fiddle with the faders.

For this recording, after sadly letting go of Nigel Gray because of the debacle of *Zenyatta Mondatta,* we have a new engineer/co-producer in the person of Hugh Padgham, a soft-spoken middle-class sort of chap who is confronted with three raging egos. The drums, the bass, and the guitar are going down onto tape, but his voice is faint as we battle it out. There is a humiliating episode in the studio one day when as a result of all this tension and loss of perspective, Sting goes berserk on me, calling me every name under the sun with considerable vehemence, leaving everyone in the room white-faced and in shock. It's an excruciating moment. I don't know whether I feel my pain or his pain more, but it is a deep wound, an outward manifestation of the frustration Sting must feel on the inside.

We get past it later with "sorry, man," and "I love you—sorry, mate," because underneath the layers of tension there is genuine affection. But I feel pain because—why? Why the fuck why? How long, I wonder, how long?

The next morning I get a call from Kate, who tells me with hardly a breath that she wants a divorce. The buzzing flies and drifting palms become a roar in my ears as I sink to the floor. I argue on the phone with her, but it is useless. She is intractable; she has made her decision, that's it. I walk outside into the white light, feeling numb. Gone? She's gone? I can't imagine not waking up next to her—the pyramid of golden hair, the slender waist, the soft voice, the subtle humor, the incisive intelligence, the relationship, our child. The smell of paradise fills my head like a sour perfume, the bushes a few feet away across the small manicured lawn staring back at me like a hellish vision, and it feels as if a beautiful object has just slipped through my fingers and smashed. I feel the urge to return immediately to Ireland to try to rescue the situation, but she doesn't want me to come back, says she'll see me in Canada to work things out. I stare up at the burning disc of sun and shiver, feel like throwing up.

I go back to the studio as usual that day, but with the sense that I inhabit a different world. I don't feel free, I just feel fucked up. I don't want this, don't want it. Love is the ultimate cruelty.

We work our way through the rest of the new songs: "Invisible Sun,"

"Hungry for You," "Too Much Information," "Rehumanize Yourself," and "One World." In the studio Sting is going through a phase of playing alto saxophone, and on many of these songs he adds little sax riffs that give the album a more blustery rhythm and blues feel than we have had in the past. One of my favorites this time is "Secret Journey," a song he has extracted from the pages of Gurdjieff's book *Meetings with Remarkable Men.* In spirit, this one is very much of the sixties, and as if returning to an earlier stance, I try to create the sound of the Himalayas with my Roland guitar synthesizer. In the middle of all the banter, bullshit, and brutality that are par for the course, I fight the desolation in my head with a facade of bonhomie and camaraderie, but it feels thin and I find it hard to concentrate as if I am trying to ignore a bad dream. I know I will have to say something eventually. I can't think of anything except the telephone call with Kate, and I keep going over it in my head. The nights are stifling and now sleepless as my brain races from the song we have just recorded to Kate's voice to the dive-bombing whine of mosquitoes in the oppressively close heat.

Stepping away finally from the Police-speak of the first three albums, this one will be called *Ghost in the Machine,* inspired by Sting's reading of the Arthur Koestler book of the same title, which is an essay on the urge to self-destruct—a hand-in-glove fit with my brand-new life.

We finish up the album with a sense that maybe it is a good one, but we're not entirely sure. Everyone around us seems to like it, but these days people tell us what we want to hear. Personally, I like about half of the album and hate all the un-Police saxophone shit.

We pack up and head back to the airstrip. We are going to Caracas, Venezuela, for two concerts. The flight across the Caribbean is about two hours, but the only plane we can find to fly us and our equipment is an ancient-looking prop plane. Looking as if it has been repaired with elastic bands and chewing gum, it doesn't appear that it will last one hour, let alone two. Standing on the hot tarmac, we have serious misgivings about getting into this antique, but with a "live fast, die young" attitude, we climb in. With a death rattle the old dear sputters to life and rises like a parrot with a broken wing into the sky. We slowly climb to about ten thousand feet and turn toward South America.

We begin to enjoy it, as it feels as if we are in an old World War II movie.

Eventually I get up and plop myself down at the back of the plane, resting against one of my Marshall cabinets casually chained in with the rest of the gear at the back of the cabin, since there is no cargo hold. One thing the Caribbean is known for is hurricane weather, which occurs with some frequency; although we don't exactly fly into a hurricane, it starts to get fierce and from nowhere the plane starts to buffet about, lose altitude, rise again, take sudden dips. It's frightening and it seems certain that we are going to go down. I crawl up the plane from my relaxed position and pull into a seat next to the emergency exit, strapping myself in with a face pale as ash. Seconds later the emergency exit door blows off the plane completely and sails down into the Caribbean. Luckily, I am strapped in—but still only about two inches from a large hole in the side of the plane with the sea ten thousand feet below. The roar of the wind outside is like the scream of death, and I have to move. With a chain of hands and arms gripping me, I unbuckle and crawl away from the gaping banshee mouth until I reach a comparatively stable spot on the other side.

We hurtle on across the Caribbean to Venezuela with the howl of wind drowning out all our voices—though we have gone very quiet as, white faced, and white knuckled, we grip our seats. Finally we cross the coast, but as we gaze down through the gash, the mountains appear like pinpricks and we feel even sicker. We drop down to the runway and shudder to a halt. One of the pilots gets out and kneels on the ground, making the sign of the cross as the other wipes perspiration from his brow. They have both been terrified by the experience, and we wonder what the hell we were thinking. I suddenly see the appeal of believing in a higher power.

That night we play at El Poliedro de Caracas, an arena on the outskirts of the city; it is a wild show, with the warmth and energy typical of South America. After the concert as we walk across the parking area to the transport we become aware of a commotion going on at the entrance to the auditorium. Soldiers in brown and green army fatigues are rounding up teenage boys and shoving them at gunpoint into army trucks to be taken off to the Venezuela-Colombia border to fight in the war. Most of the boys look about sixteen or seventeen years old, and in their bright T-shirts and spiked hair, they look like butterflies being carried off by carrion crows. A few young girls stand on the tarmac, watching and crying as their boyfriends and brothers are hustled off into the night. I trail across the tarmac and throw my stuff in the back of a purring limo and feel useless in front of this. It is a chilling display of the realities that exist in countries outside of Europe and the United States.

In North America Reagan is God and his presidency sets a new scene that will lead in twenty years to an administration that will become servile to polluters, fossil-fuel extractors, and fanatical religious fundamentalists of every stripe except Islam; be hostile to science; embrace fiscal insolvency; and transubstantiate worldwide solidarity into worldwide anti-Americanism. But the eighties will be looked back upon as a golden era. A few years from now as the presidency of Hugo Chávez is challenged, I will spend desperate hours in the airport as a military coup takes place and my equipment gets ripped apart in search of a bomb.

From Venezuela we fly up to Canada, where we are to mix a live album. This time is marked for me by Kate's arrival to discuss the divorce. I nurse a hope that maybe when we are together she will relent, maybe we'll be able to talk it through. But despite my efforts, divorce is what she wants. My attempts to talk her out of it are useless. We lie in the dark, with the wind gently soughing through the pines outside, and I go to pieces. It is a bitter lesson and I bury my head in the pillow, flooded with remorse, devastated that I won't see my daughter as she grows up, gutted that they won't be in my life anymore. But for Kate the marriage no longer exists; I am not there, I am adrift, elsewhere. She wants a genuine supportive relationship—a husband, a father, a partner—but in this gilded moment of excess and the carousel of rock touring, I am not providing it. We do not get specific or even accusatory, but the subtext is that as well as being forever absent, I am succumbing, indulging in all the temptations. It's over, and two days later she leaves, taking Layla with her. I fragment.

We finish mixing the live album and return to the U.S., where we play a couple of shows and then return to England. Because of the ever increasing whirl of activity around the group, the live album gets put away somewhere and sadly is never seen again, never sees the light of day. In London our old flat without Kate and Layla feels empty of everything but memory, and I hate being in it, hate going to the local shops, hate buying groceries just for me, and I take to eating out and being out all the time. I decide to move out of the flat, and I buy a larger house at the other end of Putney.

Twenty-Four

In October *Ghost in the Machine* is released. With a collective sigh of relief that we haven't blown it, the press give us rave reviews. *Zenyatta Mondatta* came in for some mauling, as most critics considered it to have one or two singles and a lot of filler. To an extent, they may have been right. We rushed through that recording without time to really think about it. "Invisible Sun" is the first single off this album, and the video is immediately banned by the BBC for political content they don't want to show on the grounds that it is too controversial. Once again the institution shows that it is living in the Stone Age and with a double standard. Our video contains no violent imagery but shows kids in Belfast—the lives of people in Northern Ireland and what they are subjected to. The BBC shows violent newsreels all the time, but when the same subject matter is expressed artistically they prefer to ban it—and by doing so promote it. We make various comments to the press and take a stand, but clearly the BBC does not approve of it as *Top of the Pops* material. Nevertheless, it reaches number one on the British charts within two weeks.

This album and the video mark a shift away from the three spiky blond heads and the cheerful demeanor of our earlier incarnation. The press interviews contain remarks like "Thank God for Adam [Ant]," who can now take over that part of the market, which is a subtle put-down of his efforts. The album cover is black with a set of red marks that are supposed to represent a digital version of us and the title. Many people don't get its abstraction. None of it matters, though, as the album and the single both hit the top of the charts in the U.K. In the U.S. "Every Little Thing She Does Is Magic" goes to number one while the album climbs rapidly to the number two position on the *Billboard* chart. It stays there for six weeks while we all hold our breath; frustratingly, it does not hit the fabled number one spot. But "Magic" goes to number one everywhere else in the world (except Britain).

To support the release of *Ghost in the Machine,* we play four nights at Wembley Arena, and again we are all over the U.K. press like a wet rag. Now we sell newspapers, have moved to the center, and fired the English imagination, but already the pictures have a smoky edge. As if throwing fuel into the flames that will eventually consume us, the press looks for the dirt, sex, money, power, conflict—the human drama that sells papers. Now that we are ensconced in the spotlight, it's time to expose our fragility, time for the breakup, the fits of rage, the petty jealousies, the other woman. "You've made a new record, boys—that's nice, but let's get to the real stuff. Gimme the underbelly, the temptations, how you're fucking it up." You imagine a whole country oohing and aahing, gasping with incredulity at your exploits, and muttering, "And I thought they were so nice," or, "I knew they were no good—bloody pop stars." Along with the tits of the page-three girls, we have become perfect fodder for the machine. I imagine a fifty-five-year-old bastard with grey hair and a potbelly who has trouble with his sex life, with a name like Wackford Squeers: he leans back from his gothic desk above Fleet Street and sends the hacks out the door with orders to get us.

My broken marriage is still under wraps, but still I get whole pages in the tabloids with titles like "Red Hot Summers" in which I make pious noises about my wife being very understanding—which of course is laughably untrue. Another in the *Sun*—what was I thinking?—with yet more smutty half-truths about how difficult it is and how you need an understanding partner, etc.

This is the mating dance, the courtship ritual between us and them, but it's the little sips of poison that sustain our tango partner as they slip down its hungry gullet like nectar. "Here you go, weakness; here you go, infidelity; here you go, whopping lie; here you go, divorce, betrayal, ambition, excess, narcotic abuse. Lovely—thanks, boys, we can put this next to the tits."

To the press, we have morphed from a trio of smiling blond heads into three maniacally driven, egocentric individuals who do nothing but row with each other, lizard tongues flicking like angry flames. Sting in his corner begins portraying himself as ruthless with his headline in the *Sun*, WHY I MAY QUIT THE POLICE: "I'm out for myself and they know it." At home I practice and attempt to carry on with my own inner discourse, which I try to never have subsumed by outer events. The biz is not the music, the cesspool of the tabloid press seems like a weird payoff to the nutrients that sustain this popular success. Adding fuel to this daily fire is the newsworthy fact that Sting is also breaking up with his wife, Frances, and has a brand-new relationship with the actress Trudie Styler. Trudie, who now always appears with Sting, is funny and has a raunchy and sardonic sense of humor that fits in nicely with the three of us.

We are scheduled to return to the United States in January but are now concentrating on Europe first, beginning with England. We have a show in Birmingham at the National Exhibition Centre, which holds about fourteen thousand people. On the day of the show each one of us is to be picked up in the early afternoon to be driven up to Birmingham in time for the sound check. About one o'clock in the afternoon I am engaged in an interview with *Rolling Stone* at my house. I don't feel well during the interview and think I must just be stressed-out, exhausted, or just plain ill. I have a pain in my side like a dull ache, and nothing is making it go away. I drink cups of tea, lie down, take an aspirin, but it still hurts. The car arrives to pick me up. I bundle into the car and slump into the backseat, but by the time we reach Hammersmith Bridge I am retching violently out the window and desperately ask the driver to get me to the hospital. A few minutes later we pull up at Hammersmith Hospital. Emergency—Ward 10 has already been alerted: pop star coming, possible OD, and they are there with a stretcher. I am rushed into the emergency ward; with the neon strips overhead blinking like white snakes and the stink of hospital crawling up my nose, I faintly hear the words *kidney stone* as a giant hypodermic full of black stuff is pushed into my left arm vein and I slip, slip beneath the surface of Loch Ness—bye-bye, An—

I come to about six hours later as if pulling up from a primeval swamp, but I feel better; the thing has passed through my system and exited the urethra with the brute force of a boulder passing through a human hair. Miles and Kim are both standing at the end of the table with a small army of nurses and doctors. I feel important but also as if I am waking up in a scene from a German expressionist film. "Wha?" I croak. "You alright, mate?" I hear their voices as if in a wind tunnel: "There's fourteen thousand people waiting for you in Birmingham." "Gig . . . show, yeah . . . caan dooo," I croak, "lesgo." I am groggy but no longer in pain, and I roll off the table onto a stretcher and am carried out to the backseat of a Rolls-Royce, where I plummet back to black.

I blink my eyes open as we pull into the backstage area of the center. Everyone is staring in through the window; the beloved St. John boys are there, this time with anxious faces and kidney support machines; and it is all rather lovely and heroic. I would have full honors, but my glory is slightly dented by Sting having his arm in a sling. He has jumped through a window the day before while filming on the *Brimstone & Treacle* set and badly cut his hand, so he can't play, but Danny Quatrochi will come onstage with us and play the bass parts. About ten minutes later we shuffle out onto the stage like the walking wounded and begin the show, making a big song and dance about our plight, which only endears us to the audience. Danny does a stellar job on bass, I recover more during the show, and all in all we end up feeling quite pleased with ourselves and garner an unexpected slice of publicity.

With the success of *Ghost in the Machine,* we hit the road for a tour that will last from December 1981 until July 1982. To re-create the saxophone lines on the album, we employ three guys from New Jersey who collectively call themselves Chops. They play well and flesh out Sting's original lines, but to me it just feels like an intrusion and takes away from the interplay between Stewart, Sting, and me. But on the inside of this frenzied whirlwind, with my imminent divorce and a house without wife and child, I am in a free zone. In a weird surge of loneliness in which I am never alone, the only comfort is that of strangers. To sustain any kind of relationship other than the one you have with your band and your instrument seems just about impossible. My house becomes unfamiliar, my old friends become strangers, any kind of normal day-to-day living is unreal. The heady pace of this life floats us off into a place that increasingly seems out of touch with reality. After a few more shows in the U.K. we take off around Europe with a "mic in your face" blur of concerts, jet lag, screaming fans, carnal encounters, and the unending pressure to blow everyone away—an intense, overfueled schedule that is probably shortening our lives by a few years.

In January 1982 we return to the United States. The first show is at the Boston Garden, and here a strange thing happens. After the sound check we return to the dressing rooms below the stage. Adjacent to the area are some huge industrial-looking tanks that look like boilers. Sting and I put our instruments down, and I lean mine against the boiler thing. We go off for a couple of hours to eat and get ready. We return to the dressing room half an hour before the show. I pick up the Telecaster, plug it into a practice amp, and switch on the back pickup. No sound comes out. I tug the lead, fiddle with the switches, check the jack plug, but nothing works—the pickup remains silent. Apparently something—the boiler perhaps—has demagnetized it. It's dead, the life sucked out of it. It's a freak accident, but I am devastated. The unique sound that I was able to produce from this pickup is gone. The word goes out. My Telecaster is a guitar that everybody loves. The fact that in this high-profile group I still play this old guitar appeals to a lot of people, and it has become an icon. Eventually Seymour Duncan, a well-known guitar electronics expert, comes to the rescue with an overwound pickup to replace it—but for me, it is never quite the same. As we continue forward to some distant goal, I feel with this second loss as if I am bleeding in public.

After Boston we travel along the East Coast and through the Midwest, with the payoff on the West Coast in early February for three nights in L.A.

In Birmingham, Alabama, I stay by myself in a hotel close to the gig, as I am going up to New York the next day to attend an exhibition of my photography. The fans who check every hotel in town already know where I am staying, and there is a huge crowd in the lobby by the time I arrive. Surrounded by a large pushing mass, I check in with stress and difficulty and, knowing that it will be a sleepless night, am not in a great mood. But they know which room I am in, and they take the adjacent rooms, bang on my door, call out my name, and play Police tracks at high volume until the sun breaks into the Alabama dawn. It is intense, torturous; finally I have to drag the blankets into the bathroom and sleep on the floor in an effort to drown out the riot next door.

Now we are surrounded by muscle, and in a perverse way it is pleasant, giving a false sense of importance, as if we are a precious treasure that must be guarded at all times. Large, beefy men are everywhere; they watch out for us and occasionally overdo their job, roughing up people who even dare look in our direction. This is distressing, and sometimes we get worked up about being in the hands of these monosyllabic bozos. We are spirits in the material world, but that would be hard to discern with the deeply macho atmosphere that now appears to surround us. It makes us feel stupid and Neanderthal: like a "rock group."

At every show there is a long line of people who want to meet the group. We sit in the dressing room, trying to put it off, but Kim comes in and out, asking if we are ready to meet the director of KBIG or KFAT: "They're really important," and they have the record in rotation. And then it's the local record-store owner or the chairman of the Elks Club and there's a kid in a wheelchair, the president of the local Police fan club. A line is formed and we press flesh with several overweight and badly dressed people who all tell us, "Youse guys 'r great, thanks fer comin' t'Po'dunk, Arkansas, ma dorter rilly lurves youse." It's tiresome but we are grateful—it is positive energy, and after all, we could be back at the Hope and Anchor, so we smile a lot and try to be gracious. Once they have penetrated the inner sanctum of the dressing room, some of them don't want to leave and we have to put in a request for a "swordfish sandwich," which is our ingenious code word for "get them out, please."

Everyone backstage is supposed to wear a backstage pass, an item that is coveted as the holy grail of fandom, as it allows ingress to the court of the kings, passage from the outer rings of concentric circles that mark us like the growth of a tree. Out there, conspiracy, machination, maneuvering, and collusion between the rabid ones as they importune, offer favors, drugs, physical contact to those who guard the cave. And if one of these three-hundred-pound bruisers asks for a favor, it's hard to refuse—they are so big.

The Forum in Los Angeles is sold out for three nights. There is a delirious buzz around the event that is reaching new heights; Policemania is the word. We have arrived back here after an intense tour of the U.S., playing in arenas every night. On the scale of fame and celebrity, we are now playing the high notes, twanging the treble strings. We check into hotels under pseudonyms, go incognito, and speed away from the shows in three separate limos, our soaking stage clothes sticking to the black leather and our heat making condensation on the windows. Behind us the audience surrounds the building we have just left. It is either take off instantly or be trapped in the building for several hours, but it is a peculiar anticlimax to go within minutes from a burning stage and a crazed auditorium to the solitude and roaring silence of your pastel-papered hotel room.

As we hit the stage there is a roar and the whole audience stands up to spark the flames of their lighters, and with this gesture the auditorium becomes beautiful, an American namaste—I salute the spirit within you. We haven't seen this before, and for a second it stops me dead, my eyes tear up, my heart opens, and then Stewart's cracking snare sends me careening on down the path of the concert. Standing up front are Jack Nicholson and Michael Douglas, and grooving in his own space, complete with Blues Brothers shades, John Belushi. "Driven to Tears," "Roxanne," "So Lonely," "Walking on the Moon," "Spirits in the Material World," "Demolition Man," and "Can't Stand Losing You"—we pile-drive from one song to another in a fury until we reach a writhing symbiosis and arrive an hour and half later at a place of exstasis.

A big party has been arranged for us by A&M at a beautiful art deco mansion in the Hollywood Hills. You fall out of the backstage area and into your limos with yells of "yeah, c'mon, man, come with me, yeah, bring her, her too—whatever." You tumble into the stretch with fizzing bottles of champagne, marijuana and perfume mixing like an elixir in a limo filled with sprawling limbs, flashing underwear, high laughing voices, and chemical madness. The limousine is the chariot, the vessel of tribal celebration, as you speed across L.A. on wings of bubbles and powder to the party that celebrates you, and out there the streets of L.A., the Hollywood Hills, the Capitol Building, the movie lots, Disney, Paramount, Warner Brothers, Beverly Hills and Bel-Air, the 76 gas stations, the Hollywood sign, the Santa Monica Freeway, the open doors, Sunset Strip—you own it all, you are hot, the king, the world is watching as the dream unfolds, your dream, the ecstasy, the glory; and five minutes back, the food stamps, the fifty cents of gas, the terrors of shoplifting food from the supermarket, the scrape and grind of survival, and the music, always the music—Miles, Coltrane, Monk, Mingus, Parker, Ellington, Robert Johnson, Son House, Elmore James, Ray Charles, Mozart, Bach, Beethoven, Chopin, Debussy, Villa-Lobos, ragas, blues standards, bebop—music, music, and more music fueling this crazy ride, the song that never leaves your head—you are a starbody, and you bend over with another rolled dollar bill, thinking, *I'll be back, boys—I'll be back.*

The central hall of the mansion is packed; you cruise from one group to another as they come at you in dream waves—you pose with Jack Nicholson for photographs and he turns to you with that satanic grin and says, "Doesn't this just give you the shits?" High five and hugs with Belushi; smoke a joint with gentle, cool Michael Douglas, buddy boy himself; and spin off into the kaleidoscope of night.

I meet with Belushi the next night at the Chateau Marmont on the Sunset Strip. In John's room we slug back some Glenfiddich, smoke a joint, do a couple of lines, and float out into the neon radiance of the Strip. John has a big black limo and a big black driver, and we cruise the Strip, going in and out of bars. Everywhere we go people cheer; everybody knows Belushi, and by now many know me. They like seeing us together, we do a double act, laugh, crack jokes, stagger about, and don't disappoint them. Up and down the Strip we go like yo-yos in a storm of fluttering dollar bills, chicks, perfume, leather, dark corners, loud voices, the stink of booze, TVs suspended over bars with the Lakers game in full flight.

We pull up at the Comedy Store, and John leaps up onto the stage and does twenty minutes of fantastic improv. He is great, very fast, very funny, and stoned to the max. The audience loves him. We hit more joints, more scenes, more buildings, more lobbies, until Hollywood becomes a skid mark across our speeding brains. We fall into the Formosa Cafe at 4:30 A.M. with some vaguely formed idea that we need sustenance. Speech has become difficult, and as the sky breaks into yellow streaks over Laurel Canyon we part company in a slurred embrace. "Later, man." "Yeah, tonight." I find the rented car and in a stupor aim it back at Le Parc. I arrive there and pull up at the top of the slope that leads down to the garage, which has a huge iron gate. Climbing out of the car, I press the button to open the gate, and watch like a

zombie as the car with a mind of its own gently drives itself down the slope and into the steel gate, which crashes down out of its track and smashes the hood to a pulp. I shuffle the remains of the Mercedes into the garage and stagger off to my room to pass out. I open the door and struggle through dozens of party balloons on strings and sink, fully clothed, into blackness like an undersea diver. I wake about six P.M.; the balloons are slightly deflated; and a bill for four thousand dollars has been discreetly pushed under the door.

BRIDGEHAMPTON, AUGUST 18, 1983

I get out of bed and cross the room to pull a nylon string guitar out of its case. As we are in this place for three weeks, I brought an acoustic to practice on because it helps keep up the strength in the hands. G# minor 7 with an open E and B strings. The first chord of the "One Note Samba." Jobim wrote this famous song on the guitar in the key of E major, where it falls so easily under the left hand. This was pointed out to me by a great Brazilian guitarist who said that this is the real version. Brazilian music is another style that Sting and I also both love, and our signature song, "Roxanne," was first written as a bossa nova. I start playing down the sequence and remember arriving in Rio for the first time.

The Maracanazinho Gym in Rio de Janeiro is a huge concrete structure with nightmare acoustics. At the sound check we play in dismay as the sound reverberates around the walls to make a mocking mush of every note we play. "Who the fuck booked us in here?" we yell as we come offstage. This is our first gig in Brazil and we want it to be great, but this place is a disaster. Because of its great musical culture, Brazil holds a special place for most musicians; and we want to impress. Despite the Grand Canyon sound, the gig is an intoxicating riot in a way that only a gig in Brazil can be.

Backstage, smiling and being photographed, is Ronnie Biggs, the famous English train robber. Most visiting celebrities usually meet up with him when in Rio. He has been a resident of Brazil for quite a few years at this point and is basically a very cheery English Cockney bloke who seems completely out of place here. In a bizarre final twist of the Sex Pistols story, Biggs recorded two songs with Paul Cook and Steve Jones, "Belsen Was a Gas" and "A Punk Prayer," McClaren having flown down to Rio after his final bitter break up with John Lydon in the United States. A double-A-side single was released with "A Punk Prayer" and the Sid Vicious version of "My Way." This was all part of McClaren's plan to dupe Virgin: if they didn't accept Ronnie Biggs as the new lead singer of the Pistols, he could void the contract and take it elsewhere. Oddly enough, the single was a hit mostly because of Sid's version of the Sinatra song; unfortunately there was no future in Biggs becoming the Pistols' new lead singer—he was still on the most-wanted list in Britain—and McClaren moved on. Biggs seems relieved to see us, and I feel a twinge of sadness coming from him, a yearning for anything English.

After Rio we fly across the continent to Chile to appear at the Viña del Mar International Song Festival. Like Argentina, this country too is under the fist of the military junta. With the help of the CIA and a military coup, socialist president Allende, who many believed was leading the country toward communism and had already invited Castro for a visit, was disposed of in 1973. Henry Kissinger remarked that we don't need to stand idly by and watch a whole country go communist. Fueled by the ire of ITT, the U.S. telephone company that was furious over Allende's appropriation of the copper companies and that paid the CIA to get Allende out, the most violent coup in Chilean history took place, leaving Allende dead in the Moneda Palace the next day.

General Pinochet now rules the country and has remarked that not a leaf stirs in the country without his knowing. As we touch down, the country is full of murder, brutality, and repression. We are so buried in our group cocoon that we are not really aware of everything that has taken place here, and in consequence we will have to defend ourselves to human-rights groups. I immediately sense that there is something wrong—you can almost smell it. But, hey, just another performance for another fascist dictatorship; after all, we too are the Police.

We check into the strangely named O'Higgins Hotel, wondering why it is not the Casa del Mar or something, but later find out that Bernardo O'Higgins, the illegitimate son of an Irishman from Sligo, had risen under the service of the Spanish crown to become captain-general of Chile and viceroy of Peru. We have a very difficult time checking into the hotel. There is a strictly observed protocol that we are not used to and these days tend to circumvent. As we are not greeted with golden smiles there is an altercation at the front desk with one of our minders, and by the time we get our room keys the knives are out. As we check in, a large group of fans surround the hotel, and the road crew take it upon themselves to pose in the large front window of the hotel, hands on nose and crotch, which means "Got any gak?"—in other words, "Got any cocaine?" This is misinterpreted as something like "your mother sucks dicks," and the press take pictures that appear in the papers the next day with large headlines proclaiming that THE POLICE ARE ANIMALS, although Sting, Stewart, and I were upstairs reading Jane Austen at the time of said incident.

The same day of these headlines we have a press conference scheduled. We are led into the conference room of the hotel at midday, and the press is already there wearing vulture outfits. In the center of the table is a long line of international flags. As we sit down I sweep the whole lot off the table. Why? I don't know, I just do it, but immediately all the cameras go off like a blast of white lightning and then the barrage of questions: "Why did you do that?" "What does this gesture mean?" "What do you think of international relations?" "What are you bringing to Chile?" All the questions are hostile, and the media seem incensed by my mindless little action, an overreaction that maybe conceals something else, fear or gutless collusion with the powers above as a means of survival. In New York or L.A. they would just have laughed, and said "rock and roll," but here they seem uncomfortable, as if we are presenting them with something that they cannot have, cannot be. I believe they are experiencing shame.

Whatever it is, we come out of the press conference hating the country. I feel that I never want to come back. We play that night and it all goes well enough except for an incident that occurs when Sting refuses to use the same microphone as the singer before him, as apparently the man is sick and coughing. This again is an insult and causes another furor that has to be diplomatically calmed down by Miles, but this one puts the final nail in the coffin. We fly out the next day to return to Rio. I vow never to come back, but in fact I will return to Santiago in a few years and will fall in love with its soft Spanish streets, Indian faces, and *empanadas, cazuelas, humitas.*

We fly back to Rio to relax among the dental-floss bikinis of Ipanema. While sunning myself on the beach, I get the pleasing news that "Behind My Camel" has won a Grammy for best instrumental. "There is justice in this world after all," I mutter as a nearly naked copper-skinned beauty totters past me and my ice cream melts in my hand.

Miami, Jacksonville, Birmingham, Memphis, Baton Rouge, Houston, Dallas, Austin, Kansas City, Oklahoma City, Chicago, St. Louis, Charlotte, on and on we go like a hurricane ripping across the states until our songs fill every nook and cranny, are on every radio station, in every kid's bedroom, in tape players that repeat endlessly as hot mouths bruise up against each other in the backseats of parked cars, as the last days of vinyl spin out in orbit through the suburbs, as young single mothers feed sugar-coated corn puffs to the mouths of babies in high chairs. "Rehumanize yourself," we sing, for we are spirits in the material world, and one world is enough, there's too much information. . . . We blow out of the U.S. with three nights at the Meadowlands and cascades of female underwear falling from the stage rigging of Nassau Coliseum, the road crew in the wings sick with laughter as bras and panties fall on our heads.

In London there is no peace, no silence. I get sick of it and realize I need assistance. I hire a girl by the name of what else but . . . Roxanne, who used to work for Pete Townshend. We are now in the celebrity portion of our sojourn, and it is de rigueur to invite us to everything. Doors open, restaurant tables become suddenly available, first-name basis is established with maître d's around town, gifts arrive every day, and we get motorbikes, guitars, free travel, clothes, sporting-goods endorsements, invitations, free exclusive club memberships, and guitar strings for life. Everyone wants a slice of the Police cake, to be let in the door, to get behind bars with us. It is giddy and we have to watch out that we don't get swallowed by this new monster. There is no training for this. We have learned how to make records, perform, be rock stars, but there is a whole other side—it becomes easy to see how people end up with nothing a few years later as the fall from grace inevitably happens.

Our main financial adviser is Keith Moore. He has a charming bedside manner and a brain to go with it. We like him, listen attentively, and generally take his sage advice. But we watch in dismay as he begins to change in front of our eyes as he acquires a very sexy young Indian girlfriend who is obviously on the make, and we groan inwardly both over her very desirable body and the first signs of his getting caught up in the glitz. We have regarded him as a father/doctor figure, but he too is flawed: later, in a tragedy with all the hallmarks of a Dostoyevsky novel, he will fall and eventually be incarcerated.

It is as if the group itself sets some kind of high-water mark and people change to meet it. It tends to be a fiery embrace, and we become almost inured to seeing people self-immolate around us. Eventually we can only greet it with a raised eyebrow; another one bites the dust. I will pass through another three financial advisers before finally getting it right, one more of whom will also end up in prison. Having money, one realizes after a while, is very nice, but you need to develop a razor-edged awareness if you want to hang on to it. There is a large number of thieves disguised as angels out there who can't wait to relieve you of the burden. They slip under your door, confront you in dark hallways, slither through the letter box, whisper in tones of silk, infiltrate your life with the stealth of a cell quietly dividing. The water has fangs, and the only way to make it, to land is by keeping your head up and thinking about the next song.

One of my touchstones in the middle of this heady brew is Bob the plumber, who comes over to my house for the odd bit of pipe work, loose washer, a replumb. After his work is done we sit down and have a cup of tea together, and our conversations about lagging, washers, boilers, and Chelsea's chances in the upcoming season are laced with pithy remarks from Bob that bring me back to Earth, refocus the lens, blow out the sweet smell of gilded decay.

In terms of music, I am beginning to feel that even this group—despite everything—is becoming a cage and that I need to spread my wings for a moment, try playing with someone else to see if I can still function in the real world. I contact Robert Fripp to see if he might be interested in putting something together. Recently I have heard a solo he played on a Roches album, which strikes me as being quite soulful, and impresses me enough to think that we might find common ground. A few days later we meet in New York at the Cupping Room in SoHo, then go to an apartment nearby that belongs to a friend of his. We sit around for a couple of hours with guitars, finding areas to explore and figuring that we'll put it together in the studio. We meet two weeks later in Bournemouth, where an old friend of ours has a studio, and get to work. We emerge about ten days later with a quirky instrumental album that we call *I Advance Masked.* Initially A&M is not very interested in putting this out, but they wouldn't want to upset me at this point, so they duly release it with the result that our weird instrumental album makes it into the Top Sixty of the *Billboard* charts. The suits don't get it but are pleased.

In September we begin to tour again. We arrive in the north of England to play at Gateshead with U2, who are just beginning their upward climb. We're still playing the songs from *Ghost in the Machine,* but there is an internal pressure building toward the next record. With each new album, we have to top the last one; it's a difficult trick to pull off because you can get caught between changing your sound or style and disappointing the fans who love you for what they know, or risk not moving on and becoming stale.

Before we return to Montserrat we work our way through another giant pastiche of American cities with stages, people, interviews, radio stations, rooms, carpets, walls, limos, contracts, meetings with lawyers, corridors, and darkened windows until it is a disorientating blur. I feel as if I open the same door to the same room every night, and the tour becomes like an outtake of

Bill Murray's future film *Groundhog Day*. This is all I have ever known or will know, a Kafkaesques series of Chinese boxes and so many rooms that in their unfamiliarity, they become familiar. Unrelenting muted shades, Otis elevators, and restaurants with names like Feelings, Moments, or Memories. Each room is loaded with little bits of stand-up cardboard shit gushing about weekend specials, honeymoon rates, the Friday-night happy hour, and Dodies Hair Salon in the basement. I enter each room and toss all the crap in the trash; there is so much of this shit on every surface—I hate it. This is private space—you paid for it, it belongs to you, but still you get subjected to the relentless sell. Fuck 'em . . . what to do? . . . music—put on; clothes— throw on floor; books—read; guitar—play. I hang the DO NOT DISTURB sign on the doorknob with FUCKING written between NOT and DISTURB, pick up my guitar, and stare at the beige carpet. What? . . . oh, yeah—fuck hotels. I was going to practice but I have a very strong urge to empty a bottle of vodka over the sheets and toss a match in it—fuck the Mexican maid—and piss in the corridor, but now I feel exhausted and instead order a bottle of Chilean red and, wondering why I feel lost, watch the news, barely making sense of it. I am very specific about my needs, I have several special room re- quirements, I am a pain in the ass. "Hey, man, don't put me in a room next to the fuckin' elevator shaft, or the goddamn maids' linen closet. I don't

even wanna see a freeway, let alone hear it. No male fans within a ten-mile radius, and do not disturb me—ever—leave me the fuck alone until gig time, and no dairy creamer with the coffee or that half-and-half shit, and I'll rip the fucking phone wires out if I want to." I am a rock-and-roll asshole, an emaciated millionaire prick, and fuck everything.

Billy Francis, our tour manager, now waits for me at the front desk while I inspect two or three rooms before he bothers to go to his own room and wait for my "Okay, it'll do"; then he checks me in as Django Reinhardt or occasionally Stéphane Grappelli. Obsessed with photography, I document everything endlessly: fire hoses, curtains, maids, limo drivers, fans, front desks, views out the window, tarmac, fire escapes, parking lots, TV screens, room-service menus, dirty underwear, the sky, corners of buildings, cars, clouds. I cogitate on ways to make photographs in this hell of blandness: trap trouser legs under doorways, knock sand-filled cigarette bins to the ground, attach little rubber sharks to body parts, wrap legs in fire hose, place little toy nuns on naked female bodies—it's a passage through it, another way of dreaming.

Twenty-Five

On December 12, after a three-month rip through the States, we return to Montserrat to begin recording our fifth album. It seems as though Sting is at the North Pole, I am at the South Pole, and Stewart is in the tropics. We are the emotional opposites of when we recorded *Outlandos*. Arriving to record another album suddenly wipes the glass clear and we stare at one another as if in assessment. In the shocking calm of the studio, without the blanket of touring, the need to make it to the next gig. The mud drops to the bottom of the glass and we eye each other like strangers.

We've changed. Sting, after a year of celebrity highlights—his high-profile court case against Virgin, his movie appearance in *Brimstone & Treacle,* and endless appearances in the press—is now someone else. It changes you; how could it not? The inevitable corrosion is eating its way through the tenuous threads that have held us together so far. But whatever monster lies beneath the surface goes unremarked.

We strap on the band persona; we still have a goal, still have fire, still have desire, still want a number one record in the United States. We begin tentatively at first, mostly listening to the new batch of songs that Sting has conjured up: "Synchronicity," "King of Pain," "Every Breath You Take." As usual, there is some good material but it needs the Police signature, needs to be toughened, and we get to work. As we wrestle our way into the tracks the energy is sexual, provocative, goading, until we get the right tension that makes it sound like the Police, until it has the push and pull we need before the songs emerge from our hands writhing like wet baby snakes. There is a moment when you know; it arrives and suddenly the track—like a taut string—has that indefinable thing.

Despite the underlying degradation of the group psyche, we manage to imitate a nice camaraderie and can still enjoy the process of recording, however difficult. We are back in paradise, making an album expected to sell in the millions, living like kings, wealthy, famous—well, why shouldn't we be happy? Sting has split up with Frances, I am now divorced from Kate, Stewart has married Sonja Kristina but will eventually divorce her, Keith Moore has already taken the path that will lead to Wormwood Scrubs prison, and Miles will divorce Mary Pegg (whom he marries this year), as will Kim Turner his bride. Several people have left us after becoming emotionally distraught, and one is in a psychiatric ward—nice going, boys. But in the all-important quest to make another hit, we pull together and focus on the gold, the new record, and the elusive number one in America.

The term *synchronicity* was coined by Carl Jung, the Swiss psychologist, in 1927 after studying what he perceived to be an unusual phenomenon in some of his patients. He subsequently developed a theory of the underlying pattern, the acausal connecting principle, commonly known as coincidence. In the years previous to the Police, following Kate's lead, I spent three years with a Jungian psychotherapist in London by the name of Bonnie Shorter and have since then become immersed in the work of Jung, filling my head with theories about the numinous, the personality archetypes, intuitive extrovert, and the interpretation of dreams. Laid out like a spiritual quest, Jung's path of individuation is seductive.

On the last tour of the United States before we return to Montserrat, I saw Sting reading *Memories, Dreams, Reflections*—Jung's autobiography—and talked about it. I had never mentioned my sojourn into this realm, but it is a world that is close to my heart, and now it becomes a point of common interest. I would not have connected it to songwriting, but it has seized Sting's imagination and by the time we arrive in Montserrat he has songs that have been inspired by this unlikely source. Another book I have passed on is *The Sheltering Sky* by Paul Bowles. From this Sting has extracted the story of three girls making tea in the desert and turned it into a beautiful new song called "Tea in the Sahara."

Most of the new songs have a dark psychological undercurrent. I have one song I think I might get on the record, but I don't know—it is difficult to get anything past Sting these days. It is a psycho rendition in seven/four called "Mother." More Captain Beefheart than the Police, but Sting actually loves this song and it makes it onto the album (though, of course, I have to sing it myself). I have a small amount of anxiety about my mum's hearing this for the first time and I warn her about it, but when she does hear it she laughs her head off, thinking it a hoot.

In the studio the tension is so high that you can hear it twanging like an out-of-tune piano. As a group we seem to swing between high emotional intensity and sophomoric fraternity with frightening ease, almost like a group version of bipolar disorder. The best result is that when "it" happens, we can play with an empathy that is hard to imagine achieving with other people. But making albums is a brutal affair: you are forced to stand down, moodily let go of an idea, play someone else's idea, watch all your cherished licks go out of the window—often accompanied by boos and jeers. It's painful because none of us likes being told what to do or being controlled in any way. In truth, we are like children locked in a house with big shiny machines and a handful of explosives. But from the pain comes the growth—and that, we tell ourselves or one another after having just trashed some musical effort, is what it is all about.

As if underscoring our current mental state, we record in three separate rooms: Stewart up in the dining room of the house with miles of cable and earphones, Sting in the control room, and me alone in the actual studio. All this is for what the engineer calls perfect separation, and with this album we get it, although not quite in the way intended—a weird symbol of where and what we've become.

In the long hours of the studio there is a tendency to fall into a group mind that is kindergarten in level. One of its manifestations is a nasty habit called "taking someone to the party." Some poor soul will fall asleep from the sheer grueling effort of it all, and during naptime he will be covered in old cigarette butts, matchsticks, chocolate wrappers, and other bits of garbage. Tam Fairgrieve, my roadie, manages to pass out on the couch in front of the monitors after dinner one night and descends into a snoring sleep. We are all sniggering away at him and keep yelling his name, but like Rip Van Winkle, he does not wake up. We begin turning the music up louder and louder, to no avail, and as a last resort shove a microphone under his face and run it through the speakers, cranking it up and adding reverb, bass, treble, and phasing effects until we are beside ourselves with this jape and the very wall of the room is quaking. Finally, when we think the building is going to blow apart with the sonic bomb we have built, Tam wakes up with a startled grunt and a bug-eyed stare to ask what the fuck is going on, which puts us all on the floor. We have recorded the whole thing and eventually use the snoring to signify the Loch Ness monster on "Synchronicity II."

A few nights later we are sitting around, listening to a track we have recorded earlier in the day. I start fiddling around with a piece of silver paper from a chocolate bar. I begin sticking it in my left ear, scratching away at something and pushing it farther and farther into the canal until suddenly I can't feel the paper in my fingers anymore and realize it has disappeared right into my ear. I don't panic at first but try to work it out. No luck. I become a little bit frightened and ask Danny and Tam if they can see anything. They can see it but can't get it. This is now an interesting event, more interesting than the track we have been listening to. I lie on the floor with my left ear pointing upward; everyone crowds around, excitedly suggesting various methods to retrieve the foreign object, including my standing on my head, banging me on the side of the head, pinching my nostrils together and blowing hard, jumping up and down, and administering the Heimlich maneuver, which al-most makes me throw up. Then Tam bends a guitar string into a vicious-looking hook and tries to fish it out. Nothing works and I am starting to freak out, as it is beginning to feel very large inside my head.

Someone remembers that the island has an ear, throat, and nose medical-training facility, and by a stroke of synchronicity there is an American spe-cialist on the island. Phone calls are quickly made and I am bundled into a jeep and rushed across the island to the medical staff bungalows. Luckily, he is in and is just about to retire for the night but grasps the situation instantly, tells me to lie on the bed, and opens a little leather bag full of long silver tweezers. Picking his device like a connoisseur, he leans over me and with a deft twist removes the invader to a small round of applause and a huge sigh of relief from me. "Aah, Cadbury's," he says.

After lobster, mango chicken, and chocolate cake one night, I wander over to the bookshelf sagging under the weight of the usual vacation island fodder—thrillers, murder mysteries, holidays in Tuscany, etc.—and I pull out a book on the flora and fauna of the Caribbean and start studying it. Looking at the exotic watercolors returns me to my childhood—plants, birds, the natural world—and a wave of nostalgia passes through me. It seems like so long ago—how did I get so far from it? I decide to learn the names of the indigenous species, become one with this island habitat, ground in the earth.

But being cooped up in the studio tends to bring out perversity, and we continue playing tricks on one another, trying to fuck each other up. Sometimes these antics work and add more edge to the playing. But one afternoon in the torpor of the Caribbean heat, the ionized air of the studio, and the effects of simple boredom, we reach a point where we are paralyzed, unable to move forward. It is a moment of deep tension when we hate being together and are right on the edge of breaking up. Pain fills the room and we look at one another and would like to be anywhere else but here. Making this album has become the supreme ordeal. We need a mentor, someone to slash the Gordian knot, point the way forward, save the sinking ship. And then like a ray of light, it comes to me. The owner of the studio is on the island, the producer of the Beatles, George Martin—what about him? Suddenly it seems like a great idea, a way out of the black funk with the ultimate producer. It's either that, or this, our fifth album, is going to die halfway through—and then what? I get assigned the task of chatting him up. He lives in a beautiful old house a couple of miles away across the island, and I decide to walk there and compose my request on the way.

I start out toward his house with the burning white ellipse of sun on my unprotected scalp. Through squinty eyes and the afternoon haze, I can just make out the outline of his place, the house of hope. I pass by passion fruit, banana trees, lime trees, bougainvillea and oleander, my head swimming with hazy thoughts: the transformation of adverse conditions into the path of awakening; pain being a component of happiness; Kate and Layla, England, George Martin, the Beatles. I can't believe I'm doing this—the first time I heard "She Loves You" would I have ever thought that I would end up hoofing it across a tropical island under the beating sun to get the producer of the Fab Four? This is like Jesus—yeah, I'm like Jesus on the road to Calvary—or is it Paul on the road to Damascus? Regard all phenomena as dreams . . . hibiscus . . . bamboo . . . royal palm . . . guava . . . ginger on the road to nowhere . . . maybe a miracle will happen . . . pelican . . . parrot . . . parakeet . . . this is the fucking end, I knew this would happen sooner or later, but this is it, this is fucking "it" . . . those bastards . . . unless Georgie boy pulls it out of the hat, we're, like, sitting on a volcano . . . actually we *are* sitting on a volcano, ha-ha . . . the volcano that will destroy this island . . . if only he knew that I was coming to him now, but maybe he does know . . . Michael Henchard . . . *The Mayor of Casterbridge* . . . Lyme Regis . . . this is a tragedy . . . no, a fuckup . . . two parakeets, flamingo flower . . .

Part of me realizes that this is a moment to let go, pull back, take the long view. Thich Nhat Hanh says, "What will it matter three hundred years from now?" I hope that the next half hour goes well.

Feeling knackered and with a mild case of sunstroke, I arrive at Olveston House and rattle the mosquito screen on the front door. The maid comes out. "Yaa?" she asks. I raise my sunglasses and croak, "Is George Martin here?" "Mzzr. Martin, dere's a man f'you," she yells out. George appears in the gloom of the hallway like a pale white ghost. "Hey, come on in," he says. "Cup of tea?" We go out to the back of the house and sit on the veranda, and over tea he asks me if we are enjoying the studio and how we are getting on. I take a deep breath and tell him that the studio is fine, very nice actually, but that in fact we are going through a period of internal friction—basically we are at one another's throats. Can he help, would he like to take over, guide us through the process, do some of the old Martin magic? We could be a great team. "Hmmmm," says George, "I'm sorry to hear that you are having a bad time of it, but why don't you just try and sort it out yourselves. I'm sure you can do it." And he gives me some sage advice about carrying on and pulling through this tough stretch: "It's typical group stuff—seen it all before. We're English—'nother cup of Darjeeling?"

I feel reassured by his strength and experience, wonder if he has been a naval commander. Suddenly he appears to me as Obi Wan Kenobi. Yeah—we can get past this. We chat for a while longer. I thank him and, with my jaw pushing forward, start marching back toward the studio. I imagine that I hear Sir George calling out behind me, "May the force be with you."

By the time I get back, it was if he has waved his wand across the valley, the air seems to have cleared—maybe we had to go all the way down before we could come up again. We glide back together with a crisp new courtesy toward one another and continue on toward the completion of the album.

The linchpin of *Synchronicity* is a song called "Every Breath You Take." When Sting first plays us his demo, it sounds not unlike the group Yes with a huge rolling synthesizer part. It needs work, needs the stripped-down guitar and drums treatment, but it has something. More obvious than some of Sting's material, it has a classic pop song chord sequence with a dramatic C section but it needs clarity. This song is the one that gets the most argument. Sting and Stewart go on endlessly about the drums and bass—how they should underpin the vocal—but after a couple of weeks we get a track down with just bass and drums and a token vocal to give us some perspective.

Feeling slightly numb, we sit on the couch at a creative standstill. Sting leans over and says, "Go on, go in there, make it your own." This is either a beautiful example of trust between partners or is tantamount to being told to jump off a cliff, prove you're a man, or walk the gangplank. But there she is, a nice naked track, waiting to be ruined or trimmed with gold by yours truly. "Right," I say, "right," and heave my bum up off the deep plush and toward the direction of the big room. In the engulfing loneliness of the empty studio I am hyperaware that everyone is watching and listening. This will be the naked truth.

I pick up my Strat and stare out across the gloom. It's a simple chord sequence and shouldn't prove a problem, depending on one's imagination, inspiration, and context. What are the criteria? It should sound like the Police—big, brutal barre chords won't do, too vulgar; it has to be something that says Police but doesn't get in the way of the vocals; it should exist as music in its own right, universal but with just a hint of irony, be recognized the world over, possibly be picked up by a rapper as the guitar lick to hang a thirty-million-copy song on in eleven years or so. "Yeah, okay," "roll it," I say. The track rolls and I play a sequence of intervals that outline the chords and add a nifty little extension to each one that makes it sound like the Police, root, fifth, second, third, up and down through each chord. It is clean, succinct, immediately identifiable; it has just enough of the signature sound of el Policia. I play it straight through in one take. There is a brief silence, and then everyone in the control room stands up and cheers. It is an emotional and triumphant moment, and it will take us to number one in America.

With this lick I realize a dream that maybe I have cherished since first picking up the guitar as a teenager—to at least once in my life make something that would go around the world, create a lick that guitarists everywhere would play, be number one in America, be heard at weddings, bar mitzvahs, births, funerals, be adapted into the repertoire of brass bands in the north of England, and make my mum and dad proud. Do you ever really get beyond them? Maybe not and maybe this is where the story should fade out, with me standing there, grinning like an idiot, feeling like a hero and just happy to have pleased.

"Every Breath You Take" will go to number one on the *Billboard* charts and stay there for eight weeks. I will be asked, "How did you come up with that? Where does it come from?" as if one sits down and works out a formula for these things. My poker-faced answer is usually along the lines of "God spoke through me, I'm merely the vessel." But in fact as a guitarist, with the bloody thing hardly ever out of your hands, the fingers build their own memory and I think that you go along with pockets of information, things that you tend to play or go to when you pick up the instrument, and then they slowly morph into another set of responses. During the summer I had been playing through the forty-four Bartók violin duets, thinking I might do some of them with Fripp. They are well suited to the guitar and with their intervallic structures and modal ambience are not a thousand miles from the Police guitar sound, hence the ability to immediately lay the fitting part to "Every Breath." It was already there, even if by way of Eastern Europe.

Laying down the guitar part for "Every Breath You Take" clears the air and increases the chances that we have a hit album. Whether it will reach number one is not a certainty, but we all hope for it. From Montserrat we return once again to Le Studio in Canada to mix the album. Generally we let Hugh Padgham prepare the mixes to a point, and then we come into the control room to fine-tune the mix ourselves. But I receive a nasty shock when sitting down to hear the mix of "Every Breath." The thick creamy

Strat sound I had in Montserrat has been reduced to a thin over-reverbed whine. I become extremely upset and tell Hugh to go back immediately to the rough mix from Montserrat, check the sound, and get it back. Luckily, we still have the rough mixes. It takes a couple of days, but we get the guitar sounding almost as good as the rough mix. But to my mind, it is not quite the same. The track is almost stillborn, but it has a future to fulfill.

After the heat and light of the Caribbean, the deep snow and subzero temperatures of Quebec are brutal, but we have to finish the work. Tension continues to run high among us, as if our time is already up. We have made the album and are committed to touring behind it, but a fatalistic air seems to hang over us. We are not talking about the years to come, the rosy future, the path ahead, the next album; instead, we are separating like oil and water, even though *Synchronicity* will bring us our biggest success yet. I realize that Sting thinks that he doesn't need either Stewart or me and that he can go on alone, but this well-worn path is nothing new. We don't talk about it, but along with abrasive ego clashes, there is the desire not to be confronted, not to be challenged, have it all your own way; what makes us will eventually destroys us.

We struggle on through the mixing and end the sessions with a ridiculous scene in which we toss a coin to see which tracks will go onto the album. Will Stewart and I get our songs on? Is it fair to let the whole album be only Sting's songs? Miles valiantly tries to hold some sort of democracy together so some of us don't go away feeling pissed off and alienated. What will the final sequence be? I finally solve that one by suggesting that maybe we put all the softer songs on one side and the up-tempo stuff on the other. Sting likes this idea, and thus it is ordained.

Twenty-Six

We leave the snow and ice of Quebec, the new album, the tension, ego, and confrontation to follow our own pursuits until we begin touring. I go to New York in January 1983 to live for a few months in the American Stanhope hotel. I negotiate a rate for an extended period in a large, sunny suite at the back of the hotel and, away from the band, settle into a regal existence as I begin work on a book of photography. New York is a powerful drug that insulates you if you want, protects you from the sad jewel of loneliness, fills you with emanations from outside your own room. The metropolis seems like an escape from reality and even a place to find a kind of spiritual sustenance. For as I arrive in and embrace living in Manhattan, that is how I feel about it, a place of renewal and a reward for the rigors of the past few years. Here the chances are endless and as I get caught up in the thrill of publishing my first book, the implausibly huge success of our group, and the forthcoming album, New York feels like a bull's-eye.

My two powder blue rooms become a studio, with amps, guitars, and a sea of black-and-white photographs strewn across the carpet and bedspreads as I try to order and edit several hundred pictures. Within a short time I meet up with Ralph Gibson, a great photographer whose work I have admired for some time. He knocks on the door one day, and after a few moments of introductory chat, he picks up the Stratocaster lying on the bed, begins to play, and also remarks on the music playing through the speakers—Brian Eno's

"On Land." Ralph loves music and plays guitar. I play guitar and love photography. We connect and decide that it's time for lunch and that we should produce my book *Throb* together. Thus starts a groove that will continue on through the next twenty years with an ongoing dialogue of music, photography, and jokes of a dubious nature. Later that afternoon we go down to Ralph's loft in lower Manhattan, where we drink Armagnac and begin laying out my pictures in a thirty-foot strip. The friendship with Ralph takes me deeper into New York life, and I wonder why anyone would want to be anywhere else. This is the world capital, the city of final destination.

The heat in my head and the internal engine that races me around the city is a brew of ego powered by the elixir of success and the new feeling that I can do anything, buy anything, have anything. But in the bathroom of Area 51, with a head full of champagne and marching powder, I stare into the mirror with a face that looks numb and strange, and from the small sliver of perception that is not doused in intoxicants, I hear a small, steely voice intoning a warning message. But I step over a body and go back out into the club, grinning like an idiot as I pass by the evening's art piece—a near-naked female suspended by straps in a glass case. Maybe I need the band after all, the discipline and structure of musical performance—I miss the others. As I return to the hissing silence of the bedroom I know that these nights are bullshit, that the only thing that really matters is the work, the music; although I love New York, I am living in it as an authentic fake as I live out the requisite narrative. Maybe I am missing something, the anchor, the balance, the weight that holds you in place while you play out the lunatic side. But, I stupidly console myself, this is rock and roll. Somewhere beneath the surface of this hedonism lies the truth that I am not truly self-destructive, because I love making music—and that is the thing that keeps you one step from the edge. But for a few months and for what seems night after endless night, I almost forget it as I take to the streets of Manhattan at midnight and cruise in a limo with a couple of pals to Area 51, Limelight, the Mudd Club, or Studio 54— wherever there's a scene. It becomes a game to see how many girls we can get into a limousine in one night as we pick them up along the way. They practically line up because being in the city now is like being beneath a hot public light, and it seems that everyone knows you and wants to get next to you. Our image is everywhere. I get stopped on the street, accosted in restaurants, yelled at from cabs, and importuned by doormen. I pretend to find it tiresome, but secretly I enjoy it. This fame thing? It's fun—like a dessert slipping down your throat, and with about as much nutritional power. I walk into Charivari and the sales assistants in the groovy emporium all nudge one another, trying to act cool but instead tripping over themselves in the attempt to be the first to offer you a Perrier while bringing out some Japanese designer's trifle for a few thousand dollars. Some innocently ask you your name, as if they don't know who you are, and you answer, "Raskolnikov," or with a thick Madrid accent, "Jesus." Resistance is low, and if you casually ask a beautiful female salesperson what she might be doing tonight, "Oh, nothing" is always the reply. "Dinner?" you murmur. . . .

I go to Los Angeles and visit a woman I am interested in. We go for a walk on Venice Beach among muscled and bronzed beach types in shorts and tank tops. I wear a baggy suit made in a lurid red-and-blue check, my hair is spiked, my skin chalky white. Someone suddenly yells out my name. A crowd gathers behind me. It grows larger and larger as we walk down the boardwalk, with everyone singing "Roxanne" under the curving sky and spindly palms of California. I feel like the Pied Piper, and it is hard not to smile.

Maybe Sting, Stewart, and I all feel the sensation of being in a pressure cooker, and need to get out. Sting goes to Mexico to film his part in *Dune;* Stewart works on the soundtrack to *Rumble Fish;* I work on my book and music for another album with Fripp. It seems that we are writing our future scripts.

Some weekends I fly from Kennedy Airport to Shannon in Ireland to visit Kate and Layla. From western Ireland I take a train to Cork and then a taxi to Kinsale. After the intensity and sophistication of New York, rural Ireland is like walking into a thick wooden door. I feel as if I have just dropped in from another planet. With the thrum of New York glitter, and cutting-edge nightclubs roaring in my head, the sound of wind laced with the cries of gulls and the acrid smell of a coal fire hits me like a powerful memory that almost knocks me over. I want to stay close to Layla—be her father, not a stranger. Kate allows me this; for a few days I try to fulfill the role, but I feel like an intruder as I sit around on the floor with her and a scattering of children's books with bright simple pictures and big letters, with dolls and teddy bears. "Pat the bunny, pat the bunny," I croak as the wind rattles the windows and storm clouds gather over Kinsale Harbor.

In this time-off period we continue to do interviews and are constantly in the press. The starmaker machinery is cranking once again, and everything is set up to encourage the worst in you—the childish behavior, the arrogance, the self-indulgence—and the weird thing is that all these traits seem to be in opposition to the quality of making music, which is spiritual. But how do you become a successful musician in the exterior world without all of this— the press, the media, music television, lawyers, accountants, managers, hype?

It almost feels that the main job now is talking about what we do rather than doing it. If the time were added up, it would be so. Meanwhile, our fifth album is being manufactured, complete with thirty-six sleeve variations. For this record we have each been photographed separately, choosing our own images to illustrate our idea of synchronicity. We won't see one another's pictures until the album is released, but it seems sadly symbolic of the inner life of the group—much as playing in three separate rooms did at the time of recording.

For my shots I place eggs on a piano keyboard, set fire to a telephone, slip beneath the surface of a warm bath, signify time passing with a metronome, and have a lovely Chinese girl in most of the pictures. My favorite idea, under the influence of magical realism, is to stand in a room with a cloud of butterflies around my head. This is a difficult photograph to pull off because you have to buy the butterflies from a farm and they come to you in a box frozen, as if in a coma. My photographer is Duane Michals, who is famous in the art world for his dreamlike sequences. Together we hover over a cardboard box in a cold tenement room in Queens with rancid and peeling wallpaper, trying to get the iced insects to wake up, but it doesn't work. We heat up the room, bring in hair dryers, turn up the radiators, but still nothing works apart from a feeble tremble of the odd wing, as if to say, "Leave me alone, I am having a dream that I am a butterfly." It is sad; I don't know whether I feel more sorry for them or for us. We are sweating with the heat now, and in the end we start tossing them into the air to see if they will get the idea of flight. One or two make fluttering motions and our hearts leap, but it is over quickly and they drop to the floor like stones and our hearts sink. Instead of a morning of fun, it's turning into a morning of death, the great butterfly funeral. Duane places the insects on my shirt and face and makes a few photographs, including one amazing shot in which my eyes are somehow both open and closed at the same time. It appears later in one of his portrait books. We finally decide to leave, but we don't know what to do with the lovely Lepidoptera. Should we dump them in the trash, bury them, donate them, eat them, what? We take them with us in the cab and finally pull over into Central Park, where we leave them in a patch of sunlight, hoping that a miracle of nature will take place.

On June 10, *Synchronicity,* like the return of a seven-year plague, is released. Our faces and the album cover emerge onto billboards, storefronts, shop windows, and the backs of buses in London. Magazines, newspapers, periodicals, quarterlies—wherever you look, there we are like an infestation you can't avoid. "Go big now" is the strategy at A&M, and the word comes down from el presidente to spare no expense where these boys are concerned. We hit the media like a tsunami.

The press reaction is interesting because the word *synchronicity* throws them for a moment. It is a word that is not heard much in the rock world, and some people think we have invented it. But it is picked up and rolled around the tongue—"s-i-n-k-r-o-n-c-t-ee," they say—and the word travels around the globe into the malls of the Midwest, the record sections of department stores in Manchester, the mouths of teenage girls as they try to get the word out, the confused minds of mums and dads as they say, "Sin what? Sting-cron-isn't-he?" Students look it up; hamburgers are named after it.

A surge of interviews begins, this time with high-flown responses about Jung, the collective unconscious, the underlying fabric, the acausal connecting principle, the implicate order; in the context of the pop world, it all sounds rather grandiose and overreaching. I try to downplay it slightly and refer it to synchronistic events in the studio, as if throwing them a false scent. Stewart seems embarrassed by it and refers to it as Sting in his German scientist phase, as if he is merely tolerating a whim. (This whim will earn him several million dollars.) I have my own history of interest in Jung but am aware of how this might appear to the hacks. We pretty much get away with it.

We appear in *Time* and *Newsweek,* the album is generally regarded a masterpiece, with one or two dissenters who don't buy Sting's lyrics. Synchronicity is a commercial juggernaut that rolls forward, crushing all competition.

"Every Breath You Take" is the first single and once again enters the U.K. charts at number one and begins a fast climb on the U.S. *Billboard* charts. I have the impression that we could record "Mary Had a Little Lamb" and it too would go to number one at this point in our career. One of the side effects of our success is that we are widely imitated, with Police copy bands springing up all over the world.

My guitar style in particular has entered the lexicon. At this seminal point I am probably the most imitated guitarist in the world. Guitar players everywhere are quickly dropping their Led Zeppelin riffs and Hendrix lines to stretch their fingers out for the long reach of the added second chords and offbeat syncopation, the shining minor eleventh of "Walking on the Moon." With our success we have set a new high-water mark, and for a moment the height of cool is to be like the Police, to look like us, to sound like us; anything else is yesterday's news.

As we begin the promotion for *Synchronicity* it is like the high point of a song that will be heard for a few moments before beginning its final cadence. Videos, MTV interviews, photography sessions, lawyers, accountants, and contracts crowd into my head like a swarm of bees, and the guitar remains my place of refuge, the immutable dialogue between mind, fingers, frets, strings, the history, the still point, the matrix of spirit and love, and the path forward.

Inflated to the breaking point, we begin rehearsals for the great tour. The press now wait for us to self-destruct in public, go out in a fiery display, self-immolate, but they will be disappointed. Back together after the trials of recording the *Synchronicity* album, Sting, Stewart, and I once again rebuild some sort of group psyche to tour with to make this album a success. But I feel it is now thin and strained. Sting is more distant, more difficult to talk to, and I begin to hate the feeling that I am a guitarist in someone else's band.

MTV is in only its second year and picks us as the band to promote all summer long. They organize contests to meet the band, win free tickets, etc. The "Every Breath" video is in constant rotation, and we each do exclusive interviews that are shown over and over again. This is the hummingbird standing still, the solar-flared apogee of our sojourn, and *Synchronicity* the album and "Every Breath You Take" the single hit like Scud missiles at number one on the *Billboard* charts. The single will remain in this position for eight weeks and the album for four months, keeping even Michael Jackson at the height of his popularity out of the number one spot. We are ecstatic. We have reached the pinnacle, the last point between earth and space.

We arrive at Comiskey Park, a baseball stadium in Chicago, to begin the tour. MTV is there in force interviewing fans, wandering about the stadium, and filling the screen with our images and the "Every Breath" video. Martha Quinn, an elfinlike Veejay, arrives for a backstage interview that ends with a water-throwing fight between Stewart and Sting. We are now playing in stadiums to capacity audiences of fifty and sixty thousand people a night, and the expectation is at fever pitch. The desire to be near us or see us spreads like an epidemic. Emotions run high, and male and female fans alike break into tears when and if they get anywhere near us. Some have to be carried off. One of our girl fans in London tries to slash her wrists when we don't recognize her with a new cropped hairstyle. She survives, we breathe a sigh of relief, but it feels like a warning. We have become the locus of a huge projection, the recipients of a collective fantasy; the only comparison we can imagine at this point is in fact the Beatles. In the United States the terms *celebrity* and *success* are synonymous, and in the eyes of our fans we are seen as everything you would want to be. We are "it." When fans are allowed to get close to us for autographs, even the simple act of signing your name becomes almost impossible with the screaming and the mayhem, and you find yourself talking gently to them as tears stream down their faces. Underneath the desire, things seem fragile. The heat of the fans seems to mirror the hot coal that's burning through the band. Fame is a loaded gun.

In the hotels we have guards at each end of the corridor and we can't leave our rooms. To go into the hotel restaurant is to cause a furor. We are accompanied twenty-four hours a day by large men with bodybuilder physiques: Larry, Ron, Jeff. The cliché of the goldfish bowl is the hyperreality in which we are living. Now we are stamped with the word *icon,* and the gig at Shea Stadium—ever since the Beatles played there—is a trenchant symbol of rock-and-roll glory.

We play a show in Miami and, despite the place in our head offstage, the show is a power surge as we whip through the show opener, "Synchronicity"—on which I play an electric twelve-string on a stand with the Telecaster hanging off my back—and on through the power chords of "Synchronicity II," "Walking in Your Footsteps," selections of our earlier songs, and climaxing with "Every Breath You Take." We return for a blowout encore of "Can't Stand Losing You" and leave the stage with the crowd in a frenzied uproar. The support group is the Animals. The original groups, who seem to do nothing but argue with one another, have got back together for a reunion tour. As they finish their set and come offstage we climb the ramp to go on. As I go up I pass Eric Burdon coming down; we raise an eyebrow at each other.

I get off a plane at Kennedy Airport, and Neil Sedaka gets off right behind me. We look at each other in amazement. "So, it is you," he says as minders surround me and a limo door swings open, "we were wondering." It's a sweet moment and a couple of weeks later he will come to the Shea Stadium concert with his family. The minders start edging me toward the backseat of the limo. I wave at Neil through the darkened glass. He raises a hand to his mouth and as we pull away I hear him murmur, "Oh, my God."

Twenty-Seven

I flick the television back on. MTV pulses across the room in cartoon color. They are talking about us, the show tonight, the expected turnout—what songs will we play, will there be songs from the new album? Music television: this is a new concept that is already turning music into a visual rather than an aural medium. I don't like it, but even at this early stage it is attracting a large audience. They have chosen us as the band of the year; despite some reticence, we realize that if you can't beat them, join them. We are all over it. My face comes on the screen and I snort in disgust and suddenly become bored with watching me, Martha Quinn, Stewart, Sting, me, Martha Stewart, Sting Quinn, Martha Quinn, me, and decide to get up. Other people are now moving about the place, and suddenly it makes me feel better—we are still a family of sorts and the sound check is at three.

My suitcase is lying on the floor by the fireplace with everything spread out around it. As usual, I haven't bothered with any drawers or closets, as they just seem to confuse the issue, my philosophy being that if I am living out of a suitcase, to hell with the drawers. I stare at the contents—what to wear today? As we never seem to go anywhere without cameras going off like fireflies, a look of some sort is always a consideration. I sort through the pile: pink T-shirt—no, worn it three times, stinks; white shirt—no, too formal for a sound check; blue striped pants, green shirt—too gay; black suit—no, it's not a fucking funeral. Fuck, what? Everything is filthy. Okay, I am going for this yellow shirt and the green and white jacket, maybe some aviator shades—a faux Miles Davis look. . . .

I wander into the dining room, to a table loaded like the Last Supper, a late-morning pre–sound check brunch. The owner of this mansion and our very gracious host is a man by the name of Lenny Riggio. We are constantly treated to banquet-size breakfasts, dinners, and late-night suppers. Helicopters and limousines are also at our disposal. He loves our band and tells us one night that he is buying up a faded old chain called Barnes & Noble and that he is going to transform it. It seems like a daunting task, as this particular store chain now seems to be on the way out, but we nod and make encouraging sounds. Various members of our entourage are gathered around the table, filling their lunch plates. As I appear like a forlorn ghost with no one realizing that I've been up for hours, the usual sardonic comments come my way: "My God, it's alive—look what the cat dragged in, anybody seen the lead guitar," etc. Sting and Trudie come into the room from the garden out by the pool. They are a beautiful couple with a glimmering physicality. Together they form an appealing symbiosis; I like Trudie; she fits in well with the group and seems to add another dimension to Sting's more contained personality, like wine and champagne. But at this inflated point in our career, it feels as if Sting has already broken away, and I know there are machinations taking place in his head—murmurings about getting off now and breaking up the band are an obvious clue. Although I do not dwell on it, I can feel a shift taking place, an idea of the future Sting being worked on.

In the early days together Sting was withdrawn, introverted. Although he could cut loose onstage and perform, I often wondered how natural it was for him. Obviously he is gifted with musical talent, but the performance aspect—although he pulled it off brilliantly—seemed like a strain, something that had to be done. He had the voice, and the songs had to be sung. In Germany Eberhard remarked that he was like a child—so quiet, so . . . , and then Eberhard would look off into the distance with a puzzled look on his face. But as time went on and the heat got turned up, Sting became more vocal and started flexing his persona, confidently trying on the coat of celebrity. The film of *Quadrophenia* exponentially increased his emerging star power, and maybe in a sense that was the early death knell of the band. Amazingly enough, he didn't immediately take off and start a solo career, because the band itself was becoming a megasuccess and maybe there was a sense of loyalty, although he made remarks to the press to the contrary. To have walked out then would have been foolish—you don't walk away from that kind of power unless you don't have the stomach for it.

With success, forming new personal agendas becomes possible and ultimately has to be played out. After a few years and unparalleled success together, the fragile democracy has become a dictatorship, and Sting's agenda—his natural proclivity to do it alone—has begun to manifest itself with a kind of grumpiness around the band, an irritability at being in this situation. But with the machine roaring along, it probably has seemed impossible to jump off. The band was almighty, and Stewart and I could not be factored out, because people liked the idea of the group. All three personalities were taken up by the public in the same way the Beatles were in their time. It was too powerful to discard easily.

But Stewart and I, not being short of ego or our own control issues, naturally challenge all ideas or commands. Although veiled, it is obvious that ultimately this is not the way forward for Sting. He needs to control the crew or abandon ship. And in a way I don't blame him, because none of us want to be controlled. Maybe it is time to split—we've done our work, this is as far as we can go. But what a shame.

But the vessel containing all these stratagems, intrigues, and machinations is the music we make together. Comforting myself with this fragile idea and feeling drowsy from lunch, I lie down in a patch of warm sunlight and within seconds fall asleep.

Twenty-Eight

"Come on, mate, you're onstage in five minutes." I open my eyes to see Kim standing over me with a grin on his face. "Your chariot awaits you." "Bastard," I say, stretch, and then, "okay, let's do it."

Outside in the driveway are a couple of stretch limos with their engines purring. We pile into them and begin the drive.

Shea Stadium has been forever associated with the Beatles since their historic U.S. tour of '65. We are the first band since then to play there. It seems to be a marker of our power that we can sell out such a venue in a few hours. For me it represents a personal triumph over the city of dreams.

The stadium looms over us like a giant black monolith. Is it possible that we are actually going to play here? We start an idle conversation, wondering who is on tonight, they must be big—probably a bunch of wankers—and why would we want to waste our time? Then, sighing deeply, "Oh well, if we have to, we have to," etc. But the truth is that we are excited—the atmosphere is loaded, electric.

We pile out of the limos and are taken to the stage; the crew—Danny, Tam, Jeff, and about sixty riggers, lighting men, electricians, security guards, vendors, and other worker bees—are everywhere. We are merely the band, and weirdly insignificant: simple ghosts in the machine. Danny, Jeff, and Tam are setting up and they greet us with the usual world-weary remarks.

They live a grueling and
sleepless existence while we
are on tour, but they are a
great crew and we feel lucky
to have them with us. As we
arrive on the stage, cameras
start going off and MTV
is in attendance to do a
preshow interview with the
usual gushing inanities
about how we think it will
go tonight, what we are going to play. Will there be
anything special? Any sur-
prises? What does the fu-
ture hold for the Police?
Despite any underlying ten-

sion between us or thoughts about the demise of the band, we present a
united front that underscores the public success.

I stare out across the vast stadium, over the field the Beatles emerged
onto, drowning in the roar and screams of their fans, their tiny Vox AC30
amps a whisper in the canyon. Was this the end for them, the leap off the
mountainside, the point of no return? As if running a check on this hyperreality, the words stream like a banner through my head: "you are onstage at
Shea Stadium." The Telecaster is in my hands, my pedal board is on the
floor in front of me, the Marshalls are behind me, and my Scottish roadie
stares at me from the side of the stage at the alert. This is it.

As if to defuse the tension, Sting and Stewart go into one of their mock
fights and roll about on the stage for a few minutes. This is the highlight for
the media and signals the end of the sound check.

Back at the mansion we disappear into our various rooms to sleep, rest,
and prepare for what will be the highlight of our career. We are all in a
hyped-up state, and I find it difficult to sleep, staring into the dark with
thoughts drifting by in a strange collage: the immediate memory of the

songs we will play tonight, the feel of the Telecaster in my hands, a couple of remarks that Tam made at the sound check, and the awareness of lying here bathed in the glow of success and yet experiencing mixed feelings about the future. I am so glutted with all of it, the sheer amount that comes at us, that I almost don't care or can't take it in; and perversely I ruminate on the little black spot that is buried within every sun.

But as I roll through these thoughts I pull back for a wider view, indulge in a "what if " game. Things change—if anyone has learned that lesson, it certainly is me; almost every band I have been in has broken up—you go on. Maybe (once again) it's just something new unfolding, the endless cycle, and if I can draw back from the whirlpool of this particular moment, I'll see that. What if this is a script—wants to play own music, needs platform, creates successful rock band, moves on to own thing—what if life doesn't end here but gets even better? You have the power, don't give it away. And maybe that is what Sting—what all of us—are thinking, consciously or not.

Maybe there is someone else in my future, maybe there are more children; life as a creative musician will continue, can become the thing I have always wanted, can play out the fantasies I imagined as a kid. This was a dream; there are other dreams. The Police will have been just one of them along the way, and whatever happens, one thing is for certain: music.

A couple of hours later we assemble downstairs and drink a glass of champagne and congratulate one another for having arrived together on this particular night. We cross the lawn, hair blowing back from the chopper blades, and take off in the direction of Shea. As we circle the stadium in the night air, it glows below us like a cathedral packed with believers waiting for us, waiting to give confirmation and sacrament.

We land behind the stage and are immediately surrounded by a mob of smiling faces, jostling bodies, a feeling of high excitement. The backstage atmosphere is electric; it's not possible to feel smug or clever, but only to experience a strange mix of inward thanks and a gut feeling that we really have to pull this off tonight. The next hour goes by like a surreal dream of dressing room banter, well-wishers, presidents of record companies, radio stations, the Telecaster being gently placed in my hands. Now we are being led to the stage. We mount the steps to the platform, the edge of the stage where darkness and light touch. We walk into the center, the lumi-nescence, the incandescent blaze of electric power, and there is a deep roar like the end of the world. Eighty thousand lighters go on in the stadium, an incendiary salutation. Like a prayer, it is now, it is forever. I strike the first chord.

Afterword

Six months after Shea Stadium the band broke up. We performed our final show in Melbourne, Australia, to a raging crowd of fifty thousand Police fans. I remember the backstage scene after the show like a kind of hallucination. As we were accosted by one person after another raving about the band and the performance, gasping how great it must be to be in the Police, I felt I was drowning in a sea of something close to worship but could only smile back and say, "Yeah . . . great . . . thanks," knowing the grim truth that they had just witnessed the final gig. The feeling the next day was of an incomprehensible black reality. I got on a plane and went alone to Sri Lanka for a couple of weeks in the hope of meditating about the next step, but the white sand beaches of the Indian Ocean seemed only to emphasize the feeling of alienation. Returning to England felt depressing after the nonstop years of touring around the world, and I began drifting between L.A., New York, and London as if hoping to take root somewhere. Never short of a crowd, I found it easy enough to stick a Band-Aid on the void, to plug the ache of something unresolved. Eventually I began to record a solo album, and the act of making music and being in the studio again felt like the first steps of healing and finding the direction forward.

In 1986 a miracle happened when Kate and I—after a divorce, four and a half years apart, and attempts at relationships with other people—found our way back together. We reunited in London, and Kate became pregnant almost immediately—this time with twin boys. We started over and returned to family life. With this blessing and the feeling of getting my feet back on the ground, I felt that new things were possible. This was the real gold. Like a man returning from a long voyage, I had the treasure and finally the mind to settle into this part of my life.

A year later we returned to California, built a house, and began raising our kids. But the experience of having been in the Police and achieving that kind of success was not easily discarded because it was a life experience replete with intensity, striving, and the endless struggle in public to be the best that you can possibly be. An adventure like that—if remaining unresolved—sticks inside you like a stone in the throat. Despite my being able to move forward in a very happy way with my family and career, the memory of the group still felt like an open wound—something that would take years to heal, if ever. For a long time I dreamed about the band as if somehow trying to rebuild it, or reclaim something stolen, or make it whole again. Somewhere on the subconscious level there was need for a closure maybe impossible to obtain, and the only alternative was to live with it, do other work, and hope that maybe in time the wound would heal.

The problem with the demise of our group is that we didn't play out all our potential; we were not washed up, finished, or on a downward spiral. To compound this sense of incompleteness we never acknowledged our fans around the world with a farewell tour. Instead, we went through three years of pretense until I—at least—could not stand lying about it anymore and the truth became public.

The most exquisite moments in music are when you connect with the other players, when you fly, when you touch the spirit, and the audience is there with you. Sting, Stewart, and I experienced these moments many times. The music remains.

Index